Criminal Procedure: Laying Down the Law

ASPEN PUBLISHERS

Criminal Procedure: Laying Down the Law

Robyn Scheina Brown

Wolters Kluwer
Law & Business

AUSTIN   BOSTON   CHICAGO   NEW YORK   THE NETHERLANDS

Aspen Publishers
Attn: Permissions Department
76 Ninth Avenue, 7th Floor
New York, NY 10011-5201

To contact Customer Care, e-mail customer.care@aspenpublishers.com, call 1-800-234-1660, fax 1-800-901-9075, or mail correspondence to:

Aspen Publishers
Attn: Order Department
PO Box 990
Frederick, MD 21705

Printed in the United States of America.

1 2 3 4 5 6 7 8 9 0

ISBN 978-0-7355-7316-1

Library of Congress Cataloging-in-Publication Data

Brown, Robyn S.
   Criminal procedure : laying down the law / Robyn Scheina Brown.
      p. cm.—(Law & business)
   Includes index.
   ISBN 978-0-7355-7316-1
   1. Criminal procedure—United States. 2. Criminal procedure—United States—Cases. I. Title.

   KF9619.B73 2009
   345.73'05—dc22

                                                    2008031820

About Wolters Kluwer Law & Business

Wolters Kluwer Law & Business is a leading provider of research information and workflow solutions in key specialty areas. The strengths of the individual brands of Aspen Publishers, CCH, Kluwer Law International and Loislaw are aligned within Wolters Kluwer Law & Business to provide comprehensive, in-depth solutions and expert-authored content for the legal, professional and education markets.

CCH was founded in 1913 and has served more than four generations of business professionals and their clients. The CCH products in the Wolters Kluwer Law & Business group are highly regarded electronic and print resources for legal, securities, antitrust and trade regulation, government contracting, banking, pension, payroll, employment and labor, and healthcare reimbursement and compliance professionals.

Aspen Publishers is a leading information provider for attorneys, business professionals and law students. Written by preeminent authorities, Aspen products offer analytical and practical information in a range of specialty practice areas from securities law and intellectual property to mergers and acquisitions and pension/benefits. Aspen's trusted legal education resources provide professors and students with high-quality, up-to-date and effective resources for successful instruction and study in all areas of the law.

Kluwer Law International supplies the global business community with comprehensive English-language international legal information. Legal practitioners, corporate counsel and business executives around the world rely on the Kluwer Law International journals, loose-leafs, books and electronic products for authoritative information in many areas of international legal practice.

Loislaw is a premier provider of digitized legal content to small law firm practitioners of various specializations. Loislaw provides attorneys with the ability to quickly and efficiently find the necessary legal information they need, when and where they need it, by facilitating access to primary law as well as state-specific law, records, forms and treatises.

Wolters Kluwer Law & Business, a unit of Wolters Kluwer, is headquartered in New York and Riverwoods, Illinois. Wolters Kluwer is a leading multinational publisher and information services company.

Dedicated with gratitude to
The Honorable Raymond G. Thieme, Jr.,
an extraordinary judge, mentor, and individual

Summary of Contents

PART I: THE PRE-TRIAL PROCESS

PART II: THE TRIAL PROCESS

PART III: THE POST-TRIAL PROCESS

Table of Contents

Chapter 3: Self-Incrimination   47

Chapter 4: Identification of a Suspect   69

Chapter 5: Double Jeopardy   89

PART II: THE TRIAL PROCESS

Chapter 6: Due Process   111

Chapter 7: Assistance of Counsel   135

Chapter 8: Speedy Trial   157

Chapter 9: Jury Trial   175

Chapter 10: Confrontation   195

PART III: THE POST-TRIAL PROCESS

Chapter 11: Cruel and Unusual Punishment   217

Chapter 12: Sentencing and Appeals   241

Acknowledgments

I would like to extend my sincere gratitude to those individuals who provided their invaluable input by reviewing this book: Anna Pace Atchick, Esq., Instructor, Legal Studies Program at Saint Joseph's University; Phil Cykon, Esq., Enforcement Attorney, Vermont Division of Securities; Janine Ferraro, J.D., Nassau Community College; Kimberly M. Tatum, J.D., Assistant Professor, Department of Criminal Justice & Legal Studies, University of West Florida; and the Honorable Raymond G. Thieme, Jr., Court of Special Appeals of Maryland, Retired. Their time and expertise was greatly appreciated.

I would also like to thank Professor Kelly A. Koermer, Esq., of Anne Arundel Community College, for providing a lawyer's second opinion when I needed it; Sgt. Ronald V. Naughton of the Calvert County Sheriff's Department, for providing a cop's perspective when I needed it; and most of all, my family, for providing their unconditional love, support, and encouragement, not only through this project but the project known as "life."

Criminal Procedure: Laying Down the Law

Introduction

I'm no dummy. Most students *never* read the Introduction to a book. I know that. I've studied plenty a textbook during my days in school, and rarely, if ever, did I actually take the time to read the Introduction. No, I usually jumped right in with Chapter One. After all, the Introduction doesn't actually *teach* you anything, does it? And even more importantly, you're never tested on it. So even though it's listed as required reading on your course syllabus for the first week or two of class, the Introduction is more like a "freebie" for that week. Or, perhaps if you're one of those very studious kinds, you might skim through the pages just to make yourself feel better about having done the required work. Well, this Introduction will be a little different from all the rest. For starters, it *will* teach you a thing or two about constitutional criminal procedure. Additionally, where most introductions can go on for pages, I promise to do my best to keep this short and sweet. And finally, who knows? Maybe you *will* be tested on it. So, take a minute or two, and keep reading!

Two quick items of business before we get into the meat of this Introduction: The first is a little preview of what this book is all about. The second is also a preview, but of what this book is *not* about. First things first. Each chapter deals with a single constitutional provision related to criminal procedure. Each chapter as well is formatted in exactly the same way, containing eight separate sections: the Chapter Introduction; Student Checklist; Supreme Court Cases; Case Questions; Hypothetical with Accompanying Analysis; Hypothetical for Student Analysis; Discussion Questions; and Test Bank. It's designed to be user-friendly, to let you work through issues and scenarios dealing with constitutional criminal procedure so that by the time you've completed a chapter, you actually "*get*" it.

Now that we've determined what the book *is* supposed to do, let's take a brief moment to talk about what it's *not* supposed to do. It's not a textbook. It's not designed to instruct you on every nuance of criminal procedure. It's not 300-plus pages of lengthy chapters citing to hundreds of cases, all in a monstrous hardbound volume. In fact, if you're reading this as your *only* source on constitutional criminal procedure, you will very likely have more questions than answers. My point is that you should be using this *with* other sources on constitutional criminal procedure, whether they are classroom discussions, a textbook, power points, or the like. That way, you'll get the full benefit of this book by mastering constitutional criminal procedure.

Having taken care of our two items of business, we are left with the final, and most important, part of this Introduction. . . .

THE TOP TEN THINGS TO REMEMBER WHILE WORKING THROUGH THIS BOOK:

It might not be the Late Show with David Letterman, but if you take the advice in this Top Ten List, you'll be better equipped to analyze the issues dealing with constitutional criminal procedure throughout this book. In fact, most items on the list apply whenever you study the criminal justice system, so keep them in the back of your mind.

10. **Sometimes, there *is* no right answer. . . .** Several of the issues you'll be presented with, whether in case questions, discussion questions, or hypothetical scenarios, don't *have* answers. At least, not yet. You may be faced on occasion with what's called an "issue of first impression." That is, an issue which has never been decided by a court. If that happens to be the case, you have a clean slate. But remember, for every argument you can make in favor of what you *think* should be the answer, I guarantee that someone could make the opposite argument. The law is very seldom black or white. Many times when it comes to the law, the "winner" isn't necessarily the person who has the stronger case. Rather, it's the person who can make the stronger argument. So be passionate and don't hold back.

9. **Sometimes there *is* a right answer, but you might not like it. . . .** You don't always have to agree with the law, but that doesn't change the fact that it's still the law. I often have students who dislike a law, and they give me very compelling arguments as to why they dislike it. Sometimes so compelling, in fact, that I find myself agreeing with them. So what do I tell them? Tough. You don't have like it, but it is what it is. Unless you have aspirations to become a legislator, a judge, or even a Supreme Court Justice (and if you do, more power to you), you can't change what you don't like simply because you disagree with it. Remember when you were a little kid and you asked your parents, "Why do I have to do this?" What was their response? "Because I said so." Like it or not, the rules are the rules.

8. **Make sure to look at both sides of the coin. . . .** We *all* have opinions, and we're often very forceful in expressing them. How many of you have heard from a friend or relative, "Gee, with the way you can argue, you'd make a great lawyer." We tend to think that the more ammunition we have on our side, the more foolproof our argument is. But being able to get your point across means recognizing your weaknesses (or, in other words, your opponent's strengths) and being able to refute them. Don't be so one-sided that you can't anticipate counterarguments to your position. In fact, once or twice try to argue the *opposite* of what you believe in. Does it seem unnatural? Yes, especially at first. But, you'll find that if you can anticipate those counterarguments and head them off at the pass, you'll make a better adversary in the long run.

7. **Don't expect to hit a home run the first time at bat. . . .** Being able to understand and analyze constitutional criminal procedure takes time, and it takes practice. It doesn't happen overnight. Many of the issues in this book are extremely complicated; so complicated, in fact, that at times the Supreme Court Justices themselves can't even agree on what the law should be. Don't feel bad if at first some of it is a bit overwhelming. Consider, for example, the Supreme Court cases included in each chapter. Believe me, reading a judicial opinion can be *very* intimidating. It's nothing like reading your favorite crime novel, where you breeze through twenty pages in what

feels like less than five minutes. But with each additional case you read, you'll find it easier to grasp the writing style of an opinion, and it won't seem as though it was written in a foreign language. Keep the same basic premise in mind when you're working through the hypotheticals. There are a total of 24 hypotheticals in this book—12 that are analyzed for you, so you can practice, and another 12 without an analysis so you can test your skills. The more hypotheticals you work through, the easier they will become to analyze. Practice makes perfect.

6. **Don't always believe what you see on television. . . .** I can't even begin to tell you how many times I've been discussing an issue in class when a student raises his hand and says, "Well, when I was watching *Law & Order* the other night they said. . . ." Since when did *Law & Order* or *CSI* become the Bible of constitutional criminal procedure? Remember the purpose of these shows: entertainment. What might appear very realistic might actually be completely *un*realistic. Even "reality" based programs and shows such as *Court TV* or *Cops* can unintentionally (or even intentionally) distort the criminal justice system depending upon what they show their viewers. Learn to watch crime shows with a grain of salt, and don't get your criminal justice education from a television set!

5. **Use plain English. . . .** When analyzing the issues within this book, learn to express your thoughts in a clear, concise manner. Too many students studying the criminal justice system get caught up in using what I call "legal language." This takes two forms. One is the frequent use of Latin phrases, such as *a fortiorari* or *sina que non* (huh?). The other is the use of extra-long words (which are usually two or three little words smashed together), such as "heretofore," "hereinafter," or "henceforth." Students fall victim to both of these pitfalls in an attempt to sound impressive and knowledgeable about a subject. The problem is, their good intentions backfire. They end up sounding impressed with themselves rather than actually impressing anyone else. Forget the legal jargon.

4. **Follow the trail of breadcrumbs. . . .** Why did Hansel and Grettel leave a trail of breadcrumbs? To find their way through the dense forest and back home again. Okay, so maybe it didn't work for them. But you've got your very own breadcrumbs in each chapter; they take the form of a Student Checklist. That checklist is designed to get you through the forest by simplifying and breaking down very complicated, multifaceted issues. Each checklist will take you through a step-by-step analysis of whichever constitutional provision you happen to be reading about. You'll find key vocabulary or "buzz words" in these checklists so you can analyze issues using the proper terms. Follow the checklist not only in your thought process but in your writing as well. Your analysis of an issue will not only be more thorough and comprehensive, but it will also be more accurate. I guarantee that unlike Hansel and Grettel, if you follow those breadcrumbs, they *will* work for you.

3. **The cops aren't *always* the good guys, and the "robbers" aren't *always* the bad guys. . . .** The same goes for lawyers and judges. Well okay, perhaps *most* of the time the cops are the good guys and the robbers are the bad guys, but that isn't always the case. Inevitably, some actors within the criminal justice system may not fully understand the law. Or even, perhaps, they don't care about the law. When analyzing any scenario, don't always assume that the accused is automatically guilty (remember that good ole' saying "innocent

until proven guilty"?). By the same token, don't assume that the players on the government's side are flawless either. Everyone makes mistakes, even the guy with the badge, the three-piece suit, or the black robe.

2. **Keep those scales balanced. . . .** The law discussed throughout this book comes from the amendments to the Constitution. So then, let's return for a moment to our high school government class. What were the amendments designed to protect us from? Our nosey neighbor? Our overbearing mother? Our archenemy? No, from government. Don't forget that the protections in the Bill of Rights and other constitutional amendments don't even apply unless the government is somehow involved. Next, remember those scales of justice. Courts are constantly trying to strike a balance between two competing interests: the government and its desires to reduce crime and punish criminals, versus the individual, and his desires for liberty, freedom, and a fair trial. So when you're analyzing any issue, make sure you first determine what interests are at stake, and then try to reach a resolution that won't tip the scales.

And the Number One thing to remember when working through this book . . .

1. **Don't treat this as just *any* other book on criminal procedure. . . .** Don't read it only half-focused on the words while hoping that by osmosis the concepts magically seep into your brain. It won't happen. This book is not about seeing how quickly you can finish it so you can get back to more important things, like watching television, texting your friend, or listening to your iPod. Everything in it has a very *real* application to a very *real* world. If you happen to be that police officer, lawyer, or judge involved in the case, you could very well have an individual's freedom (or even life) in your hands. So take the time *now* to start caring. Learn about the cases, work through the issues, and follow the checklists. Instead of just dipping your big toe in the water and merely memorizing concepts for the shelf life of an exam or a semester-long course, why not dive in and get the full understanding of what constitutional criminal procedure is all about? *That* is what this book is designed to do. And I promise, if you do dive in and really *work* through it, you won't sink.

I

The Pre-Trial Process

1

Unreasonable Searches and Seizures

"The right of the people to be secure in their persons, houses, papers, and effects, against unreasonable searches and seizures, shall not be violated . . ."

—The Fourth Amendment

INTRODUCTION

The Fourth Amendment. When read in its entirety, any good high school English teacher would tell you that it's the quintessential run-on sentence. Fifty-four words, separated only by a series of commas, which spell out some of our most treasured rights as United States citizens: the rights to privacy and security. These rights appear to be straightforward, even simplistic, but the body of law interpreting them is extraordinarily complicated.

Because of the Fourth Amendment's complexity, its study can quickly become overwhelming and even discouraging. In order to grasp this mammoth subject it is necessary to break the Fourth Amendment down into workable components. First, it can be separated into the two clauses within it: The Reasonabless Clause, which will be discussed in this chapter, and the Warrant Clause, which will be discussed in Chapter 2. But breaking the amendment down into those two clauses is not enough, for a vast body of caselaw still accompanies each. We must further break each clause down into workable components. Instead of barely muddling through a Fourth Amendment analysis while feeling like we're helplessly sinking in quicksand, we need to use strategically placed stepping stones, carefully taking one step at a time so we can proceed through an analysis with the confidence that we are addressing all major issues and reaching the correct conclusion. While navigating those stepping stones keep in mind that the first two chapters of this text are unique—they must be read together in order to undertake a complete analysis of the Fourth

Amendment. Don't stop your analysis after Chapter 1, and don't begin with Chapter 2. Every other chapter in this book will stand on its own, but *not* the Fourth Amendment chapters.

We begin our journey with the first stepping stone. Not every search of a person or place, and not every seizure of someone or something, will trigger the Fourth Amendment. So before we can go any further we first need to know, exactly *when* does the Fourth Amendment apply?

STUDENT Checklist

Unreasonable Search and Seizure

1. Does the Fourth Amendment apply?

■ Was a **search** and/or **seizure** conducted?
  Seizure of a **person** = **meaningful inference** with an individual's **freedom of movement** and **submission** to the assertion of authority (whether a reasonable person would feel **free to leave**)
  Seizure of **property** = some **meaningful interference** with an individual's **possessory interests** in property

■ By **government**?
  Was the search/seizure conducted by **government**
  or
  Was the search/seizure conducted by someone **acting** as an **instrument** or **agent of government** or with the **participation or knowledge** of a government official?

■ In a place where the individual possessed a **reasonable expectation of privacy (REP)**?

To be continued in Chapter 2 . . .

SUPREME COURT CASES

KATZ v. UNITED STATES, 389 U.S. 347 (1967)

The petitioner was convicted in the District Court for the Southern District of California under an eight-count indictment charging him with transmitting wagering information by telephone from Los Angeles to Miami and Boston in violation of a federal statute. At trial the Government was permitted, over the petitioner's objection, to introduce evidence of the petitioner's end of telephone conversations, overheard by FBI agents who had attached an electronic listening and recording device to the outside of the public telephone booth from which he had placed his calls. In affirming his conviction, the Court of Appeals rejected the contention that the recordings had been obtained in violation of the Fourth Amendment, because "(t)here was no physical entrance into the area occupied by, (the petitioner)." We granted certiorari in order to consider the constitutional questions thus presented.

The petitioner had phrased those questions as follows:

A. Whether a public telephone booth is a constitutionally protected area so that evidence obtained by attaching an electronic listening recording device to the top of such a booth is obtained in violation of the right to privacy of the user of the booth.

B. Whether physical penetration of a constitutionally protected area is necessary before a search and seizure can be said to be violative of the Fourth Amendment to the United States Constitution.

We decline to adopt this formulation of the issues. In the first place the correct solution of Fourth Amendment problems is not necessarily promoted by incantation of the phrase "constitutionally protected area." Secondly, the Fourth Amendment cannot be translated into a general constitutional "right to privacy." That Amendment protects individual privacy against certain kinds of governmental intrusion, but its protections go further, and often have nothing to do with privacy at all. Other provisions of the Constitution protect personal privacy from other forms of governmental invasion. But the protection of a person's general right to privacy—his right to be let alone by other people—is, like the protection of his property and of his very life, left largely to the law of the individual States.

Because of the misleading way the issues have been formulated, the parties have attached great significance to the characterization of the telephone booth from which the petitioner placed his calls. The petitioner has strenuously argued that the booth was a "constitutionally protected area." The Government has maintained with equal vigor that it was not. But this effort to decide whether or not a given "area," viewed in the abstract, is "constitutionally protected" deflects attention from the problem presented by this case. For the Fourth Amendment protects people, not places. What a person knowingly exposes to the public, even in his own home or office, is not a subject of Fourth Amendment protection. See Lewis v. United States, 385 U.S. 206, 210, 87 S. Ct. 424, 427, 17 L. Ed. 2d 312; United States v. Lee, 274 U.S. 559, 563, 47 S. Ct. 746, 748, 71 L. Ed. 1202. But what he seeks to preserve as private, even in an area accessible to the public, may be constitutionally protected. See Rios v. United States, 364 U.S. 253, 80 S. Ct. 1431, 4 L. Ed. 2d 1688; Ex parte Jackson, 96 U.S. 727, 733, 24 L. Ed. 877.

The Government stresses the fact that the telephone booth from which the petitioner made his calls was constructed partly of glass, so that he was as visible after he entered it as he would have been if he had remained outside. But what he sought to exclude when he entered the booth was not the intruding eye—it was the uninvited ear. He did not shed his right to do so simply because he made his calls from a place where he might be seen. No less than an individual in a business office, in a friend's apartment, or in a taxicab, a person in a telephone booth may rely upon the protection of the Fourth Amendment. One who occupies it, shuts the door behind him, and pays the toll that permits him to place a call is surely entitled to assume that the words he utters into the mouthpiece will not be broadcast to the world. To read the Constitution more narrowly is to ignore the vital role that the public telephone has come to play in private communication.

The Government contends, however, that the activities of its agents in this case should not be tested by Fourth Amendment requirements, for the surveillance technique they employed involved no physical penetration of the telephone booth from which the petitioner placed his calls. It is true that the absence of such penetration was at one time thought to foreclose further Fourth Amendment inquiry, Olmstead v. United States, 277 U.S. 438, 457, 464, 466, 48 S. Ct. 564, 565, 567, 568, 72 L. Ed. 944; Goldman v. United States, 316 U.S. 129, 134-136, 62 S. Ct. 993, 995-997, 86 L. Ed. 1322, for that Amendment was thought to limit only searches and seizures of tangible property. But "(t)he premise that property interests control the right of the Government to search and seize has been discredited." Warden, Md. Penitentiary v. Hayden, 387 U.S. 294, 304, 87 S. Ct. 1642, 1648, 18 L. Ed. 2d 782. Thus, although a closely divided Court supposed in *Olmstead* that surveillance without any trespass and without the seizure of any material object fell outside the ambit of the Constitution, we have since departed from the narrow view on which that decision rested. Indeed, we have expressly held that the Fourth Amendment governs not only the seizure of tangible items, but extends as well to the recording of oral statements overheard without any "technical trespass under . . . local property law." Silverman v. United States, 365 U.S. 505, 511, 81 S. Ct. 679, 682, 5 L. Ed. 2d 734. Once this much is acknowledged, and once it is recognized that the Fourth Amendment protects people—and not simply "areas"—against unreasonable searches and seizures it becomes clear that the reach of that Amendment cannot turn upon the presence or absence of a physical intrusion into any given enclosure.

We conclude that the underpinnings of *Olmstead* and *Goldman* have been so eroded by our subsequent decisions that the "trespass" doctrine there enunciated can no longer be regarded as controlling. The Government's activities in electronically listening to and recording the petitioner's words violated the privacy upon which he justifiably relied while using the telephone booth and thus constituted a "search and seizure" within the meaning of the Fourth Amendment. The fact that the electronic device employed to achieve that end did not happen to penetrate the wall of the booth can have no constitutional significance.

The question remaining for decision, then, is whether the search and seizure conducted in this case complied with constitutional standards. In that regard, the Government's position is that its agents acted in an entirely defensible manner: They did not begin their electronic surveillance until investigation of the petitioner's activities had established a strong probability that he was using the telephone in question to transmit gambling information to persons in other States, in violation of federal law. Moreover, the surveillance was limited, both in scope and in duration, to the specific purpose of establishing the contents of the petitioner's unlawful telephonic communications. The agents confined their surveillance to the brief periods during which he used the telephone booth, and they took great care to overhear only the conversations of the petitioner himself.

Accepting this account of the Government's actions as accurate, it is clear that this surveillance was so narrowly circumscribed that a duly authorized magistrate, properly notified of the need for such investigation, specifically informed of the basis on which it was to proceed, and clearly apprised of the precise intrusion it would entail, could constitutionally have authorized, with appropriate safeguards, the very limited search and seizure that the Government asserts in fact took place. . . .

The Government urges that, because its agents relied upon the decisions in *Olmstead* and *Goldman*, and because they did no more here than they might properly have done with prior judicial sanction, we should retroactively validate their conduct. That we cannot do. It is apparent that the agents in this case acted with restraint. Yet the inescapable fact is that this restraint was imposed by the agents themselves, not by a judicial officer. They were not required, before commencing the search, to present their estimate of probable cause for detached scrutiny by a neutral magistrate. They were not compelled, during the conduct of the search itself, to observe precise limits established in advance by a specific court order. Nor were they directed, after the search had been completed, to notify the authorizing magistrate in detail of all that had been seized. In the absence of such safeguards, this Court has never sustained a search upon the sole ground that officers reasonably expected to find evidence of a particular crime and voluntarily confined their activities to the least intrusive means consistent with that end. Searches conducted without warrants have been held unlawful "notwithstanding facts unquestionably showing probable cause," Agnello v. United States, 269 U.S. 20, 33, 46 S. Ct. 4, 6, 70 L. Ed. 145, for the Constitution requires that the deliberate, impartial judgment of a judicial officer . . . be interposed between the citizen and the police. . . ." Wong Sun v. United States, 371 U.S. 471, 481-482, 83 S. Ct. 407, 414, 9 L. Ed. 2d 441. "Over and again this Court has emphasized that the mandate of the (Fourth) Amendment requires adherence to judicial processes," United States v. Jeffers, 342 U.S. 48, 51, 72 S. Ct. 93, 95, 96 L. Ed. 59, and that searches conducted outside the judicial process, without prior approval by judge or magistrate, are per se unreasonable under the Fourth Amendment—subject only to a few specifically established and well-delineated exceptions.

It is difficult to imagine how any of those exceptions could ever apply to the sort of search and seizure involved in this case. Even electronic surveillance substantially contemporaneous with an individual's arrest could hardly be deemed an "incident" of that arrest. Nor could the use of electronic surveillance without prior authorization be justified on grounds of "hot pursuit." And, of course, the very nature of electronic surveillance precludes its use pursuant to the suspect's consent.

The Government does not question these basic principles. Rather, it urges the creation of a new exception to cover this case. It argues that surveillance of a telephone booth should be exempted from the usual requirement of advance authorization by a magistrate upon a showing of probable cause. We cannot agree. Omission of such authorization "bypasses the safeguards provided by an objective predetermination of probable cause, and substitutes instead the far less reliable procedure of an after-the-event justification for the . . . search, too likely to be subtly influenced by the familiar shortcomings of hindsight judgment." Beck v. State of Ohio, 379 U.S. 89, 96, 85 S. Ct. 223, 228, 13 L. Ed. 2d 142.

And bypassing a neutral predetermination of the scope of a search leaves individuals secure from Fourth Amendment violations "only in the discretion of the police." Id., at 97, 85 S. Ct. at 229.

These considerations do not vanish when the search in question is transferred from the setting of a home, an office, or a hotel room to that of a telephone booth. Wherever a man may be, he is entitled to know that he will remain free from unreasonable searches and seizures. The government agents here ignored "the procedure of antecedent justification . . . that is central to the Fourth Amendment," a procedure that we hold to be a constitutional precondition of the kind of electronic surveillance involved in this case. Because the surveillance here failed to meet that condition, and because it led to the petitioner's conviction, the judgment must be reversed.

It is so ordered. Judgment reversed. . . .

Mr. Justice HARLAN, concurring.

I join the opinion of the Court, which I read to hold only (a) that an enclosed telephone booth is an area where, like a home, Weeks v. United States, 232 U.S.

383, 34 S. Ct. 341, 58 L. Ed. 652, and unlike a field, Hester v. United States, 265 U.S. 57, 44 S. Ct. 445, 68 L. Ed. 898, a person has a constitutionally protected reasonable expectation of privacy; (b) that electronic as well as physical intrusion into a place that is in this sense private may constitute a violation of the Fourth Amendment; and (c) that the invasion of a constitutionally protected area by federal authorities is, as the Court has long held, presumptively unreasonable in the absence of a search warrant.

As the Court's opinion states, "the Fourth Amendment protects people, not places." The question, however, is what protection it affords to those people. Generally, as here, the answer to that question requires reference to a "place." My understanding of the rule that has emerged from prior decisions is that there is a twofold requirement, first that a person have exhibited an actual (subjective) expectation of privacy and, second, that the expectation be one that society is prepared to recognize as "reasonable." Thus a man's home is, for most purposes, a place where he expects privacy, but objects, activities, or statements that he exposes to the "plain view" of outsiders are not "protected" because no intention to keep them to himself has been exhibited. On the other hand, conversations in the open would not be protected against being overheard, for the expectation of privacy under the circumstances would be unreasonable. Cf. Hester v. United States, supra.

The critical fact in this case is that "(o)ne who occupies it, (a telephone booth) shuts the door behind him, and pays the toll that permits him to place a call is surely entitled to assume" that his conversation is not being intercepted. Ante, at 511. The point is not that the booth is "accessible to the public" at other times, ante, at 511, but that it is a temporarily private place whose momentary occupants' expectations of freedom from intrusion are recognized as reasonable. Cf. Rios v. United States, 364 U.S. 253, 80 S. Ct. 1431, 4 L. Ed. 2d 1688.

In Silverman v. United States, 365 U.S. 505, 81 S. Ct. 679, 5 L. Ed. 2d 734, we held that eavesdropping accomplished by means of an electronic device that penetrated the premises occupied by petitioner was a violation of the Fourth Amendment. That case established that interception of conversations reasonably intended to be private could constitute a "search and seizure," and that the examination or taking of physical property was not required. . . . In *Silverman* we found it unnecessary to re-examine Goldman v. United States, 316 U.S. 129, 62 S. Ct. 993, 86 L. Ed. 1322, which had held that electronic surveillance accomplished without the physical penetration of petitioner's premises by a tangible object did not violate the Fourth Amendment. This case requires us to reconsider *Goldman*, and I agree that it should now be overruled. Its limitation on Fourth Amendment protection is, in the present day, bad physics as well as bad law, for reasonable expectations of privacy may be defeated by electronic as well as physical invasion.

Finally, I do not read the Court's opinion to declare that no interception of a conversation one-half of which occurs in a public telephone booth can be reasonable in the absence of a warrant. As elsewhere under the Fourth Amendment, warrants are the general rule, to which the legitimate needs of law enforcement may demand specific exception. It will be time enough to consider any such exceptions when an appropriate occasion presents itself, and I agree with the Court that this is not one.

ILLINOIS v. CABALLES, 543 U.S. 405 (2005)

Illinois State Trooper Daniel Gillette stopped respondent for speeding on an interstate highway. When Gillette radioed the police dispatcher to report the stop, a second trooper, Craig Graham, a member of the Illinois State Police Drug Interdiction Team, overheard the transmission and immediately headed for the scene with his narcotics-detection dog. When they arrived, respondent's car was on the shoulder of the road and respondent was in Gillette's vehicle. While Gillette was in the process of writing a warning ticket, Graham walked his dog around respondent's car. The dog alerted at the trunk. Based on that alert, the officers searched the trunk, found marijuana, and arrested respondent. The entire incident lasted less than 10 minutes.

Respondent was convicted of a narcotics offense and sentenced to 12 years' imprisonment and a $256,136 fine. The trial judge denied his motion to suppress the seized evidence and to quash his arrest. He held that the officers had not unnecessarily prolonged the stop and that the dog alert was sufficiently reliable to provide probable cause to conduct the search. . . .

The question on which we granted certiorari, 541 U.S. 972, 124 S. Ct. 1875, 158 L. Ed. 2d 466 (2004), is narrow: "Whether the Fourth Amendment requires reasonable, articulable suspicion to justify using a drug-detection dog to sniff a vehicle during a legitimate traffic stop." Pet. for Cert. i. Thus, we proceed on the assumption that the officer conducting the dog sniff had no information about respondent except that he had been stopped for speeding; accordingly, we have omitted any reference to facts about respondent that might have triggered a modicum of suspicion.

Here, the initial seizure of respondent when he was stopped on the highway was based on probable cause and was concededly lawful. It is nevertheless clear that a seizure that is lawful at its inception can violate the Fourth Amendment if its manner of execution unreasonably infringes interests protected by the Constitution. *United States v. Jacobsen*, 466 U.S. 109, 124, 104 S. Ct. 1652, 80 L. Ed. 2d 85 (1984). A seizure that is justified solely by the interest in issuing a warning ticket to the driver can become unlawful if it is prolonged beyond the time reasonably required to complete that mission. . . .

In the state-court proceedings, however, the judges carefully reviewed the details of Officer Gillette's conversations with respondent and the precise timing of his radio transmissions to the dispatcher to determine whether he had improperly extended the duration of the stop to enable the dog sniff to occur. We have not recounted those details because we accept the state court's conclusion that the duration of the stop in this case was entirely justified by the traffic offense and the ordinary inquiries incident to such a stop.

Despite this conclusion, the Illinois Supreme Court held that the initially lawful traffic stop became an unlawful seizure solely as a result of the canine sniff that occurred outside respondent's stopped car. That is, the court characterized the dog sniff as the cause rather than the consequence of a constitutional violation. In its view, the use of the dog converted the citizen-police encounter from a lawful traffic stop into a drug investigation, and because the shift in purpose was not supported by any reasonable suspicion that respondent possessed narcotics, it was unlawful. In our view, conducting a dog sniff would not change the character of a traffic stop that is lawful at its inception and otherwise executed in a reasonable manner, unless the dog sniff itself infringed respondent's constitutionally protected interest in privacy. Our cases hold that it did not.

Official conduct that does not "compromise any legitimate interest in privacy" is not a search subject to the Fourth Amendment. *Jacobsen*, 466 U.S., at 123, 104 S. Ct. 1652. We have held that any interest in possessing contraband cannot be deemed "legitimate," and thus, governmental conduct that *only* reveals the possession of contraband "compromises no legitimate privacy interest." *Ibid.* This is because the expectation "that certain facts will not come to the attention of the authorities" is not the same as an interest in "privacy that society is prepared to consider reasonable." *Id.*, at 122, 104 S. Ct. 1652 (punctuation omitted). In *United States v. Place*, 462 U.S. 696, 103 S. Ct. 2637,

77 L. Ed. 2d 110 (1983), we treated a canine sniff by a well-trained narcotics-detection dog as "*sui generis*" because it "discloses only the presence or absence of narcotics, a contraband item." *Id.*, at 707, 103 S. Ct. 2637; see also *Indianapolis v. Edmond*, 531 U.S. 32, 40, 121 S.Ct. 447, 148 L. Ed. 2d 333 (2000). Respondent likewise concedes that "drug sniffs are designed, and if properly conducted are generally likely, to reveal only the presence of contraband." Brief for Respondent 17. Although respondent argues that the error rates, particularly the existence of false positives, call into question the premise that drug-detection dogs alert only to contraband, the record contains no evidence or findings that support his argument. Moreover, respondent does not suggest that an erroneous alert, in and of itself, reveals any legitimate private information, and, in this case, the trial judge found that the dog sniff was sufficiently reliable to establish probable cause to conduct a full-blown search of the trunk.

Accordingly, the use of a well-trained narcotics-detection dog—one that "does not expose noncontraband items that otherwise would remain hidden from public view," *Place*, 462 U.S., at 707, 103 S. Ct. 2637—during a lawful traffic stop, generally does not implicate legitimate privacy interests. In this case, the dog sniff was performed on the exterior of respondent's car while he was lawfully seized for a traffic violation. Any intrusion on respondent's privacy expectations does not rise to the level of a constitutionally cognizable infringement.

This conclusion is entirely consistent with our recent decision that the use of a thermal-imaging device to detect the growth of marijuana in a home constituted an unlawful search. *Kyllo v. United States*, 533 U.S. 27, 121 S. Ct. 2038, 150 L. Ed. 2d 94 (2001). Critical to that decision was the fact that the device was capable of detecting lawful activity—in that case, intimate details in a home, such as "at what hour each night the lady of the house takes her daily sauna and bath." *Id.*, at 38, 121 S. Ct. 2038. The legitimate expectation that information about perfectly lawful activity will remain private is categorically distinguishable from respondent's hopes or expectations concerning the nondetection of contraband in the trunk of his car. A dog sniff conducted during a concededly lawful traffic stop that reveals no information other than the location of a substance that no individual has any right to possess does not violate the Fourth Amendment.

The judgment of the Illinois Supreme Court is vacated, and the case is remanded for further proceedings not inconsistent with this opinion. *It is so ordered.* . . .

Justice GINSBURG, with whom Justice SOUTER joins, dissenting.

Illinois State Police Trooper Daniel Gillette stopped Roy Caballes for driving 71 miles per hour in a zone with a posted speed limit of 65 miles per hour. Trooper Craig Graham of the Drug Interdiction Team heard on the radio that Trooper Gillette was making a traffic stop. Although Gillette requested no aid, Graham decided to come to the scene to conduct a dog sniff. Gillette informed Caballes that he was speeding and asked for the usual documents-driver's license, car registration, and proof of insurance. Caballes promptly provided the requested documents but refused to consent to a search of his vehicle. After calling his dispatcher to check on the validity of Caballes' license and for outstanding warrants, Gillette returned to his vehicle to write Caballes a warning ticket. Interrupted by a radio call on an unrelated matter, Gillette was still writing the ticket when Trooper Graham arrived with his drug-detection dog. Graham walked the dog around the car, the dog alerted at Caballes' trunk, and, after opening the trunk, the troopers found marijuana. . . .

In *Terry v. Ohio*, the Court upheld the stop and subsequent frisk of an individual based on an officer's observation of suspicious behavior and his reasonable belief that the suspect was armed. See 392 U.S., at 27-28, 88 S. Ct.

1868. In a *Terry*-type investigatory stop, "the officer's action [must be] justified at its inception, and . . . reasonably related in scope to the circumstances which justified the interference in the first place." *Id.*, at 20, 88 S. Ct. 1868. In applying *Terry*, the Court has several times indicated that the limitation on "scope" is not confined to the duration of the seizure; it also encompasses the manner in which the seizure is conducted. . . .

"A routine traffic stop," the Court has observed, "is a relatively brief encounter and 'is more analogous to a so-called *Terry* stop . . . than to a formal arrest.' " . . . I would apply *Terry's* reasonable-relation test, as the Illinois Supreme Court did, to determine whether the canine sniff impermissibly expanded the scope of the initially valid seizure of Caballes.

It is hardly dispositive that the dog sniff in this case may not have lengthened the duration of the stop. Cf. *ante*, at 837 ("A seizure . . . can become unlawful if it is prolonged beyond the time reasonably required to complete [the initial] mission."). *Terry*, it merits repetition, instructs that any investigation must be "reasonably related in *scope* to the circumstances which justified the interference in the first place." 392 U.S., at 20, 88 S. Ct. 1868 (emphasis added). The unwarranted and nonconsensual expansion of the seizure here from a routine traffic stop to a drug investigation broadened the scope of the investigation in a manner that, in my judgment, runs afoul of the Fourth Amendment. . . .

In my view, the Court diminishes the Fourth Amendment's force by abandoning the second *Terry* inquiry (was the police action "reasonably related in scope to the circumstances [justifying] the [initial] interference"). 392 U.S., at 20, 88 S. Ct. 1868. A drug-detection dog is an intimidating animal. Cf. *United States v. Williams*, 356 F.3d 1268, 1276 (C.A.10 2004) (McKay, J., dissenting) ("drug dogs are not lap dogs"). Injecting such an animal into a routine traffic stop changes the character of the encounter between the police and the motorist. The stop becomes broader, more adversarial, and (in at least some cases) longer. Caballes—who, as far as Troopers Gillette and Graham knew, was guilty solely of driving six miles per hour over the speed limit—was exposed to the embarrassment and intimidation of being investigated, on a public thoroughfare, for drugs. Even if the drug sniff is not characterized as a Fourth Amendment "search," cf. *Indianapolis v. Edmond*, 531 U.S. 32, 40, 121 S. Ct. 447, 148 L. Ed. 2d 333 (2000); *United States v. Place*, 462 U.S. 696, 707, 103 S. Ct. 2637, 77 L. Ed. 2d 110 (1983), the sniff surely broadened the scope of the traffic-violation-related seizure.

The Court has never removed police action from Fourth Amendment control on the ground that the action is well calculated to apprehend the guilty. . . . Under today's decision, every traffic stop could become an occasion to call in the dogs, to the distress and embarrassment of the law-abiding population.

The Illinois Supreme Court, it seems to me, correctly apprehended the danger in allowing the police to search for contraband despite the absence of cause to suspect its presence. Today's decision, in contrast, clears the way for suspicionless, dog-accompanied drug sweeps of parked cars along sidewalks and in parking lots. . . . Nor would motorists have constitutional grounds for complaint should police with dogs, stationed at long traffic lights, circle cars waiting for the red signal to turn green. . . .

The dog sniff in this case, it bears emphasis, was for drug detection only. A dog sniff for explosives, involving security interests not presented here, would be an entirely different matter. Detector dogs are ordinarily trained not as all-purpose sniffers, but for discrete purposes. For example, they may be trained for narcotics detection or for explosives detection or for agricultural products detection. . . . There is no indication in this case that the dog accompanying Trooper Graham was trained for anything other than drug detection. . . .

For the reasons stated, I would hold that the police violated Caballes' Fourth Amendment rights when, without cause to suspect wrongdoing, they conducted a dog sniff of his vehicle. I would therefore affirm the judgment of the Illinois Supreme Court.

CASE QUESTIONS

KATZ v. UNITED STATES

1. What problem did the Court have with the way the Petitioner worded his issues?

2. What if Katz had entered the public phone booth but left the door opened when making his calls; do you think the Court's holding would have been different? Explain.

3. What proposition of law did the Court's previous decision in Olmstead v. United States, 277 U.S. 438 (1928) stand for? What did the Court in *Katz* have to say about the *Olmstead* case?

4. What two-fold requirement did Justice Harlan enunciate in his concurrence for determining whether something is protected by the Fourth Amendment?

5. Subsequent Supreme Court cases and other authorities discussing the Fourth Amendment's expectation of privacy have quoted Justice Harlan's concurring opinion more frequently than the majority opinion in *Katz*. Why do you think Justice Harlan's opinion has gained more acceptability as the applicable law than the majority opinion?

ILLINOIS v. CABALLES

1. What was the majority's holding with respect to the issue of whether a canine "alerting" to the trunk of a vehicle constituted a search under the Fourth Amendment?

2. How did the majority distinguish its holding in *Caballes* from its recent decision in Kyllo v. United States, 533 U.S. 27 (2001)? Explain.

3. What if it had taken the police an hour to conduct the canine sniff of Caballes' vehicle; do you think the majority's holding would have been different? Do you think it would have had an impact on Justice Ginsburg's dissent? Explain.

4. How does Justice Ginsburg use Terry v. Ohio, 392 U.S. 1 (1968) to support her dissent?

5. What type of a "snowball effect" does Justice Ginsberg perceive is possible in light of the majority's holding? Do you think she has a valid concern? Explain.

HYPOTHETICAL WITH ACCOMPANYING ANALYSIS

Hypothetical

One summer afternoon Laurie was visiting a local park with her two small children when a uniformed police officer approached her. Officer Thomas introduced himself and then explained to Laurie that he suspected her husband, Trevor, of being involved in illegal pornography. "Not Trevor," Laurie responded skeptically, "he would never do anything like that." "Look," the officer replied, "just see for yourself. You know, do a little snooping around when he's not home. Is he secretive about anything? Are there any places in the house that he keeps to himself?" "Well, he does tell me he doesn't want me going into his closet, but he says it's because his closet is always such a mess." The officer then shook his head. "All I'm saying is that I think as his wife it's your right to know if he's involved in something shady. And if he is, don't you think it's in your children's best interest to have this all out in the open? Think of your kids, their future." "What if I find something?" asked Laurie. "Simple," replied the officer, "you bring it to me. And besides," he continued while studying the expression on Laurie's face, "if you find something and you *don't* bring it to me, well then if your husband gets caught and you knew about it and didn't do anything. . . ." Officer Thomas' voice trailed off without finishing his sentence, but he didn't have to. He gave Laurie his business card and left.

That night while Trevor was working late, Laurie entered Trevor's walk-in closet and at first she began by just casually looking around. But before she knew it she had ransacked the entire closet. While doing so she found a box, about the size of a telephone book, which had been hidden underneath a pile of Trevor's sweaters on the top shelf of his closet. The box was marked "PRIVATE" in bold lettering and it was locked. Laurie and Trevor had been married for so long that she could practically read his mind. It took her no time at all to locate the key in Trevor's sock drawer. She opened the box and found hundreds of pictures of minors engaged in explicit sexual acts.

Devastated, Laurie took the box and its contents to the police station. She found Officer Thomas. Handing him the box, she sadly said, "Here you go, you were right." Trevor was thereafter arrested for child pornography and other related offenses. Analyze whether the Fourth Amendment applies.

Analysis

The Fourth Amendment protects individuals against "unreasonable searches and seizures." In order for that protection to come into play, however, it must be determined whether the Fourth Amendment is applicable to any given set of facts.

The first requirement for the Fourth Amendment to be applicable is that a search and/or seizure occur. A "search" occurs whenever an expectation of privacy that society considers reasonable is infringed, and a "seizure" of property occurs when there is some meaningful interference with an individual's possessory interests in that property. Jacobsen v. United States, 466 U.S. 109 (1984). In the instant case Laurie conducted a search when she "ransacked" Trevor's closet while looking for any potentially incriminating evidence. She also conducted a seizure when she took possession of the box and its contents. The first requirement for the Fourth Amendment to be applicable has been met.

Next, the search/seizure must have been conducted by government officials, or it must be conducted by someone acting as an "instrument" or "agent" of the government or with their knowledge or participation. Coolidge v. New Hampshire, 403 U.S. 443 (1971). Laurie is not herself a government official. The question is whether she was acting as an instrument or agent of government when she conducted the search/seizure. During the conversation between Officer Thomas and Laurie, it became apparent that she had no inclination her husband was possibly involved in illegal activity, and thus she had no independent incentive to search Trevor's belongings. Laurie's sole motivation to search arose from Officer Thomas' persuasive tactics. He encouraged her to "snoop around," said she had a "right to know," said it would be best for her children, and indirectly implied that she could be held criminally responsible if she did not turn over any evidence to police. Officer Thomas then went so far as to provide her with his business card. Based on these facts, the evidence strongly indicates that Laurie was acting as an instrument or agent of the Officer Thomas when she conducted the search/seizure. Therefore, the second requirement for the Fourth Amendment to apply has also been met.

The final requirement that must be considered is if the search/seizure occurred where Trevor maintained a reasonable expectation of privacy. This is to be measured by both an objective and subjective standard. Katz v. United States, 389 U.S. 347 (1967). It appears from the facts that Trevor subjectively wished to maintain privacy in the box. It was stored in his closet where he had specifically told his wife on prior occasions not to go, it was hidden from view, it was marked "PRIVATE," and it was locked. From an objective standpoint, one could argue that it would not be reasonable for a husband to maintain an expectation of privacy from his wife in something that was located in their jointly owned and occupied home. However, the counterargument could be that spouses can still retain privacy from one another despite their marital status. Here, since Trevor went to great lengths to ensure that the box was hidden from everyone, including his wife, a reasonable person would likely determine that Trevor had the right to expect privacy in the contents of the box. Thus both prongs of the "reasonable expectation of privacy" standard have been satisfied.

In conclusion, a search and seizure of Trevor's property occurred by someone acting as an agent of government, and Trevor maintained a reasonable expectation of privacy in that property. Therefore, the Fourth Amendment is applicable.

Cloverville is a tiny little town where everyone knows everyone else's business. The local police have been aware for at least a year that the Smiths, Cloverville's wealthiest family, got all of their riches by running drugs for the higher-ups in the big city. Despite the talk of the town the Smiths were always one step ahead of the law, and the police could never to find any evidence against them other than the word of all the local gossips. One day, Deputy R. Ebel, a rookie on the Cloverville Police Department who was known for not playing by the rules, decided that enough was enough. He paid a visit to the Smith's home when no one was there and did a little snooping around. Lo and behold, Deputy Ebel hit the jackpot.

Upon pulling up to the Smith residence in his patrol vehicle, Ebel first noticed two green plastic garbage bags sitting on the curb propped up against the Smith's mailbox. Trash pick-up was that morning, so Ebel knew he had to act quickly before the garbage was taken. He rummaged through both bags and found several pieces of junk mail belonging to the Smiths, some baggies containing a white powdery residue, several small mirrors, and several used razor blades. Ebel deposited the items in his patrol car, and then he then walked up the driveway to their house. The entire backyard was enclosed by a six-foot high picket fence with a "No Trespassing" sign affixed to the gate. Ebel opened the gate and entered the backyard where he spotted a shed containing no windows with a padlock and a "Keep Out" sign on the door. He retrieved a crowbar from his patrol car and managed to break the padlock. Inside the shed he found several heat lamps typically used for growing marijuana and approximately fifty potted plants. Ebel wasn't sure, but in his training manual he had seen a picture of a marijuana plant and it looked identical to the potted plants in the shed. He seized a lamp and two plants. As he was on his way back to his vehicle he passed by a screened-in back porch that was attached to the house. Clearly visible on a table inside the porch was a bong and a set of scales. Recognizing the drug paraphernalia immediately, he forced open the porch door, which had been locked by a small metal latch hooked on the inside of the door, and he collected the items on the table. Ebel was ecstatic! He had finally found indisputable proof of the Smiths' criminal activity, and they were on their way to jail. Or were they?

Analyze whether the Fourth Amendment applied to Deputy Ebel's actions.

DISCUSSION QUESTIONS

1. Kyle is suspected of bringing a weapon onto the grounds of his public high school. Mr. Boxwell, the principal of the school, conducts a search of Kyle's book bag and finds a gun. Does the Fourth Amendment apply? Explain.

2. Research challenge: Who is "Popsicle" the pit bull terrier, how was he first discovered, and how has he helped United States Customs officers in seizing evidence?

3. Sam owns a hundred-acre farm that runs adjacent to a major interstate highway. On ninety-nine of those acres Sam grows corn, but in the center acre of his farm he is growing marijuana. Police officers, who happen to be in a helicopter flying over Sam's farm on traffic patrol, spot the suspicious acre and hover to get a closer look. They discover that Sam is growing marijuana and he is arrested. Will Sam have a successful argument that the police unreasonably searched his private property and violated his reasonable expectation of privacy? Why or why not? *See* California v. Ciraolo, 476 U.S. 207 (1986) and Florida v. Riley, 488 U.S. 445 (1989).

4. Given the fact that we live in such a technologically advanced era, what obstacles do you think police might encounter today that they did not encounter decades ago when executing a search or seizure? How has the "traditional" search of one's home or one's person been replaced by non-traditional searches in light of the change in times?

5. How exactly is it determined whether an individual is under arrest? Must police officers say the magic words "you are under arrest"? Must they handcuff a suspect? Can police use deadly force when effectuating an arrest? *See, e.g.,* Tennessee v. Garner, 471 U.S. 1 (1985) and California v. Hodari D., 499 U.S. 621 (1991).

6. Brad's neighbors, the Busybodies, suspect he is counterfeiting money. Late one night they break into his home and search his basement, where they find illegal equipment and several thousand bills with no serial numbers. They seize the money and take it directly to the police. Brad is charged with federal and state counterfeiting offenses. Will he succeed in having the evidence suppressed based on his Fourth Amendment rights? What consequences could the Busybodies face for their actions?

7. Kevin and Rachael are college sophomores who had been casually seeing each other for the last month. One night at a fraternity party, things apparently got a little out of hand. The next morning Rachael's mother called the police station to report that her daughter was a victim of "date rape." The police interviewed Rachael and convinced her to call Kevin and discuss the night's events, in the hopes that Kevin would admit to the rape. The police coached Rachael regarding what to say, and about ten minutes into the conversation Kevin admitted to Rachael that he had had sexual intercourse with her and that she had not consented. Unbeknownst to Kevin, the entire conversation was being recorded by police with Rachael's permission. Does the Fourth Amendment apply? *See* Rathbun v. United States, 355 U.S. 107 (1957).

8. Police suspect Mark of being a drug dealer, but they have been unable to obtain any evidence against him. Therefore, they attach a small box containing a tracking device underneath Mark's car in the hopes that they will obtain incriminating information against him. Do these actions on the part of police constitute a search and/or seizure of Mark's whereabouts or travels? Is the Fourth Amendment applicable?

9. What is a "citizen's arrest"? When can it be effectuated? What types of individuals can you think of who would likely make citizens arrests?

10. Revisit the Hypothetical with Accompanying Analysis from this chapter after carefully reading Coolidge v. New Hampshire, 403 U.S. 443 (1971). How are the facts of *Coolidge* dealing with the suspect's wife's actions distinguishable from those in the hypothetical? Why was the Fourth Amendment applicable in the Hypothetical but not in *Coolidge*? Explain.

True/False

1. A drug dog sniffing the outside of a vehicle and "alerting" to the presence of contraband would be considered a search under the Fourth Amendment.

2. Katz v. United States established that the Fourth Amendment can potentially govern the seizure of intangible items in addition to tangible items.

3. A search conducted by a private individual would never implicate the Fourth Amendment.

4. An individual has no reasonable expectation of privacy in property that has been abandoned.

5. Kim has rented a vehicle for a cross-country vacation. She is pulled over and police search her vehicle despite her protests. The government maintains she had no reasonable expectation of privacy in the vehicle because she did not own the vehicle. The government will succeed in its argument.

Multiple Choice

6. Sally owns a ten-acre farm. On her farm she has a home, a barn, a chicken coop, and a detached garage with a guest room over top. A large fence surrounds all but the chicken coop, which is located ten feet from the highway and has no doors. The barn has no electricity or running water, but it has a dead bolt on the door and a "no trespassing" sign affixed to the door. Which of the following would most likely be considered "curtilage" for the purposes of the Fourth Amendment?

   A. The chicken coop
   B. The barn and the chicken coop
   C. The barn and the detached garage
   D. The home and the detached garage

7. Under which of the following circumstances would Bobby most likely *not* be seized within the meaning of the Fourth Amendment?

   A. Police forcibly grab Bobby's arms and handcuff him while Bobby submits to their authority.
   B. Police forcibly grab Bobby's arms and handcuff him while Bobby struggles and tries unsuccessfully to break free.
   C. Police draw their weapons, state "You are under arrest," and Bobby puts his hands up in the air.
   D. Police draw their weapons, state "You are under arrest," but Bobby runs and police pursue him.

8. Sam was driving along smoking what appeared to be a hand-rolled cigarette when a police officer pulled along side of Sam and noticed him smoking. The officer pulled behind Sam to observe Sam's driving, when he observed Sam open his car window and throw out both the cigarette he had been smoking and a small plastic bag that was filled with a dark green material. Noting the plate number on Sam's car, the officer went back to where he observed Sam throw the items out of the car window, and he retrieved those items. The officer concluded that both the contents of the plastic bag and the cigarette were marijuana. A short time later, Sam was located and arrested. The plastic bag and the cigarette are:

   A. Inadmissible as evidence because the officer had no probable cause to search for them
   B. Inadmissible as evidence because the officer did not have a warrant to seize those items
   C. Inadmissible as evidence because during the brief time the officer followed Sam, the officer was not acting as an agent of the government
   D. Admissible against Sam because the items were not protected by the Fourth Amendment

9. Which of the following individuals is most likely *not* covered by the Fourth Amendment?

   A. A private security guard
   B. A high school principal
   C. Agents of the Internal Revenue Service
   D. A local sheriff's deputy

10. Which of the following would most likely *not* constitute a "search" under the Fourth Amendment?

   A. A government inspector taking urine samples from government employees to determine whether drugs are present in the employees' bodies
   B. A drug dog sniffing and "alerting" to the presence of contraband outside of a high school student's locker
   C. Police using a thermal imaging device to detect the presence of heat from inside of a private residence
   D. Police flying over a farm in an airplane looking for contraband being grown on the farm

2

The Warrant Requirement and Exceptions

"... and no Warrants shall issue, but upon probable cause, supported by Oath or affirmation, and particularly describing the place to be searched, and the persons or things to be seized."

—The Fourth Amendment

INTRODUCTION

An elementary school child hops off the bus one afternoon waiving a piece of paper in front of her mother. "What's that?" her mother inquires. "A permission slip," the child replies. The mother takes a closer look. The slip informs her that her daughter's third grade class will be taking a field trip to a local zoo, on a specified date and at a specified time, and it lists the activities that will occur once the class arrives. Then, down at the bottom of the page is a blank line where she must sign in order to give her daughter permission to attend the field trip. What on earth does a child's permission slip have to do with the Fourth Amendment? Simple. The warrant is the government's version of a permission slip, because it provides legal authority to conduct a search and seizure. A school doesn't send home a permission slip with a child that reads, "We're going to take a field trip, but we're not quite sure *where*, and we're not quite sure *when*, and we're not quite sure what we're going to *do* once we're there." Of course not. The permission slip is specific, and so too is the warrant. It describes in detail the place to be searched and the items to be seized. And perhaps most importantly, it requires the signature of a detached magistrate or judge before it will be valid, just like the young girl needs her mother's signature in order to attend the field trip. The warrant requirement is crucial in law enforcement, because if the government puts forth the time and energy to get a warrant, any resulting search and seizure will be presumed lawful. If, on the other hand, the government executes a search and/or seizure *without* a warrant, it will bear the burden at trial of proving that the Fourth Amendment was complied with despite the lack of a warrant.

That's not to say, however, that the government must *always* get a warrant. Requiring a warrant in some cases would be just as absurd as the child's vague permission slip. Imagine this: Police are hot on the tail of a man in a getaway car who has just robbed a bank. The officer is in pursuit—his lights flashing and sirens blaring. All of a sudden the officer makes a sharp left, speeds six blocks away to the courthouse where he runs inside and demands from a judge, "I need a warrant, *now*!" The scenario is ridiculous for obvious reasons. Recognizing just that fact, the Supreme Court has said to the government that under certain circumstances, "We excuse you from having to first get a warrant." Or at times the Court has permitted a limited search on less than probable cause, thus negating the warrant requirement altogether. Therefore, understanding when a warrant is or is not required is just as important as understanding what a warrant is.

This chapter, a continuation of our analysis from Chapter 1, will examine the components for obtaining and executing a warrant, and the circumstances under which a warrant need not be obtained. Finally, it will take us across our last stepping stone when we examine what to do when evidence is illegally seized from an individual.

STUDENT *Checklist*

The Warrant Requirement and Exceptions

Continued from Chapter 1 . . .

2. Was the Fourth Amendment **complied with**?

▪ Did the government obtain a **warrant** . . .

　 Was the warrant supported by **facts** which established **probable cause**?

　 Was the warrant signed by a **neutral and detached magistrate**?

　 Was the warrant **detailed** with respect to the **place to be searched** and the **things to be seized**?

　 Was the warrant **executed** in a proper manner?

　　❑ Did the government **knock and announce** presence if so required?

　　❑ Was the warrant served during **daylight hours** if so required?

　　❑ Was scope of search **reasonable** in light of items searched for?

　　❑ Was the warrant served in a **timely** manner (i.e., it had not gone **stale**)?

　　❑ Did the search **end** once the items to be seized were seized?

　　❑ Did the government provide **notice** that property had been seized?

　or

▪ Did the search/seizure fall within an **exception** to the warrant requirement. . . .

      Search incident to arrest
      Plain view and related doctrines
      Emergency Circumstances/Hot Pursuit
      Evanescent evidence
      Automobiles
      Consent**
      or

■ Was the search/seizure permissible on **less than probable cause**?
      Stop and frisk
      Public school searches
      Inspections of closely regulated industries
      Inventory searches
      Border/Airport searches
      Protective sweeps
      Sobriety checkpoints
      Consent[*]

3. If the Fourth Amendment was not complied with, was the individual afforded a **remedy**?

■ Under the **Exclusionary Rule**, was all illegally seized evidence **suppressed** at trial?

■ Under the **Fruit of the Poisonous Tree Doctrine**, was all **derivative evidence** obtained as a result of the illegal search also **suppressed**?
    or

■ Did the government persuade the judge by a **preponderance of the evidence** that the evidence should be admissible despite the illegal search because of:
      Good faith
      Inevitable discovery
      Independent source
      Attenuation of the taint

* Note: Consent is unique in that police officers may ask for consent to search while possessing probable cause, but they can also ask for consent even when no probable cause exists. In either case, if consent is granted, police need not obtain a warrant.

SUPREME COURT CASES

TERRY v. OHIO, 392 U.S. 1 (1968)

This case presents serious questions concerning the role of the Fourth Amendment in the confrontation on the street between the citizen and the policeman investigating suspicious circumstances.

    Petitioner Terry was convicted of carrying a concealed weapon and sentenced to the statutorily prescribed term of one to three years in the penitentiary. Following the denial of a pretrial motion to suppress, the prosecution introduced in evidence two revolvers and a number of bullets seized from Terry and a codefendant, Richard Chilton, by Cleveland Police Detective Martin

McFadden. At the hearing on the motion to suppress this evidence, Officer McFadden testified that while he was patrolling in plain clothes in downtown Cleveland at approximately 2:30 in the afternoon of October 31, 1963, his attention was attracted by two men, Chilton and Terry, standing on the corner of Huron Road and Euclid Avenue. He had never seen the two men before, and he was unable to say precisely what first drew his eye to them. However, he testified that he had been a policeman for 39 years and a detective for 35 and that he had been assigned to patrol this vicinity of downtown Cleveland for shoplifters and pickpockets for 30 years. He explained that he had developed routine habits of observation over the years and that he would "stand and watch people or walk and watch people at many intervals of the day." He added: "Now, in this case when I looked over they didn't look right to me at the time."

His interest aroused, Officer McFadden took up a post of observation in the entrance to a store 300 to 400 feet away from the two men. "I get more purpose to watch them when I seen their movements," he testified. He saw one of the men leave the other one and walk southwest on Huron Road, past some stores. The man paused for a moment and looked in a store window, then walked on a short distance, turned around and walked back toward the corner, pausing once again to look in the same store window. He rejoined his companion at the corner, and the two conferred briefly. Then the second man went through the same series of motions, strolling down Huron Road, looking in the same window, walking on a short distance, turning back, peering in the store window again, and returning to confer with the first man at the corner. The two men repeated this ritual alternately between five and six times apiece—in all, roughly a dozen trips. At one point, while the two were standing together on the corner, a third man approached them and engaged them briefly in conversation. This man then left the two others and walked west on Euclid Avenue. Chilton and Terry resumed their measured pacing, peering and conferring. After this had gone on for 10 to 12 minutes, the two men walked off together, heading west on Euclid Avenue, following the path taken earlier by the third man.

By this time Officer McFadden had become thoroughly suspicious. He testified that after observing their elaborately casual and oft-repeated reconnaissance of the store window on Huron Road, he suspected the two men of "casing a job, a stick-up," and that he considered it his duty as a police officer to investigate further. He added that he feared "they may have a gun." Thus, Officer McFadden followed Chilton and Terry and saw them stop in front of Zucker's store to talk to the same man who had conferred with them earlier on the street corner. Deciding that the situation was ripe for direct action, Officer McFadden approached the three men, identified himself as a police officer and asked for their names. At this point his knowledge was confined to what he had observed. He was not acquainted with any of the three men by name or by sight, and he had received no information concerning them from any other source. When the men "mumbled something" in response to his inquiries, Officer McFadden grabbed petitioner Terry, spun him around so that they were facing the other two, with Terry between McFadden and the others, and patted down the outside of his clothing. In the left breast pocket of Terry's overcoat Officer McFadden felt a pistol. He reached inside the overcoat pocket, but was unable to remove the gun. At this point, keeping Terry between himself and the others, the officer ordered all three men to enter Zucker's store. As they went in, he removed Terry's overcoat completely, removed a .38-caliber revolver from the pocket and ordered all three men to face the wall with their hands raised. Officer McFadden proceeded to pat down the outer clothing of Chilton and the third man, Katz. He discovered another revolver in the outer pocket of Chilton's overcoat, but no weapons were found on Katz. The officer testified that he only patted the men down to see whether they had weapons, and that he did not put his hands beneath the outer garments of either Terry or Chilton until he felt their guns. So far as appears from the record, he never placed his hands beneath Katz' outer garments. Officer McFadden seized Chilton's gun, asked the proprietor of the store to call a police wagon, and took all three men to the station, where Chilton and Terry were formally charged with carrying concealed weapons. . . .

After the court denied their motion to suppress, Chilton and Terry waived jury trial and pleaded not guilty. The court adjudged them guilty . . .

I

The Fourth Amendment provides that "the right of the people to be secure in their persons, houses, papers, and effects, against unreasonable searches and seizures, shall not be violated. . . ." This inestimable right of personal security belongs as much to the citizen on the streets of our cities as to the homeowner closeted in his study to dispose of his secret affairs. For, as this Court has always recognized,

> No right is held more sacred, or is more carefully guarded, by the common law, than the right of every individual to the possession and control of his own person, free from all restraint or interference of others, unless by clear and unquestionable authority of law. Union Pac. R. Co. v. Botsford, 141 U.S. 250, 251, 11 S. Ct. 1000, 1001, 35 L. Ed. 734 (1891).

We have recently held that "the Fourth Amendment protects people, not places," Katz v. United States, 389 U.S. 347, 351, 88 S. Ct. 507, 511, 19 L. Ed. 2d 576 (1967), and wherever an individual may harbor a reasonable "expectation of privacy," id., at 361, 88 S. Ct. at 507, (Mr. Justice Harlan, concurring), he is entitled to be free from unreasonable governmental intrusion. Of course, the specific content and incidents of this right must be shaped by the context in which it is asserted. For "what the Constitution forbids is not all searches and seizures, but unreasonable searches and seizures." Elkins v. United States, 364 U.S. 206, 222, 80 S. Ct. 1437, 1446, 4 L. Ed. 2d 1669 (1960). Unquestionably petitioner was entitled to the protection of the Fourth Amendment as he walked down the street in Cleveland. . . . The question is whether in all the circumstances of this on-the-street encounter, his right to personal security was violated by an unreasonable search and seizure. . . .

II

Our first task is to establish at what point in this encounter the Fourth Amendment becomes relevant. That is, we must decide whether and when Officer McFadden "seized" Terry and whether and when he conducted a "search." There is some suggestion in the use of such terms as "stop" and "frisk" that such police conduct is outside the purview of the Fourth Amendment because neither action rises to the level of a "search" or "seizure" within the meaning of the Constitution. We emphatically reject this notion. It is quite plain that the Fourth Amendment governs "seizures" of the person which do not eventuate in a trip to the station house and prosecution for crime—"arrests" in traditional terminology. It must be recognized that whenever a police officer accosts an individual and restrains his freedom to walk away, he has "seized" that person. And it is nothing less than sheer torture of the English language to suggest that a careful exploration of the outer surfaces of a person's clothing all over his or her body in an attempt to find weapons is not a "search," Moreover, it is simply fantastic to urge that such a procedure performed in public by a policeman while the citizen stands helpless, perhaps facing a wall with his hands raised, is a "petty indignity." It is a serious intrusion upon the sanctity of the person, which may inflict great indignity and arouse strong resentment, and it is not to be undertaken lightly. . . .

In this case there can be no question, then, that Officer McFadden "seized" petitioner and subjected him to a "search" when he took hold of him and patted down the outer surfaces of his clothing. We must decide whether at that point it was reasonable for Officer McFadden to have interfered with petitioner's personal security as he did. And in determining whether the seizure and search were "unreasonable" our inquiry is a dual one—whether the officer's action was justified at its inception, and whether it was reasonably related in scope to the circumstances which justified the interference in the first place.

III

If this case involved police conduct subject to the Warrant Clause of the Fourth Amendment, we would have to ascertain whether "probable cause" existed to justify the search and seizure which took place. However, that is not the case. We do not retreat from our holdings that the police must, whenever practicable, obtain advance judicial approval of searches and seizures through the warrant procedure . . . or that in most instances failure to comply with the warrant requirement can only be excused by exigent circumstances, see, e.g., Warden v. Hayden, 387 U.S. 294, 87 S. Ct. 1642, 18 L. Ed. 2d 782 (1967) (hot pursuit); cf. Preston v. United States, 376 U.S. 364, 367-368, 84 S. Ct. 881, 884, 11 L. Ed. 2d 777 (1964). But we deal here with an entire rubric of police conduct—necessarily swift action predicated upon the on-the-spot observations of the officer on the beat—which historically has not been, and as a practical matter could not be, subjected to the warrant procedure. Instead, the conduct involved in this case must be tested by the Fourth Amendment's general proscription against unreasonable searches and seizures.

Nonetheless, the notions which underlie both the warrant procedure and the requirement of probable cause remain fully relevant in this context. In order to assess the reasonableness of Officer McFadden's conduct as a general proposition, it is necessary "first to focus upon the governmental interest which allegedly justifies official intrusion upon the constitutionally protected interests of the private citizen," for there is "no ready test for determining reasonableness other than by balancing the need to search (or seize) against the invasion which the search (or seizure) entails." Camara v. Municipal Court, 387 U.S. 523, 534-535, 536-537, 87 S. Ct. 1727, 1735, 18 L. Ed. 2d 930 (1967). And in justifying the particular intrusion the police officer must be able to point to specific and articulable facts which, taken together with rational inferences from those facts, reasonably warrant that intrusion. The scheme of the Fourth Amendment becomes meaningful only when it is assured that at some point the conduct of those charged with enforcing the laws can be subjected to the more detached, neutral scrutiny of a judge who must evaluate the reasonableness of a particular search or seizure in light of the particular circumstances. And in making that assessment it is imperative that the facts be judged against an objective standard: would the facts available to the officer at the moment of the seizure or the search "warrant a man of reasonable caution in the belief" that the action taken was appropriate? Cf. Carroll v. United States, 267 U.S. 132, 45 S. Ct. 280, 69 L. Ed. 543 (1925); Beck v. State of Ohio, 379 U.S. 89, 96-97, 85 S. Ct. 223, 229, 13 L. Ed. 2d 142 (1964). Anything less would invite intrusions upon constitutionally guaranteed rights based on nothing more substantial than inarticulate hunches, a result this Court has consistently refused to sanction. . . . And simple "good faith on the part of the arresting officer is not enough." . . . If subjective good faith alone were the test, the protections of the Fourth Amendment would evaporate, and the people would be "secure in their persons, houses, papers and effects," only in the discretion of the police. Beck v. Ohio, supra, at 97, 85 S. Ct. at 229.

Applying these principles to this case, we consider first the nature and extent of the governmental interests involved. One general interest is of course that of effective crime prevention and detection; it is this interest which underlies the recognition that a police officer may in appropriate circumstances and in an appropriate manner approach a person for purposes of investigating possibly criminal behavior even though there is no probable cause to make an arrest. It was this legitimate investigative function Officer McFadden was discharging when he decided to approach petitioner and his companions He had observed Terry, Chilton, and Katz go through a series of acts, each of them perhaps innocent in itself, but which taken together warranted further investigation. There is nothing unusual in two men standing together on a street corner, perhaps waiting for someone. Nor is there anything suspicious about people in such circumstances strolling up and down the street, singly or in pairs. Store windows, moreover, are made to be looked in. But the story is quite different where, as here, two men hover about a street corner for an extended period of time, at the end of which it becomes apparent that they are not waiting for anyone or anything; where these men pace alternately along an identical route, pausing to stare in the same store window roughly 24 times; where each completion of this route is followed immediately by a conference between the two men on the corner; where they are joined in one of these conferences by a third man who leaves swiftly; and where the two men finally follow the third and rejoin him a couple of blocks away. It would have been poor police work indeed for an officer of 30 years' experience in the detection of thievery from stores in this same neighborhood to have failed to investigate this behavior further.

The crux of this case, however, is not the propriety of Officer McFadden's taking steps to investigate petitioner's suspicious behavior, but rather, whether there was justification for McFadden's invasion of Terry's personal security by searching him for weapons in the course of that investigation. We are now concerned with more than the governmental interest in investigating crime; in addition, there is the more immediate interest of the police officer in taking steps to assure himself that the person with whom he is dealing is not armed with a weapon that could unexpectedly and fatally be used against him. Certainly it would be unreasonable to require that police officers take unnecessary risks in the performance of their duties. American criminals have a long tradition of armed violence, and every year in this country many law enforcement officers are killed in the line of duty, and thousands more are wounded. Virtually all of these deaths and a substantial portion of the injuries are inflicted with guns and knives.

In view of these facts, we cannot blind ourselves to the need for law enforcement officers to protect themselves and other prospective victims of violence in situations where they may lack probable cause for an arrest. When an officer is justified in believing that the individual whose suspicious behavior he is investigating at close range is armed and presently dangerous to the officer or to others, it would appear to be clearly unreasonable to deny the officer the power to take necessary measures to determine whether the person is in fact carrying a weapon and to neutralize the threat of physical harm.

We must still consider, however, the nature and quality of the intrusion on individual rights which must be accepted if police officers are to be conceded the right to search for weapons in situations where probable cause to arrest for crime is lacking. Even a limited search of the outer clothing for weapons constitutes a severe, though brief, intrusion upon cherished personal security, and it must surely be an annoying, frightening, and perhaps humiliating experience. Petitioner contends that such an intrusion is permissible only incident to a lawful arrest, either for a crime involving the possession of weapons or for a crime the commission of which led the officer to investigate in the first place. However, this argument must be closely examined. . . .

Our evaluation of the proper balance that has to be struck in this type of case leads us to conclude that there must be a narrowly drawn authority to permit a reasonable search for weapons for the protection of the police officer, where he has reason to believe that he is dealing with an armed and dangerous individual, regardless of whether he has probable cause to arrest the individual for a crime. The officer need not be absolutely certain that the individual is armed; the issue is whether a reasonably prudent man in the circumstances would be warranted in the belief that his safety or that of others was in danger. . . . And in determining whether the officer acted reasonably in such circumstances, due weight must be given, not to his inchoate and unparticularized suspicion or "hunch," but to the specific reasonable inferences which he is entitled to draw from the facts in light of his experience. Cf. Brinegar v. United States, supra.

IV

We must now examine the conduct of Officer McFadden in this case to determine whether his search and seizure of petitioner were reasonable, both at their inception and as conducted. He had observed Terry, together with Chilton and another man, acting in a manner he took to be preface to a "stick-up." We think on the facts and circumstances Officer McFadden detailed before the trial judge a reasonably prudent man would have been warranted in believing petitioner was armed and thus presented a threat to the officer's safety while he was investigating his suspicious behavior. The actions of Terry and Chilton were consistent with McFadden's hypothesis that these men were contemplating a daylight robbery—which, it is reasonable to assume, would be likely to involve the use of weapons—and nothing in their conduct from the time he first noticed them until the time he confronted them and identified himself as a police officer gave him sufficient reason to negate that hypothesis. Although the trio had departed the original scene, there was nothing to indicate abandonment of an intent to commit a robbery at some point. Thus, when Officer McFadden approached the three men gathered before the display window at Zucker's store he had observed enough to make it quite reasonable to fear that they were armed; and nothing in their response to his hailing them, identifying himself as a police officer, and asking their names served to dispel that reasonable belief. We cannot say his decision at that point to seize Terry and pat his clothing for weapons was the product of a volatile or inventive imagination, or was undertaken simply as an act of harassment; the record evidences the tempered act of a policeman who in the course of an investigation had to make a quick decision as to how to protect himself and others from possible danger, and took limited steps to do so. . . .

The scope of the search in this case presents no serious problem in light of these standards. Officer McFadden patted down the outer clothing of petitioner and his two companions. He did not place his hands in their pockets or under the outer surface of their garments until he had felt weapons, and then he merely reached for and removed the guns. He never did invade Katz' person beyond the outer surfaces of his clothes, since he discovered nothing in his patdown which might have been a weapon. Officer McFadden confined his search strictly to what was minimally necessary to learn whether the men were armed and to disarm them once he discovered the weapons. He did not conduct a general exploratory search for whatever evidence of criminal activity he might find.

V

We conclude that the revolver seized from Terry was properly admitted in evidence against him. At the time he seized petitioner and searched him for weapons, Officer McFadden had reasonable grounds to believe that petitioner was armed and dangerous, and it was necessary for the protection of himself and others to take swift measures to discover the true facts and neutralize the threat of harm if it materialized. The policeman carefully restricted his search to what was appropriate to the discovery of the particular items which he sought. Each case of this sort will, of course, have to be decided on its own facts. We merely hold today that where a police officer observes unusual conduct which leads him reasonably to conclude in light of his experience that criminal activity may be afoot and that the persons with whom he is dealing may be armed and presently dangerous, where in the course of investigating this behavior he identifies himself as a policeman and makes reasonable inquiries, and where nothing in the initial stages of the encounter serves to dispel his reasonable fear for his own or others' safety, he is entitled for the protection of himself and others in the area to conduct a carefully limited search of the outer clothing of such persons in an attempt to discover weapons which might be used to assault him. Such a search is a reasonable search under the Fourth Amendment, and any weapons seized may properly be introduced in evidence against the person from whom they were taken.

Affirmed.

UNITED STATES v. GRUBBS, 547 U.S. 90 (2006)

Federal law enforcement officers obtained a search warrant for respondent's house on the basis of an affidavit explaining that the warrant would be executed only after a controlled delivery of contraband to that location. We address two challenges to the constitutionality of this anticipatory warrant.

I

Respondent Jeffrey Grubbs purchased a videotape containing child pornography from a Web site operated by an undercover postal inspector. Officers from the Postal Inspection Service arranged a controlled delivery of a package containing the videotape to Grubbs' residence. A postal inspector submitted a search warrant application to a Magistrate Judge for the Eastern District of California, accompanied by an affidavit describing the proposed operation in detail. The affidavit stated:

> Execution of this search warrant will not occur unless and until the parcel has been received by a person(s) and has been physically taken into the residence. . . . At that time, and not before, this search warrant will be executed by me and other United States Postal inspectors, with appropriate assistance from other law enforcement officers in accordance with this warrant's command. App. to Pet. for Cert. 72a.

In addition to describing this triggering condition, the affidavit referred to two attachments, which described Grubbs' residence and the items officers would seize. These attachments, but not the body of the affidavit, were incorporated into the requested warrant. The affidavit concluded:

> Based upon the foregoing facts, I respectfully submit there exists probable cause to believe that the items set forth in Attachment B to this affidavit and the search warrant, will be found [at Grubbs' residence], which residence is further described at Attachment A. *Ibid.*

The Magistrate Judge issued the warrant as requested. Two days later, an undercover postal inspector delivered the package. Grubbs' wife signed for it and took the unopened package inside. The inspectors detained Grubbs as he left his home a few minutes later, then entered the house and commenced the search. Roughly 30 minutes into the search, Grubbs was provided with a copy of the warrant, which included both attachments but not the supporting affidavit that explained when the warrant would be executed. Grubbs consented to interrogation by the postal inspectors and admitted ordering the videotape. He was placed under arrest, and various items were seized, including the videotape.

A grand jury for the Eastern District of California indicted Grubbs on one count of receiving a visual depiction of a minor engaged in sexually explicit conduct. See 18 U.S.C. § 2252(a)(2). He moved to suppress the evidence seized during the search of his residence, arguing as relevant here that the warrant was invalid because it failed to list the triggering condition. After an evidentiary hearing, the District Court denied the motion. Grubbs pleaded guilty, but reserved his right to appeal the denial of his motion to suppress.

The Court of Appeals for the Ninth Circuit reversed. 377 F.3d 1072, amended, 389 F.3d 1306 (C.A.9 2004). Relying on Circuit precedent, it held that "the particularity requirement of the Fourth Amendment applies with full force to the conditions precedent to an anticipatory search warrant." 377 F.3d, at 1077-1078 (citing *United States v. Hotal*, 143 F.3d 1223, 1226 (C.A.9 1998)). An anticipatory warrant defective for that reason may be "cur[ed]" if the conditions precedent are set forth in an affidavit that is incorporated in the warrant and "presented to the person whose property is being searched." 377 F.3d, at 1079. Because the postal inspectors "failed to present the affidavit—the only document in which the triggering conditions were listed"—to Grubbs or his wife, the "warrant was . . . inoperative, and the search was illegal." *Ibid.* We granted certiorari. 545 U.S. 1164, 126 S. Ct. 34, 162 L. Ed. 2d 932 (2005).

II

Before turning to the Ninth Circuit's conclusion that the warrant at issue here ran afoul of the Fourth Amendment's particularity requirement, we address the antecedent question whether anticipatory search warrants are categorically unconstitutional. An anticipatory warrant is "a warrant based upon an affidavit showing probable cause that at some future time (but not presently) certain evidence of crime will be located at a specified place." 2 W. LaFave, Search and Seizure § 3.7(c), p. 398 (4th ed. 2004). Most anticipatory warrants subject their execution to some condition precedent other than the mere passage of time—a so-called "triggering condition." The affidavit at issue here, for instance, explained that "[e]xecution of th[e] search warrant will not occur unless and until the parcel [containing child pornography] has been received by a person(s) and has been physically taken into the residence." App. to Pet. for Cert. 72a. If the government were to execute an anticipatory warrant before the triggering condition occurred, there would be no reason to believe the item described in the warrant could be found at the searched location; by definition, the triggering condition which establishes probable cause has not yet been satisfied when the warrant is issued. Grubbs argues that for this reason anticipatory warrants contravene the Fourth Amendment's provision that "no Warrants shall issue, but upon probable cause."

We reject this view, as has every Court of Appeals to confront the issue, see, e.g., *United States v. Loy*, 191 F.3d 360, 364 (C.A.3 1999) (collecting cases). Probable cause exists when "there is a fair probability that contraband or evidence of a crime will be found in a particular place." *Illinois v. Gates*, 462 U.S. 213, 238, 103 S. Ct. 2317, 76 L. Ed. 2d 527 (1983). Because the probable-cause requirement looks to whether evidence will be found *when the search is conducted*, all warrants are, in a sense, "anticipatory." In the typical case where the police seek permission to search a house for an item they believe is already located there, the magistrate's determination that there is probable cause for the search amounts to a prediction that the item will still be there when the warrant is executed. See *People v. Glen*, 30 N.Y.2d 252, 258, 331 N.Y.S.2d 656, 282 N.E.2d 614, 617 (1972) ("[P]resent possession is only probative of the likelihood of future possession."). The anticipatory nature of warrants is even clearer in the context of electronic surveillance. See, e.g., *Katz v. United States*, 389 U.S. 347, 88 S. Ct. 507, 19 L. Ed. 2d 576 (1967). When police request approval to tap a telephone line, they do so based on the probability that, during the course of the surveillance, the subject *will* use the phone to engage in crime-related conversations. The relevant federal provision requires a judge authorizing "interception of wire, oral, or electronic communications" to determine that "there is probable cause for belief that particular communications concerning [one of various listed offenses] *will be obtained* through such interception." 18 U.S.C. § 2518(3)(b) (emphasis added); see also *United States v. Ricciardelli*, 998 F.2d 8, 11, n.3 (C.A.1 1993) ("[T]he magistrate issues the warrant on the basis of a substantial probability that crime-related conversations will ensue."). Thus, when an anticipatory warrant is issued, "the fact that the contraband is not presently located at the place described in the warrant is immaterial, so long as there is probable cause to believe that it will be there when the search warrant is executed." *United States v. Garcia*, 882 F.2d 699, 702 (C.A.2 1989) (quoting *United States v. Lowe*, 575 F.2d 1193, 1194 (C.A.6 1978); internal quotation marks omitted).

Anticipatory warrants are, therefore, no different in principle from ordinary warrants. They require the magistrate to determine (1) that it is *now probable* that (2) contraband, evidence of a crime, or a fugitive *will be* on the described premises (3) when the warrant is executed. It should be noted, however, that where the anticipatory warrant places a condition (other than the mere passage of time) upon its execution, the first of these determinations goes not merely to what will probably be found *if* the condition is met. (If that were the extent of the probability determination, an anticipatory warrant could be issued for every house in the country, authorizing search and seizure *if* contraband should be delivered—though for any single location there is no likelihood that contraband will be delivered.) Rather, the probability determination for a conditioned anticipatory warrant looks also to the likelihood that the condition will occur, and thus that a proper object of seizure will be on the described premises. In other words, for a conditioned anticipatory warrant to comply with the Fourth Amendment's requirement of probable cause, two prerequisites of probability must be satisfied. It must be true not only that *if* the triggering condition occurs "there is a fair probability that contraband or evidence of a crime will be found in a particular place," *Gates, supra*, at 238, 103 S. Ct. 2317, but also that there is probable cause to believe the triggering condition *will occur*. The supporting affidavit must provide the magistrate with sufficient information to evaluate both aspects of the probable-cause determination. See *Garcia, supra*, at 703.

In this case, the occurrence of the triggering condition—successful delivery of the videotape to Grubbs' residence—would plainly establish probable cause for the search. In addition, the affidavit established probable cause to believe the triggering condition would be satisfied. Although it is possible that Grubbs could have refused delivery of the videotape he had ordered, that was unlikely. The Magistrate therefore "had a 'substantial basis for . . . conclud[ing]' that probable cause existed." *Gates*, 462 U.S., at 238-239, 103 S. Ct. 2317 (quoting *Jones v. United States*, 362 U.S. 257, 271, 80 S. Ct. 725, 4 L. Ed. 2d 697 (1960)).

III

The Ninth Circuit invalidated the anticipatory search warrant at issue here because the warrant failed to specify the triggering condition. The Fourth Amendment's particularity requirement, it held, "applies with full force to the conditions precedent to an anticipatory search warrant." 377 F.3d, at 1077-1078.

The Fourth Amendment, however, does not set forth some general "particularity requirement." It specifies only two matters that must be "particularly describ[ed]" in the warrant: "the place to be searched" and "the persons or things to be seized." We have previously rejected efforts to expand the scope of this provision to embrace unenumerated matters. In *Dalia v. United States*, 441 U.S. 238, 99 S. Ct. 1682, 60 L. Ed. 2d 177 (1979), we considered an order authorizing the interception of oral communications by means of a "bug" installed by the police in the petitioner's office. The petitioner argued that, if a covert entry is necessary to install such a listening device, the authorizing order must "explicitly set forth its approval of such entries before the fact." *Id.*, at 255, 99 S. Ct. 1682. This argument fell before the "'precise and clear'" words of the Fourth Amendment: "Nothing in the language of the Constitution or in this Court's decisions interpreting that language suggests that, in addition to the [requirements set forth in the text], search warrants also must include a specification of the precise manner in which they are to be executed." *Id.*, at 255, 99 S. Ct. 1682 (quoting *Stanford v. Texas*, 379 U.S. 476, 481, 85 S. Ct. 506, 13 L. Ed. 2d 431 (1965)), 257, 99 S. Ct. 1682. The language of the Fourth Amendment is likewise decisive here; its particularity requirement does not include the conditions precedent to execution of the warrant.

Respondent, drawing upon the Ninth Circuit's analysis below, relies primarily on two related policy rationales. First, he argues, setting forth the triggering condition in the warrant itself is necessary "to delineate the limits of the executing officer's power." Brief for Respondent 20. This is an application, respondent asserts, of the following principle: "[I]f there is a precondition to the valid exercise of executive power, that precondition must be particularly identified on the face of the warrant." *Id.*, at 23. That principle is not to be found in the Constitution. The Fourth Amendment does not require that the warrant set forth the magistrate's basis for finding probable cause, even though probable cause is the quintessential "precondition to the valid exercise of executive power." Much less does it require description of a triggering condition.

Second, respondent argues that listing the triggering condition in the warrant is necessary to "'assur[e] the individual whose property is searched or seized of the lawful authority of the executing officer, his need to search, and the limits of his power to search.'" *Id.*, at 19 (quoting *United States v. Chadwick*, 433 U.S. 1, 9, 97 S. Ct. 2476, 53 L. Ed. 2d 538 (1977)). The Ninth Circuit went even further, asserting that if the property owner were not informed of the triggering condition, he "would 'stand [no] real chance of policing the officers' conduct.'" 377 F.3d, at 1079 (quoting *Ramirez v. Butte-Silver Bow County*, 298 F.3d 1022, 1027 (C.A.9 2002)). This argument assumes that the executing officer must present the property owner with a copy of the warrant before conducting his search. See 377 F.3d, at 1079, n.9. In fact, however, neither the Fourth Amendment nor Rule 41 of the Federal Rules of Criminal Procedure imposes such a requirement. See *Groh v. Ramirez*, 540 U.S. 551, 562, n.5, 124 S. Ct. 1284, 157 L. Ed. 2d 1068 (2004). "The absence of a constitutional requirement that the warrant be exhibited at the outset of the search, or indeed until the search has ended, is . . . evidence that the requirement of particular description does not protect an interest in monitoring searches." *United States v. Stefonek*, 179 F.3d 1030, 1034 (C.A.7 1999) (citations omitted). The Constitution protects property owners not by giving them license to engage the police in a debate over the basis for the warrant, but by interposing, *ex ante*, the "deliberate, impartial judgment of a judicial officer . . . between the citizen and the police." *Wong Sun v. United States*, 371 U.S. 471, 481-482, 83 S. Ct. 407, 9 L. Ed. 2d 441 (1963), and by providing, *ex post*, a right to suppress evidence improperly obtained and a cause of action for damages.

* * *

Because the Fourth Amendment does not require that the triggering condition for an anticipatory search warrant be set forth in the warrant itself, the Court of Appeals erred in invalidating the warrant at issue here. The judgment of the Court of Appeals is reversed, and the case is remanded for further proceedings consistent with this opinion.

It is so ordered.

CASE QUESTIONS

TERRY v. OHIO

1. How does the Court respond to the argument that the officer's actions in *Terry* did not implicate the Fourth Amendment because the officer conducted neither a "search" nor a "seizure"?

2. What standard does the Court enunciate for evaluating the reasonabless of a police officer's conduct during such "stop and frisk" encounters?

3. According to the Court, when may an officer look for weapons on a suspect, and where exactly may the officer look? Is the right to search for weapons automatic once an individual has been detained? Explain.

4. What specific facts in the underlying case supported Officer McFadden's actions?

UNITED STATES v. GRUBBS

1. What is an anticipatory search warrant? Why is this particular type of warrant beneficial to law enforcement officers?

2. Why did the Court hold that *all* warrants are essentially anticipatory? What example did the Court provide when making its point?

3. What two probable cause prerequisites must occur in order for an anticipatory warrant to satisfy the Fourth Amendment?

4. What second argument did Grubbs make, and how did the Court respond to his argument?

HYPOTHETICAL WITH ACCOMPANYING ANALYSIS

Hypothetical

One afternoon while Trooper Davidson was on routine road patrol, he spotted a sports car with some rowdy teenagers inside. He became suspicious and decided to follow them. After about five minutes, the driver changed lanes without signaling, so Davidson pulled the vehicle over for the traffic infraction and to investigate his suspicions. Once on the side of the road he determined the vehicle contained two teenagers—Caleb, the driver, and Zachary, the front seat passenger. They were both acting extremely nervous and fidgety, so Davidson ordered them out of the car. As Caleb was getting out, a joint of marijuana fell from his lap onto the shoulder of the road. Davidson recovered the joint and placed Caleb under arrest. He searched Caleb's pockets and found a plastic baggie containing marijuana. Davidson then searched the passenger compartment of the car, seizing rolling papers, currency, and an address book, all of which were located in the unlocked glove compartment. During his search of the car Davidson noticed Zachary quickly toss something from his pocket into the grass along the shoulder of the road. Davidson searched in the grass for a few moments and recovered a syringe and a vial containing a clear liquid. Davidson seized both items, correctly believing the drug to be heroin. He then arrested Zachary. A search of his pockets turned up a large wad of twenty dollar bills rubber banded together. After placing both handcuffed individuals in the back of Davidson's patrol vehicle, he asked Caleb if anyone would be available to pick up his vehicle. Caleb replied no, so Davidson explained that it was standard police procedure for the vehicle to be impounded and inventoried. The vehicle was removed by a tow truck and taken to the police impoundment lot. Once there Davidson conducted the inventory, and upon opening the trunk of the car he found a duffel bag. He unzipped the bag and discovered over fifty pounds of marijuana.

Discuss whether Officer Davidson's actions were constitutional under the Fourth Amendment. Be sure to discuss the relevant pieces of evidence separately.

Analysis

The Fourth Amendment protects citizens from "unreasonable searches and seizures" by the government. When analyzing the constitutionality of Officer Davidson's actions, it is first necessary to determine whether the Fourth

Amendment applied. Three elements must be present. First, a search and/or seizure must occur. Officer Davidson searched both occupants of the car as well as the vehicle, and he took control of numerous items as a result of that search. Second, the search/seizure must be conducted by the government. At the time of the stop Officer Davidson was a police officer on routine patrol, so he clearly qualifies as government. Third, the search/seizure must have been in a place where the individuals possessed a reasonable expectation of privacy. Caleb maintained a reasonable expectation of privacy in his vehicle and on his person. Zachary also maintained a reasonable expectation of privacy on his person. However, Zachary would not have had a reasonable expectation of privacy in the heroin or syringe, because by tossing them into the grass he abandoned any expectation of privacy he may have had. Hester v. United States, 265 U.S. 57 (1924). Therefore, although the Fourth Amendment is inapplicable to the seizure of the heroin and vial, it would apply to the seizure of remaining items during Officer Davidson's encounter with the two teenagers.

The next step is determining whether Officer Davidson had a warrant for any of his actions. He did not. To satisfy the Fourth Amendment, therefore, his actions must have either fallen within an exception to the warrant requirement or have been permitted on less than probable cause. When analyzing the events in chronological order, the following occurred: Officer Davidson initially stopped the vehicle for a traffic infraction, although he was suspicious and he used the stop as a pretext to investigate his suspicions further. This "pretextual stop" was entirely constitutional, and it mattered not what Officer Davidson's subjective intentions were as long as he had a legal basis to detain the vehicle, which he did. Whren v. United States, 517 U.S. 806 (1996). At his discretion Davidson then order both occupants out of the vehicle, because when he initially observed the vehicle the occupants were "rowdy," and following the stop Caleb and Zachary were "nervous and fidgety." Officer Davidson's actions of ordering the driver (Pennsylvania v. Mimms, 434 U.S. 106 (1977)) and the passenger (Maryland v. Wilson, 519 U.S. 408 (1997)) out of the vehicle for officer safety were constitutional. While Caleb was exiting the vehicle a joint fell from his lap to the ground. Officer Davidson properly seized the joint because it was in plain view: Davidson had lawfully pulled the vehicle over and ordered Caleb out of the car, and it was immediately apparent to Davidson that the joint was evidence of a crime. Coolidge v. New Hampshire, 403 U.S. 443 (1971). Once the joint was observed Davidson then had probable cause to arrest Caleb and to conduct a search incident to arrest. The search of Caleb's pockets that led to the seizure of a plastic baggie of marijuana was therefore constitutional based on the search incident to arrest exception to the warrant requirement. Chimel v. California, 395 U.S. 752 (1969). The search incident to arrest exception also permitted Davidson to search the entire passenger compartment of the vehicle, where he constitutionally seized the rolling papers, currency and address book from the glove compartment. New York v. Belton, 453 U.S. 454 (1981). With regard to Zachary, once Officer Davidson seized the abandoned heroin and vial from the shoulder of the road, he had probable cause to arrest Zachary as well. After placing Zachary under arrest he conducted a search incident to arrest and constitutionally seized the wad of currency from Zachary's pocket. Finally, Officer Davidson conducted an inventory search of the vehicle and discovered a duffel bag containing over fifty pounds of marijuana. The inventory search was also constitutional assuming it was standard police procedure, and Officer Davidson informed Caleb that it was such. The inventory search can be conducted on less than probable cause in order to protect the owner from theft and to protect police from false claims of theft. The inventory search permitted the opening of the duffel bag, so the seizure of the marijuana was constitutional. South Dakota v. Opperman, 428 U.S. 364 (1976).

In conclusion, the Fourth Amendment applied to Officer Davidson's actions. Although he did not have a warrant, Davidson's actions either fell under exceptions recognized by the Supreme Court not requiring him to first obtain a warrant or the searches were permitted on less than probable cause. All evidence, therefore, was constitutionally seized.

On Thanksgiving afternoon the local sheriff's department control center received a call from an individual who wished to remain anonymous but gave his address as 124 Pine Street. The caller said that his next-door neighbor's basement door was opened and that he believed his neighbor was out of town for the holiday. The caller then gave the address of the neighbor's house as 126 Pine Street. Upon receiving the information the control center contacted Corporal Adams, who was on routine patrol in the area, and directed him to respond to the residence because of a possible breaking and entering. Apparently, the neighborhood in question had been subject to a string of burglaries in recent months.

Corporal Adams arrived at the house and immediately checked all doors and windows. He noticed that the basement door was wide opened, but he saw no signs of a forcible entry. Believing that a breaking and entering might be in progress, Corporal Adams called for back-up assistance before entering the house so he would not have to confront any burglars alone. While waiting for Deputy Baker to arrive, Corporal Adams called into the house, "Sheriff's office, anybody home?" He received no reply. He then walked around to the front of the house, knocked on the door and rang the doorbell. He again received no reply.

A short time later Deputy Baker arrived on the scene. The two officers entered the house from the opened basement door and they immediately noticed that the basement was a mess. They then began a room-to-room sweep of the residence to determine if any burglars or possible victims were inside. During that search Deputy Baker opened the door of what turned out to be the master bathroom. Sitting on the counter he saw as many as twenty prescription bottles. Due to excessive number of bottles and the fact that, based on his training and experience, many drug dealers were switching from street drugs to prescription drugs as the "drug of choice," Baker became suspicious that the drugs might be illegal. He picked up several of the bottles to read the name of the individual and the drug. He found pills for Xanax, Percocet, and OxyContin, all of which were drugs commonly sold illegally. Believing the drugs to be evidence of a crime, he seized them.

As it turned out, no burglary was in progress, but the prescription drugs were, in fact, illegal. Stephen and Emily Little, the homeowners, were charged with various narcotics offenses. Prior to trial they moved to have all of the prescription drugs suppressed as evidence, arguing that the police violated their Fourth Amendment rights. Discuss the likelihood that the Littles will succeed in their motion.

1. What is a "night-capped" warrant? What is its purpose, and what are some types of crimes that might commonly call for a night-capped warrant?

2. Officer Hadley investigates a crime for months, types up the facts in his application for a warrant, and delivers the application to a local magistrate

for her signature. The magistrate, however, refuses to sign off on the warrant, stating that the facts do not rise to the level of probable cause. What does Officer Hadley do then?

3. An old adage states, "Don't look for an elephant in a matchbox." How does this statement apply to the execution of search warrants?

4. Police arrest Katie in the kitchen of her apartment. While reading Katie her rights, one of the officers hears a strange noise coming from another room. He asks Katie what the noise was, but she is unresponsive. Afraid that other individuals might be in the apartment who could pose a danger to them, the officer walks through the apartment and sees drugs and drug paraphernalia on a desk in the study. Was the officer legally entitled to look through Katie's apartment? If so, where could he search? Will the drugs and paraphernalia be admissible against her at trial? Explain. *See* Maryland v. Buie, 494 U.S. 325 (1990).

5. Lisa was just found dead in her home, having been strangled to death. Her husband, Dwight, voluntarily came to the police station for questioning. During the conversation, Detective Potter noticed a spot that looked like blood on Dwight's fingernail and asked if he could take nail scrapings. Dwight refused and began vigorously rubbing his hands together and onto his clothes. Detective Potter immediately seized Dwight's hands and took the nail scrapings. Were Detective Potter's actions valid? Explain. *See* Cupp v. Murphy, 412 U.S. 291 (1973).

6. Which of the following individuals would *not* likely have the authority to consent to the respective searches described below and why? (a) The manager of a hotel consenting to the search of a paid guest's room; (b) The owner of an apartment complex consenting to the search of a tenant's apartment; (c) A husband consenting to a search of his wife's private business office which is attached to the house; or (d) A parent consenting to a search of their nineteen-year-old son's bedroom. What additional facts might you want to know in each scenario before being sure of your answers? *See, e.g.,* Chapman v. United States, 365 U.S. 610 (1961) and Stoner v. California, 376 U.S. 483 (1964).

7. Richard is suspected of murdering his roommate. Late one night the police enter Richard's residence without a warrant and without any exigencies that would permit them to go into the home. They begin thoroughly searching the premises when an officer finds a hand-drawn map of Richard's back yard shoved in a desk drawer. Near a tool shed that was drawn and labeled on the map, the officer sees a large "x" and written next to it, "body." Within a few hours the site marked on the map is excavated and police discover Richard's dead roommate. Will the map be admissible against Richard at his murder trial? The body? Explain. What if at the exact same time that police were digging in the backyard, Richard's neighbor, unaware of the activity at Richard's house, was calling police to report that the night before he saw Richard digging a large hole and dumping what appeared to be a body next to the tool shed? *See, e.g.,* Mapp v. Ohio, 367 U.S. 643 (1961), Silverthorne Lumber Co. v. United States, 251 U.S. 385 (1920), and Nix v. Williams, 467 U.S. 431 (1984).

8. What if the police blatantly violate your Fourth Amendment rights, enter your home, and seize evidence. In addition to having the evidence

suppressed at any criminal trial, what other remedies might you be entitled to against the officers, and how would you go about pursuing those remedies?

9. Detective Brady has a warrant to search a residence located at 1157 Spruce Circle, but when the warrant is prepared the clerk inadvertently typed 1157 Spruce "Court" instead of Spruce "Circle." Det. Brady, unaware of the error, searches 1157 Spruce Court and finds evidence of a crime. Will that evidence be admissible against the owners of the house on Spruce Court? Explain.

10. Police are walking along a city street one night when a man sees them and runs in the opposite direction. The police give chase and when they catch him they immediately pat him down for weapons. Is the pat-down constitutional? What if they questioned the man but he refused to answer any questions, would that entitle police to conduct a pat-down? *See* Illinois v. Wardlow, 528 U.S. 119 (2000).

11. The plain view doctrine is based on the officer's sense of sight. What about an officer's other senses—should plain view be extended, or has it been extended, to include circumstances related to the other senses such as "plain smell," "plain feel," "plain hear," or "plain taste"? *See, e.g.*, Minnesota v. Dickerson, 508 U.S. 366 (1993).

12. A police officer on routine patrol in the city sees an individual lying unconscious on the sidewalk. The officer attempts to render first aid, calls for an ambulance, and searches the woman's pockets to obtain her identification. When reaching into the pocket the officer finds crack cocaine. Do you think the search is constitutional?

13. Is a sobriety checkpoint an unconstitutional search and seizure? What about checkpoints for drugs? *See* Michigan Dep't of State Police v. Sitz, 496 U.S. 444 (1990) and City of Indianapolis v. Edmond, 531 U.S. 32 (2000).

14. What if a police officer blatantly lies in an affidavit in order to get a judge's signature on a warrant? Or, what if an officer, although not knowing the information contained in the information is false, doesn't investigate thoroughly to learn whether the information contained within the affidavit is accurate? Assuming that officer obtains the warrant and as a result obtains incriminating information against an individual, is there anything that individual can do to challenge the validity of the warrant? *See* Franks v. Delaware, 438 U.S. 154 (1978).

15. If police stop an individual on the street and ask her for identification, is she legally obligated to provide such information to the police? If she refuses to identify herself, will that give police reasonable suspicion for a stop and frisk? Do you think she should be obligated to respond? Why or why not? *See* Brown v. Texas, 443 U.S. 47 (1979) and Hiibel v. Sixth Judicial Dist. Ct., 542 U.S. 177 (2004).

16. What if police obtain information from a confidential informant that a crime is about to occur. Can police use that informant's information as their basis for probable cause? Would it matter if police had prior dealings with the informant or the degree of information provided by the informant? *See* Illinois v. Gates, 462 U.S. 213 (1983).

True/False

1. If police have probable cause to arrest an individual they may always forcibly enter the individual's home without a warrant in order to effectuate that arrest.

2. During a routine traffic stop, a police officer has the constitutional authority to order the driver out of a vehicle even without suspicion of criminal activity, but that officer does not have the constitutional authority to order any passengers out of the vehicle.

3. Officer Olsen spots a car in a ditch near some town homes. A bystander tells him that about twenty minutes ago a woman exited the vehicle who appeared to be very intoxicated. The bystander pointed to a town home and said the woman went inside. Officer Olsen knocked on the door and when no one answered he forced entry into the home. Officer Olsen's entry of the home without a warrant was valid based on the hot pursuit exception to the warrant requirement.

4. If police obtain a warrant prior to executing a search and/or seizure, their actions will be presumed lawful and the defendant will bear the burden at trial of proving that the search violated her constitutional rights.

5. If an officer asks for and obtains an individual's consent to search an area, it makes no difference whether the officer had probable cause, reasonable suspicion, or only a hunch; the search will be lawful.

Multiple Choice

6. Officer Ryan was conducting a lawful search (with a warrant) of Timmy's home. Timmy was suspected of passing bad checks. When Officer Ryan went into Timmy's den he noticed a large gun cabinet with a glass door and several guns inside. Although guns were not specifically listed in the warrant, Officer Ryan thought one of the guns may have been used in a recent burglary down the block from where Timmy lived. So, Officer Ryan removed the gun from the cabinet, turned it over, read the serial number on the butt of the gun, and determined that it was, in fact, the gun used in the burglary. Why would the "plain view" exception to the warrant requirement not apply?

   A. There was no prior valid intrusion.
   B. The gun was not in plain view.
   C. It was not immediately apparent that the gun was evidence.
   D. The gun was not included in the search warrant.

7. When comparing a stop and frisk to a search incident to an arrest:

   A. A search may be conducted automatically upon any arrest and a pat-down may be conducted automatically upon any stop.
   B. A search may be conducted automatically upon any arrest and a pat-down may be conducted only if the officer has reasonable suspicion that the suspect is armed and dangerous.
   C. An officer may automatically go into the suspect's pockets in either the search incident to arrest or the stop and frisk.
   D. An officer may automatically search the suspect's "wingspan" in either the search incident to arrest or the stop and frisk.

8. Which of the following exceptions to the warrant requirement would most likely give a police officer the ability to search the trunk of a vehicle?

   A. Search incident to arrest
   B. Automobile exception
   C. Hot pursuit
   D. A police officer must always obtain a warrant before searching the trunk of a vehicle.

9. Which of the below lists the correct order of proof, beginning with the least amount of proof and ending with the greatest amount of proof?

   A. Hunch; probable cause; reasonable suspicion; beyond a reasonable doubt
   B. Reasonable suspicion; hunch; probable cause; beyond a reasonable doubt
   C. Hunch; reasonable suspicion; probable cause; beyond a reasonable doubt
   D. Reasonable suspicion; hunch; beyond a reasonable doubt; probable cause

10. Police illegally force Tim to confess to a murder. During that confession, he tells officers that he dumped the murder weapon in a stream behind his house. Based on Tim's confession police search the stream and recover the weapon. There is no indication the police would have found the weapon had it not been for the confession. The weapon:

    A. Would be inadmissible as evidence at Tim's murder trial based on the Exclusionary Rule
    B. Would be inadmissible as evidence at Tim's murder trial based on the Fruit of the Poisonous Tree Doctrine
    C. Would be admissible as evidence at Tim's murder trial based on the Inevitable Discovery Doctrine
    D. Would be admissible as evidence at Trim's murder trial based on the Attenuation of the Taint Doctrine

3
Self-Incrimination

"No person ... shall be compelled in any criminal case to be a witness against himself[.]"

—The Fifth Amendment

INTRODUCTION

The constitutional right not to incriminate ourselves is something with which we are all familiar, so much so that when a friend asks us a question we don't want to answer, we jokingly reply "I'm going to plead the Fifth." Obviously, when our friend is asking us the question in a casual conversation, we don't actually *have* any Fifth Amendment right to remain silent. When, on the other hand, the government seeks to elicit potentially incriminating information from us, the ball game changes entirely. The laws protecting an individual's Fifth Amendment rights against compelled self-incrimination cover situations both inside and outside of the courtroom. "Inside" of the courtroom, we learn that a criminal defendant has an absolute right under the Fifth Amendment not to take the stand, and if she elects to exercise her right the prosecution cannot comment on that fact. The bulk of the law, however, has evolved with respect to the Fifth Amendment "outside" of the courtroom: The circumstances under which an individual will be constitutionally protected from making a statement against her interest. Arguably, the most recognized Supreme Court case of all time comes from the 1966 decision in Miranda v. Arizona. All we have to do is turn on any television crime show to see someone being read their "*Miranda* rights," so most of us assume that we have at least a basic knowledge of what *Miranda* is all about. However, there is a much greater significance and depth to *Miranda* than what we have commonly come to associate with the protection against self-incrimination.

This chapter will explore that depth as well as answer a number of critical questions dealing with the Self-Incrimination Clause of the Fifth Amendment, such as: When do you have the right to remain silent? What tactics can police use to get you to incriminate yourself? Are those tactics constitutional? What must the police do to ensure that your Fifth Amendment rights are protected?

And, what types of incriminating information are covered under the Fifth Amendment?

STUDENT

When completing your analysis of any issue related to the Self-Incrimination Clause of the Fifth Amendment, first determine whether you are dealing with the Fifth Amendment "inside" the courtroom or the Fifth Amendment "outside" the courtroom. Then employ the following analysis:

Self-Incrimination "Inside" of the Courtroom

1. No person

▪ Was the protection applied to a **natural person**, i.e., either the **accused** (who need not take the stand) or a **witness** (who may assert the privilege on a question by question basis)?

2. Shall be compelled

▪ Was the person made to testify **against their will**?

▪ Was a **witness** granted **immunity** in exchange for constitutionally permissible testimony?

3. In any criminal case

▪ Is the right being asserted in a criminal **prosecution** or a civil/administrative case in which incriminating answers will likely bring about **future criminal charges**?

4. To be a witness

▪ Does it relate to evidence that is **testimonial** or **communicative** by nature?

5. Against himself

▪ Was the person asserting the privilege to avoid **self**-incrimination rather than the incrimination of another?

Self-Incrimination "Outside" of the Courtroom

1. Was the suspect in official custody?

▪ Was the suspect under **arrest** or its functional equivalent (i.e., would a reasonable person in the suspect's position not feel free to leave)?

2. Was the suspect subjected to interrogation?

▪ Did police directly **question** the suspect?
or

▪ Did police engage in some tactic that was **designed to elicit an incriminating response** from the suspect?

3. Did police properly inform suspect of his *Miranda* rights prior to interrogation?

■ If **yes**:

　　Did suspect **invoke** his right to remain silent or right to counsel?
　　or
　　Did suspect **knowingly and voluntarily waive** his rights?

■ If **no**:

　　Did a **public safety exception** temporarily excuse police from giving Miranda warnings prior to questioning?
　　or
　　Did police unintentionally **omit** *Miranda* warnings or give warnings that were **incomplete** or **inaccurate**?

4. Were any improperly obtained statements suppressed by the Exclusionary Rule?

■ Was there a **mere *Miranda*** violation?
　or

■ Was the suspect's statement **involuntary** based on **due process** of law?

SUPREME COURT CASES

MIRANDA v. ARIZONA, 384 U.S. 436 (1966)

The cases before us raise questions which go to the roots of our concepts of American criminal jurisprudence: the restraints society must observe consistent with the Federal Constitution in prosecuting individuals for crime. More specifically, we deal with the admissibility of statements obtained from an individual who is subjected to custodial police interrogation and the necessity for procedures which assure that the individual is accorded his privilege under the Fifth Amendment to the Constitution not to be compelled to incriminate himself. . . .

Our holding will be spelled out with some specificity in the pages which follow but briefly stated it is this: the prosecution may not use statements, whether exculpatory or inculpatory, stemming from custodial interrogation of the defendant unless it demonstrates the use of procedural safeguards effective to secure the privilege against self-incrimination. By custodial interrogation, we mean questioning initiated by law enforcement officers after a person has been taken into custody or otherwise deprived of his freedom of action in any significant way. As for the procedural safeguards to be employed, unless other fully effective means are devised to inform accused persons of their right of silence and to assure a continuous opportunity to exercise it, the following measures are required. Prior to any questioning, the person must be warned that he has a right to remain silent, that any statement he does make may be used as evidence against him, and that he has a right to the presence of an attorney, either retained or appointed. The defendant may waive effectuation of these rights, provided the waiver is made voluntarily, knowingly and intelligently. If, however, he indicates in any manner and at any stage of the process that he wishes to consult with an attorney before speaking there can be no questioning. Likewise, if the individual is alone and indicates in any manner that he does not wish to be interrogated, the police may not question him. The mere fact that he may have answered some questions or volunteered some statements on his own does not deprive him of the right to refrain from answering any further inquiries until he has consulted with an attorney and thereafter consents to be questioned.

I

The constitutional issue we decide in each of these cases is the admissibility of statements obtained from a defendant questioned while in custody or otherwise deprived of his freedom of action in any significant way. In each, the defendant was questioned by police officers, detectives, or a prosecuting attorney in a room in which he was cut off from the outside world. In none of these cases was the defendant given a full and effective warning of his rights at the outset of the interrogation process. In all the cases, the questioning elicited oral admissions, and in three of them, signed statements as well which were admitted at their trials. They all thus share salient features— incommunicado interrogation of individuals in a police-dominated atmosphere, resulting in self-incriminating statements without full warnings of constitutional rights.

An understanding of the nature and setting of this in-custody interrogation is essential to our decisions today. The difficulty in depicting what transpires at such interrogations stems from the fact that in this country they have largely taken place incommunicado. From extensive factual studies undertaken in the early 1930's, including the famous Wickersham Report to Congress by a Presidential Commission, it is clear that police violence and the "third degree" flourished at that time. In a series of cases decided by this Court long after these studies, the police resorted to physical brutality—beatings, hanging, whipping—and to sustained and protracted questioning incommunicado in order to extort confessions. The Commission on Civil Rights in 1961 found much evidence to indicate that "some policemen still resort to physical force to obtain confessions," 1961 Comm'n on Civil Rights Rep., Justice, pt. 5, 17. The use of physical brutality and violence is not, unfortunately, relegated to the past or to any part of the country. Only recently in Kings County, New York, the police brutally beat, kicked and placed lighted cigarette butts on the back of a potential witness under interrogation for the purpose of securing a statement incriminating a third party. People v. Portelli, 15 N.Y.2d 235, 257 N.Y.S.2d 931, 205 N.E.2d 857 (1965).

The examples given above are undoubtedly the exception now, but they are sufficiently widespread to be the object of concern. Unless a proper limitation upon custodial interrogation is achieved—such as these decisions will advance—there can be no assurance that practices of this nature will be eradicated in the foreseeable future. . . .

From these representative samples of interrogation techniques, the setting prescribed by the manuals and observed in practice becomes clear. In essence, it is this: To be alone with the subject is essential to prevent distraction and to deprive him of any outside support. The aura of confidence in his guilt undermines his will to resist. He merely confirms the preconceived story the police seek to have him describe. Patience and persistence, at times relentless questioning, are employed. To obtain a confession, the interrogator must "patiently maneuver himself or his quarry into a position from which the desired objective may be attained." When normal procedures fail to produce the needed result, the police may resort to deceptive stratagems such as giving false legal advice. It is important to keep the subject off balance, for example, by trading on his insecurity about himself or his surroundings. The police then persuade, trick, or cajole him out of exercising his constitutional rights.

Even without employing brutality, the "third degree" or the specific stratagems described above, the very fact of custodial interrogation exacts a heavy toll on individual liberty and trades on the weakness of individuals. . . .

In the cases before us today, given this background, we concern ourselves primarily with this interrogation atmosphere and the evils it can bring. In No. 759, Miranda v. Arizona, the police arrested the defendant and took him to a special interrogation room where they secured a confession. . . .

In these cases, we might not find the defendants' statements to have been involuntary in traditional terms. Our concern for adequate safeguards to protect precious Fifth Amendment rights is, of course, not lessened in the slightest. In each of the cases, the defendant was thrust into an unfamiliar atmosphere and run through menacing police interrogation procedures. . . . The fact remains that in none of these cases did the officers undertake to afford appropriate safeguards at the outset of the interrogation to insure that the statements were truly the product of free choice.

It is obvious that such an interrogation environment is created for no purpose other than to subjugate the individual to the will of his examiner. This atmosphere carries its own badge of intimidation. To be sure, this is not physical intimidation, but it is equally destructive of human dignity. The current practice of incommunicado interrogation is at odds with one of our Nation's most cherished principles—that the individual may not be compelled to incriminate himself. Unless adequate protective devices are employed to dispel the compulsion inherent in custodial surroundings, no statement obtained from the defendant can truly be the product of his free choice. . . .

II

. . . [W]e may view the historical development of the privilege as one which groped for the proper scope of governmental power over the citizen. As a "noble principle often transcends its origins," the privilege has come rightfully to be recognized in part as an individual's substantive right, a "right to a private enclave where he may lead a private life. That right is the hallmark of our democracy." United States v. Grunewald, 233 F.2d 556, 579, 581-582 (Frank, J., dissenting), *rev'd*, 353 U.S. 391, 77 S. Ct. 963, 1 L. Ed. 2d 931 (1957). We have recently noted that the privilege against self-incrimination—the essential mainstay of our adversary system—is founded on a complex of values, Murphy v. Waterfront Comm. of New York Harbor, 378 U.S. 52, 55-57, n.5, 84 S. Ct. 1594, 1596-1597, 12 L. Ed. 2d 678 (1964); Tehan v. United States ex rel. Shott, 382 U.S. 406, 414-415, n.12, 86 S. Ct. 459, 464, 15 L. Ed. 2d 453 (1966). All these policies point to one overriding thought: the constitutional foundation underlying the privilege is the respect a government—state or federal—must accord to the dignity and integrity of its citizens. To maintain a "fair state-individual balance," to require the government "to shoulder the entire load," 8 Wigmore, Evidence 317 (McNaughton rev. 1961), to respect the inviolability of the human personality, our accusatory system of criminal justice demands that the government seeking to punish an individual produce the evidence against him by its own independent labors, rather than by the cruel, simple expedient of compelling it from his own mouth. Chambers v. State of Florida, 309 U.S. 227, 235-238, 60 S. Ct. 472, 476-477, 84 L. Ed. 716 (1940). In sum, the privilege is fulfilled only when the person is guaranteed the right "to remain silent unless he chooses to speak in the unfettered exercise of his own will." Malloy v. Hogan, 378 U.S. 1, 8, 84 S. Ct. 1489, 1493, 12 L. Ed. 2d 653 (1964).

The question in these cases is whether the privilege is fully applicable during a period of custodial interrogation. In this Court, the privilege has consistently been accorded a liberal construction. . . . We are satisfied that all the principles embodied in the privilege apply to informal compulsion exerted by law—enforcement officers during in—custody questioning. An individual swept from familiar surroundings into police custody, surrounded by antagonistic forces, and subjected to the techniques of persuasion described above cannot be otherwise than under compulsion to speak. As a practical matter, the compulsion to speak in the isolated setting of the police station may well be greater than in courts or other official investigations, where there are often impartial observers to guard against intimidation or trickery. . . .

III

Today, then, there can be no doubt that the Fifth Amendment privilege is available outside of criminal court proceedings and serves to protect persons in all settings in which their freedom of action is curtailed in any significant way from being compelled to incriminate themselves. We have concluded that without proper safeguards the process of in-custody interrogation of persons suspected or accused of crime contains inherently compelling pressures which work to undermine the individual's will to resist and to compel him to speak where he would not otherwise do so freely. In order to combat these pressures and to permit a full opportunity to exercise the privilege against self-incrimination, the accused must be adequately and effectively apprised of his rights and the exercise of those rights must be fully honored. . . .

At the outset, if a person in custody is to be subjected to interrogation, he must first be informed in clear and unequivocal terms that he has the right to remain silent. For those unaware of the privilege, the warning is needed simply to make them aware of it—the threshold requirement for an intelligent decision as to its exercise. More important, such a warning is an absolute prerequisite in overcoming the inherent pressures of the interrogation atmosphere. It is not just the subnormal or woefully ignorant who succumb to an interrogator's imprecations, whether implied or expressly stated, that the interrogation will continue until a confession is obtained or that silence in the face of accusation is itself damning and will bode ill when presented to a jury. Further, the warning will show the individual that his interrogators are prepared to recognize his privilege should he choose to exercise it.

In accord with our decision today, it is impermissible to penalize an individual for exercising his Fifth Amendment privilege when he is under police custodial interrogation. The prosecution may not, therefore, use at trial the fact that he stood mute or claimed his privilege in the face of accusation. . . .

The warning of the right to remain silent must be accompanied by the explanation that anything said can and will be used against the individual in court. This warning is needed in order to make him aware not only of the privilege, but also of the consequences of forgoing it. It is only through an awareness of these consequences that there can be any assurance of real understanding and intelligent exercise of the privilege. Moreover, this warning may serve to make the individual more acutely aware that he is faced with a phase of the adversary system—that he is not in the presence of persons acting solely in his interest.

The circumstances surrounding in-custody interrogation can operate very quickly to overbear the will of one merely made aware of his privilege by his interrogators. Therefore, the right to have counsel present at the interrogation is indispensable to the protection of the Fifth Amendment privilege under the system we delineate today. . . . [T]he need for counsel to protect the Fifth Amendment privilege comprehends not merely a right to consult with counsel prior to questioning, but also to have counsel present during any questioning if the defendant so desires. . . .

Accordingly we hold that an individual held for interrogation must be clearly informed that he has the right to consult with a lawyer and to have the lawyer with him during interrogation under the system for protecting the privilege we delineate today. . . .

If an individual indicates that he wishes the assistance of counsel before any interrogation occurs, the authorities cannot rationally ignore or deny his request on the basis that the individual does not have or cannot afford a retained attorney. The financial ability of the individual has no relationship to the scope of the rights involved here. The privilege against self-incrimination secured by the Constitution applies to all individuals. The need for counsel in order to protect the privilege exists for the indigent as well as the affluent. . . .

In order fully to apprise a person interrogated of the extent of his rights under this system then, it is necessary to warn him not only that he has the right to consult with an attorney, but also that if he is indigent a lawyer will be appointed to represent him. Without this additional warning, the admonition of the right to consult with counsel would often be understood as meaning only that he can consult with a lawyer if he has one or has the funds to obtain one. The warning of a right to counsel would be hollow if not couched in terms that would convey to the indigent—the person most often subjected to interrogation—the knowledge that he too has a right to have counsel present. As with the warnings of the right to remain silent and of the general right to counsel, only by effective and express explanation to the indigent of this right can there be assurance that he was truly in a position to exercise it.

Once warnings have been given, the subsequent procedure is clear. If the individual indicates in any manner, at any time prior to or during questioning, that he wishes to remain silent, the interrogation must cease. At this point he has shown that he intends to exercise his Fifth Amendment privilege; any statement taken after the person invokes his privilege cannot be other than the product of compulsion, subtle or otherwise. Without the right to cut off questioning, the setting of in-custody interrogation operates on the individual to overcome free choice in producing a statement after the privilege has been once invoked. If the individual states that he wants an attorney, the interrogation must cease until an attorney is present. At that time, the individual must have an opportunity to confer with the attorney and to have him present during any subsequent questioning. If the individual cannot obtain an attorney and he indicates that he wants one before speaking to police, they must respect his decision to remain silent. . . .

If the interrogation continues without the presence of an attorney and a statement is taken, a heavy burden rests on the government to demonstrate that the defendant knowingly and intelligently waived his privilege against self-incrimination and his right to retained or appointed counsel. Escobedo v. State of Illinois, 378 U.S. 478, 490, n.14, 84 S. Ct. 1758, 1764, 12 L. Ed. 2d 977. . . .

Whatever the testimony of the authorities as to waiver of rights by an accused, the fact of lengthy interrogation or incommunicado incarceration before a statement is made is strong evidence that the accused did not validly waive his rights. In these circumstances the fact that the individual eventually made a statement is consistent with the conclusion that the compelling influence of the interrogation finally forced him to do so. It is inconsistent with any notion of a voluntary relinquishment of the privilege. Moreover, any evidence that the accused was threatened, tricked, or cajoled into a waiver will, of course, show that the defendant did not voluntarily waive his privilege. The requirement of warnings and waiver of rights is a fundamental with respect to the Fifth Amendment privilege and not simply a preliminary ritual to existing methods of interrogation. . . .

Our decision is not intended to hamper the traditional function of police officers in investigating crime. See Escobedo v. State of Illinois, 378 U.S. 478, 492, 84 S. Ct. 1758, 1765. When an individual is in custody on probable cause, the police may, of course, seek out evidence in the field to be used at trial against him. Such investigation may include inquiry of persons not under restraint. General on-the-scene questioning as to facts surrounding a crime or other general questioning of citizens in the fact-finding process is not affected by our holding. It is an act of responsible citizenship for individuals to give whatever information they may have to aid in law enforcement. In such situations the compelling atmosphere inherent in the process of in-custody interrogation is not necessarily present.

In dealing with statements obtained through interrogation, we do not purport to find all confessions inadmissible. Confessions remain a proper element in law enforcement. Any statement given freely and voluntarily without any compelling influences is, of course, admissible in evidence. The fundamental import of the privilege while an individual is in custody is not whether he is allowed to talk to the police without the benefit of warnings and counsel, but whether he can be interrogated. There is no requirement that police stop a person who enters a police station and states that he wishes to confess to a crime, or a person who calls the police to offer a confession or any other statement he desires to make. Volunteered statements of any kind are not barred by the Fifth Amendment and their admissibility is not affected by our holding today.

To summarize, we hold that when an individual is taken into custody or otherwise deprived of his freedom by the authorities in any significant way and is subjected to questioning, the privilege against self-incrimination is jeopardized. Procedural safeguards must be employed to protect the privilege and unless other fully effective means are adopted to notify the person of his right of silence and to assure that the exercise of the right will be scrupulously honored, the following measures are required. He must be warned prior to any questioning that he has the right to remain silent, that anything he says can be used against him in a court of law, that he has the right to the presence of an attorney, and that if he cannot afford an attorney one will be appointed for him prior to any questioning if he so desires. Opportunity to exercise these rights must be afforded to him throughout the interrogation. After such warnings have been given, and such opportunity afforded him, the individual may knowingly and intelligently waive these rights and agree to answer questions or make a statement. But unless and until such warnings and waiver are demonstrated by the prosecution at trial, no evidence obtained as a result of interrogation can be used against him.

IV

A recurrent argument made in these cases is that society's need for interrogation outweighs the privilege. . . .

In announcing these principles, we are not unmindful of the burdens which law enforcement officials must bear, often under trying circumstances. We also fully recognize the obligation of all citizens to aid in enforcing the criminal laws. This Court, while protecting individual rights, has always given ample latitude to law enforcement agencies in the legitimate exercise of their duties. The limits we have placed on the interrogation process should not constitute an undue interference with a proper system of law enforcement. As we have noted, our decision does not in any way preclude police from carrying out their traditional investigatory functions. Although confessions may play an important role in some convictions, the cases before us present graphic examples of the overstatement of the "need" for confessions. . . .

V

Because of the nature of the problem and because of its recurrent significance in numerous cases, we have to this point discussed the relationship of the Fifth Amendment privilege to police interrogation without specific concentration on the facts of the cases before us. We turn now to these facts to consider the application to these cases of the constitutional principles discussed above. In each instance, we have concluded that statements were obtained from the defendant under circumstances that did not meet constitutional standards for protection of the privilege.

No. 759. Miranda v. Arizona

On March 13, 1963, petitioner, Ernesto Miranda, was arrested at his home and taken in custody to a Phoenix police station. He was there identified by the complaining witness. The police then took him to "Interrogation Room No. 2" of the detective bureau. There he was questioned by two police officers. The officers admitted at trial that Miranda was not advised that he had a right to have an attorney present. Two hours later, the officers emerged from the interrogation room with a written confession signed by Miranda. At the top of the statement was a typed paragraph stating that the confession was made voluntarily, without threats or promises of immunity and "with full knowledge of my legal rights, understanding any statement I make may be used against me."

At his trial before a jury, the written confession was admitted into evidence over the objection of defense counsel, and the officers testified to the prior oral confession made by Miranda during the interrogation. Miranda was found guilty of kidnapping and rape. He was sentenced to 20 to 30 years' imprisonment on each count, the sentences to run concurrently. On appeal, the Supreme Court of Arizona held that Miranda's constitutional rights were not violated in obtaining the confession and affirmed the conviction. 98 Ariz. 18, 401 P.2d 721. . . .

We reverse. From the testimony of the officers and by the admission of respondent, it is clear that Miranda was not in any way apprised of his right to consult with an attorney and to have one present during the interrogation, nor was his right not to be compelled to incriminate himself effectively protected in any other manner. Without these warnings the statements were inadmissible. The mere fact that he signed a statement which contained a typed-in clause stating that he had "full knowledge" of his "legal rights" does not approach the knowing and intelligent waiver required to relinquish constitutional rights. . . .

MISSOURI v. SEIBERT, 542 U.S. 600 (2004)

I

Respondent Patrice Seibert's 12-year-old son Jonathan had cerebral palsy, and when he died in his sleep she feared charges of neglect because of bedsores on his body. In her presence, two of her teenage sons and two of their friends devised a plan to conceal the facts surrounding Jonathan's death by incinerating his body in the course of burning the family's mobile home, in which they planned to leave Donald Rector, a mentally ill teenager living with the family, to avoid any appearance that Jonathan had been unattended. Seibert's son Darian and a friend set the fire, and Donald died.

Five days later, the police awakened Seibert at 3 a.m. at a hospital where Darian was being treated for burns. In arresting her, Officer Kevin Clinton followed instructions from Rolla, Missouri, Officer Richard Hanrahan that he refrain from giving *Miranda* warnings. After Seibert had been taken to the police station and left alone in an interview room for 15 to 20 minutes, Officer Hanrahan questioned her without *Miranda* warnings for 30 to 40 minutes, squeezing her arm and repeating "Donald was also to die in his sleep." App. 59 (internal quotation marks omitted). After Seibert finally admitted she knew Donald was meant to die in the fire, she was given a 20-minute coffee and cigarette break. Officer Hanrahan then turned on a tape recorder, gave Seibert the Miranda warnings, and obtained a signed waiver of rights from her. He resumed the questioning with "Ok, 'trice, we've been talking for a little while about what happened on Wednesday the twelfth, haven't we?" App. 66, and confronted her with her prewarning statements:

> **Hanrahan:** Now, in discussion you told us, you told us that there was a[n] understanding about Donald.
> **Seibert:** Yes.
> **Hanrahan:** Did that take place earlier that morning?
> **Seibert:** Yes.
> **Hanrahan:** And what was the understanding about Donald?
> **Seibert:** If they could get him out of the trailer, to take him out of the trailer.
> **Hanrahan:** And if they couldn't?
> **Seibert:** I, I never even thought about it. I just figured they would.
> **Hanrahan:** Trice, didn't you tell me that he was supposed to die in his sleep?
> **Seibert:** If that would happen, cause he was on that new medicine, you know . . . .
> **Hanrahan:** The Prozac? And it makes him sleepy. So he was supposed to die in his sleep?
> **Seibert:** Yes.

Id., at 70.

After being charged with first-degree murder for her role in Donald's death, Seibert sought to exclude both her prewarning and postwarning statements. At the suppression hearing, Officer Hanrahan testified that he made a "conscious decision" to withhold Miranda warnings, thus resorting to an interrogation technique he had been taught: question first, then give the warnings, and then repeat the question "until I get the answer that she's already provided once." App. 31-34. He acknowledged that Seibert's ultimate statement was "largely a repeat of information . . . obtained" prior to the warning. *Id.*, at 30.

The trial court suppressed the prewarning statement but admitted the responses given after the Miranda recitation. A jury convicted Seibert of second-degree murder. On appeal, the Missouri Court of Appeals affirmed[.] . . .

II

"In criminal trials, in the courts of the United States, wherever a question arises whether a confession is incompetent because not voluntary, the issue is controlled by that portion of the Fifth Amendment . . . commanding that no person 'shall be compelled in any criminal case to be a witness against himself.'" Bram v. United States, 168 U.S. 532, 542, 18 S. Ct. 183, 42 L. Ed. 568 (1897). . . .

In *Miranda*, we explained that the "voluntariness doctrine in the state cases . . . encompasses all interrogation practices which are likely to exert such pressure upon an individual as to disable him from making a free and rational choice," *id.*, at 464-465, 86 S. Ct. 1602. We appreciated the difficulty of judicial enquiry *post hoc* into the circumstances of a police interrogation, Dickerson v. United States, 530 U.S. 428, 444, 120 S. Ct. 2326, 147 L. Ed. 2d 405 (2000), and recognized that "the coercion inherent in custodial interrogation blurs the line between voluntary and involuntary statements, and thus heightens the risk" that the privilege against self-incrimination will not be observed, *id.*, at 435, 120 S. Ct. 2326. Hence our concern that the "traditional totality-of-the-circumstances" test posed an "unacceptably great" risk that involuntary custodial confessions would escape detection. *Id.*, at 442, 120 S. Ct. 2326.

Accordingly, "to reduce the risk of a coerced confession and to implement the Self-Incrimination Clause," Chavez v. Martinez, 538 U.S. 760, 790, 123 S. Ct. 1994, 155 L. Ed. 2d 984 (2003) (Kennedy, J., concurring in part and dissenting in part), this Court in *Miranda* concluded that "the accused must be adequately and effectively apprised of his rights and the exercise of those rights must be fully honored," 384 U.S., at 467, 86 S. Ct. 1602. *Miranda* conditioned the admissibility at trial of any custodial confession on warning a suspect of his rights: failure to give the prescribed warnings and obtain a waiver of rights before custodial questioning generally requires exclusion of any statements obtained. Conversely, giving the warnings and getting a waiver has generally produced a virtual ticket of admissibility; maintaining that a statement is involuntary even though given after warnings and voluntary waiver of rights requires unusual stamina, and litigation over voluntariness tends to end with the finding of a valid waiver. . . . To point out the obvious, this common consequence would not be common at all were it not that *Miranda* warnings are customarily given under circumstances allowing for a real choice between talking and remaining silent.

III

There are those, of course, who preferred the old way of doing things, giving no warnings and litigating the voluntariness of any statement in nearly every instance. In the aftermath of *Miranda*, Congress even passed a statute seeking to restore that old regime, 18 U.S.C. § 3501, although the Act lay dormant for years until finally invoked and challenged in Dickerson v. United States, *supra. Dickerson* reaffirmed *Miranda* and held that its constitutional character prevailed against the statute.

The technique of interrogating in successive, unwarned and warned phases raises a new challenge to *Miranda.* Although we have no statistics on the frequency of this practice, it is not confined to Rolla, Missouri. An officer of that police department testified that the strategy of withholding *Miranda* warnings until after interrogating and drawing out a confession was promoted not only by his own department, but by a national police training organization and other departments in which he had worked. App. 31-32. Consistently with the officer's testimony, the Police Law Institute, for example, instructs that "officers may conduct a two-stage interrogation. . . . At any point during the pre-*Miranda* interrogation, usually after arrestees have confessed, officers may then read the *Miranda* warnings and ask for a waiver. If the arrestees waive their *Miranda* rights, officers will be able to repeat any *subsequent* incriminating statements later in court." Police Law Institute, Illinois Police Law Manual 83 (Jan. 2001-Dec. 2003) (available in Clerk of Court's case file) (hereinafter Police Law Manual) (emphasis in original). The upshot of all this advice is a question-first practice of some popularity, as one can see from the reported cases describing its use, sometimes in obedience to departmental policy.

IV

When a confession so obtained is offered and challenged, attention must be paid to the conflicting objects of *Miranda* and question-first. *Miranda* addressed "interrogation practices . . . likely . . . to disable [an individual] from making a free and rational choice" about speaking, 384 U.S., at 464-465, 86 S. Ct. 1602, and held that a suspect must be "adequately and effectively" advised of the choice the Constitution guarantees, *id.*, at 467, 86 S. Ct. 1602. The object of question-first is to render *Miranda* warnings ineffective by waiting for a particularly opportune time to give them, after the suspect has already confessed.

Just as "no talismanic incantation [is] required to satisfy [*Miranda's*] strictures," California v. Prysock, 453 U.S. 355, 359, 101 S. Ct. 2806, 69 L. Ed. 2d 696 (1981) *(per curiam)*, it would be absurd to think that mere recitation of the litany suffices to satisfy *Miranda* in every conceivable circumstance. "The inquiry is simply whether the warnings reasonably 'conve[y] to [a suspect] his rights as required by *Miranda*.'" Duckworth v. Eagan, 492 U.S. 195, 203, 109 S. Ct. 2875, 106 L. Ed. 2d 166 (1989) (quoting *Prysock, supra*, at 361, 101 S. Ct. 2806). The threshold issue when interrogators question first and warn later is thus whether it would be reasonable to find that in these circumstances the warnings could function "effectively" as *Miranda* requires. Could the warnings effectively advise the suspect that he had a real choice about giving an admissible statement at that juncture? Could they reasonably convey that he could choose to stop talking even if he had talked earlier? For unless the warnings could place a suspect who has just been interrogated in a position to make such an informed choice, there is no practical justification for accepting the formal warnings as compliance with *Miranda*, or for treating the second stage of interrogation as distinct from the first, unwarned and inadmissible segment.

There is no doubt about the answer that proponents of question-first give to this question about the effectiveness of warnings given only after successful interrogation, and we think their answer is correct. By any objective measure, applied to circumstances exemplified here, it is likely that if the interrogators employ the technique of withholding warnings until after interrogation succeeds in eliciting a confession, the warnings will be ineffective in preparing the suspect for successive interrogation, close in time and similar in content. After all, the reason that question-first is catching on is as obvious as its manifest purpose, which is to get a confession the suspect would not make if he understood his rights at the outset; the sensible underlying assumption is that with one confession in hand before the warnings, the interrogator can count on getting its duplicate, with trifling additional trouble. Upon hearing warnings only in the aftermath of interrogation and just after making a confession, a suspect would hardly think he had a genuine right to remain silent, let alone persist in so believing once the police began to lead him over the same ground again. A more likely reaction on a suspect's part would be perplexity about the reason for discussing rights at that point, bewilderment being an unpromising frame of mind for knowledgeable decision. What is worse, telling a suspect that "anything you say can and will be used against you," without expressly excepting the statement just given, could lead to an entirely reasonable inference that what he has just said will be used, with subsequent silence being of no avail. Thus, when *Miranda* warnings are inserted in the midst of coordinated and continuing interrogation, they are likely to mislead and "depriv[e] a defendant of knowledge essential to his ability to understand the nature of his rights and the consequences of abandoning them." Moran v. Burbine, 475 U.S. 412, 424, 106 S. Ct. 1135, 89 L. Ed. 2d 410 (1986). By the same token, it would ordinarily be unrealistic to treat two spates of integrated and proximately conducted questioning as independent interrogations subject to independent evaluation simply because *Miranda* warnings formally punctuate them in the middle.

V

Missouri argues that a confession repeated at the end of an interrogation sequence envisioned in a question-first strategy is admissible on the authority of Oregon v. Elstad, 470 U.S. 298, 105 S. Ct. 1285, 84 L. Ed. 2d 222 (1985), but the argument disfigures that case. In *Elstad*, the police went to the young suspect's house to take him into custody on a charge of burglary. Before the arrest, one officer spoke with the suspect's mother, while the other one joined the suspect in a "brief stop in the living room," *id.*, at 315, 105 S. Ct. 1285, where the officer said he "felt" the young man was involved in a burglary, *id.*, at 301, 105 S. Ct. 1285 (internal quotation marks omitted). The suspect acknowledged he had been at the scene. *Ibid.* This Court noted that the pause in the living room "was not to interrogate the suspect but to notify his mother of the reason for his arrest," *id.*, at 315, 105 S. Ct. 1285, and described the incident as having "none of the earmarks of coercion," *id.*, at 316, 105 S. Ct. 1285. The Court, indeed, took care to mention that the officer's initial failure to warn was an "oversight" that "may have been the result of confusion as to whether the brief exchange qualified as 'custodial interrogation' or . . . may simply have reflected . . . reluctance to initiate an alarming police procedure before [an officer] had spoken with respondent's mother." *Id.*, at 315-316, 105 S. Ct. 1285. At the outset of a later and systematic station house interrogation going well beyond the scope of the laconic prior admission, the suspect was given *Miranda* warnings and made a full confession. *Elstad, supra*, at 301, 314-315, 105 S. Ct. 1285. In holding the second statement admissible and voluntary, *Elstad* rejected the "cat out of the bag" theory that any short, earlier admission, obtained in arguably innocent neglect of *Miranda*, determined the character of the later, warned confession, *Elstad*, 470 U.S., at 311-314, 105 S. Ct. 1285; on the facts of that case, the Court thought any causal connection between the first and second responses to the police was "speculative and attenuated," *id.*, at 313, 105 S. Ct. 1285. Although the *Elstad* Court expressed no explicit conclusion about either officer's state of mind, it is fair to read *Elstad* as treating the living room conversation as a good-faith *Miranda* mistake, not only open to correction by careful warnings before systematic questioning in that particular case, but posing no threat to warn-first practice generally. See *Elstad, supra*, at 309, 105 S. Ct. 1285. . . .

The contrast between *Elstad* and this case reveals a series of relevant facts that bear on whether *Miranda* warnings delivered midstream could be effective enough to accomplish their object: the completeness and detail of the questions and answers in the first round of interrogation, the overlapping content of the two statements, the timing and setting of the first and the second, the continuity of police personnel, and the degree to which the interrogator's questions treated the second round as continuous with the first. In *Elstad*, it was not unreasonable to see the occasion for questioning at the station house as presenting a markedly different experience from the short conversation at home; since a reasonable person in the suspect's shoes could have seen the station house questioning as a new and distinct experience, the *Miranda* warnings could have made sense as presenting a genuine choice whether to follow up on the earlier admission.

At the opposite extreme are the facts here, which by any objective measure reveal a police strategy adapted to undermine the *Miranda* warnings. The unwarned interrogation was conducted in the station house, and the questioning was systematic, exhaustive, and managed with psychological skill. When the police were finished there was little, if anything, of incriminating potential left unsaid. The warned phase of questioning proceeded after a pause of only 15 to 20 minutes, in the same place as the unwarned segment. When the same officer who had conducted the first phase recited the *Miranda* warnings, he said nothing to counter the probable misimpression that the advice that anything Seibert said could be used against her also applied to the details of the inculpatory statement previously elicited. In particular, the police did not advise that her prior statement could not be used. Nothing was said or done to dispel the oddity of warning about legal rights to silence and counsel right after the police had led her through a systematic interrogation, and any uncertainty on her part about a right to stop talking about matters previously discussed would only have been aggravated by the way Officer Hanrahan set the scene by saying "we've been talking for a little while about what happened on Wednesday the twelfth, haven't we?" App. 66. The impression that the further questioning was a mere continuation of the earlier questions and responses was fostered by references back to the confession already given. It would have been reasonable to regard the two sessions as parts of a continuum, in which it would have been unnatural to refuse to repeat at the second stage what had been said before. These circumstances must be seen as challenging the comprehensibility and efficacy of the *Miranda* warnings to the point that a reasonable person in the suspect's shoes would not have understood them to convey a message that she retained a choice about continuing to talk.

VI

Strategists dedicated to draining the substance out of *Miranda* cannot accomplish by training instructions what *Dickerson* held Congress could not do by statute. Because the question-first tactic effectively threatens to thwart *Miranda's* purpose of reducing the risk that a coerced confession would be admitted, and because the facts here do not reasonably support a conclusion that the warnings given could have served their purpose, Seibert's postwarning statements are inadmissible. The judgment of the Supreme Court of Missouri is affirmed. . . .

CASE QUESTIONS

MIRANDA v. ARIZONA

1. Miranda v. Arizona is what is known as a "companion case." What is a companion case? What benefits are there in deciding companion cases? Can you locate any other examples of notable Supreme Court decisions that were companion cases?

2. According to *Miranda*, what are the four rights a suspect must be informed of when in police custody prior to being interrogated? When will a suspect's waiver of those rights be constitutionally acceptable?

3. What are some examples provided by the Court of situations in which a citizen provides police with a statement yet *Miranda* would not apply? Why would *Miranda* not apply under those circumstances?

4. In *Miranda* the Supreme Court is balancing competing interests. What are those interests? What balance does the Court strike and why?

5. The Supreme Court explicitly stated that the prosecution is prohibited from using "exculpatory or inculpatory" statements of a suspect during custodial interrogation unless *Miranda* warnings had first been given to the suspect. What did the Court mean by this?

6. The decision in Miranda v. Arizona was not retroactive. What does this mean and how does it affect cases decided prior to *Miranda*?

MISSOURI v. SEIBERT

1. Missouri v. Seibert is an example of what is known as a "plurality opinion" by the Supreme Court. What is a plurality opinion? How does it affect the impact of the Court's decision?

2. Explain in detail the "question-first" tactic used by police officers in order to gain a confession from a suspect. How did the police in Missouri specifically use this tactic in order to gain a confession in *Seibert*?

3. How does the Court factually distinguish *Seibert* from its earlier decision in Oregon v. Elstad, 470 U.S. 298 (1985)? In comparing the cases what factors does the Court enunciate with regard to whether *Miranda* warnings given between two instances of interrogation would sufficiently protect a suspect's constitutional rights?

4. What if the time lapse between the initial pre-*Miranda* questioning of Seibert and subsequent post-*Miranda* questioning had been 24 hours rather than only 15-20 minutes; do you think the outcome of the case would have been different? Why or why not?

5. How does Missouri v. Seibert uphold and reinforce the principals enunciated by the Court in *Miranda* almost 40 years earlier?

HYPOTHETICAL WITH ACCOMPANYING ANALYSIS

Hypothetical

One weekday afternoon, Officer Olney was on routine patrol in his vehicle when he heard a broadcast over the police radio that an armed gunman had just run into a nearby elementary school. The broadcast gave a very specific physical description of the suspect and stated that the gunman had just robbed a local bank at gunpoint. Olney, who was less than a mile from the school, was the first one on the scene. The moment he opened the door to the school he spotted someone who fit the detailed description running at the far end of the hallway. Realizing it was his suspect, Officer Olney yelled "Stop! Police!" The suspect fled around a corner. Olney lost sight of the suspect for a few moments, but as he turned the corner where the suspect had disappeared he noticed a hallway door slightly ajar. Olney found the suspect hiding in a custodian's closet.

Olney immediately informed the suspect he was under arrest and simultaneously began searching him. During the search, Olney noticed that the suspect had an empty gun holster around his waist. Olney asked the suspect, "Where's the gun?" to which the suspect replied, "The gun is in the trash can in the girls' bathroom." Olney sent another officer who had since arrived on the scene to recover the gun, and Olney proceeded to handcuff the suspect. The second officer soon returned, showed Olney a handgun, and confirmed that it had been retrieved from a trashcan in a girls' bathroom. Olney then said, "You were the one who just robbed the local bank. You might as well admit it, because I know it was you." The suspect shook his head and replied, "Yeah, I robbed the bank." Officer Olney *Mirandized* the suspect and took him to police headquarters for further questioning.

Analyze whether the suspect's Fifth Amendment rights against compelled self-incrimination applied in the above scenario and whether they were violated. In the course of your analysis, be sure to discuss separately whether the statements, "The gun is in the trash can in the girls' bathroom;" and "Yeah, I robbed the bank," should be admissible against him at trial.

Analysis

In Miranda v. Arizona, the Supreme Court extended the Fifth Amendment privilege against compelled self-incrimination to situations of custodial interrogation by police. The issue here is whether the suspect was protected by the Fifth Amendment, and if so, whether his constitutional rights were violated. The Court in *Miranda* held that a suspect must be informed of his constitutional rights if two conditions are met. First, the suspect must be in custody. Second, the warnings must be read before the suspect can be interrogated. Each consideration will be examined separately.

The first consideration is whether the suspect was in custody at the time he made the statements at issue. "Custody" has been defined by the courts as arrest or its functional equivalent, or whether a reasonable person would feel free to leave under the circumstances. As soon as Officer Olney located the suspect hiding in the custodian's closet, he verbally informed the suspect that he was under arrest and then Olney began an immediate search incident to arrest. Therefore, the suspect was in police custody at the time he made both statements because he was under arrest and a reasonable person in the suspect's position would not feel free to leave.

The second consideration is whether the suspect was subjected to police interrogation. In the case at hand, two separate instances of possible interrogation occurred. The initial instance occurred when Officer Olney asked the suspect, "Where's the gun?" This was a direct question posed to the suspect and designed to elicit a response, i.e., the location of the weapon. Clearly, the suspect was being interrogated in the initial instance. In the subsequent instance, Officer Olney said to the suspect, "You were the one who robbed the local bank.

You might as well admit it, because I know it was you." In the second instance Officer Olney was not asking a direct question but rather making a statement. Therefore, the prosecution could argue that the officer's statement should not be considered interrogation. However, the better argument would be that the officer's remarks were clearly designed to elicit a response from the suspect (i.e., "you might as well admit it") and would be considered an interrogation of the suspect. In conclusion, both instances discussed amounted to interrogation on the part of Officer Olney.

Because the suspect was (1) in police custody and (2) being interrogated, *Miranda* warnings should have been given. The last issue to address is whether any additional circumstances would render the suspect's statements admissible despite the fact that *Miranda* warnings had not been given prior to interrogation. In New York v. Quarles, 467 U.S. 649 (1984), the Supreme Court recognized a narrow exception to the *Miranda* rule and stated that if police are faced with an immediate public emergency, the need to obtain information for the safety of individuals outweighs the procedural needs to inform a suspect of his *Miranda* rights. Applying the principles announced in *Quarles* to the instant case, the first statement made by the suspect, "The gun is in the trash can in the girls' bathroom," would be admissible against him. Immediately prior to locating and arresting the suspect, Officer Olney possessed information that the suspect was armed and had just robbed a local bank, supporting a reasonable conclusion that the suspect was dangerous. During the officer's search of the suspect, Olney came upon an empty shoulder holster, signifying to the officer that the suspect had disposed of his weapon at some point in time. Given the fact that the suspect had fled into an elementary school, where a young child could conceivably find the weapon, Officer Olney was justified in asking the defendant "Where's the gun?" despite the lack of *Miranda* warnings. The second statement made by the suspect, however, would be inadmissible against him. The suspect answered "Yeah, I robbed the bank," to Officer Olney's attempt to get the suspect to confess to the crime. At the time Olney told the suspect he "might as well confess," the public emergency no longer existed. The second officer had successfully retrieved the weapon at issue and Office Olney had direct knowledge of this. Hence, no exigency existed which would have legally permitted Olney to continue questioning the suspect without having first informed the suspect of his *Miranda* rights.

In conclusion, both statements made by the suspect were protected by the procedural safeguards enunciated in Miranda v. Arizona. The public safety exception established in New York v. Quarles will allow for the admission of the suspect's first statement because of a genuine emergency. However, the public safety exception will not apply to the second statement made by the suspect, and that statement will be suppressed as evidence against him because it was obtained in violation of his Fifth Amendment rights.

The Bakersville Police Department just got their big break; they finally cracked the case of what the media had dubbed the "Bakersville Bandits," a team of men in their early twenties who had burglarized numerous homes over the past several months. The suspects were brothers Larry and Barry Thompson. On Friday the 13th the two men were arrested and transported to police headquarters.

Upon his arrival at the station, Larry was placed in Interrogation Room #1. Corporal Cohen entered the room approximately ten minutes later and informed Larry of his *Miranda* rights. Larry stated that he didn't want to talk to anyone. Corporal Cohen replied, "Fine, that's your decision," and he left the room. Approximately thirty minutes later, Corporal Cohen returned. He then said to Larry, "Listen, you don't have to talk to me if you don't want to, but I'll be honest with you. Look at you, and look at your brother. Barry's smart, he's got a great job, he's got a beautiful wife, he's got a nice home. You gonna let him take the rap for this mess and have it ruin his whole life? Look at you—you got no job, no girl, and no life. Why don't you just come clean and take responsibility for this? Be a man. Show Barry what brothers are for." Larry looked down and shook his head, muttering "Man, I don't know what to do," several times. Cohen, sensing that Larry was just about to break, decided to put the last nail in the coffin. "Besides," Cohen continued, "remember the Miller house that you broke into? Well the house had security cameras all over the place and it shows someone limping through the house." Larry had had a limp since childhood; unbeknownst to Larry, the home did not have any security cameras. After requesting a cigarette, Larry broke down, signed a written waiver of his *Miranda* rights, and confessed to six burglaries.

Meanwhile, Barry sat waiting in Interrogation Room #2. Deputy Dennison entered, advised Barry of his *Miranda* rights, and asked if Barry would be willing to talk. Barry simply replied "I've got nothing to say." Deputy Dennison, however, wasn't going to give up quite so easily. He sat down next to Barry and put a hand on Barry's shoulder. "Listen, me and the District Attorney, well, we're like this," he said, holding up his hand and crossing his fingers. "You've got a rack of charges against you. You come clean with me, tell me all about it, and I give you my word I'll talk to the DA and see to it that we get most of these charges dropped." "Really?" Barry asked Dennison, "You could do that?" "I gave you my word, didn't I?" Dennison answered. Barry then confessed to the six burglaries.

Analyze whether the Fifth Amendment right against compelled self-incrimination applied in the above scenario, and if so, whether it was adhered to. Be sure to analyze each suspect separately and discuss both the relevant (a) facts, and (b) law, that support your ultimate conclusion.

DISCUSSION QUESTIONS

1. Brandon was driving well in excess of the posted speed limit when he looked into his rearview mirror and saw flashing lights behind him.

Brandon pulled over to the shoulder and watched as a police officer exited his patrol car and walked up alongside of Brandon's window. The officer said to Brandon, "Excuse me sir, do you know how fast you were going?" Is the officer required to inform Brad of his *Miranda* rights prior to asking Brad how fast he was going? Why or why not? *See* Berkemer v. McCarty, 468 U.S. 420 (1984).

2. If a woman walks into a police station and confesses a crime to the first police officer she encounters, will that confession be admissible against her? Is the police officer obligated to stop her mid-confession and *Mirandize* her, or could the officer let the woman talk as long as she wants?

3. Assume the police arrest a juvenile for an armed robbery who is seventeen and eleven months old. The juvenile explains to police officers that the only way he will make a statement is with his parents present. Are the police obligated to allow the juvenile access to his parents? What if the juvenile does not request to see his parents, but instead his parents demand to see their son before he is permitted to talk to the police. Are the police obligated under those circumstances? Would your answers to any of the above questions change if the juvenile were twelve years old? Explain.

4. Research challenge: What ultimately happened to Ernesto Miranda following the Supreme Court's reversal of his convictions?

5. Read the case of Dickerson v. United States, 520 U.S. 428 (2000) that was referenced in Missouri v. Seibert. What was the potential impact of that case on the earlier precedent of Miranda v. Arizona? What was the majority's conclusion? What was the dissent's main argument? Did you agree with the majority or the dissent?

6. Jerry had just been arrested at his home for the rape and murder of a young child. He was read his *Miranda* rights and told Detective Dan that he wished to remain silent. Jerry was placed in the back of a patrol car, and Detective Dan commenced the twenty-minute ride to the police station. About five minutes into the car ride Detective Dan turned on a religious radio station he enjoyed listening to while on duty that broadcasted sermons. During this particular sermon the preacher urged sinners to "repent of their sins, ask for forgiveness," and to "cleanse yourself of all your wrongdoing." Meanwhile, religious hymns played in the background. Within ten minutes of Jerry listening to the station, he began sobbing and gave Dan a full confession to the crimes. Detective Dan never said one word to Jerry during the ride. Was Jerry's confession obtained in violation of his Fifth Amendment rights? *See* Rhode Island v. Innis, 446 U.S. 291 (1979).

7. Jane had been a secretary at Madison High School for decades. She is currently on trial for embezzling thousands of dollars from the school. Betty, Jane's best friend and another secretary at the school, is called to the stand as a State's witness. The prosecutor asks Betty, "Did you ever see Jane taking cash from the school's safe?" Betty refuses to answer the question under the Fifth Amendment, afraid that her answer might incriminate her best friend. Will Betty's attempt to avoid answering the question be successful? Explain.

8. Mary was suspected of having abused her three-year-old daughter Cindy. When the local Child Protective Services representative visited Mary and

inquired about the alleged abuse as well as the child's whereabouts, Mary refused to answer any questions based on her Fifth Amendment rights for fear that her answers could potentially incriminate her. Can Mary successfully invoke her rights? Explain. *See* Baltimore City Dep't of Social Servs. v. Bouknight, 493 U.S. 549 (1990).

9. Given the fact that our nation is comprised of many different cultures and ethnicities, do you think all police officers should be required to be able to read *Miranda* warnings in more than one language? Why or why not?

10. A defense attorney will often have a very good idea even before trial begins whether the defendant will take the stand and testify. Oftentimes, if the defendant is not planning to take the stand, the attorney will question potential jurors during the jury selection process about whether they would hold it against a defendant if he chose to exercise his Fifth Amendment rights. If you were one of those potential jurors, do you think *you* would hold it against a defendant who failed to testify at trial? What might be some reasons the defendant is not testifying?

11. Revisit the Hypothetical with Accompanying Analysis in this chapter. Based on what you learned in Chapters 1 and 2 dealing with the Fourth Amendment, *supra*, would the gun that was seized from the trashcan of the girls' bathroom be admissible against the suspect at trial? Explain.

12. Can you think of exigent circumstances other than a missing weapon that would permit police in delaying *Miranda* warnings until the exigency has dissipated?

13. If a police officer pulls an individual over for suspected drunk driving and proceeds to ask the suspect a series of routine questions in order to record the suspect's answers (i.e., field sobriety tests), is the officer first obligated to provide the suspect with her *Miranda* rights? *See* Pennsylvania v. Muniz, 496 U.S. 582 (1990).

14. Research challenge: Prior to the court's decision in *Miranda*, how did courts determine whether a suspect's confession was admissible against him? What constitutional provisions were implicated? How did the decision in *Miranda* arguably clarify the law for determining the voluntariness of a confession?

15. What is immunity and how does it impact the protections against compelled self-incrimination? What is the distinction between "transactional" immunity and "use-and-derivative-use" immunity? *See* Kastigar v. United States, 406 U.S. 441 (1972).

True/False

1. A criminal defendant does not have to take the stand and testify based on the Fifth Amendment.

2. A witness in a criminal trial does not have to take the stand and testify based on the Fifth Amendment.

3. Miranda v. Arizona stands for the proposition that police must inform a suspect of his rights prior to interrogation if he is in custody.

4. The Fifth Amendment right against compelled self-incrimination applies in civil as well as criminal cases.

5. New York v. Quarles stands for the proposition that officers must always read suspects their *Miranda* rights before interrogating them, regardless of circumstances.

Multiple Choice

6. If an individual waives her *Miranda* rights, to be acceptable that waiver must be:

    A. Knowingly made
    B. Voluntarily made
    C. Knowingly and voluntarily made
    D. Neither knowingly nor voluntarily made

7. When must an individual be read her *Miranda* rights?

    A. When she is in custody
    B. When she is in custody and prior to being interrogated
    C. When she has been formally charged with a crime
    D. When she is at the police station

8. Which of the following would most likely *not* be considered "interrogation" once a suspect has been arrested for the purposes of *Miranda*?

    A. An officer says to a suspect, "Did you commit the crime?"
    B. An officer says to a suspect, "I want you to tell me if you committed the crime."
    C. An officer presents to the suspect a set of written questions that inquire whether the suspect committed the crime and ask for details.
    D. All of the above would likely constitute interrogation.

9. In which of the following scenarios will an individual *not* have the right to assert her Fifth Amendment right to remain silent?

   A. A suspect testifying before a Grand Jury
   B. A juvenile testifying during her delinquency hearing
   C. A witness testifying in a criminal case where answers could incriminate her
   D. All of the above are situations in which the individual has a Fifth Amendment right to remain silent.

10. Which of the following is *not* one of the *Miranda* warnings?

    A. The right to remain silent
    B. The right to counsel
    C. The right to be informed of all charges
    D. The right to have counsel appointed if the suspect cannot afford an attorney

4

Identification of a Suspect

INTRODUCTION

"He did it, he's the one," she says in an unsteady voice as she points a shaky finger towards the man standing in line with several other men. "Are you sure?" "Yes, I'm positive." The police officer standing next to her scribbles something down on a pad of paper, and the procedure is over. At least for the moment it's over. A similar scene will be repeated several months later in the courtroom when that same woman will again point her finger at the defendant sitting across from her, telling the jury, "He's the one." His fate is all but sealed. The implications of the woman's finger pointing are monumental. Put yourself in the place of one of the jurors for a moment—if you learned that the victim of a crime positively identified the perpetrator not only once but *twice*, wouldn't you believe her?

Identification of the perpetrator of a crime by either the victim or a witness can occur both before trial and during the trial. In terms of pre-trial identification, the most common methods include the line-up, show-up, or photo array. But those methods are by no means all-inclusive. Other pre-trial identification techniques include collecting samples of blood, DNA, handwriting, or even voice recordings. The list is endless, and with the continual advancements in technology, the methods used to positively identify the perpetrator of a crime will only expand in the future. In-court identifications are just as important. There, the witness comes face to face with her accuser and tells the people who will ultimately decide his fate that, yes, he is in fact the one who committed the crime.

Although the identification of a suspect is a crucial part of almost every criminal case, it is nowhere explicitly mentioned in the constitutional amendments; there is no "Identification of a Suspect" Clause like there is a Self-Incrimination, Double Jeopardy, or Speedy Trial Clause. Nevertheless, the Supreme Court has recognized that several constitutional protections *are* implicated when an identification of a suspect occurs, whether in or out of court. Specifically, the Court has clarified when issues related to the Fourth Amendment's right to be free from unreasonable searches and seizures are implicated; whether a pre-trial identification violates the suspect's Fifth Amendment rights against compelled self-incrimination; and, how the identification procedures have to comply with the Sixth Amendment right to the assistance of counsel and the either the Fifth or Fourteenth Amendment right to due process. For the most part, these constitutional standards set by the Supreme Court occurred during the 1960s through the early 1980s, and the issue of suspect identification hasn't seen much activity from the Court since that time. But that lack of activity doesn't diminish its importance, for when the victim points her finger and accuses the suspect of a crime, it just might be the proverbial last nail in his coffin. This chapter, therefore, will explore how identification of a suspect should be done to comply with relevant constitutional provisions.

STUDENT *Checklist*

Identification of a Suspect

1. **Fourth Amendment** right against **unreasonable searches and seizures**:

▓ Did the person have a **reasonable expectation of privacy** in the place searched and items seized? If so . . .

▓ Did the government have a **warrant** for the seizure of evidence
or

▓ Did an **emergency situation** exist where the delay in obtaining a warrant could result in the **destruction of evidence**?

2. **Fifth Amendment** right against **compelled self-incrimination**:

▓ Was the identification method **communicative** or **testimonial** in nature?

3. **Sixth Amendment** right to **assistance of counsel**:

▓ Did the identification method occur at or after the **initiation of adversary judicial criminal proceedings,** and did the identification procedure require the **physical presence** of the accused? If so . . .

▓ Was **counsel provided** to the suspect during the identification procedure or did the suspect **intelligently waive** the right to counsel?

4. **Fifth** or **Fourteenth Amendment** right to **due process of law**:

▓ Was the identification procedure so **suggestive** that it would likely lead to a **misidentification** based on a **totality of the circumstances**? If so. . . .

▓ Was it determined whether the identification was **reliable** even though the pre-trial confrontation procedure was suggestive?

5. **Remedy** for violation of constitutional protections:

▓ Was any pre-trial identification obtained in violation of the suspect's constitutional rights **suppressed** as evidence based on **Exclusionary Rule**?

▓ Was **in-court** identification based on an **independent origin** rather than previous tainted identification?

SUPREME COURT CASES

UNITED STATES v. WADE, 388 U.S. 218 (1967)

The question here is whether courtroom identifications of an accused at trial are to be excluded from evidence because the accused was exhibited to the witnesses before trial at a post-indictment lineup conducted for identification purposes without notice to and in the absence of the accused's appointed counsel.

The federally insured bank in Eustace, Texas, was robbed on September 21, 1964. A man with a small strip of tape on each side of his face entered the bank, pointed a pistol at the female cashier and the vice president, the only persons in the bank at the time, and forced them to fill a pillowcase with the bank's money. The man then drove away with an accomplice who had been waiting in a stolen car outside the bank. On March 23, 1965, an indictment was returned against respondent, Wade, and two others for conspiring to rob the bank, and against Wade and the accomplice for the robbery itself. Wade was arrested on April 2, and counsel was appointed to represent him on April 26. Fifteen days later an FBI agent, without notice to Wade's lawyer, arranged to have the two bank employees observe a lineup made up of Wade and five or six other prisoners and conducted in a courtroom of the local county courthouse. Each person in the line wore strips of tape such as allegedly worn by the robber and upon direction each said something like "put the money in the bag," the words allegedly uttered by the robber. Both bank employees identified Wade in the lineup as the bank robber.

At trial the two employees, when asked on direct examination if the robber was in the courtroom, pointed to Wade. The prior lineup identification was then elicited from both employees on cross-examination. At the close of testimony, Wade's counsel moved for a judgment of acquittal or, alternatively, to strike the bank officials' courtroom identifications on the ground that conduct of the lineup, without notice to and in the absence of his appointed counsel, violated his Fifth Amendment privilege against self-incrimination and his Sixth Amendment right to the assistance of counsel. The motion was denied, and Wade was convicted. The Court of Appeals for the Fifth Circuit reversed the conviction and ordered a new trial at which the in-court identification evidence was to be excluded, holding that, though the lineup did not violate Wade's Fifth Amendment rights, "the lineup, held as it was, in the absence of counsel, already chosen to represent appellant, was a violation of his Sixth Amendment rights. . . ." 358 F.2d 557, 560. We granted certiorari, 385 U.S. 811, 87 S. Ct. 81, 17 L. Ed. 2d 53, and set the case for oral argument with No. 223, Gilbert v. State of California, 388 U.S. 263, 87 S. Ct. 1951, 18 L. Ed. 2d 1178, and No. 254, Stovall v. Denno, 386 U.S. 293, 87 S. Ct. 1967, 18 L. Ed. 2d 1199, which present similar questions. We reverse the judgment of the Court of Appeals and remand to that court with direction to enter a new judgment vacating the conviction and remanding the case to the District Court for further proceedings consistent with this opinion.

I

Neither the lineup itself nor anything shown by this record that Wade was required to do in the lineup violated his privilege against self-incrimination. We have only recently reaffirmed that the privilege "protects an accused only from being compelled to testify against himself, or otherwise provide the State with evidence of a testimonial or communicative nature. . . ." Schmerber v. State of California, 384 U.S. 757, 761, 86 S. Ct. 1826, 1830, 16 L. Ed. 2d 908. We there held that compelling a suspect to submit to a withdrawal of a sample of his blood for analysis for alcohol content and the admission in evidence of the analysis report were not compulsion to those ends. That holding was supported by the opinion in Holt v. United States, 218 U.S. 245, 31 S. Ct. 2, 54 L. Ed. 1021, in which case a question arose as to whether a blouse belonged to the defendant. A witness testified at trial that the defendant put on the blouse and it had fit him. The defendant argued that the admission of the testimony was error because compelling him to put on the blouse was a violation of his privilege. The Court rejected the claim as "an extravagant extension of the Fifth Amendment," Mr. Justice Holmes saying for the Court:

> (T)he prohibition of compelling a man in a criminal court to be witness against himself is a prohibition of the use of physical or moral compulsion to extort communications from him, not an exclusion of his body as evidence when it may be material. 218 U.S., at 252-253, 31 S. Ct. at 6.

The Court in Holt, however, put aside any constitutional questions which might be involved in compelling an accused, as here, to exhibit himself before victims of or witnesses to an alleged crime; the Court stated, "we need now consider how far a court would go in compelling a man to exhibit himself." Id., at 253, 31 S. Ct. at 6.

We have no doubt that compelling the accused merely to exhibit his person for observation by a prosecution witness prior to trial involves no compulsion of the accused to give evidence having testimonial significance. It is compulsion of the accused to exhibit his physical characteristics, not compulsion to disclose any knowledge he might have. It is no different from compelling Schmerber to provide a blood sample or Holt to wear the blouse, and, as in those instances, is not within the cover of the privilege. Similarly, compelling Wade to speak within hearing distance of the witnesses, even to utter words purportedly uttered by the robber, was not compulsion to utter statements of a "testimonial" nature; he was required to use his voice as an identifying physical characteristic, not to speak his guilt. We held in Schmerber, supra, 384 U.S. at 761, 86 S. Ct. at 1830, that the distinction to be drawn under the Fifth Amendment privilege against self-incrimination is one between an accused's "communications" in whatever form, vocal or physical, and "compulsion which makes a suspect or accused the source of 'real or physical evidence,'" Schmerber, supra, at 764, 86 S. Ct. at 1832. We recognized that "both federal and state courts have usually held that . . . (the privilege) offers no protection against compulsion to submit to fingerprinting, photography, or measurements, to write or speak for identification, to appear in court, to stand, to assume a stance, to walk, or to make a particular gesture." Id., at 764, 86 S. Ct. at 1832. None of these activities becomes testimonial within the scope of the privilege because required of the accused in a pretrial lineup.

Moreover, it deserves emphasis that this case presents no question of the admissibility in evidence of anything Wade said or did at the lineup which implicates his privilege. The Government offered no such evidence as part of its case, and what came out about the lineup proceedings on Wade's cross-examination of the bank employees involved no violation of Wade's privilege.

II

The fact that the lineup involved no violation of Wade's privilege against self-incrimination does not, however, dispose of his contention that the courtroom identifications should have been excluded because the lineup was conducted without notice to and in the absence of his counsel. Our rejection of the right to counsel claim in Schmerber rested on our conclusion in that case that "(n)o issue of counsel's ability to assist petitioner in respect of any rights he did possess is presented." 384 U.S., at 766, 86 S. Ct. at 1833. In contrast, in this case it is urged that the assistance of counsel at the lineup was indispensable to protect Wade's most basic right as a criminal defendant—his right to a fair trial at which the witnesses against him might be meaningfully cross-examined. . . .

As early as Powell v. State of Alabama, supra, we recognized that the period from arraignment to trial was "perhaps the most critical period of the proceedings . . ." id., at 57, 53 S. Ct. at 59, during which the accused "requires the guiding hand of counsel . . ." id., at 69, 53 S. Ct. at 64 if the guarantee is not to prove an empty right. . . .

[I]n addition to counsel's presence at trial, the accused is guaranteed that he need not stand alone against the State at any stage of the prosecution, formal or informal, in court or out, where counsel's absence might derogate from the accused's right to a fair trial. The security of that right is as much the aim of the right to counsel as it is of the other guarantees of the Sixth Amendment—the right of the accused to a speedy and public trial by an impartial jury, his right to be informed of the nature and cause of the accusation, and his right to be confronted with the witnesses against him and to have compulsory process for obtaining witnesses in his favor. The presence of counsel at such critical confrontations, as at the trial itself, operates to assure that the accused's interests will be protected consistently with our adversary theory of criminal prosecution. Cf. Pointer v. State of Texas, 380 U.S. 400, 85 S. Ct. 1065, 13 L. Ed. 2d 923.

In sum, the principle of Powell v. Alabama and succeeding cases requires that we scrutinize any pretrial confrontation of the accused to determine whether the presence of his counsel is necessary to preserve the defendant's basic right to a fair trial as affected by his right meaningfully to cross-examine the witnesses against him and to have effective assistance of counsel at the trial itself. It calls upon us to analyze whether potential substantial prejudice to defendant's rights inheres in the particular confrontation and the ability of counsel to help avoid that prejudice.

III

The Government characterizes the lineup as a mere preparatory step in the gathering of the prosecution's evidence, not different—for Sixth Amendment purposes—from various other preparatory steps, such as systematized or scientific analyzing of the accused's fingerprints, blood sample, clothing, hair, and the like. We think there are differences which preclude such stages being characterized as critical stages at which the accused has the right to the presence of his counsel. Knowledge of the techniques of science and technology is sufficiently available, and the variables in techniques few enough, that the accused has the opportunity for a meaningful confrontation of the Government's case at trial through the ordinary processes of cross-examination of the Government's expert witnesses and the presentation of the evidence of his own experts. The denial of a right to have his counsel present at such analyses does not therefore violate the Sixth Amendment; they are not critical stages since there is minimal risk that his counsel's absence at such stages might derogate from his right to a fair trial.

IV

But the confrontation compelled by the State between the accused and the victim or witnesses to a crime to elicit identification evidence is peculiarly riddled with innumerable dangers and variable factors which might seriously, even crucially, derogate from a fair trial. The vagaries of eyewitness identification are well-known; the annals of criminal law are rife with instances of mistaken identification. Mr. Justice Frankfurter once said:"What is the worth of identification testimony even when uncontradicted? The identification of strangers is proverbially untrustworthy. The hazards of such testimony are established by a formidable number of instances in the records of English and American trials. These instances are recent—not due to the brutalities of ancient criminal procedure." The Case of Sacco and Vanzetti 30 (1927). A major factor contributing to the high incidence of miscarriage of justice from mistaken identification has been the degree of suggestion inherent in the manner in which the prosecution presents the suspect to witnesses for pretrial identification. A commentator has observed that "(t)he influence of improper suggestion upon identifying witnesses probably accounts for more miscarriages of justice than any other single factor—perhaps it is responsible for more such errors than all other factors combined." Wall, Eye-Witness Identification in Criminal Cases 26. Suggestion can be created intentionally or unintentionally in many subtle ways. And the dangers for the suspect are particularly grave when the witness' opportunity for observation was insubstantial, and thus his susceptibility to suggestion the greatest.

Moreover,"(i)t is a matter of common experience that, once a witness has picked out the accused at the line-up, he is not likely to go back on his word later on, so that in practice the issue of identity may (in the absence of other relevant evidence) for all practical purposes be determined there and then, before the trial."

The pretrial confrontation for purpose of identification may take the form of a lineup, also known as an "identification parade" or "showup," as in the present case, or presentation of the suspect alone to the witness, as in Stovall v. Denno, supra. It is obvious that risks of suggestion attend either form of confrontation and increase the dangers inhering in eyewitness identification. But as is the case with secret interrogations, there is serious difficulty in depicting what transpires at lineups and other forms of identification confrontations. "Privacy results in secrecy and this in turn results in a gap in our knowledge as to what in fact goes on. . . ." Miranda v. State of Arizona, supra, 384 U.S. at 448, 86 S. Ct. at 1614. For the same reasons, the defense can seldom reconstruct the manner and mode of lineup identification for judge or jury at trial. Those participating in a lineup with the accused may often be police officers; in any event, the participants' names are rarely recorded or divulged at trial. The impediments to an objective observation are increased when the victim is the witness. Lineups are prevalent in rape and robbery prosecutions and present a particular hazard that a victim's understandable outrage may excite vengeful or spiteful motives. In any event, neither witnesses nor lineup participants are apt to be alert for conditions prejudicial to the suspect. And if they were, it would likely be of scant benefit to the suspect since neither witnesses nor lineup participants are likely to be schooled in the detection of suggestive influences. Improper influences may go undetected by a suspect, guilty or not, who experiences the emotional tension which we might expect in one being confronted with potential accusers. Even when he does observe abuse, if he has a criminal record he may be reluctant to take the stand and open up the admission of prior convictions. Moreover any protestations by the suspect of the fairness of the lineup made at trial are likely to be in vain; the jury's choice is between the accused's unsupported version and that of the police officers present. In short, the accused's inability effectively to reconstruct at trial any unfairness that occurred at the lineup may deprive him of his only opportunity meaningfully to attack the credibility of the witness' courtroom identification. . . .

The potential for improper influence is illustrated by the circumstances, insofar as they appear, surrounding the prior identifications in the three cases we decide today. In the present case, the testimony of the identifying witnesses elicited on cross-examination revealed that those witnesses were taken to the courthouse and seated in the courtroom to await assembly of the lineup. The courtroom faced on a hallway observable to the witnesses through an open door. The cashier testified that she saw Wade "standing in the hall" within sight of an FBI agent. Five or six other prisoners later appeared in the hall. The vice president testified that he saw a person in the hall in the custody of the agent who "resembled the person that we identified as the one that had entered the bank". . . .

The few cases that have surfaced therefore reveal the existence of a process attended with hazards of serious unfairness to the criminal accused and strongly suggest the plight of the more numerous defendants who are unable to ferret out suggestive influences in the secrecy of the confrontation. We do not assume that these risks are the result of police procedures intentionally designed to prejudice an accused. Rather we assume they derive from the dangers inherent in eyewitness identification and the suggestibility inherent in the context of the pretrial identification. Williams & Hammelmann, in one of the most comprehensive studies of such forms of identification, said,"(T)he fact that the police themselves have, in a given case, little or no doubt that the man put up for identification has committed the offense, and that their chief pre-occupation is with the problem of getting sufficient proof, because he has not 'come clean,' involves a danger that this persuasion may communicate itself even in a doubtful case to the witness in some way. . . ." Identification Parades, Part I, (1963) Crim. L. Rev. 479, 483.

Insofar as the accused's conviction may rest on a courtroom identification in fact the fruit of a suspect pretrial identification which the accused is helpless to subject to effective scrutiny at trial, the accused is deprived of that right of cross-examination which is an essential safeguard to his right to confront the witnesses against him. Pointer v. State of Texas, 380 U.S. 400, 85 S. Ct. 1065, 13 L. Ed. 2d 923. And even though cross-examination is a precious safeguard to a fair trial, it cannot be viewed as an absolute assurance of accuracy and reliability. Thus in the present context, where so many variables and pitfalls exist, the first line of defense must be the prevention of unfairness and the lessening of the hazards of eyewitness identification at the lineup itself. The trial which might determine the accused's fate may well not be that in the courtroom but that at the pretrial confrontation, with the State aligned against the accused, the witness the sole jury, and the accused unprotected against the overreaching, intentional or unintentional, and with little or no effective appeal from the judgment there rendered by the witness—"that's the man."

Since it appears that there is grave potential for prejudice, intentional or not, in the pretrial lineup, which may not be capable of reconstruction at trial, and since presence of counsel itself can often avert prejudice and assure a meaningful confrontation at trial there can be little doubt that for Wade the postindictment lineup was a critical stage of the prosecution at which he was "as much entitled to such aid (of counsel) . . . as at the trial itself." Powell v. State of Alabama, 287 U.S. 45, at 57, 53 S. Ct. 55, at 60, 77 L. Ed. 158. Thus both Wade and his counsel should have been notified of the impending lineup, and counsel's presence should have been a requisite to conduct of the lineup, absent an "intelligent waiver." See Carnley v. Cochran, 369 U.S. 506, 82 S. Ct. 884, 8 L. Ed. 2d 70. No substantial countervailing policy considerations have been advanced against the requirement of the presence of counsel. Concern is expressed that the requirement will forestall prompt identifications and result in obstruction of the confrontations. As for the first, we note that in the two cases in which the right to counsel is today held to apply, counsel had already been appointed and no argument is made in either case that notice to counsel would have prejudicially delayed the confrontations. Moreover, we leave open the question whether the presence of substitute counsel might not suffice where notification and presence of the suspect's own counsel would result in prejudicial delay. And to refuse to recognize the right to counsel for fear that counsel will obstruct the course of justice is contrary to the basic assumptions upon which this Court has operated in Sixth Amendment cases. . . .

In our view counsel can hardly impede legitimate law enforcement; on the contrary, for the reasons expressed, law enforcement may be assisted by preventing the infiltration of taint in the prosecution's identification evidence. That result cannot help the guilty avoid conviction but can only help assure that the right man has been brought to justice. . . .

V

We come now to the question whether the denial of Wade's motion to strike the courtroom identification by the bank witnesses at trial because of the absence of his counsel at the lineup required, as the Court of Appeals held, the grant of a new trial at which such evidence is to be excluded. We do not think this disposition can be justified without first giving the Government the opportunity to establish by clear and convincing evidence that the in-court identifications were based upon observations of the suspect other than the lineup identification. See Murphy v. Waterfront Commission, 378 U.S. 52, 79, n.18, 84 S. Ct. 1594, 1609, 12 L. Ed. 2d 678. Where, as here, the admissibility of evidence of the lineup identification itself is not involved, a per se rule of exclusion of courtroom identification would be unjustified. See Nardone v. United States, 308 U.S. 338, 341, 60 S. Ct. 266, 267, 84 L. Ed. 307. A rule limited solely to the exclusion of testimony concerning identification at the lineup itself, without regard to admissibility of the courtroom identification, would render the right to counsel an empty one. The lineup is most often used, as in the present case, to crystallize the witnesses' identification of the defendant for future reference. We have already noted that the lineup identification will have that effect. The State may then rest upon the witnesses' unequivocal courtroom identifications, and not mention the pretrial identification as part of the State's case at trial. Counsel is then in the predicament in which Wade's counsel found himself— realizing that possible unfairness at the lineup may be the sole means of attack upon the unequivocal courtroom identification, and having to probe in the dark in an attempt to discover and reveal unfairness, while bolstering the government witness' courtroom identification by bringing out and dwelling upon his prior identification. Since counsel's presence at the lineup would equip him to attack not only the lineup identification but the courtroom identification as well, limiting the impact of violation of the right to counsel to exclusion of evidence only of identification at the lineup itself disregards a critical element of that right.

We think it follows that the proper test to be applied in these situations is that quoted in Wong Sun v. United States, 371 U.S. 471, 488, 83 S. Ct. 407, 417, 9 L. Ed. 2d 441, "(W)hether, granting establishment of the primary illegality, the evidence to which instant objection is made has been come at by exploitation of that illegality or instead by means sufficiently distinguishable to be purged of the primary taint." Maguire, Evidence of Guilt, 221 (1959). See also Hoffa v. United States, 385 U.S. 293, 309, 87 S. Ct. 408, 17 L. Ed. 2d 374. Application of this test in the present context requires consideration of various factors; for example, the prior opportunity to observe the alleged criminal act, the existence of any discrepancy between any pre-lineup description and the defendant's actual description, any identification prior to lineup of another person, the identification by picture of the defendant prior to the lineup, failure to identify the defendant on a prior occasion, and the lapse of time between the alleged act and the lineup identification. It is also relevant to consider those facts which, despite the absence of counsel, are disclosed concerning the conduct of the lineup. . . .

On the record now before us we cannot make the determination whether the in-court identifications had an independent origin. This was not an issue at trial, although there is some evidence relevant to a determination. That inquiry is most properly made in the District Court. We therefore think the appropriate procedure to be followed is to vacate the conviction pending a hearing to determine whether the in-court identifications had an independent source, or whether, in any event, the introduction of the evidence was harmless error, Chapman v. State of California, 386 U.S. 18, 87 S. Ct. 824, 17 L. Ed. 2d 705, and for the District Court to reinstate the conviction or order a new trial, as may be proper. See United States v. Shotwell Mfg. Co., 355 U.S. 233, 245-246, 78 S. Ct. 245, 253, 2 L. Ed. 2d 234.

The judgment of the Court of Appeals is vacated and the case is remanded to that court with direction to enter a new judgment vacating the conviction and remanding the case to the District Court for further proceedings consistent with this opinion. It is so ordered.

NEIL v. BIGGERS, 409 U.S. 188 (1972)

In 1965, after a jury trial in a Tennessee court, respondent was convicted of rape and was sentenced to 20 years' imprisonment. The State's evidence consisted in part of testimony concerning a station-house identification of respondent by the victim. The Tennessee Supreme Court affirmed. Biggers v. State, 219 Tenn. 553, 411 S.W.2d 696 (1967). On certiorari, the judgment of the Tennessee Supreme Court was affirmed by an equally divided Court. Biggers v. Tennessee, 390 U.S. 404, 88 S. Ct. 979, 19 L. Ed. 2d 1267 (1968) (Marshall, J., not participating). . . .

We granted certiorari to decide whether . . . the identification procedure violated due process. 405 U.S. 954, 92 S. Ct. 1167, 31 L. Ed. 2d 230 (1972). . . .

II

We proceed, then, to consider respondent's due process claim. As the claim turns upon the facts, we must first review the relevant testimony at the jury trial and at the habeas corpus hearing regarding the rape and the identification. The victim testified at trial that on the evening of January 22, 1965, a youth with a butcher knife grabbed her in the doorway to her kitchen:

> **A:** (H)e grabbed me from behind, and grappled—twisted me on the floor. Threw me down on the floor.
> **Q:** And there was no light in that kitchen?
> **A:** Not in the kitchen.
> **Q:** So you couldn't have seen him then?
> **A:** Yet, I could see him, when I looked up in his face.
> **Q:** In the dark?
> **A:** He was right in the doorway—it was enough light from the bedroom shining through. Yes, I could see who he was.
> **Q:** You could see? No light? And you could see him and know him then?
> **A:** Yes.

Tr. of Rec. in No. 237, O.T.1967, pp. 33-34.

When the victim screamed, her 12-year-old daughter came out of her bedroom and also began to scream. The assailant directed the victim to "tell her (the daughter) to shut up, or I'll kill you both." She did so, and was then walked at knifepoint about two blocks along a railroad track, taken into a woods, and raped there. She testified that "the moon was shining brightly, full moon." After the rape, the assailant ran off, and she returned home, the whole incident having taken between 15 minutes and half an hour.

She then gave the police what the Federal District Court characterized as "only a very general description," describing him as "being fat and flabby with smooth skin, bushy hair and a youthful voice." Additionally, though not mentioned by the District Court, she testified at the habeas corpus hearing that she had described her assailant as being between 16 and 18 years old and between five feet ten inches and six feet, tall, as weighing between 180 and 200 pounds, and as having a dark brown complexion. This testimony was substantially corroborated by that of a police officer who was testifying from his notes.

On several occasions over the course of the next seven months, she viewed suspects in her home or at the police station, some in lineups and others in showups, and was shown between 30 and 40 photographs. She told the police that a man pictured in one of the photographs had features similar to those of her assailant, but identified none of the suspects. On August 17, the police called her to the station to view respondent, who was being detained on another charge. In an effort to construct a suitable lineup, the police checked the city jail and the city juvenile home. Finding no one at either place fitting respondent's unusual physical description, they conducted a showup instead.

The showup itself consisted of two detectives walking respondent past the victim. At the victim's request, the police directed respondent to say "shut up or I'll kill you." The testimony at trial was not altogether clear as to whether the victim first identified him and then asked that he repeat the words or made her identification after he had spoken. In any event, the victim testified that she had "no doubt" about her identification. At the habeas corpus hearing, she elaborated in response to questioning.

We must decide whether, as the courts below held, this identification and the circumstances surrounding it failed to comport with due process requirements.

III

We have considered on four occasions the scope of due process protection against the admission of evidence deriving from suggestive identification procedures. In Stovall v. Denno, 388 U.S. 293, 87 S. Ct. 1967, 18 L. Ed. 2d 1199 (1967), the Court held that the defendant could claim that "the confrontation conducted . . . was so unnecessarily suggestive and conductive to irreparable mistaken identification that he was denied due process of law." Id., at 301-302, 87 S. Ct., at 1972. This we held, must be determined "on the totality of the circumstances." We went on to find that on the facts of the case then before us, due process was not violated, emphasizing that the critical condition of the injured witness justified a showup in her hospital room. At trial, the witness, whose view of the suspect at the time of the crime was brief, testified to the out-of-court identification, as did several police officers present in her hospital room, and also made an in-court identification.

Subsequently, in a case where the witnesses made in-court identifications arguably stemming from previous exposure to a suggestive photographic array, the Court restated the governing test:

"(W)e hold that each case must be considered on its own facts, and that convictions based on eye-witness identification at trial following a pretrial identification by photograph will be set aside on that ground only if the photographic identification procedure was so impermissibly suggestive as to give rise to a very substantial likelihood of irreparable misidentification." Simmons v. United States, 390 U.S. 377, 384, 88 S. Ct. 967, 971, 19 L. Ed. 2d 1247 (1968).

Again we found the identification procedure to be supportable, relying both on the need for prompt utilization of other investigative leads and on the likelihood that the photographic identifications were reliable, the witnesses having viewed the bank robbers for periods of up to five minutes under good lighting conditions at the time of the robbery.

The only case to date in which this Court has found identification procedures to be violative of due process is Foster v. California, 394 U.S. 440, 442, 89 S. Ct. 1127, 1128, 22 L. Ed. 2d 402 (1969). There, the witness failed to identify Foster the first time he confronted him, despite a suggestive lineup. The police then arranged a showup, at which the witness could make only a tentative identification. Ultimately, at yet another confrontation, this time a lineup, the witness was able to muster a definite identification. We held all of the identifications inadmissible, observing that the identifications were "all but inevitable" under the circumstances. Id., at 443, 89 S. Ct., at 1129.

In the most recent case of Coleman v. Alabama, 399 U.S. 1, 90 S. Ct. 1999, 26 L. Ed. 2d 387 (1970), we held admissible an in-court identification by a witness who had a fleeting but "real good look" at his assailant in the headlights of a passing car. The witness testified at a pretrial suppression hearing that he identified one of the petitioners among the participants in the lineup before the police placed the participants in a formal line. Mr. Justice Brennan for four members of the Court stated that this evidence could support a finding that the in-court identification was "entirely based upon observations at the time of the assault and not at all induced by the conduct of the lineup." Id., at 5-6, 90 S. Ct., at 2001.

Some general guidelines emerge from these cases as to the relationship between suggestiveness and misidentification. It is, first of all, apparent that the primary evil to be avoided is "a very substantial likelihood of irreparable misidentification." Simmons v. United States, 390 U.S., at 384, 88 S. Ct., at 971. While the phrase was coined as a standard for determining whether an in-court identification would be admissible in the wake of a suggestive out-of-court identification, with the deletion of "irreparable" it serves equally well as a standard for the admissibility of testimony concerning the out-of-court identification itself. It is the likelihood of misidentification which violates a defendant's right to due process, and it is this which was the basis of the exclusion of evidence in Foster. Suggestive confrontations are disapproved because they increase the likelihood of misidentification, and unnecessarily suggestive ones are condemned for the further reason that the increased chance of misidentification is gratuitous. But as Stovall makes clear, the admission of evidence of a showup without more does not violate due process.

What is less clear from our cases is whether, as intimated by the District Court, unnecessary suggestiveness alone requires the exclusion of evidence. While we are inclined to agree with the courts below that the police did not exhaust all possibilities in seeking persons physically comparable to respondent, we do not think that the evidence must therefore be excluded. The purpose of a strict rule barring evidence of unnecessarily suggestive confrontations would be to deter the police from using a less reliable procedure where a more reliable one may be available, and would not be based on the assumption that in every instance the admission of evidence of such a confrontation offends due process. Clemons v. United States, 133 U.S. App. D.C. 27, 48, 408 F.2d 1230, 1251 (1968) (Leventhal, J., concurring); cf. Gilbert v. California, 388 U.S. 263, 273, 87 S. Ct. 1951, 1957, 18 L. Ed. 2d 1178 (1967); Mapp v. Ohio, 367 U.S. 643, 81 S. Ct. 1684, 6 L. Ed. 2d 1081 (1961). Such a rule would have no place in the present case, since both the confrontation and the trial preceded Stovall v. Denno, supra, when we first gave notice that the suggestiveness of confrontation procedures was anything other than a matter to be argued to the jury.

We turn, then, to the central question, whether under the "totality of the circumstances" the identification was reliable even though the confrontation procedure was suggestive. As indicated by our cases, the factors to be considered in evaluating the likelihood of misidentification include the opportunity of the witness to view the criminal at the time of the crime, the witness' degree of attention, the accuracy of the witness' prior description of the criminal, the level of certainty demonstrated by the witness at the confrontation, and the length of time between the crime and the confrontation. Applying these factors, we disagree with the District Court's conclusion.

In part, as discussed above, we think the District Court focused unduly on the relative reliability of a lineup as opposed to a showup, the issue on which expert testimony was taken at the evidentiary hearing. It must be kept in mind also that the trial was conducted before Stovall and that therefore the incentive was lacking for the parties to make a record at trial of facts corroborating or undermining the identification. The testimony was addressed to the jury, and the jury apparently found the identification reliable. Some of the State's testimony at the federal evidentiary hearing may well have been self-serving in that it too neatly fit the case law, but it surely does nothing to undermine the state record, which itself fully corroborated the identification.

We find that the District Court's conclusions on the critical facts are unsupported by the record and clearly erroneous. The victim spent a considerable period of time with her assailant, up to half an hour. She was with him under adequate artificial light in her house and under a full moon outdoors, and at least twice, once in the house and later in the woods, faced him directly and intimately. She was no casual observer, but rather the victim of one of the most personally humiliating of all crimes. Her description to the police, which included the assailant's approximate age, height, weight, complexion, skin texture, build, and voice, might not have satisfied Proust but was more than ordinarily thorough. She had "no doubt" that respondent was the person who raped her. In the nature of the crime, there are rarely witnesses to a rape other than the victim, who often has a limited opportunity of observation. The victim here, a practical nurse by profession, had an unusual opportunity to observe and identify her assailant. She testified at the habeas corpus hearing that there was something about his face "I don't think I could ever forget." App. 127.

There was, to be sure, a lapse of seven months between the rape and the confrontation. This would be a seriously negative factor in most cases. Here, however, the testimony is undisputed that the victim made no previous identification at any of the showups, lineups, or photographic showings. Her record for reliability was thus a good one, as she had previously resisted whatever suggestiveness inheres in a showup. Weighing all the factors, we find no substantial likelihood of misidentification. The evidence was properly allowed to go to the jury.

Affirmed in part, reversed in part, and remanded.

CASE QUESTIONS

UNITED STATES v. WADE

1. How did the Court resolve the issue of whether the pre-trial identification procedure violated the defendant's Fifth Amendment right against compelled self-incrimination? What authority did the Court use when reaching its decision?

2. What was the Court's response to the argument made by the government that a line-up is merely a "preparatory step" in the prosecution's process of gathering evidence for trial and hence counsel is unnecessary?

3. What were some of the problems articulated by the Court regarding either the defendant's inability or unwillingness to attack the fairness of a line-up?

4. If a pre-trial line-up is invalid because the accused was denied his right to counsel, will that pre-trial identification automatically be excluded as evidence at trial? Explain.

5. Does a suggestive pre-trial identification procedure have to be intentional on the part of law enforcement in order for it to be considered unconstitutional? Explain.

NEIL v. BIGGERS

1. What did the Court mean when it stated that whether a line-up is unfairly suggestive is determined "based on a totality of the circumstances"?

2. What were the facts of the one case referenced by the Court where the pre-trial identification procedure *was* unnecessarily suggestive? Do you agree with the outcome of that case?

3. According to the Court, what is the "primary evil" to be avoided when analyzing pre-trial identification procedures?

4. If a pre-trial identification procedure is suggestive, does that mean it will automatically be excluded as evidence from trial? Explain.

5. What factors does the Court set forth for considering whether an identification was reliable even though the pre-trial confrontation procedure was suggestive?

6. What were the unique facts of the victim's pre-trial identification in this case? Did the Supreme Court find that those procedures violated due process? Explain.

HYPOTHETICAL WITH ACCOMPANYING ANALYSIS

Hypothetical

Tropical Tan is a small tanning salon located on the outskirts of town. One evening as two employees were closing up shop for the night, a gunman entered the store and demanded money. Chloe, the receptionist, began taking the money out of the cash register. "Put it in the bag," the gunman demanded, pointing to a bright red travel bag for sale on a nearby display counter. Chloe filled the bag with the money and the man fled. Jessica, the second employee, was in one of the back rooms wiping down a tanning bed. She did not see the man although she heard his voice. The entire incident lasted approximately ten minutes. As soon as the man left Chloe called the police, and they arrived within minutes. Out of earshot of her co-worker, Chloe described the perpetrator for Corporal Cox: "I got a really good look at him. He was very, very tall, well over six feet I'm sure. He had an olive complexion, very dark brown hair, almost black, and although he was clean-shaven you could still see a five o'clock shadow. He also had an accent of some sort, Italian maybe." Corporal Cox radioed dispatch with the description given by Chloe, and an APB was put out.

For fifteen minutes Corporal Cox remained on the scene interviewing the two employees when he received a call that an officer canvassing the area located a man fitting Chloe's description carrying a bright red bag. The officer said he was bringing the man back to the scene for possible identification. Corporal Cox separated the two women so that each could make an independent identification while neither woman would have to be confronted directly with the possible suspect; he placed Chloe behind the reception counter where she had a clear view outside the front window onto the sidewalk, and he placed Jessica in the back seat of his patrol car with the window partially opened. Chloe asked Corporal Cox, "Did you find him? Did you find the man who robbed us?" Cox, however, refused to answer her questions. Officer Ortega arrived with Tony, the man fitting the description, and walked him slowly past the front window of the salon. As soon as Chloe saw the man and before Corporal Cox could say a word she said, "That's definitely him. He did it, not a doubt in my mind." Corporal Cox then went outside and got into the back of the patrol vehicle with Jessica. Officer Ortega walked Tony near the vehicle and began a conversation with him. After listening to his voice for approximately five minutes, Corporal Cox asked Jessica, "Do you recognize that voice at all?" Jessica thought for a minute. "Well, I'm not positive, but it does sound kind of like the one I heard when we got robbed. It could be him."

Tony was arrested and charged with armed robbery and related offenses. At trial, the pre-trial identifications made by both Chloe and Jessica were admitted into evidence, and they each took the stand and made in-court identifications as well. Tony was convicted on all counts. He is now appealing, claiming his constitutional rights were violated in light of the pre-trial identification procedures. Analyze his likelihood of success, discussing all relevant constitutional provisions.

Analysis

In the above case Tony is challenging the pre-trial identification procedure stemming from his convictions of armed robbery and related offenses.

In order for the identification to be valid, it must comply with several constitutional provisions.

First of all, the Supreme Court has held that a suspect is entitled to the assistance of counsel during a pre-trial identification procedure if (a) adversarial judicial criminal proceedings have been initiated against the suspect, and (b) the procedure requires the physical presence of the defendant. In the instant case, although the show-up technique used by police did require Tony's physical presence, he had not yet been formally accused of a crime. Tony was not constitutionally entitled to the assistance of counsel, and no Sixth Amendment violation occurred.

Identification procedures must also comply with the Due Process Clauses of the Fifth and Fourteenth Amendments. The Supreme Court has held that the primary evil to be avoided in pre-trial identification procedures is "a very substantial likelihood of irreparable misidentification." Neil v. Biggers, 409 U.S. 188 (1972). The facts of each individual case must be examined to determine whether, based on a totality of the circumstances, the identification was reliable. In the instant case, the facts which support the finding that no due process violation occurred are as follows: Chloe had a good opportunity to observe the suspect since she had direct contact with him for ten minutes, she was able to provide a very detailed description to police, and by her own account she "got a really good look at" the gunman. The show-up occurred only fifteen minutes after the robbery, and upon seeing the suspect through the store window Chloe quickly made a positive identification, stating that Tony was "definitely" the armed robber and there was "no doubt" in her mind. Jessica, on the other hand, made a tentative voice identification. Although not as confident in her identification as Chloe, Jessica stated that Tony "could be" the perpetrator, and his voice was "kind of like" the armed gunman's voice. The only fact leaning towards suggestiveness of the procedure is the fact that a show-up was conducted rather than presenting Tony to the witnesses in the form of a line-up or photo array. However, the fact of a show-up alone will not violate due process. Stovall v. Denno, 388 U.S. 293 (1967). Corporal Cox took specific steps to minimize any potential suggestiveness; he separated the two witnesses to ensure that their identifications were based on their own independent recollection, and he refused to answer Chloe's questions when she inquired as to whether the police had caught the perpetrator. Therefore, the totality of the circumstances indicate that the show-up complied with due process requirements.

Finally, Tony can attempt to argue that his Fifth Amendment right against compelled self-incrimination and his Fourth Amendments right against unreasonable searches and seizures were violated. Neither argument will succeed. The Court has held that the right against compelled self-incrimination is only implicated if the method was communicative or testimonial in nature. Officer Ortega engaged Tony in conversation within earshot of Jessica so that she could make a possible voice identification. Tony's words were used for the sound of his voice only and not for the content of his words. Additionally, the Court has held that characteristics held out to the public, such as one's physical appearance, handwriting, or voice, are not protected by the Fourth Amendment because a person has no reasonable expectation of privacy in those traits.

In conclusion, the pre-trial identification of Tony by the employees of Tropical Tan was constitutionally valid and would be admissible at trial as well as their in-court identifications.

Ron is a veteran police officer who has been on the force for over twenty years. During that time he has worked road patrol and criminal investigations. In order to earn a few extra dollars, Ron often moonlit at a local warehouse as a security guard. One night at about midnight while Ron was sitting in his unmarked patrol car around the back of the building, he noticed the door to the emergency exit of the warehouse open suddenly. He then watched as a man ran out of the door and scaled a chain link fence that was about twenty feet from the door. Ron immediately got out of his cruiser and yelled for the man to stop, but the man fled. Ron gave chase but eventually lost him. Only seconds later several marked police cars arrive on the scene. Lieutenant O'Leary informed Ron that the silent burglar alarm recently installed at the warehouse had been activated. Ron then explained that he saw an individual run from the emergency exit of the warehouse. The following conversation ensued:

Lieutenant O'Leary: Did you get a good look at the guy?
Ron: Well, he was running pretty fast and it was dark out, but the flood light in back of the building was right on his face. I'd say he was about 6'2", slim build, dark brown hair with some facial hair. He was wearing blue jeans and a black turtleneck or jacket of some sort.
Lieutenant O'Leary: How long did you see him?
Ron: Not that long, a minute or two maybe.
Lieutenant O'Leary: Anything else?
Ron: Yeah, it looked like he had a pretty big scar going down his cheek.
Lieutenant O'Leary: Wait a minute, you said he had a scar on his cheek?
Ron: Yeah.
Lieutenant O'Leary: Which cheek?
Ron: His left cheek.
Lieutenant O'Leary: Hang on, don't go anywhere.

Lieutenant O'Leary walked over to his police cruiser where he shuffled some papers in his back seat. After about five minutes the lieutenant returned to Ron, holding a single photograph of Benjamin Ryder, a suspect in another burglary from a neighboring county. O'Leary presented the photograph to Ron. "Is this the guy?" he asked. "Yep, without a doubt," Ron replied. "That's the guy I saw. That's him."

Benjamin Ryder was arrested a few days later and charged with the burglary of the warehouse. His attorney has moved to suppress Ron's pre-trial identification based on a violation of Benjamin's Fourteenth Amendment due process rights. Assume you are the judge. Rule on whether the identification should be suppressed at trial, explaining your holding in detail.

DISCUSSION QUESTIONS

1. Research challenge: On November 22, 1963, President John F. Kennedy was assassinated. Lee Harvey Oswald, the prime suspect at the time, was also

accused of murdering Dallas police officer J.D. Tippet shortly after the president's assassination. Oswald was apprehended within hours and placed in a line-up for identification by a witness to the Tippet murder. What were the circumstances of his line-up? Would Oswald have had a valid constitutional challenge to the line-up? Explain.

2. Lydia was recently the victim of a robbery. Detective Donohue visited Lydia at the video shop where she works and asked if he could talk to her in order to get more information about the perpetrator. Lydia agreed and suggested the two go to the coffee shop next door, get something to drink, and discuss matters there. They purchased their coffee and were seated at a table near the window. Lydia began describing the events when all of a sudden a man walked past the window and into the coffee shop. Lydia pointed her finger and exclaimed,"That's him! That's the man who robbed me!" Detective Donohue proceeded to arrest the man. Is Lydia's identification valid?

3. Research challenge: Locate one or more of the most recent cases from your jurisdiction dealing with the pre-trial identification of a suspect. Be prepared to discuss the issues raised in those cases and their respective holdings.

4. When a suspect is asked to participate in a line-up, where might the police obtain the other individuals involved in that line-up?

5. The Supreme Court has held that police may not impermissibly use pre-trial identification techniques that "shock the conscience." What did the Court mean by this? What examples can you think of that might fall under this type of identification technique? *See, e.g.*, Rochin v. California, 342 U.S. 165 (1952).

6. What if an accused is ordered to take part in an identification procedure that requires his active participation (e.g., a line-up, giving a handwriting sample or speaking for voice identification) and he refuses to do so; how can he be legally compelled to cooperate?

7. Betty is the victim of a rape. She identifies her assailant from a photo array prior to trial, but because the photo array was impermissibly suggestive the trial court suppresses evidence of the pre-trial identification. At trial, if Betty takes the stand and testifies, will she be permitted to identify her assailant? How might the in-court identification present a "fruit of the poisonous tree" problem?

8. Make a list of ways in which a photo-array might be considered impermissibly suggestive and in violation of due process.

9. Bryan is accused of attacking Shirley. He is brought to the police station to take part in a line-up. All participants in the line-up are required to say,"If you scream you're dead," the words used by the perpetrator during the attack. Shirley positively identifies Bryan as the perpetrator. Bryan subsequently challenges the line-up on two grounds; (1) his Fifth Amendment right against compelled self-incrimination, since he was required to utter the words said by the perpetrator, and (2) his Fourth Amendment right against unreasonable searches and seizures, since the line-up constituted

a "seizure" of his person and physical characteristics. Will either challenge succeed? Explain.

10. Given the constant advancements in technology, what ways of identifying a suspect are possible now that were not possible twenty years ago? What ways would you predict might come about in the next twenty years?

11. Several suspects are arrested for a variety of unrelated crimes. As part of the pre-trial identification process, they are asked by police to provide the following: (a) Sara, suspected of forgery, is asked to provide a handwriting sample; (b) Jimmy, suspected of extortion, is asked to provide a recording of his voice; (c) Wayne, suspected of rape, is asked to provide a DNA sample; and (d) Burt, suspected of burglary, is asked to provide fingerprints. Which of the previous pre-trial identification methods implicate the Fourth Amendment and why? *See, e.g.,* Schmerber v. California, 384 U.S. 757 (1968) and United States v. Dionisio, 410 U.S. 1 (1973).

12. Research challenge: Ted Bundy, one of America's most notorious serial killers, was executed on January 24, 1989, for the murder of twelve-year-old Kimberly Leach. What were the unique circumstances that aided a witness in making a pre-trial identification of Bundy as the culprit? Did the Supreme Court of Florida accept this method of identification? Explain. *See* Bundy v. State, 471 So. 2d 9 (Fla. 1985), *cert. denied*, 479 U.S. 894 (1986).

True/False

Read the below hypothetical, then answer the following true/false questions:

Jennifer is suspected of shoplifting numerous articles of clothing from an upscale department store, but she has not yet been arrested. She is placed in a line-up with five men, and police require her to put on a bright red dress worn by the culprit that was recovered from a dumpster behind the store. Jennifer asks for counsel but her request is denied. The store owner is brought to the station and asked to identify the perpetrator. The owner positively identifies Jennifer as the culprit.

1. Jennifer's Sixth Amendment right to the assistance of counsel was violated.

2. Jennifer will have a strong argument that her Fourteenth Amendment due process rights were violated.

3. Requiring Jennifer to put on the red dress violated her Fifth Amendment right against compelled self-incrimination.

4. Requiring Jennifer to appear in the line-up violated her Fourth Amendment right against unreasonable searches and seizures.

5. If Jennifer had not been made to put on the red dress, the identification procedure would have been constitutional in all aspects.

Multiple Choice

6. Of the below pre-trial identification methods, which is the most *inherently* suggestive by nature?

   A. Line-up
   B. Show-up
   C. Photo array
   D. None are inherently suggestive.

7. Which of the following statements is *true*:

   A. A pre-trial identification obtained through impermissibly suggestive identification procedures *is not* per se inadmissible at trial, while a pre-trial identification procedure obtained in violation of the right to counsel *is* per se inadmissible at trial.
   B. A pre-trial identification obtained through impermissibly suggestive identification procedures *is* per se inadmissible at trial, while a pre-trial identification procedure obtained in violation of the right to counsel *is not* per se inadmissible at trial.

C. Both a pre-trial identification obtained through impermissibly suggestive identification procedures, and a pre-trial identification procedure
obtained in violation of the right to counsel are per se inadmissible at
trial.

D. Neither a pretrial identification obtained through impermissibly suggestive identification procedures *is not* per se inadmissible at trial, nor a
pre-trial identification procedure obtained in violation of the right to
counsel is per se inadmissible at trial.

8. A suspect is constitutionally entitled to the assistance of counsel during a
photo array:

A. At all times
B. Never
C. If it occurs at or after the initiation of adversarial judicial criminal pro-
ceedings
D. If the witness making the identification consents

9. A suspect is constitutionally entitled to the assistance of counsel during a
line-up:

A. At all times
B. Never
C. If it occurs at or after the initiation of adversarial judicial criminal pro-
ceedings
D. If the witness making the identification consents

10. Which of the following is *not* one of the factors set forth in Neil v. Biggers
for determining whether an identification is reliable even though the pre-
trial confrontation procedure was suggestive?

A. The opportunity of the witness to view the suspect at the time of the
crime
B. The witness' degree of attention
C. The time that has elapsed between the crime and the confrontation
D. The age and intelligence of the witness

5 Chapter
Double Jeopardy

"No person shall . . . be subject for the same offence to be twice put in jeopardy of life or limb[.]"

—The Fifth Amendment

INTRODUCTION

The Double Jeopardy Clause of the Fifth Amendment is likely one of the least understood provisions within the Bill of Rights. For most individuals, their knowledge begins and ends with the simple premise that once someone is acquitted of a crime, she cannot be tried again for that same crime. Even for students in the criminal justice field, their understanding does not extend significantly beyond that premise. The majority of textbooks covering criminal procedure do little to bridge our gap in understanding; they devote chapters to search and seizure, self-incrimination, and the right to counsel, yet double jeopardy is mentioned only in a few brief paragraphs if at all. On occasion, popular movies such as *Double Jeopardy* (1999) or *Fracture* (2007) are released, which only add to our misconceptions of the clause. Those of us who do have a very basic understanding of the amendment perceive it at best as a mere "technicality" of the law, or, at worst as a means to let a guilty man walk free. Our shallowness of comprehension has, therefore, relegated the Double Jeopardy Clause to a position of obscurity among our constitutional protections.

Nevertheless, the protections against twice being put in jeopardy for the same offense are crucial to an individual's freedoms from inappropriate governmental intrusion. The amendment itself is unquestionably one of the more complex and difficult to understand. In fact, it isn't unusual for Supreme Court Justices themselves to disagree on the scope of various protections provided by it, and perhaps its complexity adds to our hesitation to learn double jeopardy in detail. Yet it is just as significant as the other provisions related to constitutional criminal procedure. Therefore, this chapter will break double jeopardy into components which make it easy to both understand and analyze while answering straightforward yet critical questions such as why do we have a protection against double jeopardy, and how exactly does it work?

STUDENT *Checklist*

Double Jeopardy

1. No person, for the **same offense** . . .

■ Do the crimes have the **same elements**
   or

■ Is one crime a **lesser included offense** of the other?
   and

■ Are the crimes being applied to the **same conduct**?

2. Shall **twice** . . .

■ Is the second trial constitutionally **impermissible** because:
   The defendant was **acquitted** at the first trial;
   The defendant was **convicted** at the first trial;
   The defendant is subjected to **multiple punishments** for the same offense; or
   Collateral estoppel bas the prosecution of the crimes because the ultimate issue of fact has already been litigated in favor of the accused?
   or

■ Is the second trial constitutionally **permissible** because:
   It is for an **incomplete crime**;
   It is for an **ongoing crime**;
   The **defendant is responsible** for the retrial by either taking a successful **appeal** of the first conviction or successfully objecting to **joinder** of offenses; or
   A **mistrial** was declared that was either a **manifest necessity** or **consented to** or **requested by** the defendant?

3. Be **put in jeopardy** . . .

■ Has jeopardy **attached**?

4. In a **criminal case** . . .

■ Is it a criminal **prosecution**
   or

■ Does the sanction constitute **criminal punishment**?

5. By the **same sovereign.**

■ Are separate prosecutions permissible under the **Dual Sovereignty Doctrine**?

SUPREME COURT CASES

BLOCKBERGER v. UNITED STATES, 284 U.S. 299 (1932)

The petitioner was charged with violating provisions of the Harrison Narcotic Act, c. 1, § 1, 38 Stat. 785, as amended by c. 18, § 1006, 40 Stat. 1057, 1131 (U.S.C. Title 26, § 692 [26 USCA § 692]); and c. 1, § 2, 38 Stat. 785, 786 (U.S.C., Title 26, § 696 [26 USCA § 696]). The indictment contained five counts. The jury returned a verdict against petitioner upon the second, third, and fifth counts only. Each of these counts charged a sale of morphine hydrochloride to the same purchaser. The second count charged a sale on a specified day of ten grains of the drug not in or from the original stamped package; the third count charged a sale on the following day of eight grains of the drug not in or from the original stamped package; the fifth count charged the latter sale also as having been made not in pursuance of a written order of the purchaser as required by the statute. The court sentenced petitioner to five years' imprisonment and a fine of $2,000 upon each count, the terms of imprisonment to run consecutively; and this judgment was affirmed on appeal. (C.C.A.) 50 F.(2d) 795.

The principal contentions here made by petitioner are as follows: (1) That, upon the facts, the two sales charged in the second and third counts as having been made to the same person constitute a single offense; and (2) that the sale charged in the third count as having been made not from the original stamped package, and the same sale charged in the fifth count as having been made not in pursuance of a written order of the purchaser, constitute but one offense, for which only a single penalty lawfully may be imposed.

One. The sales charged in the second and third counts, although made to the same person, were distinct and separate sales made at different times. It appears from the evidence that, shortly after delivery of the drug which was the subject of the first sale, the purchaser paid for an additional quantity, which was delivered the next day. But the first sale had been consummated, and the payment for the additional drug, however closely following, was the initiation of a separate and distinct sale completed by its delivery.

The contention on behalf of petitioner is that these two sales, having been made to the same purchaser and following each other, with no substantial interval of time between the delivery of the drug in the first transaction and the payment for the second quantity sold, constitute a single continuing offense. The contention is unsound. The distinction between the transactions here involved and an offense continuous in its character is well settled, as was pointed out by this court in the case of In re Snow, 120 U.S. 274, 7 S. Ct. 556, 30 L. Ed. 658. There it was held that the offense of cohabiting with more than one woman, created by the Act of March 22, 1882, c. 47, 22 Stat. 31 (now 18 USCA § 514) was a continuous offense, and was committed, in the sense of the statute, where there was a living or dwelling together as husband and wife. The court said (pages 281, 286 of 120 U.S., 7 S. Ct. 556, 559):

> It is, inherently, a continuous offense, having duration; and not an offense consisting of an isolated act. . . .
>   A distinction is laid down in adjudged cases and in text-writers between an offense continuous in its character, like the one at bar, and a case where the statute is aimed at an offense that can be committed uno ictu.

The Narcotic Act does not create the offense of engaging in the business of selling the forbidden drugs, but penalizes any sale made in the absence of either of the qualifying requirements set forth. Each of several successive sales constitutes a distinct offense, however closely they may follow each other. The distinction stated by Mr. Wharton is that, "when the impulse is single, but one indictment lies, no matter how long the action may continue. If successive impulses are separately given, even though all unite in swelling a common stream of action, separate indictments lie." Wharton's Criminal Law (11th Ed.) § 34. Or, as stated in note 3 to that section, "The test is whether the individual acts are prohibited, or the course of action which they constitute. If the former, then each act is punishable separately. . . . If the latter, there can be but one penalty."

In the present case, the first transaction, resulting in a sale, had come to an end. The next sale was not the result of the original impulse, but of a fresh one-that is to say, of a new bargain. The question is controlled, not by the Snow Case, but by such cases as that of Ebeling v. Morgan, 237 U.S. 625, 35 S. Ct. 710, 59 L. Ed. 1151. There the accused was convicted under several counts of a willful tearing, etc., of mail bags with intent to rob. The court (page 628 of 237 U.S., 35 S. Ct. 710, 711) stated the question to be "whether one who, in the same transaction, tears or cuts successively mail bags of the United States used in conveyance of the mails, with intent to rob or steal any such mail, is guilty of a single offense, or of additional offenses because of each successive cutting with the criminal intent charged." Answering this question, the court, after quoting the statute, section 189, Criminal Code, (U.S.C. title 18, § 312 [18 USCA § 312]) said (page 629 of 237 U.S., 35 S. Ct. 710, 711):

> These words plainly indicate that it was the intention of the lawmakers to protect each and every mail bag from felonious injury and mutilation. Whenever any one mail bag is thus torn, cut, or injured, the offense is complete. Although the transaction of cutting the mail bags was in a sense continuous, the complete statutory offense was committed every time a mail bag was cut in the manner described, with the intent charged. The offense as to each separate bag was complete when that bag was cut, irrespective of any attack upon, or mutilation of, any other bag. . . .

Two. Section 1 of the Narcotic Act creates the offense of selling any of the forbidden drugs except in or from the original stamped package; and section 2 creates the offense of selling any of such drugs not in pursuance of a written order of the person to whom the drug is sold. Thus, upon the face of the statute, two distinct offenses are created. Here there was but one sale, and the question is whether, both sections being violated by the same act, the accused committed two offenses or only one.

The statute is not aimed at sales of the forbidden drugs qua sales, a matter entirely beyond the authority of Congress, but at sales of such drugs in violation of the requirements set forth in sections 1 and 2, enacted as aids to the enforcement of the stamp tax imposed by the act. See Alston v. United States, 274 U.S. 289, 294, 47 S. Ct. 634, 71 L. Ed. 1052; Nigro v. United States, 276 U.S. 332, 341, 345, 351, 48 S. Ct. 388, 72 L. Ed. 600.

Each of the offenses created requires proof of a different element. The applicable rule is that, where the same act or transaction constitutes a violation of two distinct statutory provisions, the test to be applied to determine whether there are two offenses or only one, is whether each provision requires proof of a fact which the other does not. Gavieres v. United States, 220 U.S. 338, 342, 31 S. Ct. 421, 55 L. Ed. 489, and authorities cited. In that case this court quoted from and adopted the language of the Supreme Court of Massachusetts in Morey v. Commonwealth, 108 Mass. 433: "A single act may be an offense against two statutes; and if each statute requires proof of an additional fact which the other does not, an acquittal or conviction under either statute does not exempt the defendant from prosecution and punishment under the other." Compare Albrecht v. United States, 273 U.S. 1, 11, 12, 47 S. Ct. 250, 71 L. Ed. 505, and cases there cited. Applying the test, we must conclude that here, although both sections were violated by the one sale, two offenses were committed. . . .

Judgment affirmed.

SATTAZAHN v. PENNSYLVANIA, 537 U.S. 101 (2003)

In this case, we consider once again the applicability of the Fifth Amendment's Double Jeopardy Clause in the context of capital-sentencing proceedings.

I

On Sunday evening, April 12, 1987, petitioner David Allen Sattazahn and his accomplice, Jeffrey Hammer, hid in a wooded area waiting to rob Richard Boyer, manager of the Heidelberg Family Restaurant. Sattazahn carried a .22-caliber Ruger semiautomatic pistol and Hammer a .41-caliber revolver. They accosted Boyer in the restaurant's parking lot at closing time. With guns drawn, they demanded the bank deposit bag containing the day's receipts. Boyer threw the bag toward the roof of the restaurant. Petitioner commanded Boyer to retrieve the bag, but instead of complying Boyer tried to run away. Both petitioner and Hammer fired shots, and Boyer fell dead. The two men then grabbed the deposit bag and fled.

The Commonwealth of Pennsylvania prosecuted petitioner and sought the death penalty. On May 10, 1991, a jury returned a conviction of first-, second-, and third-degree murder, and various other charges. In accordance with Pennsylvania law the proceeding then moved into a penalty phase. See Pa. Stat. Ann., Tit. 18, § 1102(a)(1) (Purdon 1998); Pa. Stat. Ann., Tit. 42, § 9711(a)(1) (Purdon Supp. 2002). The Commonwealth presented evidence of one statutory aggravating circumstance: commission of the murder while in the perpetration of a felony. See § 9711(d)(6). Petitioner presented as mitigating circumstances his lack of a significant history of prior criminal convictions and his age at the time of the crime. See §§ 9711(e)(1), (4). 563 Pa. 533, 539, 763 A.2d 359, 362 (2000). . . .

After both sides presented their evidence, the jury deliberated for some 3½ hours, App. 23, after which it returned a note signed by the foreman which read: "We, the jury are hopelessly deadlocked at 9-3 for life imprisonment. Each one is deeply entrenched in their [sic] position. We do not expect anyone to change his or her position." *Id.*, at 25. Petitioner then moved "under 9711(c), subparagraph 1, subparagraph Roman Numeral 5, that the jury be discharged and that [the court] enter a sentence of life imprisonment." *Id.*, at 22. The trial judge, in accordance with Pennsylvania law, discharged the jury as hung, and indicated that he would enter the required life sentence, *id.*, at 23-24, which he later did, *id.*, at 30-33.

Petitioner appealed to the Pennsylvania Superior Court. That court concluded that the trial judge had erred in instructing the jury in connection with various offenses with which petitioner was charged, including first-degree murder. It accordingly reversed petitioner's first-degree murder conviction and remanded for a new trial. Commonwealth v. Sattazahn, 428 Pa. Super. 413, 631 A.2d 597 (1993).

On remand, Pennsylvania filed a notice of intent to seek the death penalty. In addition to the aggravating circumstance alleged at the first sentencing hearing, the notice also alleged a second aggravating circumstance, petitioner's significant history of felony convictions involving the use or threat of violence to the person. (This was based on guilty pleas to a murder, multiple burglaries, and a robbery entered after the first trial.) Petitioner moved to prevent Pennsylvania from seeking the death penalty and from adding the second aggravating circumstance on retrial. The trial court denied the motion, the Superior Court affirmed the denial, App. 73, and the Pennsylvania Supreme Court declined to review the ruling, Commonwealth v. Sattazahn, 547 Pa. 742, 690 A.2d 1162 (1997). At the second trial, the jury again convicted petitioner of first-degree murder, but this time imposed a sentence of death.

On direct appeal, the Pennsylvania Supreme Court affirmed both the verdict of guilt and the sentence of death on retrial. 563 Pa., at 551, 763 A.2d, at 369. Relying on its earlier decision in Commonwealth v. Martorano, 535 Pa. 178, 634 A.2d 1063 (1993), the court concluded that neither the Double Jeopardy Clause nor the Due Process Clause barred Pennsylvania from seeking the death penalty at petitioner's retrial. 563 Pa., at 545-551, 763 A.2d, at 366-369. We granted certiorari. 535 U.S. 926, 122 S. Ct. 1294, 152 L. Ed. 2d 207 (2002).

II

A

The Double Jeopardy Clause of the Fifth Amendment commands that "[n]o person shall . . . be subject for the same offence to be twice put in jeopardy of life or limb." Under this Clause, once a defendant is placed in jeopardy for an offense, and jeopardy terminates with respect to that offense, the defendant may neither be tried nor punished a second time for the same offense. North Carolina v. Pearce, 395 U.S. 711, 717, 89 S. Ct. 2072, 23 L. Ed. 2d 656 (1969). Where, as here, a defendant is convicted of murder and sentenced to life imprisonment, but appeals the conviction and succeeds in having it set aside, we have held that jeopardy has not terminated, so that the life sentence imposed in connection with the initial conviction raises no double-jeopardy bar to a death sentence on retrial. Stroud v. United States, 251 U.S. 15, 40 S. Ct. 50, 64 L. Ed. 103 (1919).

In *Stroud*, the only offense at issue was that of murder, and the sentence was imposed by a judge who did not have to make any further findings in order to impose the death penalty. *Id.*, at 18, 40 S. Ct. 50. In Bullington v. Missouri, 451 U.S. 430, 101 S. Ct. 1852, 68 L. Ed. 2d 270 (1981), however, we held that the Double Jeopardy Clause does apply to capital-sentencing proceedings where such proceedings "have the hallmarks of the trial on guilt or innocence." *Id.*, at 439, 101 S. Ct. 1852. We identified several aspects of Missouri's sentencing proceeding that resembled a trial, including the requirement that the prosecution prove certain statutorily defined facts beyond a reasonable doubt to support a sentence of death. *Id.*, at 438, 101 S. Ct. 1852. Such a procedure, we explained, "*explicitly requires* the jury to determine whether the prosecution has 'proved its case.'" *Id.*, at 444, 101 S. Ct. 1852. Since, we concluded, a sentence of life imprisonment signifies that "'the jury has already acquitted the defendant of whatever was necessary to impose the death sentence,'" the Double Jeopardy Clause bars a State from seeking the death penalty on retrial. *Id.*, at 445, 101 S. Ct. 1852 (quoting State ex rel. Westfall v. Mason, 594 S.W.2d 908, 922 (Mo. 1980) (Bardgett, C. J., dissenting)).

We were, however, careful to emphasize that it is not the mere imposition of a life sentence that raises a double-jeopardy bar. We discussed *Stroud*, a case in which a defendant who had been convicted of first-degree murder and sentenced to life imprisonment obtained a reversal of his conviction and a new trial when the Solicitor General confessed error. In *Stroud*, the Court unanimously held that the Double Jeopardy Clause did not bar imposition of the death penalty at the new trial. 251 U.S., at 17-18, 40 S. Ct. 50. What distinguished *Bullington* from *Stroud*, we said, was the fact that in *Stroud* "there was no separate sentencing proceeding at which the prosecution was required to prove-beyond a reasonable doubt or otherwise-additional facts in order to justify the particular sentence." *Bullington*, 451 U.S., at 439, 101 S. Ct. 1852. We made clear that an "acquittal" at a trial-like sentencing phase, rather than the mere imposition of a life sentence, is required to give rise to double-jeopardy protections. *Id.*, at 446, 101 S. Ct. 1852.

Later decisions refined *Bullington's* rationale. In Arizona v. Rumsey, 467 U.S. 203, 104 S. Ct. 2305, 81 L. Ed. 2d 164 (1984), the State had argued in the sentencing phase, based on evidence presented during the guilt phase, that three statutory aggravating circumstances were present. The trial court, however, found that no statutory aggravator existed, and accordingly entered judgment in the accused's favor on the issue of death. On the State's cross-appeal, the Supreme Court of Arizona concluded that the trial court had erred in its interpretation of one of the statutory aggravating circumstances, and remanded for a new sentencing proceeding, which produced a sentence of death. *Id.*, at 205-206, 104 S. Ct. 2305. In setting that sentence aside, we explained that "[t]he double jeopardy principle relevant to [Rumsey's] case is the same as that invoked in *Bullington:* an acquittal on the merits by the sole decisionmaker in the proceeding is final and bars retrial on the same charge." *Id.*, at 211, 104 S. Ct. 2305. . . .

Rumsey thus reaffirmed that the relevant inquiry for double-jeopardy purposes was not whether the defendant received a life sentence the first time around, but rather whether a first life sentence was an "acquittal" based on findings sufficient to establish legal entitlement to the life sentence—*i.e.*, findings that the government failed to prove one or more aggravating circumstances beyond a reasonable doubt. . . .

B

Normally, "a retrial following a 'hung jury' does not violate the Double Jeopardy Clause." Richardson v. United States, 468 U.S. 317, 324, 104 S. Ct. 3081, 82 L. Ed. 2d 242 (1984). Petitioner contends, however, that given the unique treatment afforded capital-sentencing proceedings under *Bullington*, double-jeopardy protections were triggered when the jury deadlocked at his first sentencing proceeding and the court prescribed a sentence of life imprisonment pursuant to Pennsylvania law.

We disagree. Under the *Bullington* line of cases just discussed, the touchstone for double-jeopardy protection in capital-sentencing proceedings is whether there has been an "acquittal." Petitioner here cannot establish that the jury or the court "acquitted" him during his first capital-sentencing proceeding. As to the jury: The verdict form returned by the foreman stated that the jury deadlocked 9-to-3 on whether to impose the death penalty; it made no findings with respect to the alleged aggravating circumstance. That result—or more appropriately, that non-result—cannot fairly be called an acquittal "based on findings sufficient to establish legal entitlement to the life sentence." *Rumsey, supra*, at 211, 104 S. Ct. 2305. . . .

III

A

When *Bullington, Rumsey,* and *Poland* were decided, capital-sentencing proceedings were understood to be just that: *sentencing proceedings.* Whatever "hallmarks of [a] trial" they might have borne, *Bullington*, 451 U.S., at 439, 101 S. Ct. 1852, they differed from trials in a respect crucial for purposes of the Double Jeopardy Clause: They dealt only with the *sentence* to be imposed for the "offence" of capital murder. Thus, in its search for a rationale to support *Bullington* and its "progeny," the Court continually tripped over the text of the Double Jeopardy Clause.

Recent developments, however, have illuminated this part of our jurisprudence. Our decision in Apprendi v. New Jersey, 530 U.S. 466, 120 S. Ct. 2348, 147 L. Ed. 2d 435 (2000), clarified what constitutes an "element" of an offense for purposes of the Sixth Amendment's jury-trial guarantee. Put simply, if the existence of any fact (other than a prior conviction) increases the maximum punishment that may be imposed on a defendant, that fact—no matter how the State labels it—constitutes an element, and must be found by a jury beyond a reasonable doubt. *Id.*, at 482-484, 490, 120 S. Ct. 2348. . . .

B

For purposes of the Double Jeopardy Clause, then, "first-degree murder" under Pennsylvania law—the offense of which petitioner was convicted during the guilt phase of his proceedings is properly understood to be a lesser included offense of "first-degree murder plus aggravating circumstance(s)." See *Ring, supra*, at 609, 122 S. Ct. 2428. Thus, if petitioner's first sentencing jury had unanimously concluded that Pennsylvania failed to prove any aggravating circumstances, that conclusion would operate as an "acquittal" of the greater offense—which would bar Pennsylvania from retrying petitioner on that greater offense (and thus, from seeking the death penalty) on retrial. Cf. *Rumsey, supra*, at 211, 104 S. Ct. 2305.

But that is not what happened. Petitioner was convicted in the guilt phase of his first trial of the lesser offense of first-degree murder. During the sentencing phase, the jury deliberated without reaching a decision on death or life, and without making any findings regarding aggravating or mitigating circumstances. After 3½ hours the judge dismissed the jury as hung and entered a life sentence in accordance with Pennsylvania law. As explained, *supra*, at 738-739, neither judge nor jury "acquitted" petitioner of the greater offense of "first-degree murder plus aggravating circumstance(s)." Thus, when petitioner appealed and succeeded in invalidating his conviction of the lesser offense, there was no double-jeopardy bar to Pennsylvania's retrying petitioner on both the lesser and the greater offense; his "jeopardy" never terminated with respect to either. . . .

IV

The dissent reads the Court's decision in United States v. Scott, 437 U.S. 82, 98 S. Ct. 2187, 57 L. Ed. 2d 65 (1978), as supporting the proposition that where, as here, a defendant's "case was fully tried and the court, on its own motion, entered a final judgment-a life sentence-terminating the trial proceedings," *post*, at 747 (opinion of Ginsburg, J.), the Double Jeopardy Clause bars retrial. There are several problems with this reasoning.

First, it is an understatement to say that "*Scott* . . . did not home in on a case like [petitioner's]," *post*, at 746. The statement upon which the dissent relies-that double jeopardy "may" attach when the "trial judge terminates the proceedings favorably to the defendant on a basis not related to factual guilt or innocence," 437 U.S., at 92, 98 S. Ct. 2187, at least where the defendant "had either been found not guilty *or . . . had at least insisted on having the issue of guilt submitted to the first trier of fact*," *id.*, at 96, 98 S. Ct. 2187 (emphasis added)—was nothing more than dictum, and a tentative one ("may") at that. It would be a thin reed on which to rest a hitherto unknown constitutional prohibition of the entirely rational course of making a hung jury's failure to convict provisionally final, subject to change if the case must be retried anyway.

Second, the dictum in *Scott* does not even embrace the present case. The petitioner here did not "insist" upon a merits determination, but to the contrary asked that the jury be dismissed as hung. As the dissent recognizes, when the jury announced that it was deadlocked, petitioner "move[d] 'that the jury be discharged' and that a life sentence be entered under [Pa. Stat. Ann., Tit. 42,] § 9711(c)(1)(v)." *Post*, at 747, n.5. It is no response to say that "[t]he judge did not grant [the] motion," but instead made a legal determination whether petitioner was entitled to the judgment he sought. *Ibid.* Surely double-jeopardy protections cannot hinge on whether a trial court characterizes its action as self-initiated or in response to motion. Cf. *Scott, supra*, at 96, 98 S. Ct. 2187. What actually happened in this case is the same as what happened in *Scott*, where we *denied* double-jeopardy protection: (1) the defendant moved for entry of a judgment in his favor on procedural grounds (there, delay in indictment; here, a hung jury); (2) the judge measured facts (there, the length of delay; here, the likelihood of the jury's producing a verdict) against a legal standard to determine whether such relief was appropriate; and (3) concluding that it was, granted the relief.

Nor, in these circumstances, does the prospect of a second capital-sentencing proceeding implicate any of the "perils against which the Double Jeopardy Clause seeks to protect." *Post*, at 746 (Ginsburg, J., dissenting). The dissent stresses that a defendant in such circumstances is "subject to the 'ordeal' of a second full-blown life or death trial," which "'compel[s][him] to live in a continuing state of anxiety and insecurity.'" *Ibid.* (quoting *Green v. United States, supra*, at 187, 78 S. Ct. 221); see also *post*, at 748. But as even the dissent must admit, *post*, at 746-747, we have not found this concern determinative of double jeopardy in all circumstances. And it should not be so here. This case hardly presents the specter of "an all-powerful state relentlessly pursuing a defendant who had either been found not guilty or who had at least insisted on having the issue of guilt submitted to the first trier of fact." *Scott, supra*, at 96, 98 S. Ct. 2187. Instead, we see here a State which, for any number of perfectly understandable reasons, *supra*, at 739, has quite reasonably agreed to accept the default penalty of life imprisonment when the conviction is affirmed and the case is, except for that issue, at an end-but to pursue its not-yet-vindicated interest in "'one complete opportunity to convict those who have violated its laws'" where the case must be retried anyway, *post*, at 746 (quoting Arizona v. Washington, 434 U.S. 497, 509, 98 S. Ct. 824, 54 L. Ed. 2d 717 (1978)). . . .

The Pennsylvania Supreme Court correctly concluded that neither the Fifth Amendment's Double Jeopardy Clause nor the Fourteenth Amendment's Due Process Clause barred Pennsylvania from seeking the death penalty against petitioner on retrial. The judgment of that court is, therefore,

Affirmed. . . .

Justice GINSBURG, with whom Justice STEVENS, Justice SOUTER, and Justice BREYER join, dissenting.

This case concerns the events that "terminat[e] jeopardy" for purposes of the Double Jeopardy Clause. Richardson v. United States, 468 U.S. 317, 325, 104 S. Ct. 3081, 82 L. Ed. 2d 242 (1984). The specific controversy before the Court involves the entry of final judgment, as mandated by state law, after a jury deadlock. The question presented is whether a final judgment so entered qualifies as a jeopardy-terminating event. The Court concludes it does not. I would hold that it does. . . .

In no prior case have we decided whether jeopardy is terminated by the entry of a state-mandated sentence when the jury has deadlocked on the sentencing question. As I see it, the question is genuinely debatable, with tenable argument supporting each side. Comprehending our double jeopardy decisions in light of the underlying purposes of the Double Jeopardy Clause, I conclude that jeopardy does terminate in such circumstances. I would hold, as herein explained, that once the trial court entered a final judgment of life for Sattazahn, the Double Jeopardy Clause barred Pennsylvania from seeking the death penalty a second time.

I

The standard way for a defendant to secure a final judgment in her favor is to gain an acquittal. This case involves the atypical situation in which a defendant prevails by final judgment *without* an acquittal. Unusual as the situation is, our double jeopardy jurisprudence recognizes its existence. In *Scott*, the Court stated that the "primary purpose" of the Double Jeopardy Clause is to "protect the integrity" of final determinations of guilt or innocence. 437 U.S., at 92, 98 S. Ct. 2187. We acknowledged, however, that "this Court has also developed a body of law guarding the separate but related interest of a defendant in avoiding multiple prosecutions even where no final determination of guilt or innocence has been made." *Ibid.* "Such interests," we observed, "may be involved in two different situations: the first, in which the trial judge declares a mistrial; the second, in which the trial judge terminates the proceedings favorably to the defendant on a basis not related to factual guilt or innocence." *Ibid.* . . .

The second category described in *Scott*—"termination of [a] trial in [a defendant's] favor before any determination of factual guilt or innocence," *id.*, at 94, 98 S. Ct. 2187—is distinguished from the first based on the quality of finality a termination order imports. "When a trial court declares a mistrial, it all but invariably contemplates that the prosecutor will be permitted to proceed a new notwithstanding the defendant's plea of double jeopardy." *Id.*, at 92, 98 S. Ct. 2187. When a motion to terminate is granted, in contrast, the trial court "obviously contemplates that the proceedings will terminate then and there in favor of the defendant." *Id.*, at 94, 98 S. Ct. 2187. In *Scott*, for example, the trial court granted the defendant's motion to dismiss one count of the indictment, prior to its submission to the jury, on the ground of preindictment delay. If the prosecution had wanted to "reinstate the proceedings in the face of such a ruling," it could not simply have refiled the indictment; instead, it would have had to "seek reversal of the decision of the trial court" by pursuing an appeal. *Ibid.*

Sattazahn's case falls within *Scott's* second category. After the jury deadlocked at the sentencing stage, no mistrial was declared, for Pennsylvania law provided that the trial proceedings would terminate "then and there" in Sattazahn's favor. The government could not simply retry the sentencing issue at will. The hung jury in Sattazahn's case did not "mak[e] . . . completion" of the first proceeding "impossible," Wade v. Hunter, 336 U.S. 684, 689, 69 S. Ct. 834, 93 L. Ed. 974 (1949); instead, Pennsylvania law *required* the judge to bring that proceeding to a conclusion by entering a final judgment imposing a life sentence, see Pa. Stat. Ann., Tit. 42, § 9711(c)(1)(v) (Purdon Supp.2002). . . .

II

Scott, it is true, did not home in on a case like Sattazahn's. The Court's reasoning, nevertheless, lends credence to the view that a trial-terminating judgment for life, not prompted by a procedural move on the defendant's part, creates a legal entitlement protected by the Double Jeopardy Clause. Cf. *Rumsey*, 467 U.S., at 211, 104 S. Ct. 2305 (judgment based on factual findings sufficient to establish "legal entitlement" to a life sentence bars retrial). *Scott* recognized that defendants have a double jeopardy interest in avoiding multiple prosecutions even when there has been no determination of guilt or innocence, and that this interest is implicated by preverdict judgments terminating trials. 437 U.S., at 92, 98 S. Ct. 2187. The interest in avoiding a renewed prosecution following a final judgment is surely engaged here. Sattazahn's life sentence had significantly greater finality than the dismissal for preindictment delay in *Scott*, for under Pennsylvania law, as noted earlier, see *supra*, at 743, the government could not have sought to retry the sentencing question even through an appeal.

Moreover—and discrete from the Court's analysis in *Scott*—the perils against which the Double Jeopardy Clause seeks to protect are plainly implicated by the prospect of a second capital sentencing proceeding. A determination that defendants in Sattazahn's position are subject to the "ordeal" of a second full-blown life or death trial "compel[s] [them] to live in a continuing state of anxiety and insecurity." *Green*, 355 U.S., at 187, 78 S. Ct. 221.

Despite the attendant generation of anxiety and insecurity, we have allowed retrial after hung jury mistrials in order to give the State "one complete opportunity to convict those who have violated its laws." *Washington*, 434 U.S., at 509, 98 S. Ct. 824; see *Wade*, 336 U.S., at 689, 69 S. Ct. 834 ("a defendant's valued right to have his trial completed by a particular tribunal must in some instances be subordinated to the public's interest in fair trials designed to end in just judgments"). But here, the Commonwealth has already had such an opportunity: The prosecution presented its evidence to the jury, and after the jury deadlocked, final judgment was entered at the direction of the state legislature itself. This was not an instance in which "the Government was quite willing to continue with its production of evidence," but was thwarted by a defense-proffered motion. *Scott*, 437 U.S., at 96, 98 S. Ct. 2187. . . .

I recognize that this is a novel and close question: Sattazahn was not "acquitted" of the death penalty, but his case was fully tried and the court, on its own motion, entered a final judgment—a life sentence—terminating the trial proceedings. I would decide the double jeopardy issue in Sattazahn's favor, for the reasons herein stated, and giving weight to two ultimate considerations. First, the Court's holding confronts defendants with a perilous choice, one we have previously declined to impose in other circumstances. See *Green*, 355 U.S., at 193-194, 78 S. Ct. 221. Under the Court's decision, if a defendant sentenced to life after a jury deadlock chooses to appeal her underlying conviction, she faces the possibility of death if she is successful on appeal but convicted on retrial. If, on the other hand, the defendant loses her appeal, or chooses to forgo an appeal, the final judgment for life stands. In other words, a defendant in Sattazahn's position must relinquish either her right to file a potentially meritorious appeal, or her state-granted entitlement to avoid the death penalty.

We have previously declined to interpret the Double Jeopardy Clause in a manner that puts defendants in this bind. . . .

Second, the punishment Sattazahn again faced on retrial was death, a penalty "unique in both its severity and its finality." Monge v. California, 524 U.S. 721, 732, 118 S. Ct. 2246, 141 L. Ed. 2d 615 (1998) (internal quotation marks omitted). These qualities heighten Sattazahn's double jeopardy interest in avoiding a second prosecution. The "hazards of [a second] trial and possible conviction," *Green*, 355 U.S., at 187, 78 S. Ct. 221, the "continuing state of anxiety and insecurity" to which retrial subjects a defendant, *ibid.*, and the "financial" as well as the "emotional burden" of a second trial, *Washington*, 434 U.S., at 503-504, 98 S. Ct. 824, are all exacerbated when the subsequent proceeding may terminate in death. Death, moreover, makes the "dilemma" a defendant faces when she decides whether to appeal all the more "incredible." *Green*, 355 U.S., at 193, 78 S. Ct. 221. As our elaboration in *Gregg v. Georgia*, 428 U.S. 153, 188, 96 S. Ct. 2909, 49 L. Ed. 2d 859 (1976) (joint opinion of Stewart, Powell, and Stevens, JJ.), and later cases demonstrates, death is indeed a penalty "different" from all others.

For the reasons stated, I would hold that jeopardy terminated as to Sattazahn's sentence after the judge entered a final judgment for life. I would therefore reverse the judgment of the Supreme Court of Pennsylvania.

CASE QUESTIONS

BLOCKBERGER v. UNITED STATES

1. What was the Court's basis for holding that the second and third counts charged were not the "same offense" for double jeopardy purposes? Do you agree with the Court's conclusion? Why or why not?

2. Given the Court's analysis in question #1 above, what if the defendant had sold drugs to the same person *thirty* successive times rather than only twice? Do you think the Court would have concluded that the defendant was guilty of 30 separate and distinct offenses? Explain. What additional facts might you want to know in order to formulate your answer?

3. Why did the Court hold that the underlying offense which comprised the third count against the defendant could be the subject of two separate violations of the Narcotics Act without violating double jeopardy? Can you think of any other instances where the same act of criminal conduct could give rise to two or more distinct offenses?

4. Blockberger v. United States is sometimes referred to as a "landmark" decision. What does that mean and what principals of law enunciated in *Blockberger* make it such a case with regard to double jeopardy?

SATTAZAHN v. PENNSYLVANIA

1. What procedural background of this case gave rise to the appeal on double jeopardy grounds?

2. Why is it that in some death penalty cases, if a defendant received a life sentence and he successfully appeals, he *can* receive the death penalty on retrial, whereas in other cases the most he can receive on retrial is another life sentence? How is this not inconsistent?

3. How did the dissent use the Court's prior decision in Scott v. United States, 437 U.S. 82 (1978), to support its viewpoint? How did the majority in *Sattazahn* distinguish *Scott* and, therefore, refute the dissent's position?

4. What two "offenses" did the majority conclude were the "same offense" for double jeopardy purposes given the facts of the case?

HYPOTHETICAL WITH ACCOMPANYING ANALYSIS

Hypothetical

Patrick was brought to trial for the murder of his long-time rival, Brian. "Murder" is defined by State statute as "the intentional infliction of bodily harm upon the victim resulting in the victim's death." The prosecution alleged that Patrick beat Brian over the head with a baseball bat until Brian lost consciousness and eventually died. After a five-day trial, the case went to the jury. The jury deliberated only 20 minutes before acquitting Patrick of murder. Penelope Winemall, the State's most voracious prosecuting attorney, was furious. She was convinced she had a "dud" jury and she couldn't stand the fact that Patrick had literally gotten away with murder. So, Penelope had an idea. The day after the acquittal Penelope initiated charges against Patrick for battery, which is defined by statute as "the intentional infliction of bodily harm upon the victim." The battery charges also stemmed from the incident in which Patrick fatally beat Brian over the head with the baseball bat. A battery conviction only carries a maximum penalty of ten years in that jurisdiction, but Penelope figured ten years was better than nothing, since she was convinced of Patrick's guilt.

Analyze whether Patrick's Fifth Amendment rights against double jeopardy apply to the above scenario and whether those rights would be violated by his trial for battery.

Analysis

The Double Jeopardy Clause of the Fifth Amendment protects an individual from being subjected to multiple trials or multiple punishments for the same offense. In order for double jeopardy to be implicated, five factors must be present. Each of those factors will be examined separately and applied to the facts of Patrick's situation to see if his second trial would be barred by double jeopardy.

First, the subsequent trial must be for the "same offense" for which the person had already been tried. A crime can be defined as the same offense for double jeopardy purposes in one of two ways: both crimes could have the same elements or one crime could be a lesser included offense of the other. Additionally, in order to constitute the same offense for double jeopardy, both offenses must be applied to the same conduct. Patrick was first charged with the crime of murder, which consists of four elements: (1) intentional; (2) infliction of bodily harm; (3) upon the victim; (4) resulting in the victim's death. Penelope then brought charges against Patrick for battery. That crime, when broken down into its elements, consists of: (1) intentional; (2) infliction of bodily harm; (3) upon the victim. Because the battery charge contains all the same elements as murder, and murder has one additional element, battery is a "lesser included offense" of murder. The subsequent trial of lesser-included offenses is one of the categories prohibited by the Double Jeopardy Clause. Because both the murder and battery charges pertained to the incident in which Patrick fatally beat Brian over the head with a baseball bat, they both arise from the same conduct.

Second, the Double Jeopardy Clause prohibits being tried "twice" for the same offense. A retrial following an acquittal is one of the primary evils the clause seeks to prevent. Patrick was acquitted of his murder charges. Hence, Penelope's initiation of battery charges would ultimately subject Patrick to a second trial.

Third, double jeopardy is only implicated if jeopardy has "attached." During a jury trial, jeopardy attaches when the jury is first sworn and empanelled. In Patrick's murder trial, the jury had rendered a not guilty verdict. Thus, jeopardy had clearly attached in the first trial for murder.

Fourth, the Double Jeopardy Clause only prohibits multiple "criminal" prosecutions. It is not implicated by civil trials. In this situation, Patrick was first tried for murder in a criminal prosecution. The battery charge was also criminal in nature. Hence, a trial for battery would subject Patrick to multiple criminal trials.

Finally, multiple trials by the "same sovereign" are prohibited. The Dual Sovereignty Doctrine allows successive trials if by different sovereigns, such as a federal and state prosecution, or prosecutions by two separate states. In this scenario, the jurisdiction where Patrick's trial took place has not been specified. However, Penelope was the prosecutor in the first trial for murder, and she additionally initiated charges against Patrick for battery. Because Penelope would be prosecuting the battery charges if they came to trial, it is reasonable to infer that both trials would be conducted by the same sovereign and hence prohibited by the Double Jeopardy Clause.

After examining the five factors of the Double Jeopardy Clause and applying them to the case at hand, it is clear that a trial for battery would violate Patrick's Fifth Amendment rights. Although "murder" and "battery" are not the exact same crime, they qualify for double jeopardy purposes because one is a lesser-included offense of the other. To summarize, all five of the elements that the clause seeks to prohibit are present in this scenario: The prosecution would place Patrick twice in jeopardy by trying him in a criminal prosecution by the same sovereign for the same offense. Thus, Patrick's second trial for battery would be in violation of his constitutional rights.

One afternoon, Tim approached an elderly woman walking along a neighborhood street. He pulled out a pocket knife, switched the blade opened, and said to her, "Give me all your cash or I'll kill you." The woman, obviously frightened, removed $200 from her purse and handed it to Tim. Tim fled the scene. Approximately three hours later, Tim approached an elderly man on the other side of town. He repeated the same threat to the man, but this time Tim was unarmed. The man handed over $50 from his wallet and Tim again fled. A short while later, Tim was apprehended and identified as the robber of both victims. Tim was brought to trial for armed robbery of the elderly woman and acquitted.

The same day that Tim committed his two robberies, Jim approached a young woman in a shopping center parking lot on the other side of town. He pulled out a handgun, pointed it at the woman, and said, "Hand over your money or you're dead." The woman handed her purse to Jim, which contained some credit cards and $100 in cash. Jim fled. He was subsequently apprehended for the offense. Jim stood trial for armed robbery and was acquitted.

The State has now initiated charges against Tim for simple robbery against the elderly man. It has also initiated charges against Jim for simple robbery against the young woman in the parking lot. Analyze whether the Fifth Amendment prohibitions against double jeopardy apply in either of the above scenarios and, if so, whether those constitutional rights would be violated by the second prosecution of Tim and/or Jim.

DISCUSSION QUESTIONS

1. Cindy is taken to the police station for questioning in the mysterious death of her husband. After questioning, the authorities let her go. The case remains unsolved for five years, until one day police get a tip from Cindy's best friend that she committed the murder, and her friend leads police to the weapon. Cindy is subsequently charged with murder and brought to trial. Cindy claims she cannot be tried because she was twice put in jeopardy—the first time when police questioned her and the second time when she was brought to trial. Will Cindy's claims be successful?

2. Henry is the victim of a very bad beating. He is in the hospital, in a coma, for six months. Charlie, the man responsible for the beating, is tried for attempted murder and convicted. The day after the verdict is rendered, Henry dies from his injuries. The state then brings charges against Charlie for murder. Is there a double jeopardy violation? Explain. *See* Diaz v. United States, 223 U. S. 442 (1912). What if the prosecutor had decided to wait it out and see how long the victim lived before bringing any charges against Charlie—what other constitutional provisions could be implicated and possibly violated by this strategy?

3. Tim is convicted of raping a young woman. Tim appeals his decision on the basis that the trial court improperly admitted hearsay evidence. The appellate court agrees with Tim and reverses. Will the state be permitted to retry Tim for the rape offense? Why or why not? What if Tim's argument on appeal had been that there was insufficient evidence of his guilt at trial, and the appellate court reversed the case on those grounds? Would a second trial be permitted under those circumstances? Explain. *See* Burks v. United States, 437 U.S. 1 (1978).

4. What is the "Dual Sovereignty Doctrine"? What is its purpose and how does it implicate the Double Jeopardy Clause?

5. Research challenge: In 1963, Civil Rights activist Medgar Evers was murdered outside of his home. Byron De La Beckwith was believed to be responsible for the murder, and he was eventually brought to trial on three separate occasions for Evers' murder. Research the unique procedural history of the case against De La Beckwith and explain how the Double Jeopardy Clause was not violated by three prosecutions for the crime.

6. Julie White is in the middle of prosecuting a burglary case against the defendant, Tim Green. Julie can tell her case isn't going well, and she is afraid that Tim will be acquitted. Therefore, she decides to "throw" the trial by bringing forth inadmissible evidence which she knows will force the defendant to ask for and the judge to grant a mistrial. After the mistrial is declared, Julie reinitiates burglary charges in the hopes that during the new trial she can correct her previous mistakes and she will get a conviction. Does Julie's strategy violate Tim's Fifth Amendment double jeopardy rights?

7. What are the purposes of the Double Jeopardy Clause? What protections does it afford an individual and why?

8. Alex is convicted of kidnapping and sentenced to 15 years imprisonment. He appeals his conviction, wins a reversal, and the State retries him. He is once again convicted of kidnapping, but this time another judge sentences him to 25 years imprisonment. Were Alex's double jeopardy rights violated because of the increased punishment following the second trial? Explain. How is this situation distinguishable from *Sattazahn*?

9. In 1995 O.J. Simpson was acquitted of the double homicide of Nicole Brown Simpson and Ronald Goldman. Subsequently a civil suit was initiated against Simpson by the Brown and Goldman families for wrongful death. In 1997, a jury found Simpson liable for wrongful death and handed down a multi-million dollar verdict against him. Why did the second lawsuit not violate Simpson's double jeopardy rights?

10. (a) Linda is pulled over for drunk driving. At an administrative hearing, she has her license suspended. The state then brings criminal charges against her for driving while intoxicated. (b) Tom is a gynecologist. After a patient complains that she was sexually molested by Tom during an examination, Tom has his license revoked by a medical board. The State then brings sexual assault charges against Tom. (c) Mary abuses her one-year-old son. The state successfully institutes proceedings to terminate her parental rights, and her child is taken away. The state then charges Mary with

child abuse. (d) Kelly is a senior in high school. She is expelled from school for smoking marijuana. The state then brings juvenile delinquency proceedings against Kelly for narcotics violations. In which of the four situations, if any, would the prosecution of charges violate the respective defendants' rights against double jeopardy? Why? *See* Hudson v. United States, 522 U.S. 93 (1997).

11. Research challenge: Research the case of Mel Ignatow, a man who admitted to murdering his girlfriend Brenda Schaefer in Kentucky in 1988. How was double jeopardy implicated in that case? What was the outcome? Do you agree with the ultimate result? Explain.

12. Timothy McVeigh was successfully prosecuted by the federal government and sentenced to death for the 168 homicide victims of the 1995 Oklahoma City bombing. If the state of Oklahoma had wanted to, could it have prosecuted McVeigh in state court for those murders following the federal court case? Explain. Would your answer change if McVeigh had been acquitted at the conclusion of the federal trial?

13. What is the doctrine of "collateral estoppel"? How does it relate to the Double Jeopardy Clause? *See* Ashe v. Swenson, 397 U.S. 436 (1970).

14. (a) Tom is on trial for murder, although the victim's body had not been found. Tom is acquitted and two weeks later the victim's body is found, conclusively proving that Tom committed the murder. (b) Jerry is on trial for rape and acquitted. Following the acquittal it is learned that Jerry secretly paid the jurors in his case $1,000 each to hand down a not guilty verdict. In which of the two situations, if either, would a second trial *not* be barred by double jeopardy?

True/False

1. A criminal trial for rape followed by a civil trial for the medical expenses and emotional damages sustained as a result of that rape would not violate double jeopardy.

2. A civil trial for medical expenses and emotional damages sustained as a result of a rape followed by a criminal trial for rape would not violate double jeopardy.

3. Any time a mistrial is granted, a retrial will be permissible and not in violation of double jeopardy.

4. Collateral estoppel is a legal doctrine that bars the prosecution of an offense if the issue of ultimate fact has already been litigated in favor of the accused.

5. Double jeopardy only bars multiple prosecutions for the same offense: it does not prohibit multiple punishments for the same offense.

Multiple Choice

6. Under which of the following circumstances would a retrial be in violation of double jeopardy?

   A. The defendant is acquitted for a crime following a court trial because he bribed the judge to render a verdict in his favor.
   B. The defendant is convicted of a crime and wins a reversal on appeal on the ground that the trial judge erroneously admitted hearsay evidence.
   C. The defendant's jury is hopelessly deadlocked and the judge declares a mistrial.
   D. A retrial would be permitted under any of the above circumstances.

7. Max and Jack are arrested for committing an armed bank robbery together. Max is brought to trial first and acquitted of all charges. Jack is subsequently brought to trial, but he argues his trial would violate double jeopardy. Will Jack's challenge be successful?

   A. Yes, because under the doctrine of collateral estoppel, the jury in Max's trial conclusively litigated the fact that Max and Jack were not the bank robbers, thereby determining the ultimate issue in Jack's favor.
   B. Yes, because the State was required to bring Max and Jack to trial together since their crimes were based on the same conduct.
   C. No, because Jack has not twice been placed in jeopardy.
   D. No, because the State could appeal Max's acquittal and possibly retry Max for his involvement in the robbery.

8. Which of the following statements is *inaccurate*?

    A. Jeopardy attaches in a jury trial when the first witness is called and sworn.
    B. Jeopardy attaches in a court trial when the first witness is called and sworn.
    C. Jeopardy attaches in a guilty plea when the judge formally accepts the defendant's plea and enters a conviction.
    D. All of the above statements are accurate.

9. Which of the following situations would violate the Dual Sovereignty Doctrine, assuming both trials are for the same offense?

    A. A trial in State X followed by a trial in State Y
    B. A federal trial followed by a state trial
    C. A state trial followed by a federal trial
    D. A state trial in State X followed by a municipal trial in State X

10. Sean is tried for the murder of Wanda in federal court and acquitted. Sean's surviving parents then bring a civil lawsuit against Wanda, also in federal court, for wrongful death. Is the lawsuit filed by Wanda's parents in violation of double jeopardy?

    A. Yes, because Sean was acquitted at the murder trial, thus conclusively proving he did not murder Wanda.
    B. Yes, because the first trial carries a more onerous burden of proof than the second trial.
    C. Yes, because both the first trial and the civil lawsuit were brought by the same sovereign since they were both in federal court.
    D. No

Part II

The Trial Process

6
Due Process

INTRODUCTION

Due *what*??? The protections guaranteed to a criminal defendant throughout the Bill of Rights are, for the most part, self-explanatory: the right to a speedy trial; the right to a jury trial; the right to counsel; the right to be free from compelled self-incrimination. Although students initially may not know the intricacies of each right, they at least have a grasp of the basic protection by doing nothing more than reading the relevant clause itself. No great mystery exists as to what each of those rights means. Unfortunately, when it comes to due process, the large majority of students hit a brick wall. Why? Perhaps because the wording of the clause is somewhat ambiguous. Or perhaps because the right to due process doesn't protect a single part of the criminal trial, but it is more fluid in nature. As a professor of criminal justice, it becomes all too clear just how lost students are when I ask my class for a basic definition of due process. What do I get in return? Usually the complex definition of "the process that is due to someone," with the student's voice trailing off into a faint question instead of a confident assertion of his knowledge. Needless to say, students typically have a very poor understanding (if any at all) of what the right to due process is all about.

It's a little unsettling that due process is so misunderstood (or even un-understood) considering that of all of the protections in the Bill of Rights it has likely been around the longest, with its origins dating back to the Magna Charta of 1215. Perhaps that's part of the problem though—due process has been around *so* long that it has taken on a life of its own, with twists and turns in the law over the centuries that leave us confused at the muddled law. One point of confusion comes from the fact that the Amendments contain not just one but *two* due process clauses that are virtually identical—one in the Fifth Amendment and the other in the Fourteenth Amendment. Why two? Was Congress feeling particularly redundant when it ratified the Fourteenth Amendment in 1868? Understanding which clause to apply in any given case is only the first hurdle, for then we discover that due process actually encompasses two separate protections—"substantive" due process and "procedural" due process. But what exactly is the difference between the two? Another area implicated in due process is "incorporation," or the Court's piecemeal recognition that most of the protections mentioned in the Bill of Rights apply not only to the federal government but also to the states via the Fourteenth Amendment. The doctrine of incorporation is complicated and controversial to say the least. Finally, to further complicate matters, the Due Process Clauses of the Fifth and Fourteenth Amendments apply to both criminal *and* civil cases, unlike the other Amendments discussed in this text which apply exclusively to criminal cases. Due process has been implicated in areas from abortion to birth control to capital punishment and everything in between. The reach of due process is vast.

So many basic questions about due process, but so few basic answers. As a student, if you are looking for that quick solution, that nice, neat checklist for a due process analysis, you won't find it. There *is* no such thing. As Justice Oliver Wendell Holmes, Jr. noted almost one hundred years ago: "What is due process of law depends on circumstances. It varies with the subject-matter and the necessities of the situation." In other words, what amounts to due process of law depends *entirely* on the facts of each case. The best way, therefore, to analyze whether an individual's due process rights have been violated is to do two things. First, learn by example. Look to past cases to predict what the Court might do under a similar set of circumstances. Second, go with your gut. The key ingredient to any due process challenge is the notion that an individual's basic liberty interests were somehow violated. What does your gut tell you? Is there something about the law, or the way it was implemented, that just isn't right? Perhaps due process can best be compared to a sports game. The game itself has to be fair, *and* it has to played by the rules. Or, in the words of former Chief Justice Earl Warren, due process can be summarized as quite simply, *Fair play.*

STUDENT *Checklist*

Due Process

1. Determine which Due Process Clause is implicated:

■ **Fifth Amendment**: Federal government

■ **Fourteenth Amendment**: State governments

2. Determine whether **Procedural** or **Substantive** due process is implicated:

■ **Procedural Due Process**:* Before depriving an individual of life, liberty, or property, did the government ensure that adequate procedures were in place, potentially including:

Notice of the charges/sanction?
An **opportunity to be heard** and **present a defense**?
An opportunity to **confront** and **cross-examine** witnesses?
The assistance of **counsel**?
Use of **evidentiary rules** to limit the type of evidence admissible?
An **impartial decision maker**?
A transcribed **record** of the proceedings?
An **appeal** based on the record?

■ **Substantive Due Process**:
Did the government's conduct **shock the conscience** because it was so outrageous?
Did the government's conduct interfere with rights **implicit in the concept of ordered liberty**? (eg., right to **privacy**)

* **Note:** Not all of the procedural safeguards will apply in every case where a challenge to procedural due process is undertaken. What procedures must be provided depends on the interest the government seeks to terminate; the more important the individual's interest, the more procedural protections that will be available.

SUPREME COURT CASES

BELL v. WOLFISH, 441 U.S. 520 (1979)

Over the past five Terms, this Court has in several decisions considered constitutional challenges to prison conditions or practices by convicted prisoners. This case requires us to examine the constitutional rights of pretrial detainees—those persons who have been charged with a crime but who have not yet been tried on the charge. The parties concede that to ensure their presence at trial, these persons legitimately may be incarcerated by the Government prior to a determination of their guilt or innocence, *infra*, at 1871, and n.15; see 18 U.S.C. §§ 3146, 3148, and it is the scope of their rights during this period of confinement prior to trial that is the primary focus of this case.

This lawsuit was brought as a class action in the United States District Court for the Southern District of New York to challenge numerous conditions of confinement and practices at the Metropolitan Correctional Center (MCC), a federally operated short-term custodial facility in New York City designed primarily to house pretrial detainees. . . .

On November 28, 1975, less than four months after the MCC had opened, the named respondents initiated this action by filing in the District Court a petition for a writ of habeas corpus. The District Court certified the case as a class action on behalf of all persons confined at the MCC, pretrial detainees and sentenced prisoners alike. The petition served up a veritable potpourri of complaints that implicated virtually every facet of the institution's conditions and practices. Respondents charged, *inter alia*, that they had been deprived of their statutory and constitutional rights because of overcrowded conditions, undue length of confinement, improper searches, inadequate recreational, educational, and employment opportunities, insufficient staff, and objectionable restrictions on the purchase and receipt of personal items and books. . . .

II

As a first step in our decision, we shall address "double-bunking" as it is referred to by the parties, since it is a condition of confinement that is alleged only to deprive pretrial detainees of their liberty without due process of law in contravention of the Fifth Amendment.

B

In evaluating the constitutionality of conditions or restrictions of pretrial detention that implicate only the protection against deprivation of liberty without due process of law, we think that the proper inquiry is whether those conditions amount to punishment of the detainee. For under the Due Process Clause, a detainee may not be punished prior to an adjudication of guilt in accordance with due process of law. . . . A person lawfully committed to pretrial detention has not been adjudged guilty of any crime. He has had only a "judicial determination of probable cause as a prerequisite to [the] extended restraint of [his] liberty following arrest." *Gerstein v. Pugh, supra,* 420 U.S., at 114, 95 S. Ct., at 863; see *Virginia v. Paul,* 148 U.S. 107, 119, 13 S. Ct. 536, 540, 37 L. Ed. 386 (1893). And, if he is detained for a suspected violation of a federal law, he also has had a bail hearing. See 18 U.S.C. §§ 3146, 3148. Under such circumstances, the Government concededly may detain him to ensure his presence at trial and may subject him to the restrictions and conditions of the detention facility so long as those conditions and restrictions do not amount to punishment, or otherwise violate the Constitution.

Not every disability imposed during pretrial detention amounts to "punishment" in the constitutional sense, however. Once the Government has exercised its conceded authority to detain a person pending trial, it obviously is entitled to employ devices that are calculated to effectuate this detention. Traditionally, this has meant confinement in a facility which, no matter how modern or how antiquated, results in restricting the movement of a detainee in a manner in which he would not be restricted if he simply were free to walk the streets pending trial. Whether it be called a jail, a prison, or a custodial center, the purpose of the facility is to detain. Loss of freedom of choice and privacy are inherent incidents of confinement in such a facility. And the fact that such detention interferes with the detainee's understandable desire to live as comfortably as possible and with as little restraint as possible during confinement does not convert the conditions or restrictions of detention into "punishment."

This Court has recognized a distinction between punitive measures that may not constitutionally be imposed prior to a determination of guilt and regulatory restraints that may. . . . In *Kennedy v. Mendoza-Martinez, supra,* the Court examined the automatic forfeiture-of-citizenship provisions of the immigration laws to determine whether that sanction amounted to punishment or a mere regulatory restraint. While it is all but impossible to compress the distinction into a sentence or a paragraph, the Court there described the tests traditionally applied to determine whether a governmental act is punitive in nature:

> Whether the sanction involves an affirmative disability or restraint, whether it has historically been regarded as a punishment, whether it comes into play only on a finding of *scienter,* whether its operation will promote the traditional aims of punishment—retribution and deterrence, whether the behavior to which it applies is already a crime, whether an alternative purpose to which it may rationally be connected is assignable for it, and whether it appears excessive in relation to the alternative purpose assigned are all relevant to the inquiry, and may often point in differing directions. 372 U.S., at 168-169, 83 S. Ct., at 567-568 (footnotes omitted). . . .

The factors identified in *Mendoza-Martinez* provide useful guideposts in determining whether particular restrictions and conditions accompanying pretrial detention amount to punishment in the constitutional sense of that word. A court must decide whether the disability is imposed for the purpose of punishment or whether it is but an incident of some other legitimate governmental purpose. See *Flemming v. Nestor, supra,* 363 U.S., at 613-617, 80 S. Ct., at 1374-1376. Absent a showing of an expressed intent to punish on the part of detention facility officials, that determination generally will turn on "whether an alternative purpose to which [the restriction] may rationally be connected is assignable for it, and whether it appears excessive in relation to the alternative purpose assigned [to it]." *Kennedy v. Mendoza-Martinez,* 372 U.S., at 168-169, 83 S. Ct., at 567-568; see *Flemming v. Nestor, supra,* 363 U.S., at 617, 80 S. Ct., at 1376. Thus, if a particular condition or restriction of pretrial detention is reasonably related to a legitimate governmental objective, it does not, without more, amount to "punishment." Conversely, if a restriction or condition is not reasonably related to a legitimate goal—if it is arbitrary or purposeless—a court permissibly may infer that the purpose of the governmental action is punishment that may not constitutionally be inflicted upon detainees *qua* detainees. See *ibid.* Courts must be mindful that these inquiries spring from constitutional requirements and that judicial answers to them must reflect that fact rather than a court's idea of how best to operate a detention facility. . . .

C

Judged by this analysis, respondents' claim that "double-bunking" violated their due process rights fails. . . . On this record, we are convinced as a matter of law that "double-bunking" as practiced at the MCC did not amount to punishment and did not, therefore, violate respondents' rights under the Due Process Clause of the Fifth Amendment.

Each of the rooms at the MCC that house pretrial detainees has a total floor space of approximately 75 square feet. Each of them designated for "double-bunking," . . . contains a double bunkbed, certain other items of furniture, a wash basin, and an uncovered toilet. Inmates generally are locked into their rooms from 11 p.m. to 6:30 a.m. and for brief periods during the afternoon and evening head counts. During the rest of the day, they may move about freely between their rooms and the common areas. . . .

Detainees are required to spend only seven or eight hours each day in their rooms, during most or all of which they presumably are sleeping. The rooms provide more than adequate space for sleeping. During the remainder of the time, the detainees are free to move between their rooms and the common area. While "double-bunking" may have taxed some of the equipment or particular facilities in certain of the common areas, *United States ex rel. Wolfish v. United States,* 428 F. Supp., at 337, this does not mean that the conditions at the MCC failed to meet the standards required by the Constitution. Our conclusion in this regard is further buttressed by the detainees' length of stay at the MCC. See *Hutto v. Finney,* 437 U.S. 678, 686-687, 98 S. Ct. 2565, 2571-2572, 57 L. Ed. 2d 522 (1978). Nearly all of the detainees are released within 60 days. . . . We simply do not believe that requiring a detainee to share toilet facilities and this admittedly rather small sleeping place with another person for generally a maximum period of 60 days violates the Constitution.

III

Respondents also challenged certain MCC restrictions and practices that were designed to promote security and order at the facility on the ground that these restrictions violated the Due Process Clause of the Fifth Amendment. . . .

Our cases have established several general principles that inform our evaluation of the constitutionality of the restrictions at issue. First, we have held that convicted prisoners do not forfeit all constitutional protections by reason of their conviction and confinement in prison. . . . "There is no iron curtain drawn between the Constitution and the prisons of this country." *Wolff v. McDonnell, supra,* 418 U.S., at 555-556, 94 S. Ct., at 2974-2975. . . .

But our cases also have insisted on a second proposition: simply because prison inmates retain certain constitutional rights does not mean that these rights are not subject to restrictions and limitations. "Lawful incarceration brings about the necessary withdrawal or limitation of many privileges and rights, a retraction justified by the considerations underlying our penal system." *Price v. Johnston,* 334 U.S. 266, 285, 68 S. Ct. 1049, 1060, 92 L. Ed. 1356 (1948). . . . The fact of confinement as well as the legitimate goals and policies of the penal institution limits these retained constitutional rights. *Jones v. North Carolina Prisoners' Labor Union, supra,* 433 U.S., at 125, 97 S. Ct., at 2538; *Pell v. Procunier, supra,* 417 U.S., at 822, 94 S. Ct., at 2804. There must be a "mutual accommodation between institutional needs and objectives and the provisions of the Constitution that are of general application." *Wolff v. McDonnell, supra,* 418 U.S., at 556, 94 S. Ct., at 2975. This principle applies equally to pretrial detainees and convicted prisoners. A detainee simply does not possess the full range of freedoms of an unincarcerated individual.

Third, maintaining institutional security and preserving internal order and discipline are essential goals that may require limitation or retraction of the retained constitutional rights of both convicted prisoners and pretrial detainees. "[C]entral to all other corrections goals is the institutional consideration of internal security within the corrections facilities themselves." *Pell v. Procunier, supra,* 417 U.S., at 823, 94 S. Ct., at 2804; see *Jones v. North Carolina Prisoners' Labor Union, supra,* 433 U.S., at 129, 97 S. Ct., at 2540; *Procunier v. Martinez,* 416 U.S. 396, 412, 94 S. Ct. 1800, 1810, 40 L. Ed. 2d 224 (1974). Prison officials must be free to take appropriate action to ensure the safety of inmates and corrections personnel and to prevent escape or unauthorized entry. Accordingly, we have held that even when an institutional restriction infringes a specific constitutional guarantee, such as the First Amendment, the practice must be evaluated in the light of the central objective of prison administration, safeguarding institutional security. . . .

Finally, as the Court of Appeals correctly acknowledged, the problems that arise in the day-to-day operation of a corrections facility are not susceptible of easy solutions. Prison administrators therefore should be accorded wide-ranging deference in the adoption and execution of policies and practices that in their judgment are needed to preserve internal order and discipline and to maintain institutional security. *Jones v. North Carolina Prisoners' Labor Union, supra,* 433 U.S., at 128, 97 S. Ct., at 2539; *Procunier v. Martinez, supra,* 416 U.S., at 404-405, 94 S. Ct., at 1807-1808; *Cruz v. Beto, supra,* 405 U.S., at 321, 92 S. Ct., at 1081; see *Meachum v. Fano,* 427 U.S., at 228-229, 96 S. Ct., at 2540-2541. "Such considerations are peculiarly within the province and professional expertise of corrections officials, and, in the absence of substantial evidence in the record to indicate that the officials have exaggerated their response to these considerations, courts should ordinarily defer to their expert judgment in such matters." *Pell v. Procunier,* 417 U.S., at 827, 94 S. Ct., at 2806. . . .

A

At the time of the lower courts' decisions, the Bureau of Prisons' "publisher-only" rule, which applies to all Bureau facilities, permitted inmates to receive books and magazines from outside the institution only if the materials were mailed directly from the publisher or a book club. 573 F.2d, at 129-130. The warden of the MCC stated in an affidavit that "serious" security and administrative problems were caused when bound items were received by inmates from unidentified sources outside the facility. App. 24. He noted that in order to make a "proper and thorough" inspection of such items, prison officials would have to remove the covers of hardback books and to leaf through every page of all books and magazines to ensure that drugs, money, weapons, or other contraband were not secreted in the material. "This search process would take a substantial and inordinate amount of available staff time." *Ibid.* However, "there is relatively little risk that material received directly from a publisher or book club would contain contraband, and therefore, the security problems are significantly reduced without a drastic drain on staff resources." *Ibid.* . . .

It is desirable at this point to place in focus the precise question that now is before this Court. Subsequent to the decision of the Court of Appeals, the Bureau of Prisons amended its "publisher-only" rule to permit the receipt of books and magazines from bookstores as well as publishers and book clubs. 43 Fed. Reg. 30576 (1978) (to be codified in 28 CFR § 540.71). In addition, petitioners have informed the Court that the Bureau proposes to amend the rule further to allow receipt of paperback books, magazines, and other soft-covered materials from any source. Brief for Petitioners 66 n.49, 69, and n.51. The Bureau regards hardback books as the "more dangerous source of risk to institutional security," however, and intends to retain the prohibition against receipt of hardback books unless they are mailed directly from publishers, book clubs, or bookstores. *Id.* at 69 n.51. Accordingly, petitioners request this Court to review the District Court's injunction only to the extent it enjoins petitioners from prohibiting receipt of hard-cover books that are not mailed directly from publishers, book clubs, or bookstores. *Id.*, at 69; Tr. of Oral Arg. 59-60. . . .

B

Inmates at the MCC were not permitted to receive packages from outside the facility containing items of food or personal property, except for one package of food at Christmas. This rule was justified by MCC officials on three grounds. First, officials testified to "serious" security problems that arise from the introduction of such packages into the institution, the "traditional file in the cake kind of situation" as well as the concealment of drugs "in heels of shoes [and] seams of clothing." App. 80; see *id.*, at 24, 84-85. As in the case of the "publisher-only" rule, the warden testified that if such packages were allowed, the inspection process necessary to ensure the security of the institution would require a "substantial and inordinate amount of available staff time." *Id.*, at 24. Second, officials were concerned that the introduction of personal property into the facility would increase the risk of thefts, gambling, and inmate conflicts, the "age-old problem of you have it and I don't." *Id.*, at 80; see *id.*, at 85. Finally, they noted storage and sanitary problems that would result from inmates' receipt of food packages. *Id.*, at 67, 80. Inmates are permitted, however, to purchase certain items of food and personal property from the MCC commissary. . . .

C

The MCC staff conducts unannounced searches of inmate living areas at irregular intervals. These searches generally are formal unit "shakedowns" during which all inmates are cleared of the residential units, and a team of guards searches each room. Prior to the District Court's order, inmates were not permitted to watch the searches. Officials testified that permitting inmates to observe room inspections would lead to friction between the inmates and security guards and would allow the inmates to attempt to frustrate the search by distracting personnel and moving contraband from one room to another ahead of the search team. . . .

D

Inmates at all Bureau of Prison facilities, including the MCC, are required to expose their body cavities for visual inspection as a part of a strip search conducted after every contact visit with a person from outside the institution. Corrections officials testified that visual cavity searches were necessary not only to discover but also to deter the smuggling of weapons, drugs, and other contraband into the institution. App. 70-72, 83-84. . . .

IV

Nor do we think that the four MCC security restrictions and practices described in Part III, *supra*, constitute "punishment" in violation of the rights of pretrial detainees under the Due Process Clause of the Fifth Amendment. Neither the District Court nor the Court of Appeals suggested that these restrictions and practices were employed by MCC officials with an intent to punish the pretrial detainees housed there. Respondents do not even make such a suggestion; they simply argue that the restrictions were greater than necessary to satisfy petitioners' legitimate interest in maintaining security. Brief for Respondents 51-53. Therefore, the determination whether these restrictions and practices constitute punishment in the constitutional sense depends on whether they are rationally related to a legitimate nonpunitive governmental purpose and whether they appear excessive in relation to that purpose. See *supra*, at 1873-1874. Ensuring security and order at the institution is a permissible nonpunitive objective, whether the facility houses pretrial detainees, convicted inmates, or both. *Supra*, at 1874; see *id.*, at 1878, and n.28. For the reasons set forth in Part III, *supra*, we think that these particular restrictions and practices were reasonable responses by MCC officials to legitimate security concerns. Respondents simply have not met their heavy burden of showing that these officials have exaggerated their response to the genuine security considerations that actuated these restrictions and practices. . . . And as might be expected of restrictions applicable to pretrial detainees, these restrictions were of only limited duration so far as the MCC pretrial detainees were concerned. . . .

The judgment of the Court of Appeals is, accordingly, reversed, and the case is remanded for proceedings consistent with this opinion.

It is so ordered.

UNITED STATES v. SALERNO, 481 U.S. 739 (1987)

The Bail Reform Act of 1984 (Act) allows a federal court to detain an arrestee pending trial if the Government demonstrates by clear and convincing evidence after an adversary hearing that no release conditions "will reasonably assure . . . the safety of any other person and the community." The United States Court of Appeals for the Second Circuit struck down this provision of the Act as facially unconstitutional, because, in that court's words, this type of pretrial detention violates "substantive due process." We granted certiorari because of a conflict among the Courts of Appeals regarding the validity of the Act. 479 U.S. 929, 107 S. Ct. 397, 93 L. Ed. 2d 351 (1986). We hold that, as against the facial attack mounted by these respondents, the Act fully comports with constitutional requirements. We therefore reverse.

I

Responding to "the alarming problem of crimes committed by persons on release," S. Rep. No. 98-225, p. 3 (1983), U.S. Code Cong. & Admin. News 1984, pp. 3182, 3185 Congress formulated the Bail Reform Act of 1984, 18 U.S.C. § 3141 *et seq.* (1982 ed., Supp. III), as the solution to a bail crisis in the federal courts. The Act represents the National Legislature's considered response to numerous perceived deficiencies in the federal bail process. By providing for sweeping changes in both the way federal courts consider bail applications and the circumstances under which bail is granted, Congress hoped to "give the courts adequate authority to make release decisions that give appropriate recognition to the danger a person may pose to others if released." S. Rep. No. 98-225, at 3, U.S. Code Cong. & Admin. News 1984, p. 3185.

To this end, § 3141(a) of the Act requires a judicial officer to determine whether an arrestee shall be detained. Section 3142(e) provides that "[i]f, after a hearing pursuant to the provisions of subsection (f), the judicial officer finds that no condition or combination of conditions will reasonably assure the appearance of the person as required and the safety of any other person and the community, he shall order the detention of the person prior to trial." Section 3142(f) provides the arrestee with a number of procedural safeguards. He may request the presence of counsel at the detention hearing, he may testify and present witnesses in his behalf, as well as proffer evidence, and he may cross-examine other witnesses appearing at the hearing. If the judicial officer finds that no conditions of pretrial release can reasonably assure the safety of other persons and the community, he must state his findings of fact in writing, § 3142(i), and support his conclusion with "clear and convincing evidence," § 3142(f).

The judicial officer is not given unbridled discretion in making the detention determination. Congress has specified the considerations relevant to that decision. These factors include the nature and seriousness of the charges, the substantiality of the Government's evidence against the arrestee, the arrestee's background and characteristics, and the nature and seriousness of the danger posed by the suspect's release. § 3142(g). Should a judicial officer order detention, the detainee is entitled to expedited appellate review of the detention order. §§ 3145(b), (c).

Respondents Anthony Salerno and Vincent Cafaro were arrested on March 21, 1986, after being charged in a 29-count indictment alleging various Racketeer Influenced and Corrupt Organizations Act (RICO) violations, mail and wire fraud offenses, extortion, and various criminal gambling violations. The RICO counts alleged 35 acts of racketeering activity, including fraud, extortion, gambling, and conspiracy to commit murder. At respondents' arraignment, the Government moved to have Salerno and Cafaro detained pursuant to § 3142(e), on the ground that no condition of release would assure the safety of the community or any person. The District Court held a hearing at which the Government made a detailed proffer of evidence. The Government's case showed that Salerno was the "boss" of the Genovese crime family of La Cosa Nostra and that Cafaro was a "captain" in the Genovese family. According to the Government's proffer, based in large part on conversations intercepted by a court-ordered wiretap, the two respondents had participated in wide-ranging conspiracies to aid their illegitimate enterprises through violent means. The Government also offered the testimony of two of its trial witnesses, who would assert that Salerno personally participated in two murder conspiracies. Salerno opposed the motion for detention, challenging the credibility of the Government's witnesses. He offered the testimony of several character witnesses as well as a letter from his doctor stating that he was suffering from a serious medical condition. Cafaro presented no evidence at the hearing, but instead characterized the wiretap conversations as merely "tough talk."

The District Court granted the Government's detention motion, concluding that the Government had established by clear and convincing evidence that no condition or combination of conditions of release would ensure the safety of the community or any person. . . .

Respondents appealed, contending that to the extent that the Bail Reform Act permits pretrial detention on the ground that the arrestee is likely to commit future crimes, it is unconstitutional on its face. . . .

II

A facial challenge to a legislative Act is, of course, the most difficult challenge to mount successfully, since the challenger must establish that no set of circumstances exists under which the Act would be valid. The fact that the Bail Reform Act might operate unconstitutionally under some conceivable set of circumstances is insufficient to render it wholly invalid, since we have not recognized an "overbreadth" doctrine outside the limited context of the First Amendment. *Schall v. Martin, supra,* at 269, n.18, 104 S. Ct., at 2412, n.18. We think respondents have failed to shoulder their heavy burden to demonstrate that the Act is "facially" unconstitutional. . . .

A

The Due Process Clause of the Fifth Amendment provides that "No person shall . . . be deprived of life, liberty, or property, without due process of law. . . ." This Court has held that the Due Process Clause protects individuals against two types of government action. So-called "substantive due process" prevents the government from engaging in conduct that "shocks the conscience," *Rochin v. California,* 342 U.S. 165, 172, 72 S. Ct. 205, 209, 96 L. Ed. 183 (1952), or interferes with rights "implicit in the concept of ordered liberty," *Palko v. Connecticut,* 302 U.S. 319, 325-326, 58 S. Ct. 149, 152, 82 L. Ed. 288 (1937). When government action depriving a person of life, liberty, or property survives substantive due process scrutiny, it must still be implemented in a fair manner. *Mathews v. Eldridge,* 424 U.S. 319, 335, 96 S. Ct. 893, 903, 47 L. Ed. 2d 18 (1976). This requirement has traditionally been referred to as "procedural" due process.

Respondents first argue that the Act violates substantive due process because the pretrial detention it authorizes constitutes impermissible punishment before trial. See *Bell v. Wolfish,* 441 U.S. 520, 535, and n.16, 99 S. Ct. 1861, 1872, and n.16, 60 L. Ed. 2d 447 (1979). The Government, however, has never argued that pretrial detention could be upheld if it were "punishment." . . .

We conclude that the detention imposed by the Act falls on the regulatory side of the dichotomy. The legislative history of the Bail Reform Act clearly indicates that Congress did not formulate the pretrial detention provisions as punishment for dangerous individuals. See S. Rep. No. 98-225, at 8. Congress instead perceived pretrial detention as a potential solution to a pressing societal problem. *Id.,* at 4-7. There is no doubt that preventing danger to the community is a legitimate regulatory goal. *Schall v. Martin, supra.*

Nor are the incidents of pretrial detention excessive in relation to the regulatory goal Congress sought to achieve. The Bail Reform Act carefully limits the circumstances under which detention may be sought to the most serious of crimes. See 18 U.S.C. § 3142(f) (detention hearings available if case involves crimes of violence, offenses for which the sentence is life imprisonment or death, serious drug offenses, or certain repeat offenders). The arrestee is entitled to a prompt detention hearing, *ibid.,* and the maximum length of pretrial detention is limited by the stringent time limitations of the Speedy Trial Act. See 18 U.S.C. § 3161 *et seq.* (1982 ed. and Supp. III). Moreover, as in *Schall v. Martin,* the conditions of confinement envisioned by the Act "appear to reflect the regulatory purposes relied upon by the" Government. 467 U.S., at 270, 104 S. Ct., at 2413. As in *Schall,* the statute at issue here requires that detainees be housed in a "facility separate, to the extent practicable, from persons awaiting or serving sentences or being held in custody pending appeal." 18 U.S.C. § 3142(i)(2). We conclude, therefore, that the pretrial detention contemplated by the Bail Reform Act is regulatory in nature, and does not constitute punishment before trial in violation of the Due Process Clause. . . .

The government's interest in preventing crime by arrestees is both legitimate and compelling. *De Veau v. Braisted,* 363 U.S. 144, 155, 80 S. Ct. 1146, 1152, 4 L. Ed. 2d 1109 (1960). In *Schall, supra,* we recognized the strength of the State's interest in preventing juvenile crime. This general concern with crime prevention is no less compelling when the suspects are adults. Indeed, "[t]he harm suffered by the victim of a crime is not dependent upon the age of the perpetrator." *Schall v. Martin, supra,* 467 U.S., at 264-265, 104 S. Ct., at 2410. The Bail Reform Act of 1984 responds to an even more particularized governmental interest than the interest we sustained in *Schall.* The statute we upheld in *Schall* permitted pretrial detention of any juvenile arrested on any charge after a showing that the individual might commit some undefined further crimes. The Bail Reform Act, in contrast, narrowly focuses on a particularly acute problem in which the Government interests are overwhelming. The Act operates only on individuals who have been arrested for a specific category of extremely serious offenses. 18 U.S.C. § 3142(f). Congress specifically found that these individuals are far more likely to be responsible for dangerous acts in the community after arrest. See S. Rep. No. 98-225, at 6-7. Nor is the Act by any means a scattershot attempt to incapacitate those who are merely suspected of these serious crimes. The Government must first of all demonstrate probable cause to believe that the charged crime has been committed by the arrestee, but that is not enough. In a full-blown adversary hearing, the Government must convince a neutral decisionmaker by clear and convincing evidence that no conditions of release can reasonably assure the safety of the community or any person. 18 U.S.C. § 3142(f). While the Government's general interest in preventing crime is compelling, even this interest is heightened when the Government musters convincing proof that the arrestee, already indicted or held to answer for a serious crime, presents a demonstrable danger to the community. Under these narrow circumstances, society's interest in crime prevention is at its greatest.

On the other side of the scale, of course, is the individual's strong interest in liberty. We do not minimize the importance and fundamental nature of this right. But, as our cases hold, this right may, in circumstances where the government's interest is sufficiently weighty, be subordinated to the greater needs of society. We think that Congress' careful delineation of the circumstances under which detention will be permitted satisfies this standard. When the Government proves by clear and convincing evidence that an arrestee presents an identified and articulable threat to an individual or the community, we believe that, consistent with the Due Process Clause, a court may disable the arrestee from executing that threat. Under these circumstances, we cannot categorically state that pretrial detention "offends some principle of justice so rooted in the traditions and conscience of our people as to be ranked as fundamental." *Snyder v. Massachusetts,* 291 U.S. 97, 105, 54 S. Ct. 330, 332, 78 L. Ed. 674 (1934).

Finally, we may dispose briefly of respondents' facial challenge to the procedures of the Bail Reform Act. To sustain them against such a challenge, we need only find them "adequate to authorize the pretrial detention of at least some [persons] charged with crimes," *Schall, supra,* 467 U.S., at 264, 104 S. Ct., at 2409, whether or not they might be insufficient in some particular circumstances. We think they pass that test. As we stated in *Schall,* "there is nothing inherently unattainable about a prediction of future criminal conduct." 467 U.S., at 278, 104 S. Ct., at 2417. . . .

Under the Bail Reform Act, the procedures by which a judicial officer evaluates the likelihood of future dangerousness are specifically designed to further the accuracy of that determination. Detainees have a right to counsel at the detention hearing. 18 U.S.C. § 3142(f). They may testify in their own behalf, present information by proffer or otherwise, and cross-examine witnesses who appear at the hearing. *Ibid.* The judicial officer charged with the responsibility of determining the appropriateness of detention is guided by statutorily enumerated factors, which include the nature and the circumstances of the charges, the weight of the evidence, the history and characteristics of the putative offender, and the danger to the community. § 3142(g). The Government must prove its case by clear and convincing evidence. § 3142(f). Finally, the judicial officer must include written findings of fact and a written statement of reasons for a decision to detain. § 3142(i). The Act's review provisions, § 3145(c), provide for immediate appellate review of the detention decision.

We think these extensive safeguards suffice to repel a facial challenge. The protections are more exacting than those we found sufficient in the juvenile context, see *Schall, supra,* 467 U.S., at 275-281, 104 S. Ct., at 2415-2418, and they far exceed what we found necessary to effect limited postarrest detention in *Gerstein v. Pugh,* 420 U.S. 103, 95 S. Ct. 854, 43 L. Ed. 2d 54 (1975). Given the legitimate and compelling regulatory purpose of the Act and the procedural protections it offers, we conclude that the Act is not facially invalid under the Due Process Clause of the Fifth Amendment. . . .

The judgment of the Court of Appeals is therefore *Reversed.*

DECK v. MISSOURI, 544 U.S. 622 (2005)

We here consider whether shackling a convicted offender during the penalty phase of a capital case violates the Federal Constitution. We hold that the Constitution forbids the use of visible shackles during the penalty phase, as it forbids their use during the guilt phase, *unless* that use is "justified by an essential state interest"—such as the interest in courtroom security—specific to the defendant on trial. . . .

I

In July 1996, petitioner Carman Deck robbed, shot, and killed an elderly couple. In 1998, the State of Missouri tried Deck for the murders and the robbery. At trial, state authorities required Deck to wear leg braces that apparently were not visible to the jury. App. 5; Tr. of Oral Arg. 21, 25, 29. Deck was convicted and sentenced to death. The State Supreme Court upheld Deck's conviction but set aside the sentence. 68 S.W.3d 418, 432 (2002) (en banc). The State then held a new sentencing proceeding.

From the first day of the new proceeding, Deck was shackled with leg irons, handcuffs, and a belly chain. App. 58. Before the jury *voir dire* began, Deck's counsel objected to the shackles. The objection was overruled. *Ibid.*; see also *id.*, at 41-55. During the *voir dire*, Deck's counsel renewed the objection. The objection was again overruled, the court stating that Deck "has been convicted and will remain in leg irons and a belly chain." *Id.*, at 58. After the *voir dire*, Deck's counsel once again objected, moving to strike the jury panel "because of the fact that Mr. Deck is shackled in front of the jury and makes them think that he is . . . violent today." *Id.*, at 58-59. The objection was again overruled, the court stating that his "being shackled takes any fear out of their minds." *Id.*, at 59. The penalty phase then proceeded with Deck in shackles. Deck was again sentenced to death. 136 S.W.3d 481, 485 (Mo. 2004) (en banc). . . .

We granted certiorari to review Deck's claim that his shackling violated the Federal Constitution.

II

We first consider whether, as a general matter, the Constitution permits a State to use visible shackles routinely in the guilt phase of a criminal trial. The answer is clear: The law has long forbidden routine use of visible shackles during the guilt phase; it permits a State to shackle a criminal defendant only in the presence of a special need. . . .

More recently, this Court has suggested that a version of this rule forms part of the Fifth and Fourteenth Amendments' due process guarantee. Thirty-five years ago, when considering the trial of an unusually obstreperous criminal defendant, the Court held that the Constitution sometimes permitted special measures, including physical restraints. *Allen*, 397 U.S., at 343-344, 90 S. Ct. 1057. The Court wrote that "binding and gagging might possibly be the fairest and most reasonable way to handle" such a defendant. *Id.*, at 344, 90 S. Ct. 1057. But the Court immediately added that "even to contemplate such a technique . . . arouses a feeling that no person should be tried while shackled and gagged except as a last resort." *Ibid.*

Sixteen years later, the Court considered a special courtroom security arrangement that involved having uniformed security personnel sit in the first row of the courtroom's spectator section. The Court held that the Constitution allowed the arrangement, stating that the deployment of security personnel during trial is not "the sort of inherently prejudicial practice that, like shackling, should be permitted only where justified by an essential state interest specific to each trial." *Holbrook*, 475 U.S., at 568-569, 106 S. Ct. 1340. . . .

Lower courts have treated these statements as setting forth a constitutional standard that embodies Blackstone's rule. Courts and commentators share close to a consensus that, during the guilt phase of a trial, a criminal defendant has a right to remain free of physical restraints that are visible to the jury; that the right has a constitutional dimension; but that the right may be overcome in a particular instance by essential state interests such as physical security, escape prevention, or courtroom decorum. . . .

Lower courts have disagreed about the specific procedural steps a trial court must take prior to shackling, about the amount and type of evidence needed to justify restraints, and about what forms of prejudice might warrant a new trial, but they have not questioned the basic principle. They have emphasized the importance of preserving trial court discretion (reversing only in cases of clear abuse), but they have applied the limits on that discretion described in *Holbrook, Allen*, and the early English cases. In light of this precedent, and of a lower court consensus disapproving routine shackling dating back to the 19th century, it is clear that this Court's prior statements gave voice to a principle deeply embedded in the law. We now conclude that those statements identify a basic element of the "due process of law" protected by the Federal Constitution. Thus, the Fifth and Fourteenth Amendments prohibit the use of physical restraints visible to the jury absent a trial court determination, in the exercise of its discretion, that they are justified by a state interest specific to a particular trial. Such a determination may of course take into account the factors that courts have traditionally relied on in gauging potential security problems and the risk of escape at trial.

III

We here consider shackling not during the guilt phase of an ordinary criminal trial, but during the punishment phase of a capital case. And we must decide whether that change of circumstance makes a constitutional difference. To do so, we examine the reasons that motivate the guilt-phase constitutional rule and determine whether they apply with similar force in this context.

A

Judicial hostility to shackling may once primarily have reflected concern for the suffering—the "tortures" and "torments"—that "very painful" chains could cause. . . . More recently, this Court's opinions have not stressed the need to prevent physical suffering (for not all modern physical restraints are painful). Instead they have emphasized the importance of giving effect to three fundamental legal principles.

First, the criminal process presumes that the defendant is innocent until proved guilty. *Coffin v. United States*, 156 U.S. 432, 453, 15 S. Ct. 394, 39 L. Ed. 481 (1895) (presumption of innocence "lies at the foundation of the administration of our criminal law"). Visible shackling undermines the presumption of innocence and the related fairness of the factfinding process. Cf. *Estelle, supra*, at 503, 96 S. Ct. 1691. It suggests to the jury that the justice system itself sees a "need to separate a defendant from the community at large." *Holbrook, supra*, at 569, 106 S. Ct. 1340. . . .

Second, the Constitution, in order to help the accused secure a meaningful defense, provides him with a right to counsel. See, e.g., Amdt. 6; *Gideon v. Wainwright*, 372 U.S. 335, 340-341, 83 S. Ct. 792, 9 L. Ed. 2d 799 (1963). The use of physical restraints diminishes that right. Shackles can interfere with the accused's "ability to communicate" with his lawyer. *Allen*, 397 U.S., at 344, 90 S. Ct. 1057. Indeed, they can interfere with a defendant's ability to participate in his own defense, say, by freely choosing whether to take the witness stand on his own behalf. . . .

Third, judges must seek to maintain a judicial process that is a dignified process. The courtroom's formal dignity, which includes the respectful treatment of defendants, reflects the importance of the matter at issue, guilt or innocence, and the gravity with which Americans consider any deprivation of an individual's liberty through criminal punishment. And it reflects a seriousness of purpose that helps to explain the judicial system's power to inspire the confidence and to affect the behavior of a general public whose demands for justice our courts seek to serve. The routine use of shackles in the presence of juries would undermine these symbolic yet concrete objectives. As this Court has said, the use of shackles at trial "affront[s]" the "dignity and decorum of judicial proceedings that the judge is seeking to uphold." *Allen, supra*, at 344, 90 S. Ct. 1057. . . .

There will be cases, of course, where these perils of shackling are unavoidable. See *Allen, supra*, at 344, 90 S. Ct. 1057. We do not underestimate the need to restrain dangerous defendants to prevent courtroom attacks, or the need to give trial courts latitude in making individualized security determinations. We are mindful of the tragedy that can result if judges are not able to protect themselves and their courtrooms. But given their prejudicial effect, due process does not permit the use of visible restraints if the trial court has not taken account of the circumstances of the particular case.

B

The considerations that militate against the routine use of visible shackles during the guilt phase of a criminal trial apply with like force to penalty proceedings in capital cases. This is obviously so in respect to the latter two considerations mentioned, securing a meaningful defense and maintaining dignified proceedings. It is less obviously so in respect to the first consideration mentioned, for the defendant's conviction means that the presumption of innocence no longer applies. Hence shackles do not undermine the jury's effort to apply that presumption.

Nonetheless, shackles at the penalty phase threaten related concerns. Although the jury is no longer deciding between guilt and innocence, it is deciding between life and death. That decision, given the " 'severity' " and " 'finality' " of the sanction, is no less important than the decision about guilt. . . .

Neither is accuracy in making that decision any less critical. The Court has stressed the "acute need" for reliable decisionmaking when the death penalty is at issue. *Monge, supra*, at 732, 118 S. Ct. 2246 (citing *Lockett v. Ohio*, 438 U.S. 586, 604, 98 S. Ct. 2954, 57 L. Ed. 2d 973 (1978) (plurality opinion)). The appearance of the offender during the penalty phase in shackles, however, almost inevitably implies to a jury, as a matter of common sense, that court authorities consider the offender a danger to the community—often a statutory aggravator and nearly always a relevant factor in jury decisionmaking, even where the State does not specifically argue the point. Cf. Brief for Respondent 25-27. It also almost inevitably affects adversely the jury's perception of the character of the defendant. . . . And it thereby inevitably undermines the jury's ability to weigh accurately all relevant considerations—considerations that are often unquantifiable and elusive—when it determines whether a defendant deserves death. In these ways, the use of shackles can be a "thumb [on] death's side of the scale." *Sochor v. Florida*, 504 U.S. 527, 532, 112 S. Ct. 2114, 119 L. Ed. 2d 326 (1992) (internal quotation marks omitted). . . .

Given the presence of similarly weighty considerations, we must conclude that courts cannot routinely place defendants in shackles or other physical restraints visible to the jury during the penalty phase of a capital proceeding. The constitutional requirement, however, is not absolute. It permits a judge, in the exercise of his or her discretion, to take account of special circumstances, including security concerns, that may call for shackling. In so doing, it accommodates the important need to protect the courtroom and its occupants. But any such determination must be case specific; that is to say, it should reflect particular concerns, say, special security needs or escape risks, related to the defendant on trial. . . .

V

For these reasons, the judgment of the Missouri Supreme Court is reversed, and the case is remanded for further proceedings not inconsistent with this opinion.

It is so ordered.

CASE QUESTIONS

BELL v. WOLFISH

1. What is a writ of habeas corpus and why did the detainees use that in order to initiate legal proceedings?

2. What other constitutional amendments do you think might be implicated given the facts of this case and why?

3. What factors are to be considered when determining whether a government sanction constitutes "punishment" for purposes of due process?

4. What specific challenges to the conditions of confinement did the detainees make, and how did the Court respond to each challenge?

UNITED STATES v. SALERNO

1. What law was being challenged in *Salerno* and on what ground(s) was the challenge made?

2. According to the Court, what is the distinction between "substantive" and "procedural" due process?

3. What competing interests were being balanced in this case?

DECK v. MISSOURI

1. What purpose(s) does the general rule serve that an individual should not stand trial in shackles except for compelling circumstances?

2. What reason(s) did the Court give for prohibiting shackling during the penalty phase of a death penalty trial?

3. Do you agree with the proposition that normally an accused should not be required to stand trial in front of a jury while in shackles? Explain.

HYPOTHETICAL WITH ACCOMPANYING ANALYSIS

Hypothetical

Denny is a convicted murderer serving a mandatory life sentence at The Department of Corrections (DoC), one of the state's maximum security correctional facilities. Denny, however, was anything but the model prisoner. In the two years that he had been housed at DoC, he had been involved in numerous fights, he had thrown feces on a correctional officer, he had tried to escape from custody twice, and he became the leader of a prison gang. The last straw came when Denny instigated a prison riot, which resulted in serious injury to three correctional officers. Based on the culmination of Denny's behavior over those two years, the warden at DoC ordered that he be transferred to the state's Supermax Prison. Supermax is a facility designed specifically to house inmates from all over the state who are considered "problem" inmates due to their behavior or dangerousness to the general inmate population. The conditions at Supermax are far worse than any other prison facility in the state: inmates remain in their cells 23 hours of each day; they are permitted no contact with visitors; they lose any opportunity for parole; and, they are assigned to Supermax for an indefinite time period.

Denny was informed the morning after the riot that he would be transferred to Supermax effective immediately. He was moved to the facility within 12 hours of receiving notice of his transfer. Denny admits that the applicable state law permitting the transfer of inmates to Supermax under appropriate circumstances is constitutional. However, he argues that his case does not warrant such a transfer and that he was not given the opportunity to refute the transfer. Denny is therefore challenging his transfer to Supermax on the grounds that his due process rights were violated. Discuss the likelihood that Denny will succeed.

Analysis

Due process ensures that the laws are fair and that they are implemented in a fair manner. The protections of due process can be found in both the Fifth Amendment, which applies to the federal government, and the Fourteenth Amendment, which applies to state governments. Because Denny is challenging a state policy regarding his transfer to Supermax, the Fourteenth Amendment applies. It provides that no state shall "deprive any person of life, liberty, or property, without due process of law."

Two types of due process exist: substantive due process and procedural due process. Substantive due process is conduct that either "shocks the conscience" or interferes with rights "implicit in the concept of ordered liberty." United States v. Salerno, 481 U.S. 739 (1987). Substantive due process claims address whether the laws themselves are fair. Denny is not claiming that the state law permitting the transfer of inmates to Supermax is invalid; therefore, he is not challenging his transfer based on substantive due process. Procedural due process requires that any governmental actions which seek to deprive a person of life, liberty, or property be implemented in a fair manner. *Id.* In the instant case, Denny is challenging is the manner in which his transfer to Supermax occurred. Therefore, he is arguing that his procedural due process rights have been violated.

Inmates typically have no liberty interest in transfers from one prison facility to another because they are in the custody of the department of corrections generally and not any one particular prison facility. Thus, transfers can occur for a wide range of reasons and the inmates have no right to challenge the transfer. Meachum v. Fano, 427 U.S. 215 (1976). However, in Wilkinson v. Austin, 545 U.S. 209 (2005), the Supreme Court held that inmates have a liberty interest in avoiding placement at a Supermax facility because of the admittedly harsh conditions at those facilities. The Ohio Supermax facility involved in *Wilkinson* prohibited almost all human contact, cells had lights on 24 hours each day, and exercise was permitted an hour a day in a small room. Ohio had extensive procedures in place before a transfer to the Supermax prison would be accomplished. Such procedures included a hearing, an opportunity for the inmate to be heard, and numerous levels of review both before and after placement at Supermax. Based on those procedures the Court found no violation of due process. In comparison to *Wilkinson*, Denny was provided with no such procedural protections. He was informed of his transfer by the warden and was moved within 12 hours, he had no opportunity to challenge his transfer, and there was no independent review of whether the transfer was justified. None of the traditional protections afforded in procedural due process, such as adequate notice of the sanction, the opportunity to be heard and present a defense, the opportunity to confront adverse witnesses, potentially even the assistance of counsel, were made available to Denny prior to his transfer. Because the state failed to recognize Denny's liberty interest in avoiding placement at Supermax, he will have a strong argument that his due process rights were violated.

In response to the overwhelming rate of infidelity among the nation's married couples as well as the skyrocketing divorce rate, the State has enacted the following law:

§ 102 Prohibition of Marriage: Adulterers

> **(a) Any individual whose marriage results in a divorce for the reason that the individual has committed adultery shall be indefinitely prohibited from entering into another marriage.**
>> **(1) The non-adulterous partner in marriage is not prohibited from remarrying;**
>> **(2) In the event that both partners in the marriage committed adultery, then neither party may remarry.**
>
> **(b) An individual who violates this provision shall be guilty of a misdemeanor and shall be subject to incarceration not to exceed six months, a fine not to exceed $10,000, or both.**

When researching the history of the statute, the legislature of the State disclosed that the dual purposes of the statute were to encourage monogamy in marriages and to punish the marital partner who committed adultery.

David recently filed for divorce from his wife Susan. A short time later he was granted the divorce on the grounds that Susan had committed adultery. Susan now wishes to marry Andrew, the man with whom she was having an affair, but she is unable to do so because of § 102. Susan does not contest the fact that she committed adultery, but she argues that the statute violates her due process rights. Discuss whether Susan will succeed in her arguments. Be sure to discuss the relevant constitutional provision(s) as well as any Supreme Court decisions that may be applicable.

DISCUSSION QUESTIONS

1. Research challenge: The 1950s and 1960s are often referred to as the "Due Process Revolution" in our nation. Why did these two decades earn this nickname?

2. On the evening of October 9, 2003, a string of burglaries all occurred in the same neighborhood. On December 19, 2007, the state indicted Doug on the burglary charges. Doug filed a motion to dismiss the indictment, arguing that the state had allowed too much time to elapse between the commission of the crime and the indictment, thereby violating his due process rights. Will Doug's argument succeed? *See* United States v. Marion, 404 U.S. 307 (1971) and United States v. Lovasco, 431 U.S. 783 (1977). What if Doug had argued that in addition to his due process rights, his speedy trial rights of the Sixth Amendment were also violated; would that argument succeed? Why or why not? *See* Chapter 8, *infra.*

3. Abraham was recently convicted of felony murder for his participation in a bank robbery with two other individuals where a security officer was shot and killed. After he was sentenced to death, Abraham learned the prosecutor had failed to disclose that another conspirator had previously confessed to the killing. Abraham is now appealing and claiming that his due process rights were violated by the prosecutor withholding this potentially exculpatory information. Will Abraham's argument prevail? Would it matter to you if the prosecutor had intentionally or accidentally withheld the information from Abraham? *See* Brady v. Maryland, 373 U.S. 83 (1963) and Arizona v. Youngblood, 488 U.S. 51 (1988).

4. One night while at a local bar, Jason got into a scuffle with the bartender. He was convicted of misdemeanor assault and sentenced to two months incarceration. Following his conviction, Jason appealed *de novo*. The prosecutor, frustrated that she would have to go through another trial, charged Jason with felony assault based on the same altercation with the bartender. Jason has moved to dismiss the felony charges on due process grounds, arguing that the prosecutor was angry at the fact that Jason appealed. Will Jason prevail? *Compare* Blackledge v. Perry, 417 U.S. 21 (1974) *with* United States v. Goodwin, 457 U.S. 368 (1982).

5. In a small town a young girl was kidnapped, sexually assaulted, and brutally murdered. Early the following morning, James was arrested for the crimes. During the course of the next three days, the local media broadcast a taped confession given by James at the police station. The confession aired at least nine times on television during those three days and it was printed in the town's newspaper. James was later indicted on all offenses. He immediately moved for a change of venue to a location where the community had not received such extensive pretrial publicity of the crimes, but his motion was denied. James was convicted of all charges. On appeal he argued that his due process rights were violated when the court refused to grant his request for a change of venue. Will James' argument prevail? *See* Rideau v. Louisiana, 373 U.S. 723 (1963). On what other constitutional grounds could Jason potentially appeal? Explain.

6. Felix was charged with first-degree rape. During plea negotiations, his counsel advised him to plead guilty to second-degree rape for a lesser sentence. However, at no time did Felix's defense attorney explain to him the elements of either offense. When entering his plea before the court, the judge made no inquiry as to whether Felix understood the nature of his plea. Felix was convicted and sentenced to 20 years' imprisonment. He later claimed that his plea was entered in violation of his due process rights. Will Felix's argument succeed? *See, e.g.*, Henderson v. Morgan, 426 U.S. 637 (1976).

7. Revisit above questions 2 through 6. What generalizations can you make about due process and its application to the criminal justice process?

8. Research challenge: Watch the 1995 movie *Murder in the First*, which is very loosely based on the story of Alcatraz inmate Henri Young. If you were Young's defense attorney, what argument(s) would you make that his due process rights were violated? Do you think you would succeed in those arguments? Next, research the facts of the actual case. What discrepancies can you find between the real case and the movie?

9. Aside from the circumstances described in Bell v. Wolfish and the Hypothetical with Accompanying Analysis, *supra*, what other challenges have incarcerated individuals brought based on due process? Why were the majority of challenges brought as class action lawsuits?

10. What laws were challenged based on due process in Griswold v. Connecticut, 381 U.S. 479 (1965), Loving v. Virginia, 388 U.S. 1 (1967), Roe v. Wade, 410 U.S. 113 (1973), and Bowers v. Hardwick, 478 U.S. 186 (1986)? What did all of the laws have in common? Are each of these cases still good law?

11. Research challenge: Tommy Silverstein, originally incarcerated for armed robbery, was subsequently convicted of murdering a correctional officer at the United States Penitentiary located in Marion, Illinois in 1983. Following his conviction, what conditions of his confinement could give rise to potential due process violations?

True/False

1. All of the protections in the Bill of Rights have been incorporated against the states via the Fourteenth Amendment Due Process Clause.

2. Due process protections apply only to the trial portion of the criminal justice process.

3. Prisoners will never have a liberty interest in remaining at a certain correctional facility and not being transferred.

4. What is considered a violation of due process will depend heavily on the facts of each particular case.

5. Procedural due process protections may include adequate notice of a sanction and the opportunity to present a defense.

Multiple Choice

6. Due process potentially protects an individual from inappropriate actions by:

   A. The police
   B. The prosecutor
   C. The judge
   D. All of the above

7. Congress recently enacted a law making it a crime for any man who wrongfully failed to pay child support to father additional children until all child support obligations were fulfilled. This law would most likely be challenged on what grounds?

   A. Substantive due process
   B. Procedural due process
   C. Both substantive and procedural due process
   D. Neither substantive nor procedural due process

8. In question #7 above, which constitutional amendment would apply?

   A. The Fifth Amendment
   B. The Fourteenth Amendment
   C. The Fifth and Fourteenth Amendments
   D. Neither the Fifth nor the Fourteenth Amendments

9. The right to due process extends to:

   A. The right to counsel
   B. The right to be free from self-incrimination

    C. The right to be free from unreasonable search and seizures

    D. All of the above

10. According to Deck v. Missouri, which of the following is *not* a reason why courts should currently avoid shackling the defendant during his trial unless absolutely necessary?

    A. Shackles undermine the concept of "innocent until proven guilty."

    B. Shackles pose a significant danger of physical injury to the defendant.

    C. Shackles can interfere with the defendant's ability to communicate with his counsel.

    D. Shackles could undermine the perception of the trial process and the court as dignified.

7
Assistance of Counsel

"In all criminal prosecutions, the accused shall enjoy the right to ... have the Assistance of Counsel for his defence."

—The Sixth Amendment

INTRODUCTION

Counselor, attorney, lawyer, esquire, member of the bar. All different names, some of them fancier than others, for that person who the accused criminal clutches the bars of his cell at two o'clock in the morning and yells: "*I want my lawyer!*" The accused, gripped with fear, frantic about the uncharted road ahead of him and the potential consequences at the end of that road, is desperate for the comfort of knowing *someone* is on his side. Someone who will guide him through the intricate maze of the criminal justice system, who will ensure that his legal rights are protected along the way, and who will look out for his best interests. That "someone" is a lawyer—a key player in the criminal justice system and someone whom, if you ask the man behind bars, the system simply cannot do without.

The right to the assistance of counsel is in a class by itself when it comes to our constitutional protections. Why? Because it is guaranteed to the accused by no less than three separate provisions within the constitutional amendments. The bulk of the protection comes from the Sixth Amendment itself, the only provision that *expressly* provides the right to counsel. But by its very language the Sixth Amendment applies only to "criminal prosecutions." Therefore, other constitutional protections come into play by filling the gaps created by the limited coverage of the Sixth Amendment. The Due Process and Equal Protection Clauses of the Fourteenth Amendment help alleviate this gap. Also, the Supreme Court's decision in Miranda v. Arizona provides assistance of counsel in certain custodial settings in order to protect an individual's Fifth Amendment right against compelled self-incrimination (*see* Chapter 3). In order to get the "big picture" of the right to counsel, we need to understand not only the Sixth Amendment, but we also need a firm grasp on other constitutional provisions that may be implicated.

135

The man behind bars likely has many questions when it comes to his right to counsel: When am I entitled to a lawyer? Can I choose my own lawyer? What if I can't afford one? What if I'm refused a lawyer? And, just how good a job does my lawyer have to do when defending me? Once we have studied the right to counsel in this chapter, we will be able to answer all of those questions with precision and confidence.

STUDENT *Checklist*

Assistance of Counsel

1. Was the person **accused** of a crime?

■ Were formal **charges** initiated or was the person **indicted** for a crime?

2. Was it a **criminal prosecution?**

■ Was the crime a **felony** or **misdemeanor** where **jail time imposed** and

■ Was it a **critical stage** of the proceedings (i.e., stages in which **substantial rights** of the accused may be affected by counsel's absence)? and

■ Did it occur between the time period when **adversarial judicial proceedings** were initiated through **sentencing** (6th Amendment coverage), or at the accused's **first appeal as of right** (14th Amendment coverage)?

3. Did the accused receive **assistance** of counsel?

■ Was the accused permitted to **retain** counsel or, if **indigent**, was counsel **appointed** to represent the accused? or

■ Did the accused voluntarily, knowingly, and intelligently **waive** the right to assistance of counsel?

4. Was there a **violation** of the accused's right to counsel?

■ Was counsel improperly **denied** to accused or

■ Did the accused receive **ineffective assistance of counsel?**
   Was counsel's performance **incompetent** based on an objective standard of reasonableness?
   and
   Did the accused suffer **prejudice** amounting to a reasonable probability that, but for counsel's errors, the outcome of the proceeding would have been different?

5. Was the accused provided with a **remedy** for a violation of his right to counsel?

■ Was evidence obtained at a critical stage in violation of right to counsel suppressed under **Exclusionary Rule?**

SUPREME COURT CASES

POWELL v. ALABAMA, 287 U.S. 45 (1932)

The petitioners, hereinafter referred to as defendants, are negroes charged with the crime of rape, committed upon the persons of two white girls. The crime is said to have been committed on March 25, 1931. The indictment was returned in a state court of first instance on March 31, and the record recites that on the same day the defendants were arraigned and entered pleas of not guilty. There is a further recital to the effect that upon the arraignment they were represented by counsel. But no counsel had been employed, and aside from a statement made by the trial judge several days later during a colloquy immediately preceding the trial, the record does not disclose when, or under what circumstances, an appointment of counsel was made, or who was appointed. During the colloquy referred to, the trial judge, in response to a question, said that he had appointed all the members of the bar for the purpose of arraigning the defendants and then of course anticipated that the members of the bar would continue to help the defendants if no counsel appeared. Upon the argument here both sides accepted that as a correct statement of the facts concerning the matter.

There was a severance upon the request of the state, and the defendants were tried in three several groups, as indicated above. As each of the three cases was called for trial, each defendant was arraigned, and, having the indictment read to him, entered a plea of not guilty. Whether the original arraignment and pleas were regarded as ineffective is not shown. Each of the three trials was completed within a single day. Under the Alabama statute the punishment for rape is to be fixed by the jury, and in its discretion may be from ten years imprisonment to death. The juries found defendants guilty and imposed the death penalty upon all. The trial court overruled motions for new trials and sentenced the defendants in accordance with the verdicts. The judgments were affirmed by the state supreme court. . . .

The record shows that on the day when the offense is said to have been committed, these defendants, together with a number of other negroes, were upon a freight train on its way through Alabama. On the same train were seven white boys and the two white girls. A fight took place between the negroes and the white boys, in the course of which the white boys, with the exception of one named Gilley, were thrown off the train. A message was sent ahead, reporting the fight and asking that every negro be gotten off the train. The participants in the fight, and the two girls, were in an open gondola car. The two girls testified that each of them was assaulted by six different negroes in turn, and they identified the seven defendants as having been among the number. None of the white boys was called to testify, with the exception of Gilley, who was called in rebuttal. . . .

However guilty defendants, upon due inquiry, might prove to have been, they were, until convicted, presumed to be innocent. It was the duty of the court having their cases in charge to see that they were denied no necessary incident of a fair trial. With any error of the state court involving alleged contravention of the state statutes or Constitution we, of course, have nothing to do. The sole inquiry which we are permitted to make is whether the federal Constitution was contravened (Rogers v. Peck, 199 U.S. 425, 434, 26 S. Ct. 87, 50 L. Ed. 256; Hebert v. State of Louisiana, 272 U.S. 312, 316, 47 S. Ct. 103, 71 L. Ed. 270, 48 A.L.R. 1102); and as to that, we confine ourselves, as already suggested, to the inquiry whether the defendants were in substance denied the right of counsel, and if so, whether such denial infringes the due process clause of the Fourteenth Amendment.

First. The record shows that immediately upon the return of the indictment defendants were arraigned and pleaded not guilty. Apparently they were not asked whether they had, or were able to employ, counsel, or wished to have counsel appointed; or whether they had friends or relatives who might assist in that regard if communicated with. That it would not have been an idle ceremony to have given the defendants reasonable opportunity to communicate with their families and endeavor to obtain counsel is demonstrated by the fact that very soon after conviction, able counsel appeared in their behalf. . . .

It is hardly necessary to say that the right to counsel being conceded, a defendant should be afforded a fair opportunity to secure counsel of his own choice. Not only was that not done here, but such designation of counsel as was attempted was either so indefinite or so close upon the trial as to amount to a denial of effective and substantial aid in that regard. . . .

It thus will be seen that until the very morning of the trial no lawyer had been named or definitely designated to represent the defendants. Prior to that time, the trial judge had "appointed all the members of the bar" for the limited "purpose of arraigning the defendants." Whether they would represent the defendants thereafter, if no counsel appeared in their behalf, was a matter of speculation only, or, as the judge indicated, of mere anticipation on the part of the court. Such a designation, even if made for all purposes, would, in our opinion, have fallen far short of meeting, in any proper sense, a requirement for the appointment of counsel. . . .

It is true that great and inexcusable delay in the enforcement of our criminal law is one of the grave evils of our time. Continuances are frequently granted for unnecessarily long periods of time, and delays incident to the disposition of motions for new trial and hearings upon appeal have come in many cases to be a distinct reproach to the administration of justice. The prompt disposition of criminal cases is to be commended and encouraged. But in reaching that result a defendant, charged with a serious crime, must not be stripped of his right to have sufficient time to advise with counsel and prepare his defense. To do that is not to proceed promptly in the claim spirit of regulated justice but to go forward with the haste of the mob. . . .

Second. The Constitution of Alabama (Const. 1901, § 6) provides that in all criminal prosecutions the accused shall enjoy the right to have the assistance of counsel; and a state statute (Code 1923, § 5567) requires the court in a capital case, where the defendant is unable to employ counsel, to appoint counsel for him. The state Supreme Court held that these provisions had not been infringed, and with that holding we are powerless to interfere. The question, however, which it is our duty, and within our power, to decide, is whether the denial of the assistance of counsel contravenes the due process clause of the Fourteenth Amendment to the Federal Constitution. . . .

It never has been doubted by this court, or any other so far as we know, that notice and hearing are preliminary steps essential to the passing of an enforceable judgment, and that they, together with a legally competent tribunal having jurisdiction of the case, constitute basic elements of the constitutional requirement of due process of law. . . .

What, then, does a hearing include? Historically and in practice, in our own country at least, it has always included the right to the aid of counsel when desired and provided by the party asserting the right. The right to be heard would be, in many cases, of little avail if it did not comprehend the right to be heard by counsel. Even the intelligent and educated layman has small and sometimes no skill in the science of law. If charged with crime, he is incapable, generally, of determining for himself whether the indictment is good or bad. He is unfamiliar with the rules of evidence. Left without the aid of counsel he may be put on trial without a proper charge, and convicted upon incompetent evidence, or evidence irrelevant to the issue or otherwise inadmissible. He lacks both the skill and knowledge adequately to prepare his defense, even though he have a perfect one. He requires the guiding hand of counsel at every step in the proceedings against him. Without it, though he be not guilty, he faces the danger of conviction because he does not know how to establish his innocence. If that be true of men of intelligence, how much more true is it of the ignorant and illiterate, or those of feeble intellect. If in any case, civil of criminal, a state or federal court were arbitrarily to refuse to hear a party by counsel, employed by and appearing for him, it reasonably may not be doubted that such a refusal would be a denial of a hearing, and, therefore, of due process in the constitutional sense. . . .

In the light of the facts outlined in the forepart of this opinion—the ignorance and illiteracy of the defendants, their youth, the circumstances of public hostility, the imprisonment and the close surveillance of the defendants by the military forces, the fact that their friends and families were all in other states and communication with them necessarily difficult, and above all that they stood in deadly peril of their lives—we think the failure of the trial court to give them reasonable time and opportunity to secure counsel was a clear denial of due process.

But passing that, and assuming their inability, even if opportunity had been given, to employ counsel, as the trial court evidently did assume, we are of opinion that, under the circumstances just stated, the necessity of counsel was so vital and imperative that the failure of the trial court to make an effective appointment of counsel was likewise a denial of due process within the meaning of the Fourteenth Amendment. Whether this would be so in other criminal prosecutions, or under other circumstances, we need not determine. All that it is necessary now to decide, as we do decide, is that in a capital case, where the defendant is unable to employ counsel, and is incapable adequately of making his own defense because of ignorance, feeble-mindedness, illiteracy, or the like, it is the duty of the court, whether requested or not, to assign counsel for him as a necessary requisite of due process of law; and that duty is not discharged by an assignment at such a time or under such circumstances as to preclude the giving of effective aid in the preparation and trial of the case. To hold otherwise would be to ignore the fundamental postulate, already adverted to, "that there are certain immutable principles of justice which inhere in the very idea of free government which no member of the Union may disregard." Holden v. Hardy, supra. . . .

The United States by statute and every state in the Union by express provision of law, or by the determination of its courts, make it the duty of the trial judge, where the accused is unable to employ counsel, to appoint counsel for him. In most states the rule applies broadly to all criminal prosecutions, in others it is limited to the more serious crimes, and in a very limited number, to capital cases. A rule adopted with such unanimous accord reflects, if it does not establish the inherent right to have counsel appointed at least in cases like the present, and lends convincing support to the conclusion we have reached as to the fundamental nature of that right.

The judgments must be reversed and the causes remanded for further proceedings not inconsistent with this opinion.

Judgments reversed.

STRICKLAND v. WASHINGTON, 466 U.S. 668 (1984)

This case requires us to consider the proper standards for judging a criminal defendant's contention that the Constitution requires a conviction or death sentence to be set aside because counsel's assistance at the trial or sentencing was ineffective.

I

A

During a 10-day period in September 1976, respondent planned and committed three groups of crimes, which included three brutal stabbing murders, torture, kidnaping, severe assaults, attempted murders, attempted extortion, and theft. After his two accomplices were arrested, respondent surrendered to police and voluntarily gave a lengthy statement confessing to the third of the criminal episodes. The State of Florida indicted respondent for kidnaping and murder and appointed an experienced criminal lawyer to represent him.

Counsel actively pursued pretrial motions and discovery. He cut his efforts short, however, and he experienced a sense of hopelessness about the case, when he learned that, against his specific advice, respondent had also confessed to the first two murders. By the date set for trial, respondent was subject to indictment for three counts of first-degree murder and multiple counts of robbery, kidnaping for ransom, breaking and entering and assault, attempted murder, and conspiracy to commit robbery. Respondent waived his right to a jury trial, again acting against counsel's advice, and pleaded guilty to all charges, including the three capital murder charges.

In the plea colloquy, respondent told the trial judge that, although he had committed a string of burglaries, he had no significant prior criminal record and that at the time of his criminal spree he was under extreme stress caused by his inability to support his family. App. 50-53. He also stated, however, that he accepted responsibility for the crimes. E.g., id., at 54, 57. The trial judge told respondent that he had "a great deal of respect for people who are willing to step forward and admit their responsibility" but that he was making no statement at all about his likely sentencing decision. Id., at 62.

Counsel advised respondent to invoke his right under Florida law to an advisory jury at his capital sentencing hearing. Respondent rejected the advice and waived the right. He chose instead to be sentenced by the trial judge without a jury recommendation.

In preparing for the sentencing hearing, counsel spoke with respondent about his background. He also spoke on the telephone with respondent's wife and mother, though he did not follow up on the one unsuccessful effort to meet with them. He did not otherwise seek out character witnesses for respondent. App. to Pet. for Cert. A265. Nor did he request a psychiatric examination, since his conversations with his client gave no indication that respondent had psychological problems. Id., at A266.

Counsel decided not to present and hence not to look further for evidence concerning respondent's character and emotional state. That decision reflected trial counsel's sense of hopelessness about overcoming the evidentiary effect of respondent's confessions to the gruesome crimes. See id., at A282. It also reflected the judgment that it was advisable to rely on the plea colloquy for evidence about respondent's background and about his claim of emotional stress: the plea colloquy communicated sufficient information about these subjects, and by forgoing the opportunity to present new evidence on these subjects, counsel prevented the State from cross-examining respondent on his claim and from putting on psychiatric evidence of its own. Id., at A223-A225.

Counsel also excluded from the sentencing hearing other evidence he thought was potentially damaging. He successfully moved to exclude respondent's "rap sheet." Id., at A227; App. 311. Because he judged that a presentence report might prove more detrimental than helpful, as it would have included respondent's criminal history and thereby would have undermined the claim of no significant history of criminal activity, he did not request that one be prepared. App. to Pet. for Cert. A227-A228, A265-A266.

At the sentencing hearing, counsel's strategy was based primarily on the trial judge's remarks at the plea colloquy as well as on his reputation as a sentencing judge who thought it important for a convicted defendant to own up to his crime. Counsel argued that respondent's remorse and acceptance of responsibility justified sparing him from the death penalty. Id., at A265-A266. Counsel also argued that respondent had no history of criminal activity and that respondent committed the crimes under extreme mental or emotional disturbance, thus coming within the statutory list of mitigating circumstances. He further argued that respondent should be spared death because he had surrendered, confessed, and offered to testify against a codefendant and because respondent was fundamentally a good person who had briefly gone badly wrong in extremely stressful circumstances. The State put on evidence and witnesses largely for the purpose of describing the details of the crimes. Counsel did not cross-examine the medical experts who testified about the manner of death of respondent's victims. . . .

In short, the trial judge found numerous aggravating circumstances and no (or a single comparatively insignificant) mitigating circumstance. With respect to each of the three convictions for capital murder, the trial judge concluded: "A careful consideration of all matters presented to the court impels the conclusion that there are insufficient mitigating circumstances . . . to outweigh the aggravating circumstances." See Washington v. State, 362 So.2d 658, 663-664 (Fla. 1978), (quoting trial court findings), cert. denied, 441 U.S. 937, 99 S. Ct. 2063, 60 L. Ed. 2d 666 (1979). He therefore sentenced respondent to death on each of the three counts of murder and to prison terms for the other crimes. The Florida Supreme Court upheld the convictions and sentences on direct appeal.

B

Respondent subsequently sought collateral relief in state court on numerous grounds, among them that counsel had rendered ineffective assistance at the sentencing proceeding. Respondent challenged counsel's assistance in six respects. He asserted that counsel was ineffective because he failed to move for a continuance to prepare for sentencing, to request a psychiatric report, to investigate and present character witnesses, to seek a presentence investigation report, to present meaningful arguments to the sentencing judge, and to investigate the medical examiner's reports or cross-examine the medical experts. In support of the claim, respondent submitted 14 affidavits from friends, neighbors, and relatives stating that they would have testified if asked to do so. He also submitted one psychiatric report and one psychological report stating that respondent, though not under the influence of extreme mental or emotional disturbance, was "chronically frustrated and depressed because of his economic dilemma" at the time of his crimes. App. 7; see also id., at 14. . . .

II

In a long line of cases that includes Powell v. Alabama, 287 U.S. 45, 53 S. Ct. 55, 77 L. Ed. 158 (1932), Johnson v. Zerbst, 304 U.S. 458, 58 S. Ct. 1019, 82 L. Ed. 1461 (1938), and Gideon v. Wainwright, 372 U.S. 335, 83 S. Ct. 792, 9 L. Ed. 2d 799 (1963), this Court has recognized that the Sixth Amendment right to counsel exists, and is needed, in order to protect the fundamental right to a fair trial. The Constitution guarantees a fair trial through the Due Process Clauses, but it defines the basic elements of a fair trial largely through the several provisions of the Sixth Amendment, including the Counsel Clause . . .

Thus, a fair trial is one in which evidence subject to adversarial testing is presented to an impartial tribunal for resolution of issues defined in advance of the proceeding. The right to counsel plays a crucial role in the adversarial system embodied in the Sixth Amendment, since access to counsel's skill and knowledge is necessary to accord defendants the "ample opportunity to meet the case of the prosecution" to which they are entitled. . . . That a person who happens to be a lawyer is present at trial alongside the accused, however, is not enough to satisfy the constitutional command. The Sixth Amendment recognizes the right to the assistance of counsel because it envisions counsel's playing a role that is critical to the ability of the adversarial system to produce just results. An accused is entitled to be assisted by an attorney, whether retained or appointed, who plays the role necessary to ensure that the trial is fair.

For that reason, the Court has recognized that "the right to counsel is the right to the effective assistance of counsel." . . . Counsel, however, can also deprive a defendant of the right to effective assistance, simply by failing to render "adequate legal assistance," Cuyler v. Sullivan, 446 U.S., at 344, 100 S. Ct., at 1716. Id., at 345-350, 100 S. Ct., at 1716-1719 (actual conflict of interest adversely affecting lawyer's performance renders assistance ineffective).

The Court has not elaborated on the meaning of the constitutional requirement of effective assistance in the latter class of cases—that is, those presenting claims of "actual ineffectiveness." In giving meaning to the requirement, however, we must take its purpose—to ensure a fair trial—as the guide. The benchmark for judging any claim of ineffectiveness must be whether counsel's conduct so undermined the proper functioning of the adversarial process that the trial cannot be relied on as having produced a just result. . . .

III

A convicted defendant's claim that counsel's assistance was so defective as to require reversal of a conviction or death sentence has two components. First, the defendant must show that counsel's performance was deficient. This requires showing that counsel made errors so serious that counsel was not functioning as the "counsel" guaranteed the defendant by the Sixth Amendment. Second, the defendant must show that the deficient performance prejudiced the defense. This requires showing that counsel's errors were so serious as to deprive the defendant of a fair trial, a trial whose result is reliable. Unless a defendant makes both showings, it cannot be said that the conviction or death sentence resulted from a breakdown in the adversary process that renders the result unreliable.

A

As all the Federal Courts of Appeals have now held, the proper standard for attorney performance is that of reasonably effective assistance. . . . When a convicted defendant complains of the ineffectiveness of counsel's assistance, the defendant must show that counsel's representation fell below an objective standard of reasonableness. . . .

Representation of a criminal defendant entails certain basic duties. Counsel's function is to assist the defendant, and hence counsel owes the client a duty of loyalty, a duty to avoid conflicts of interest. See Cuyler v. Sullivan, supra, 446 U.S., at 346, 90 S. Ct., at 1717. From counsel's function as assistant to the defendant derive the overarching duty to advocate the defendant's cause and the more particular duties to consult with the defendant on important decisions and to keep the defendant informed of important developments in the course of the prosecution. Counsel also has a duty to bring to bear such skill and knowledge as will render the trial a reliable adversarial testing process. See Powell v. Alabama, 287 U.S., at 68-69, 53 S. Ct., at 63-64.

These basic duties neither exhaustively define the obligations of counsel nor form a checklist for judicial evaluation of attorney performance. In any case presenting an ineffectiveness claim, the performance inquiry must be whether counsel's assistance was reasonable considering all the circumstances. Prevailing norms of practice as reflected in American Bar Association standards and the like, e.g., ABA Standards for Criminal Justice 4-1.1 to 4-8.6 (2d ed. 1980) ("The Defense Function"), are guides to determining what is reasonable, but they are only guides. No particular set of detailed rules for counsel's conduct can satisfactorily take account of the variety of circumstances faced by defense counsel or the range of legitimate decisions regarding how best to represent a criminal defendant. Any such set of rules would interfere with the constitutionally protected independence of counsel and restrict the wide latitude counsel must have in making tactical decisions. See United States v. Decoster, 199 U.S. App. D.C., at 371, 624 F.2d, at 208. Indeed, the existence of detailed guidelines for representation could distract counsel from the overriding mission of vigorous advocacy of the defendant's cause. Moreover, the purpose of the effective assistance guarantee of the Sixth Amendment is not to improve the quality of legal representation, although that is a goal of considerable importance to the legal system. The purpose is simply to ensure that criminal defendants receive a fair trial.

Judicial scrutiny of counsel's performance must be highly deferential. It is all too tempting for a defendant to second-guess counsel's assistance after conviction or adverse sentence, and it is all too easy for a court, examining counsel's defense after it has proved unsuccessful, to conclude that a particular act or omission of counsel was unreasonable. Cf. Engle v. Isaac, 456 U.S. 107, 133-134, 102 S. Ct. 1558, 1574-1575, 71 L. Ed. 2d 783 (1982). A fair assessment of attorney performance requires that every effort be made to eliminate the distorting effects of hindsight, to reconstruct the circumstances of counsel's challenged conduct, and to evaluate the conduct from counsel's perspective at the time. Because of the difficulties inherent in making the evaluation, a court must indulge a strong presumption that counsel's conduct falls within the wide range of reasonable professional assistance; that is, the defendant must overcome the presumption that, under the circumstances, the challenged action "might be considered sound trial strategy." See Michel v. Louisiana, supra, 350 U.S., at 101, 76 S. Ct., at 164. There are countless ways to provide effective assistance in any given case. Even the best criminal defense attorneys would not defend a particular client in the same way. . . .

Thus, a court deciding an actual ineffectiveness claim must judge the reasonableness of counsel's challenged conduct on the facts of the particular case, viewed as of the time of counsel's conduct. A convicted defendant making a claim of ineffective assistance must identify the acts or omissions of counsel that are alleged not to have been the result of reasonable professional judgment. The court must then determine whether, in light of all the circumstances, the identified acts or omissions were outside the wide range of professionally competent assistance. In making that determination, the court should keep in mind that counsel's function, as elaborated in prevailing professional norms, is to make the adversarial testing process work in the particular case. At the same time, the court should recognize that counsel is strongly presumed to have rendered adequate assistance and made all significant decisions in the exercise of reasonable professional judgment. . . .

B

An error by counsel, even if professionally unreasonable, does not warrant setting aside the judgment of a criminal proceeding if the error had no effect on the judgment. Cf. United States v. Morrison, 449 U.S. 361, 364-365, 101 S. Ct. 665, 667-668, 66 L. Ed. 2d 564 (1981). The purpose of the Sixth Amendment guarantee of counsel is to ensure that a defendant has the assistance necessary to justify reliance on the outcome of the proceeding. Accordingly, any deficiencies in counsel's performance must be prejudicial to the defense in order to constitute ineffective assistance under the Constitution. . . .

[A]ctual ineffectiveness claims alleging a deficiency in attorney performance are subject to a general requirement that the defendant affirmatively prove prejudice. The government is not responsible for, and hence not able to prevent, attorney errors that will result in reversal of a conviction or sentence. Attorney errors come in an infinite variety and are as likely to be utterly harmless in a particular case as they are to be prejudicial. They cannot be classified according to likelihood of causing prejudice. Nor can they be defined with sufficient precision to inform defense attorneys correctly just what conduct to avoid. Representation is an art, and an act or omission that is unprofessional in one case may be sound or even brilliant in another. Even if a defendant shows that particular errors of counsel were unreasonable, therefore, the defendant must show that they actually had an adverse effect on the defense. . . .

The governing legal standard plays a critical role in defining the question to be asked in assessing the prejudice from counsel's errors. When a defendant challenges a conviction, the question is whether there is a reasonable probability that, absent the errors, the factfinder would have had a reasonable doubt respecting guilt. When a defendant challenges a death sentence such as the one at issue in this case, the question is whether there is a reasonable probability that, absent the errors, the sentencer—including an appellate court, to the extent it independently reweighs the evidence—would have concluded that the balance of aggravating and mitigating circumstances did not warrant death. . . . [A] court making the prejudice inquiry must ask if the defendant has met the burden of showing that the decision reached would reasonably likely have been different absent the errors.

IV

A number of practical considerations are important for the application of the standards we have outlined. Most important, in adjudicating a claim of actual ineffectiveness of counsel, a court should keep in mind that the principles we have stated do not establish mechanical rules. Although those principles should guide the process of decision, the ultimate focus of inquiry must be on the fundamental fairness of the proceeding whose result is being challenged. In every case the court should be concerned with whether, despite the strong presumption of reliability, the result of the particular proceeding is unreliable because of a breakdown in the adversarial process that our system counts on to produce just results. . . .

Although we have discussed the performance component of an ineffectiveness claim prior to the prejudice component, there is no reason for a court deciding an ineffective assistance claim to approach the inquiry in the same order or even to address both components of the inquiry if the defendant makes an insufficient showing on one. In particular, a court need not determine whether counsel's performance was deficient before examining the prejudice suffered by the defendant as a result of the alleged deficiencies. The object of an ineffectiveness claim is not to grade counsel's performance. If it is easier to dispose of an ineffectiveness claim on the ground of lack of sufficient prejudice, which we expect will often be so, that course should be followed. Courts should strive to ensure that ineffectiveness claims not become so burdensome to defense counsel that the entire criminal justice system suffers as a result. . . .

V . . .

Application of the governing principles is not difficult in this case. The facts as described above, see supra, at 2056-2060, make clear that the conduct of respondent's counsel at and before respondent's sentencing proceeding cannot be found unreasonable. They also make clear that, even assuming the challenged conduct of counsel was unreasonable, respondent suffered insufficient prejudice to warrant setting aside his death sentence.

With respect to the performance component, the record shows that respondent's counsel made a strategic choice to argue for the extreme emotional distress mitigating circumstance and to rely as fully as possible on respondent's acceptance of responsibility for his crimes. Although counsel understandably felt hopeless about respondent's prospects, see App. 383-384, 400-401, nothing in the record indicates, . . . that counsel's sense of hopelessness distorted his professional judgment. Counsel's strategy choice was well within the range of professionally reasonable judgments, and the decision not to seek more character or psychological evidence than was already in hand was likewise reasonable.

The trial judge's views on the importance of owning up to one's crimes were well known to counsel. The aggravating circumstances were utterly overwhelming. Trial counsel could reasonably surmise from his conversations with respondent that character and psychological evidence would be of little help. Respondent had already been able to mention at the plea colloquy the substance of what there was to know about his financial and emotional troubles. Restricting testimony on respondent's character to what had come in at the plea colloquy ensured that contrary character and psychological evidence and respondent's criminal history, which counsel had successfully moved to exclude, would not come in. On these facts, there can be little question, even without application of the presumption of adequate performance, that trial counsel's defense, though unsuccessful, was the result of reasonable professional judgment.

With respect to the prejudice component, the lack of merit of respondent's claim is even more stark. The evidence that respondent says his trial counsel should have offered at the sentencing hearing would barely have altered the sentencing profile presented to the sentencing judge. As the state courts and District Court found, at most this evidence shows that numerous people who knew respondent thought he was generally a good person and that a psychiatrist and a psychologist believed he was under considerable emotional stress that did not rise to the level of extreme disturbance. Given the overwhelming aggravating factors, there is no reasonable probability that the omitted evidence would have changed the conclusion that the aggravating circumstances outweighed the mitigating circumstances and, hence, the sentence imposed. . . .

Failure to make the required showing of either deficient performance or sufficient prejudice defeats the ineffectiveness claim. Here there is a double failure. More generally, respondent has made no showing that the justice of his sentence was rendered unreliable by a breakdown in the adversary process caused by deficiencies in counsel's assistance. Respondent's sentencing proceeding was not fundamentally unfair.

We conclude, therefore, that the District Court properly declined to issue a writ of habeas corpus. The judgment of the Court of Appeals is accordingly Reversed.

FLORIDA v. NIXON, 543 U.S. 175 (2004)

This capital case concerns defense counsel's strategic decision to concede, at the guilt phase of the trial, the defendant's commission of murder, and to concentrate the defense on establishing, at the penalty phase, cause for sparing the defendant's life. Any concession of that order, the Florida Supreme Court held, made without the defendant's express consent—however gruesome the crime and despite the strength of the evidence of guilt—automatically ranks as prejudicial ineffective assistance of counsel necessitating a new trial. We reverse the Florida Supreme Court's judgment. . . .

I

On Monday, August 13, 1984, near a dirt road in the environs of Tallahassee, Florida, a passing motorist discovered Jeanne Bickner's charred body. *Nixon v. State*, 572 So.2d 1336, 1337 (Fla. 1990) *(Nixon I);* 13 Record 2464-2466. Bickner had been tied to a tree and set on fire while still alive. *Id.,* at 2475, 2483-2484. Her left leg and arm, and most of her hair and skin, had been burned away. *Id.,* at 2475-2476. The next day, police found Bickner's car, abandoned on a Tallahassee street corner, on fire. *Id.,* at 2520. Police arrested 23-year-old Joe Elton Nixon later that morning, after Nixon's brother informed the sheriff's office that Nixon had confessed to the murder. *Id.,* at 2559. . . .

The State gathered overwhelming evidence establishing that Nixon had committed the murder in the manner he described. . . .

In late August 1984, Nixon was indicted in Leon County, Florida, for first-degree murder, kidnaping, robbery, and arson. See App. 1, 55. Assistant public defender Michael Corin, assigned to represent Nixon, see *id.,* at 232, filed a plea of not guilty, *id.,* at 468-469, and deposed all of the State's potential witnesses, *id.,* at 53-58. Corin concluded, given the strength of the evidence, that Nixon's guilt was not "subject to any reasonable dispute." *Id.,* at 490. Corin thereupon commenced plea negotiations, hoping to persuade the prosecution to drop the death penalty in exchange for Nixon's guilty pleas to all charges. *Id.,* at 336-338, 507. Negotiations broke down when the prosecutors indicated their unwillingness to recommend a sentence other than death. See *id.,* at 339, 508.

Faced with the inevitability of going to trial on a capital charge, Corin turned his attention to the penalty phase, believing that the only way to save Nixon's life would be to present extensive mitigation evidence centering on

Nixon's mental instability. *Id.*, at 261, 473; see also *id.*, at 102. Experienced in capital defense, see *id.*, at 248-250, Corin feared that denying Nixon's commission of the kidnaping and murder during the guilt phase would compromise Corin's ability to persuade the jury, during the penalty phase, that Nixon's conduct was the product of his mental illness. See *id.*, at 473, 490, 505. Corin concluded that the best strategy would be to concede guilt, thereby preserving his credibility in urging leniency during the penalty phase. *Id.*, at 458, 505.

Corin attempted to explain this strategy to Nixon at least three times. *Id.*, at 254-255. Although Corin had represented Nixon previously on unrelated charges and the two had a good relationship in Corin's estimation, see *id.*, at 466-467, Nixon was generally unresponsive during their discussions, *id.*, at 478-480. He never verbally approved or protested Corin's proposed strategy. *Id.*, at 234-238, 255, 501. Overall, Nixon gave Corin very little, if any, assistance or direction in preparing the case, *id.*, at 478, and refused to attend pretrial dispositions of various motions, *Nixon I*, 572 So.2d, at 1341; App. 478. Corin eventually exercised his professional judgment to pursue the concession strategy. As he explained: "There are many times lawyers make decisions because they have to make them because the client does nothing." *Id.*, at 486.

When Nixon's trial began on July 15, 1985, his unresponsiveness deepened into disruptive and violent behavior. . . .

The guilt phase of the trial thus began in Nixon's absence. In his opening statement, Corin acknowledged Nixon's guilt and urged the jury to focus on the penalty phase . . .

At the start of the penalty phase, Corin argued to the jury that "Joe Elton Nixon is not normal organically, intellectually, emotionally or educationally or in any other way." *Id.*, at 102. Corin presented the testimony of eight witnesses. Relatives and friends described Nixon's childhood emotional troubles and his erratic behavior in the days preceding the murder. See, e.g., *id.*, at 108-120. A psychiatrist and a psychologist addressed Nixon's antisocial personality, his history of emotional instability and psychiatric care, his low IQ, and the possibility that at some point he suffered brain damage. *Id.*, at 143-147, 162-166. The State presented little evidence during the penalty phase, simply incorporating its guilt-phase evidence by reference, and introducing testimony, over Corin's objection, that Nixon had removed Bickner's underwear in order to terrorize her. *Id.*, at 105-106.

In his closing argument, Corin emphasized Nixon's youth, the psychiatric evidence, and the jury's discretion to consider any mitigating circumstances, *id.*, at 194-199; Corin urged that, if not sentenced to death, "Joe Elton Nixon would [n]ever be released from confinement," *id.*, at 207. The death penalty, Corin maintained, was appropriate only for "intact human being[s]," and "Joe Elton Nixon is not one of those. He's never been one of those. He never will be one of those." *Id.*, at 209. Corin concluded: "You know, we're not around here all that long. And it's rare when we have the opportunity to give or take life. And you have that opportunity to give life. And I'm going to ask you to do that. Thank you." *Ibid.* After deliberating for approximately three hours, the jury recommended that Nixon be sentenced to death. See 21 Record 4013.

In accord with the jury's recommendation, the trial court imposed the death penalty. *Nixon I*, 572 So.2d, at 1338. . . .

We granted certiorari, 540 U.S. 1217, 124 S. Ct. 1509, 158 L. Ed. 2d 152 (2004), to resolve an important question of constitutional law, *i.e.*, whether counsel's failure to obtain the defendant's express consent to a strategy of conceding guilt in a capital trial automatically renders counsel's performance deficient, and whether counsel's effectiveness should be evaluated under *Cronic* or *Strickland*. We now reverse the judgment of the Florida Supreme Court.

II

An attorney undoubtedly has a duty to consult with the client regarding "important decisions," including questions of overarching defense strategy. *Strickland*, 466 U.S., at 688, 104 S. Ct. 2052. That obligation, however, does not require counsel to obtain the defendant's consent to "every tactical decision." *Taylor v. Illinois*, 484 U.S. 400, 417-418, 108 S. Ct. 646, 98 L. Ed. 2d 798 (1988). . . .

Corin was obliged to, and in fact several times did, explain his proposed trial strategy to Nixon. See *supra*, at 557, 559-560. Given Nixon's constant resistance to answering inquiries put to him by counsel and court, see *Nixon III*, 857 So.2d, at 187-188 (Wells, J., dissenting), Corin was not additionally required to gain express consent before conceding Nixon's guilt. The two evidentiary hearings conducted by the Florida trial court demonstrate beyond doubt that Corin fulfilled his duty of consultation by informing Nixon of counsel's proposed strategy and its potential benefits. Nixon's characteristic silence each time information was conveyed to him, in sum, did not suffice to render unreasonable Corin's decision to concede guilt and to home in, instead, on the life or death penalty issue. . . .

On the record thus far developed, Corin's concession of Nixon's guilt does not rank as a "fail[ure] to function in any meaningful sense as the Government's adversary." *Id.*, at 666. Although such a concession in a run-of-the-mine trial might present a closer question, the gravity of the potential sentence in a capital trial and the proceeding's two-phase structure vitally affect counsel's strategic calculus. Attorneys representing capital defendants face daunting challenges in developing trial strategies, not least because the defendant's guilt is often clear. Prosecutors are more likely to seek the death penalty, and to refuse to accept a plea to a life sentence, when the evidence is overwhelming and the crime heinous. . . .

Counsel therefore may reasonably decide to focus on the trial's penalty phase, at which time counsel's mission is to persuade the trier that his client's life should be spared. Unable to negotiate a guilty plea in exchange for a life sentence, defense counsel must strive at the guilt phase to avoid a counterproductive course. . . . In this light, counsel cannot be deemed ineffective for attempting to impress the jury with his candor and his unwillingness to engage in "a useless charade." See *Cronic*, 466 U.S., at 656-657, n.19, 104 S. Ct. 2039. . . .

To summarize, in a capital case, counsel must consider in conjunction both the guilt and penalty phases in determining how best to proceed. When counsel informs the defendant of the strategy counsel believes to be in the defendant's best interest and the defendant is unresponsive, counsel's strategic choice is not impeded by any blanket rule demanding the defendant's explicit consent. Instead, if counsel's strategy, given the evidence bearing on the defendant's guilt, satisfies the *Strickland* standard, that is the end of the matter; no tenable claim of ineffective assistance would remain.

For the reasons stated, the judgment of the Florida Supreme Court is reversed, and the case is remanded for further proceedings not inconsistent with this opinion.

It is so ordered.

CASE QUESTIONS

POWELL v. ALABAMA

1. Why did the Supreme Court base its holding on the Due Process Clause of the Fourteenth Amendment rather than the Assistance of Counsel Clause of the Sixth Amendment?

2. How did the Supreme Court limit its holding in *Powell*? Why do you think the Court handed down such a narrow holding?

3. Research challenge: What ultimately happened to the men accused of rape in Powell v. Alabama following the Court's reversal of their convictions?

STRICKLAND v. WASHINGTON

1. What two prongs did the Court establish for determining whether an accused has been denied the effective assistance of counsel? Which prong should be considered first?

2. Does the defendant have the burden of proving that counsel's conduct prejudiced him in some way, or does the state have the burden of proving nonprejudice? Why do you think the Court made the decision it did in this regard?

3. Why did the Court refuse to set more rigid guidelines for determining claims of ineffective assistance of counsel?

4. Did the Court find either of the two prongs present in the facts of the case before it? Explain.

FLORIDA v. NIXON

1. Do you agree with the Court's holding in this case? What about the fact that "death is different," and, as will be discussed in Chapter 11, death penalty cases have historically been treated very differently than any other type of case within the criminal justice system? Do you think the Supreme Court gave due recognition to this premise when deciding the case before it?

2. Did the fact that Nixon failed to expressly consent to his defense counsel's strategy to concede guilt affect the Court's holding? Why or why not?

HYPOTHETICAL WITH ACCOMPANYING ANALYSIS

Hypothetical

Bobby McIntyre, nineteen years old with only an eighth grade education, was arrested for carjacking. Shortly after his arrest, Bobby, along with a group of about twenty other recently arrested felons, was brought to the courthouse for his bail hearing. Rather than immediately appearing before a judge, the group was escorted into a small room adjacent to the courtroom where they were shown a five-minute videotape. On the videotape a judge provided information regarding the defendants' constitutional rights. The judge specifically said, "One of your most important rights is your right to have an attorney present to help you. If you cannot afford to hire your own attorney and you want legal representation, you will be provided with an attorney." After the group watched the video they were escorted into the courtroom and brought before Judge Thomas, who asked the court clerk, "Have these individuals seen the video advising them of their rights?" The clerk answered in the affirmative. The judge then addressed the group and stated, "If any of you has questions about the video you just watched, now is the time to articulate those questions." Everyone in the group, including Bobby, remained silent. "Very well," the judge declared, "you may all be seated." Judge Thomas thereafter went through each case individually and set bail. He made no further mention of the videotape or the constitutional rights of the respective defendants.

Subsequently, Bobby was formally charged with carjacking and related offenses. Bobby's next court appearance was his arraignment before Judge Howe. Bobby was not represented by counsel, and the judge inquired as to whether Bobby planned to represent himself. Bobby just shrugged, said he was confused, and explained he didn't realize that an attorney could be appointed for him if he could not afford one. The following then occurred:

> **Judge Howe:** Did you watch the video at your bail review hearing?
> **Bobby:** Yes.
> **Judge Howe:** Did you pay attention to what you were watching?
> **Bobby:** Yes.
> **Judge Howe:** And did you ask any questions after watching the video?
> **Bobby:** No.
> **Judge Howe:** Well if you were confused, then why didn't you ask any questions?
> **Bobby:** I don't know.

Based on the previous conversation, Judge Howe determined that Bobby had waived his right to counsel and ordered the arraignment to proceed. Bobby pleaded guilty to all counts and was later sentenced to a lengthy term of incarceration.

Bobby has since obtained court-appointed counsel. He is appealing his guilty plea, arguing that his Sixth Amendment right to the assistance of counsel was violated. Analyze Bobby's likelihood of success.

Analysis

The Sixth Amendment provides that "in all criminal prosecutions, the accused shall enjoy the right to . . . have the assistance of counsel for his defense." In order to analyze whether Bobby's constitutional rights were violated, it must first be determined whether he was legally entitled to counsel, and if so, whether he effectively waived his right to counsel.

An individual has the right to assistance of counsel if he has been "accused" of a crime, which occurs when either formal charges are initiated or the individual has been indicted for a crime. In the instant case, Bobby was charged with carjacking and other offenses; hence he was formally accused of a crime.

The right to counsel extends to critical stages of a criminal prosecution, and it is applicable to felonies or misdemeanors where jail time is imposed. Bobby was arrested for carjacking, a felony, which falls under the protection of the Sixth Amendment. Additionally, the Supreme Court has held that an arraignment is considered a "critical stage" where substantial rights of the accused could be affected by counsel's absence. Therefore, because Bobby was the accused in a criminal prosecution, he was constitutionally entitled to the assistance of counsel at his arraignment.

When Bobby appeared at his arraignment, he did not have counsel, so it must next be determined whether Bobby waived his right to the assistance of counsel. The Supreme Court has held that a waiver of counsel will only be effective if made "knowingly and voluntarily," and a strong presumption exists *against* the accused's waiver of counsel. Johnson v. Zerbst, 304 U.S. 458 (1938). Circumstantial evidence indicating the accused's waiver of his right to counsel is not enough—the accused must have explicitly been informed of his right and explicitly waived it after confirming he understood the nature of the right. A waiver will not be presumed from a silent record. Carnley v. Cochran, 369 U.S. 506 (1962). In the instant case, although it appears as though Bobby waived his right to counsel, the evidence strongly suggests that waiver was not made knowingly or voluntarily. Bobby was informed of his right to counsel through a five-minute video, during which time neither he nor any of the rest of the group could interject questions. When presented before Judge Thomas at the bail hearing the only inquiry made by the judge was whether the group as a whole had any questions. Bobby's reluctance to voice any concerns may well have been for reasons of intimidation or overall confusion. At no time was Bobby individually questioned about whether he understood the contents of the video or whether he appreciated the nature of the right to counsel. At Bobby's arraignment Judge Howe did nothing to elaborate upon or clarify Bobby's right to counsel. Furthermore, due to Bobby's young age and limited education, he likely may not have understood the video. In fact, at his arraignment Bobby informed the judge that he was "confused" and didn't realize he was entitled to appointed counsel. Therefore, although Bobby was advised of his right to counsel, his waiver of counsel was not "knowing and voluntary" as required by law.

Since Bobby was entitled to counsel at his arraignment and he did not waive that right, Bobby's Sixth Amendment right to the assistance of counsel was violated. The guilty plea entered at his arraignment must be excluded, and Bobby should be entitled to the assistance of counsel for his defense.

Tom Trailblazer is a high profile attorney who defends only the rich and famous. His clients have included actors, sports figures, heiresses, and even high-ranking government officials. His latest client is Misty Goldsworth, a twenty-something socialite who inherited her father's billion-dollar fortune when he died suddenly last year. Misty is best known for being one of the richest young women in America, but she is also very well known for always taking the straight and narrow. She often does public service announcements in which she speaks out against drugs or drunk driving, and she spends much of her time helping out at charities and fundraisers for the needy. Recently, however, Misty has been plastered all over the front page of the newspapers. She has been charged with extortion for allegedly trying to blackmail Kurt, her ex-boyfriend. If convicted, Misty could face some serious jail time.

Tom knows that the state's case against Misty is a very weak one—Kurt is not a believable witness, and the state has no hard evidence against her other than the hearsay testimony of several of Kurt's friends. So Tom develops a strategy that in his opinion can't fail. During the state's case-in-chief, Tom cross-examines all of the state's witnesses and completely destroys their credibility. The prosecutor rests her case, and then the following occurs:

Judge: Mr. Trailblazer, you may proceed with your defense.
Tom: Your Honor, the defense rests.
Judge: You're not going to put forth any evidence?
Tom: No, Your Honor. The defense would argue that the state has failed to meet its burden of proof in this case, and the defense, therefore, rests.
Judge: Very well, counsel, you may give your closing arguments.

Gasps could be heard throughout the courtroom following Tom's shocking pronouncement. Even Misty herself looked stunned. Of course, Tom had previously discussed his strategy with his client, and Misty said she "implicitly trusted" Tom with anything he wanted to do. But even she couldn't hide her surprise when Tom actually went through with his "no-defense, defense" as he put it. Both attorneys concluded by presenting their closing arguments to the jury. During his argument, Tom stated the following:

Ladies and gentlemen of the jury, I have no doubt that each and every one of you leads very busy lives, and I appreciate the fact that you took the time out of your lives to come in here and fulfill your civic duty by being a part of this jury. But folks, the state has wasted your time by bringing such ludicrous charges against my client. The state has wasted your time, my time, Ms. Goldsworth's time, and the court's time. The prosecutor has presented *no* evidence that my client is guilty of extortion. And, well, ladies and gentlemen, I didn't want to waste any more of your time than the state already has. Have you ever been in the situation where someone made an accusation about you that was just so utterly ridiculous you didn't even see the need to respond to it? Well ladies and gentlemen, that is *precisely* the predicament we have here today. My client, a young, vibrant, upstanding member of our community who consistently goes out of her way to help others, would never in a million years commit such a crime. Therefore, rather than dignify such a sham of a charge we will let the state's complete *lack* of evidence speak for itself. The state miserably failed to prove to you that my client committed the crime, and I therefore ask each of you to do the right thing and acquit her.

Unfortunately for Misty, Tom's "no-defense defense" strategy failed miserably. Misty was convicted of extortion and received the maximum sentence for her crime. Since then she has hired herself a new high-profile attorney. She has appealed her conviction and his claiming ineffective assistance of counsel at trial. Analyze the likelihood of Misty's success.

DISCUSSION QUESTIONS

1. What collateral consequences could an attorney face, other than the possible reversal of his client's conviction, for failing to represent his client according to the standards set forth in *Strickland*?

2. Do you think you could be a criminal defense attorney and represent someone whom you know is guilty of a crime? What explanations might an attorney have for representing an admittedly guilty client?

3. Suppose a defense attorney shows up on the day of trial and is intoxicated, but she is somehow still able to defend her client in a vigorous manner. Or, suppose a defense attorney falls asleep during periods of the trial, but it does not appear as though the defense case was damaged in any way because of it. Should such outrageous conduct qualify as a type of ineffective assistance of counsel "per se"? Why or why not? *See, eg.*, United States v. Cronic, 466 U.S. 648 (1984).

4. Revisit Chapter 3 dealing with self-incrimination. When an individual is in custody and has been read his *Miranda* rights prior to interrogation, what difference does it make to police whether the suspect invokes his right to counsel as opposed to his right to remain silent? Is the analysis the same? Explain.

5. Compare the right to a speedy trial (Chapter 8, *infra*) with the Sixth Amendment right to counsel: both provide protections to the "accused." Is the "accused" defined the same way under both provisions? Explain.

6. Research challenge: Jose Padilla, a United States citizen, was suspected of having been involved with the global terrorist organization Al Qaeda. Following the September 11, 2001, terrorist attacks, Padilla was placed on a government "watch list." He was apprehended on May 8, 2002, and on June 9, 2002, President Bush declared Padilla an "enemy combatant" and ordered Padilla detained. Between June of 2002 and March of 2004 Padilla was prohibited from communicating with his attorney in any way. On what basis was the government able to detain Padilla for almost two years without providing him with counsel? Were his Sixth Amendment rights to counsel violated? Explain.

7. An old adage states, "A man who represents himself has a fool for a client." What does this mean? Do you agree with it? What if that "man" happened to be an attorney already, would your answer change?

8. Research challenge: Track the progression of Supreme Court decisions that have expanded the right to counsel following Powell v. Alabama. Make a timeline of those cases including the years they were decided, their significance, and which constitutional provisions they relied upon for their respective holdings.

9. Sally is a public defender assigned to represent Harry at his rape trial. Despite zealously representing him, Harry is convicted. Harry wants to appeal, but after carefully studying the trial transcripts, Sally is convinced that any appeal would be meritless. Can Sally refuse to pursue the appeal on behalf of Harry, or would this violate Harry's right to counsel? Are there any steps that Sally must take before deciding his appeal has no basis? *See* Anders v. California, 386 U.S. 738 (1967).

10. Does an individual have a Sixth Amendment right to counsel in a misdemeanor case? Explain. *See* Argersinger v. Hamlin, 407 U.S. 25 (1972) and Scott v. Illinois, 440 U.S. 367 (1979).

11. Joey is charged with several counts of burglary and theft. He opts to represent himself at trial, and after completely botching his defense by failing to make objections and forgetting to call alibi witnesses to testify, Joey is convicted on all counts. He appeals and claims, based on *Strickland*, that his trial counsel (i.e., himself) was ineffective. Will his appeal be successful? Explain.

12. Research challenge: Locate some infamous criminals who have acted *pro se*. What were the outcomes of their respective trials? Do you think those individuals were at an advantage or disadvantage in the legal system? Explain.

13. Does a juvenile have a constitutional right to counsel in delinquency proceedings? In your opinion, should juveniles be afforded such rights? *See* In re Gault, 387 U.S. 1 (1967).

14. What is a "conflict of interest"? How can it serve to compromise an accused's Sixth Amendment right to counsel? What examples can you think of that might present a conflict of interest? *See* Cuyler v. Sullivan, 446 U.S. 335 (1980).

15. At English common law, a person on trial for a felony *was not* entitled to the assistance of counsel, while a person on trial for a misdemeanor *was* so entitled. Why do you think this seemingly backwards common law rule existed?

True/False

1. In order for the accused to waive his right to counsel, that waiver must be knowing, intelligent, and voluntary.

2. An individual is entitled to consult with counsel when in police custody prior to being interrogated, based on the Supreme Court's decision in Miranda v. Arizona.

3. Jenny has been arrested for forgery. She is taken to the police station and read her *Miranda* rights. She requests an attorney and is denied one. Jenny then confesses to police. Jenny's confession will be inadmissible at her trial based on the Exclusionary Rule because she incriminated herself after having been denied her right to counsel.

4. The standard for ineffective assistance of counsel set forth in *Strickland* applies only to counsel hired by the accused; it does not apply to counsel appointed to represent indigent accused.

5. The police have Jack in custody following his arrest for rape. Jack's attorney finds out that he is in custody and calls the police station, requesting to speak with Jack as soon as possible. The police are constitutionally obligated to inform Jack that his attorney wants to speak with him.

Multiple Choice

6. Which of the following would *not* be considered a "critical stage" for purposes of the Sixth Amendment's right to counsel?

   A. A pre-trial identification procedure where the victim is shown a mug shot of the accused
   B. An arraignment
   C. A preliminary hearing
   D. Sentencing

7. In order to show ineffective assistance of counsel under the test devised in *Strickland*, the accused must show:

   A. Incompetent representation based on an objective standard of reasonableness, or prejudice resulting in the reasonable probability that, but for counsel's errors, the outcome of the proceeding would have been different
   B. Incompetent representation based on an objective standard of reasonableness, and prejudice resulting in the reasonable probability that, but for counsel's errors, the outcome of the proceeding would have been different

    C. Incompetent representation based on an objective standard of reasonableness, or prejudice that could have had some conceivable effect on the proceeding

    D. Incompetent representation based on an objective standard of reasonableness, and prejudice that could have had some conceivable effect on the proceeding

8. The Sixth Amendment requires that an indigent defendant be provided:

    A. Competent counsel for felonies only

    B. Competent counsel for felonies and misdemeanors when a conviction results in actual imprisonment

    C. Counsel of her choice for felonies only

    D. Counsel of her choice for felonies and misdemeanors when a conviction results in actual imprisonment

9. Matt is taken into police custody after being arrested for narcotics offenses. After being informed of his *Miranda* rights, he tells a detective that he wants a lawyer and that he will not talk to police without a lawyer. The detective:

    A. Can disregard Matt's demand for a lawyer and can continue to question Matt because it is not "critical stage" of the criminal justice process

    B. Must initially respect Matt's wishes, but the detective can reinitiate questioning after about twenty minutes to try to get Matt to make a statement

    C. Must cease all questioning until either an attorney has been made available to Matt or until Matt initiates further communication with the police

    D. May continue to question Matt as long as it is about a case other than the narcotics case for which he demanded an attorney

10. An indigent defendant has a right to appointed counsel at his first appeal as of right based on which constitutional provision?

    A. The Fifth Amendment Self-Incrimination Clause

    B. The Sixth Amendment Assistance of Counsel Clause

    C. The Fourteenth Amendment Due Process Clause

    D. The Fourteenth Amendment Equal Protection Clause

8

Speedy Trial

"In all criminal prosecutions, the accused
shall enjoy the right to a speedy ... trial[.]"

—The Sixth Amendment

INTRODUCTION

The clock is ticking. So many events in the criminal justice system all come down to a ticking clock and, more importantly, when that clock stops ticking: time limits to initiate criminal prosecutions; time limits to file motions or pleadings with the court; time limits within which to note appeals. The law is all about deadlines and ensuring that individuals and the government alike respect them. Oftentimes, failure to meet a crucial deadline can spell disaster for a case.

By our very nature, some of us are procrastinators. We drag our feet and wait until the last possible minute to finish a task. Others of us pace ourselves and are of the mindset that the sooner something is accomplished the better. The Speedy Trial Clause of the Sixth Amendment represents the quintessential time limit placed on the government in a criminal case: the time within which to bring the accused to trial. It is an unequivocal message to the government that it cannot take the former road and drag its feet when prosecuting an individual for a crime. If it does, then the ultimate price may indeed be paid—the accused could go free. This chapter will examine the accused's right to a speedy trial, how courts are to determine whether that constitutional right has been violated, and the consequences the government will face for such a violation.

STUDIENT *Checklist*

Speedy Trial

1. Has the person been **accused** of a crime?

■ Has the right **attached** (i.e., has person either been **arrested** for or **formally charged** with a crime)?

2. Was the accused denied his right to a **speedy** trial?

■ Was the **length** of delay so excessive as to trigger a speedy trial analysis?

■ Was the **reason** for the delay attributable to the government?

■ Did the accused **assert** his right to a speedy trial, and if so, when?

■ Did the accused suffer any **prejudice** from the delay in his trial?

3. Did the accused receive the proper **remedy** for any violation of his right to a speedy trial?

■ Were charges against the accused **dismissed** due to a violation of his constitutional rights?

SUPREME COURT CASES

BARKER v. WINGO, 407 U.S. 514 (1972)

Although a speedy trial is guaranteed the accused by the Sixth Amendment to the Constitution, this Court has dealt with that right on infrequent occasions. . . . The Court's opinion in Kloper v. North Carolina, 386 U.S. 213, 87 S. Ct. 988, 18 L. Ed. 2d 1 (1967), established that the right to a speedy trial is "fundamental" and is imposed by the Due Process Clause of the Fourteenth Amendment on the States. See Smith v. Hooey, 393 U.S. 374, 89 S. Ct. 575, 21 L. Ed. 2d 607 (1969); Dickey v. Florida, 398 U.S. 30, 90 S. Ct. 1564, 26 L. Ed. 2d 26 (1970). As Mr. Justice Brennan pointed out in his concurring opinion in Dickey, in none of these cases have we attempted to set out the criteria by which the speedy trial right is to be judged. 398 U.S., at 40-41, 90 S. Ct. at 1570. This case compels us to make such an attempt.

I

On July 20, 1958, in Christian County, Kentucky, an elderly couple was beaten to death by intruders wielding an iron tire tool. Two suspects, Silas Manning and Willie Barker, the petitioner, were arrested shortly thereafter. The grand jury indicted them on September 15. Counsel was appointed on September 17, and Barker's trial was set for October 21. The Commonwealth had a stronger case against Manning, and it believed that Barker could not be convicted unless Manning testified against him. Manning was naturally unwilling to incriminate himself. Accordingly, on October 23, the day Silas Manning was brought to trial, the Commonwealth sought and obtained the first of what was to be a series of 16 continuances of Barker's trial. Barker made no objection. By first convicting Manning, the Commonwealth would remove possible problems of self-incrimination and would be able to assure his testimony against Barker.

The Commonwealth encountered more than a few difficulties in its prosecution of Manning. The first trial ended in a hung jury. A second trial resulted in a conviction, but the Kentucky Court of Appeals reversed because of the admission of evidence obtained by an illegal search. Manning v. Commonwealth, 328 S.W.2d 421 (1959). At his third trial, Manning was again convicted, and the Court of Appeals again reversed because the trial court had not granted a change of venue. Manning v. Commonwealth, 346 S.W.2d 755 (1961). A fourth trial resulted in a hung jury. Finally, after five trials, Manning was convicted, in March 1962, of murdering one victim, and after a sixth trial, in December 1962, he was convicted of murdering the other.

The Christian County Circuit Court holds three terms each year-in February, June, and September. Barker's initial trial was to take place in the September term of 1958. The first continuance postponed it until the February 1959 term. The second continuance was granted for one month only. Every term thereafter for as long as the Manning prosecutions were in process, the Commonwealth routinely moved to continue Barker's case to the next term. When the case was continued from the June 1959 term until the following September, Barker, having spent 10 months in jail, obtained his release by posting a $5,000 bond. He thereafter remained free in the community until his trial. Barker made no objection, through his counsel, to the first 11 continuances.

When on February 12, 1962, the Commonwealth moved for the twelfth time to continue the case until the following term, Barker's counsel filed a motion to dismiss the indictment. The motion to dismiss was denied two weeks later, and the Commonwealth's motion for a continuance was granted. The Commonwealth was granted further continuances in June 1962 and September 1962, to which Barker did not object.

In February 1963, the first term of court following Manning's final conviction, the Commonwealth moved to set Barker's trial for March 19. But on the day scheduled for trial, it again moved for a continuance until the June term. It gave as its reason the illness of the ex-sheriff who was the chief investigating officer in the case. To this continuance, Barker objected unsuccessfully.

The witness was still unable to testify in June, and the trial, which had been set for June 19, was continued again until the September term over Barker's objection. This time the court announced that the case would be dismissed for lack of prosecution if it were not tried during the next term. The final trial date was set for October 9, 1963. On that date, Barker again moved to dismiss the indictment, and this time specified that his right to a speedy trial had been violated. The motion was denied; the trial commenced with Manning as the chief prosecution witness; Barker was convicted and given a life sentence.

Barker appealed his conviction to the Kentucky Court of Appeals, relying in part on his speedy trial claim. The court affirmed. Barker v. Commonwealth, 385 S.W.2d 671 (1964). In February 1970 Barker petitioned for habeas corpus in the United States District Court for the Western District of Kentucky. Although the District Court rejected the petition without holding a hearing, the court granted petitioner leave to appeal in forma pauperis and a certificate of probable cause to appeal. On appeal, the Court of Appeals for the Sixth Circuit affirmed the District Court. 442 F.2d 1141 (1971). . . . We granted Barker's petition for certiorari. 404 U.S. 1037, 92 S. Ct. 719, 30 L. Ed. 2d 729 (1972).

II

The right to a speedy trial is generically different from any of the other rights enshrined in the Constitution for the protection of the accused. In addition to the general concern that all accused persons be treated according to decent and fair procedures, there is a societal interest in providing a speedy trial which exists separate from, and at times in opposition to, the interests of the accused. The inability of courts to provide a prompt trial has contributed to a large backlog of cases in urban courts which, among other things, enables defendants to negotiate more effectively for pleas of guilty to lesser offenses and otherwise manipulate the system. In addition, persons released on bond for lengthy periods awaiting trial have an opportunity to commit other crimes. It must be of little comfort to the residents of Christian County, Kentucky, to know that Barker was at large on bail for over four years while accused of a vicious and brutal murder of which he was ultimately convicted. Moreover, the longer an accused is free awaiting trial, the more tempting becomes his opportunity to jump bail and escape. Finally, delay between arrest and punishment may have a detrimental effect on rehabilitation.

If an accused cannot make bail, he is generally confined, as was Barker for 10 months, in a local jail. This contributes to the overcrowding and generally deplorable state of those institutions. Lengthy exposure to these conditions has a destructive effect on human character and makes the rehabilitation of the individual offender much more difficult. At times the result may even be violent rioting. Finally, lengthy pretrial detention is costly. The cost of maintaining a prisoner in jail varies from $3 to $9 per day, and this amounts to millions across the Nation. In addition, society loses wages which might have been earned, and it must often support families of incarcerated breadwinners.

A second difference between the right to speedy trial and the accused's other constitutional rights is that deprivation of the right may work to the accused's advantage. Delay is not an uncommon defense tactic. As the time between the commission of the crime and trial lengthens, witnesses may become unavailable or their memories may fade. It the witnesses support the prosecution, its case will be weakened, sometimes seriously so. And it is the prosecution which carries the burden of proof. Thus, unlike the right to counsel or the right to be free from compelled self-in-crimination, deprivation of the right to speedy trial does not per se prejudice the accused's ability to defend himself.

Finally, and perhaps most importantly, the right to speedy trial is a more vague concept than other procedural rights. It is, for example, impossible to determine with precision when the right has been denied. We cannot definitely say how long is too long in a system where justice is supposed to be swift but deliberate. As a consequence, there is no fixed point in the criminal process when the State can put the defendant to the choice of either exercising or waiving the right to a speedy trial. If, for example, the State moves for a 60-day continuance, granting that continuance is not a violation of the right to speedy trial unless the circumstances of the case are such that further delay would endanger the values the right protects. It is impossible to do more than generalize about when those circumstances exist. There is nothing comparable to the point in the process when a defendant exercises or waives his right to counsel or his right to a jury trial. . . .

The amorphous quality of the right also leads to the unsatisfactorily severe remedy of dismissal of the indictment when the right has been deprived. This is indeed a serious consequence because it means that a defendant who may be guilty of a serious crime will go free, without having been tried. Such a remedy is more serious than an exclusionary rule or a reversal for a new trial, but it is the only possible remedy.

III

Perhaps because the speedy trial right is so slippery, two rigid approaches are urged upon us as ways of eliminating some of the uncertainty which courts experience in protecting the right. The first suggestion is that we hold that the Constitution requires a criminal defendant to be offered a trial within a specified time period. The result of such a ruling would have the virtue of clarifying when the right is infringed and of simplifying courts' application of it. Recognizing this, some legislatures have enacted laws, and some courts have adopted procedural rules which more narrowly define the right. The United States Court of Appeals for the Second Circuit has promulgated rules for the district courts in that Circuit establishing that the government must be ready for trial within six months of the date of arrest, except in unusual circumstances, or the charge will be dismissed. This type of rule is also recommended by the American Bar Association.

But such a result would require this Court to engage in legislative or rule-making activity, rather than in the adjudicative process to which we should confine our efforts. We do not establish procedural rules for the States, except when mandated by the Constitution. We find no constitutional basis for holding that the speedy trial right can be quantified into a specified number of days or months. The States, of course, are free to prescribe a reasonable period consistent with constitutional standards, but our approach must be less precise.

The second suggested alternative would restrict consideration of the right to those cases in which the accused has demanded a speedy trial. Most States have recognized what is loosely referred to as the "demand rule," although eight States reject it. It is not clear, however, precisely what is meant by that term. Although every federal court of appeals that has considered the question has endorsed some kind of demand rule, some have regarded the rule within the concept of waiver, whereas others have viewed it as a factor to be weighed in assessing whether there has been a deprivation of the speedy trial right. We shall refer to the former approach as the demand-waiver doctrine. The demand-waiver doctrine provides that a defendant waives any consideration of his right to speedy trial for any period prior to which he has not demanded a trial. Under this rigid approach, a prior demand is a necessary condition to the consideration of the speedy trial right. . . .

In excepting the right to speedy trial from the rule of waiver we have applied to other fundamental rights, courts that have applied the demand-waiver rule have relied on the assumption that delay usually works for the benefit of the accused and on the absence of any readily ascertainable time in the criminal process for a defendant to be given the choice of exercising or waiving his right. But it is not necessarily true that delay benefits the defendant. There are cases in which delay appreciably harms the defendant's ability to defend himself. Moreover, a defendant confined to jail prior to trial is obviously disadvantaged by delay as is a defendant released on bail but unable to lead a normal life because of community suspicion and his own anxiety.

The nature of the speedy trial right does make it impossible to pinpoint a precise time in the process when the right must be asserted or waived, but that fact does not argue for placing the burden of protecting the right solely on defendants. A defendant has no duty to bring himself to trial; the State has that duty as well as the duty of insuring that the trial is consistent with due process. Moreover, for the reasons earlier expressed, society has a particular interest in bringing swift prosecutions, and society's representatives are the ones who should protect that interest. . . .

We reject, therefore, the rule that a defendant who fails to demand a speedy trial forever waives his right. This does not mean, however, that the defendant has no responsibility to assert his right. We think the better rule is that the defendant's assertion of or failure to assert his right to a speedy trial is one of the factors to be considered in an inquiry into the deprivation of the right. Such a formulation avoids the rigidities of the demand-waiver rule and the resulting possible unfairness in its application. It allows the trial court to exercise a judicial discretion based on the circumstances, including due consideration of any applicable formal procedural rule. It would permit, for example, a court to attach a different weight to a situation in which the defendant knowingly fails to object from a situation in which his attorney acquiesces in long delay without adequately informing his client, or from a situation in which no counsel is appointed. It would also allow a court to weigh the frequency and force of the objections as opposed to attaching significant weight to a purely pro forma objection. . . .

We, therefore, reject both of the inflexible approaches—the fixed-time period because it goes further than the Constitution requires; the demand-waiver rule because it is insensitive to a right which he have deemed fundamental. The approach we accept is a balancing test, in which the conduct of both the prosecution and the defendant are weighed.

IV

A balancing test necessarily compels courts to approach speedy trial cases on an ad hoc basis. We can do little more than identify some of the factors which courts should assess in determining whether a particular defendant has been deprived of his right. Though some might express them in different ways, we identify four such factors: Length of delay, the reason for the delay, the defendant's assertion of his right, and prejudice to the defendant. . . .

The length of the delay is to some extent a triggering mechanism. Until there is some delay which is presumptively prejudicial, there is no necessity for inquiry into the other factors that go into the balance. Nevertheless, because of the imprecision of the right to speedy trial, the length of delay that will provoke such an inquiry is necessarily dependent upon the peculiar circumstances of the case. To take but one example, the delay that can be tolerated for an ordinary street crime is considerably less than for a serious, complex conspiracy charge.

Closely related to length of delay is the reason the government assigns to justify the delay. Here, too, different weights should be assigned to different reasons. A deliberate attempt to delay the trial in order to hamper the defense should be weighted heavily against the government. A more neutral reason such as negligence or overcrowded courts should be weighted less heavily but nevertheless should be considered since the ultimate responsibility for such circumstances must rest with the government rather than with the defendant. Finally, a valid reason, such as a missing witness, should serve to justify appropriate delay.

We have already discussed the third factor, the defendant's responsibility to assert his right. Whether and how a defendant asserts his right is closely related to the other factors we have mentioned. The strength of his efforts will be affected by the length of the delay, to some extent by the reason for the delay, and most particularly by the personal prejudice, which is not always readily identifiable, that he experiences. The more serious the deprivation, the more likely a defendant is to complain. The defendant's assertion of his speedy trial right, then, is entitled to strong evidentiary weight in determining whether the defendant is being deprived of the right. We emphasize that failure to assert the right will make it difficult for a defendant to prove that he was denied a speedy trial.

A fourth factor is prejudice to the defendant. Prejudice, of course, should be assessed in the light of the interests of defendants which the speedy trial right was designed to protect. This Court has identified three such interests: (i) to prevent oppressive pretrial incarceration; (ii) to minimize anxiety and concern of the accused; and (iii) to limit the possibility that the defense will be impaired. Of these, the most serious is the last, because the inability of a defendant adequately to prepare his case skews the fairness of the entire system. If witnesses die or disappear during a delay, the prejudice is obvious. There is also prejudice if defense witnesses are unable to recall accurately events of the distant past. Loss of memory, however, is not always reflected in the record because what has been forgotten can rarely be shown. . . .

We regard none of the four factors identified above as either a necessary or sufficient condition to the finding of a deprivation of the right of speedy trial. Rather, they are related factors and must be considered together with such other circumstances as may be relevant. In sum, these factors have no talismanic qualities; courts must still engage in a difficult and sensitive balancing process. But, because we are dealing with a fundamental right of the accused, this process must be carried out with full recognition that the accused's interest in a speedy trial is specifically affirmed in the Constitution.

V

The difficulty of the task of balancing these factors is illustrated by this case, which we consider to be close. It is clear that the length of delay between arrest and trial—well over five years—was extraordinary. Only seven months of that period can be attributed to a strong excuse, the illness of the ex-sheriff who was in charge of the investigation. Perhaps some delay would have been permissible under ordinary circumstances, so that Manning could be utilized as a witness in Barker's trial, but more than four years was too long a period, particularly since a good part of that period was attributable to the Commonwealth's failure or inability to try Manning under circumstances that comported with due process.

Two counterbalancing factors, however, outweigh these deficiencies. The first is that prejudice was minimal. Of course, Barker was prejudiced to some extent by living for over four years under a cloud of suspicion and anxiety. Moreover, although he was released on bond for most of the period, he did spend 10 months in jail before trial. But there is no claim that any of Barker's witnesses died or otherwise became unavailable owing to the delay. The trial transcript indicates only two very minor lapses of memory—one on the part of a prosecution witness—which were in no way significant to the outcome.

More important than the absence of serious prejudice, is the fact that Barker did not want a speedy trial. Counsel was appointed for Barker immediately after his indictment and represented him throughout the period. No question is raised as to the competency of such counsel. Despite the fact that counsel had notice of the motions for continuances, the record shows no action whatever taken between October 21, 1958, and February 12, 1962, that could be construed as the assertion of the speedy trial right. On the latter date, in response to another motion for continuance, Barker moved to dismiss the indictment. The record does not show on what ground this motion was based, although it is clear that no alternative motion was made for an immediate trial. Instead the record strongly suggests that while he hoped to take advantage of the delay in which he had acquiesced, and thereby obtain a dismissal of the charges, he definitely did not want to be tried. . . .

We do not hold that there may never be a situation in which an indictment may be dismissed on speedy trial grounds where the defendant has failed to object to continuances. There may be a situation in which the defendant was represented by incompetent counsel, was severely prejudiced, or even cases in which the continuances were granted ex parte. But barring extraordinary circumstances, we would be reluctant indeed to rule that a defendant was denied this constitutional right on a record that strongly indicates, as does this one, that the defendant did not want a speedy trial. We hold, therefore, that Barker was not deprived of his due process right to a speedy trial.

The judgment of the Court of Appeals is affirmed.

DOGGETT v. UNITED STATES, 505 U.S. 647 (1992)

In this case we consider whether the delay of 8½ years between petitioner's indictment and arrest violated his Sixth Amendment right to a speedy trial. We hold that it did.

I

On February 22, 1980, petitioner Marc Doggett was indicted for conspiring with several others to import and distribute cocaine. See 84 Stat. 1265, 1291, as amended, 21 U.S.C. §§ 846, 963. Douglas Driver, the Drug Enforcement Administration's (DEA's) principal agent investigating the conspiracy, told the United States Marshal's Service that the DEA would oversee the apprehension of Doggett and his confederates. On March 18, 1980, two police officers set out under Driver's orders to arrest Doggett at his parents' house in Raleigh, North Carolina, only to find that he was not there. His mother told the officers that he had left for Colombia four days earlier.

To catch Doggett on his return to the United States, Driver sent word of his outstanding arrest warrant to all United States Customs stations and to a number of law enforcement organizations. He also placed Doggett's name in the Treasury Enforcement Communication System (TECS), a computer network that helps Customs agents screen people entering the country, and in the National Crime Information Center computer system, which serves similar ends. The TECS entry expired that September, however, and Doggett's name vanished from the system.

In September 1981, Driver found out that Doggett was under arrest on drug charges in Panama and, thinking that a formal extradition request would be futile, simply asked Panama to "expel" Doggett to the United States. Although the Panamanian authorities promised to comply when their own proceedings had run their course, they freed Doggett the following July and let him go to Colombia, where he stayed with an aunt for several months. On September 25, 1982, he passed unhindered through Customs in New York City and settled down in Virginia. Since his return to the United States, he has married, earned a college degree, found a steady job as a computer operations manager, lived openly under his own name, and stayed within the law.

Doggett's travels abroad had not wholly escaped the Government's notice, however. In 1982, the American Embassy in Panama told the State Department of his departure to Colombia, but that information, for whatever reason, eluded the DEA, and Agent Driver assumed for several years that his quarry was still serving time in a Panamanian prison. Driver never asked DEA officials in Panama to check into Doggett's status, and only after his own fortuitous assignment to that country in 1985 did he discover Doggett's departure for Colombia. Driver then simply assumed Doggett had settled there, and he made no effort to find out for sure or to track Doggett down, either abroad or in the United States. Thus Doggett remained lost to the American criminal justice system until

September 1988, when the Marshal's Service ran a simple credit check on several thousand people subject to outstanding arrest warrants and, within minutes, found out where Doggett lived and worked. On September 5, 1988, nearly 6 years after his return to the United States and 8½ years after his indictment, Doggett was arrested.

He naturally moved to dismiss the indictment, arguing that the Government's failure to prosecute him earlier violated his Sixth Amendment right to a speedy trial. The Federal Magistrate hearing his motion . . . contended that this failure to demonstrate particular prejudice sufficed to defeat Doggett's speedy trial claim.

The District Court took the recommendation and denied Doggett's motion. Doggett then entered a conditional guilty plea under Federal Rule of Criminal Procedure 11(a)(2), expressly reserving the right to appeal his ensuing conviction on the speedy trial claim.

A split panel of the Court of Appeals affirmed. 906 F.2d 573 (CA11 1990). . . . We granted Doggett's petition for certiorari, 498 U.S. 1119, 111 S. Ct. 1070, 112 L. Ed. 2d 1176 (1991), and now reverse.

II

The Sixth Amendment guarantees that, "[i]n all criminal prosecutions, the accused shall enjoy the right to a speedy . . . trial. . . ." On its face, the Speedy Trial Clause is written with such breadth that, taken literally, it would forbid the government to delay the trial of an "accused" for any reason at all. Our cases, however, have qualified the literal sweep of the provision by specifically recognizing the relevance of four separate enquiries: whether delay before trial was uncommonly long, whether the government or the criminal defendant is more to blame for that delay, whether, in due course, the defendant asserted his right to a speedy trial, and whether he suffered prejudice as the delay's result. See *Barker, supra*, 407 U.S., at 530, 92 S. Ct., at 2192.

The first of these is actually a double enquiry. Simply to trigger a speedy trial analysis, an accused must allege that the interval between accusation and trial has crossed the threshold dividing ordinary from "presumptively prejudicial" delay, 407 U.S., at 530-531, 92 S. Ct., at 2192, since, by definition, he cannot complain that the government has denied him a "speedy" trial if it has, in fact, prosecuted his case with customary promptness. If the accused makes this showing, the court must then consider, as one factor among several, the extent to which the delay stretches beyond the bare minimum needed to trigger judicial examination of the claim. See *id.*, at 533-534, 92 S. Ct., at 2193-2194. This latter enquiry is significant to the speedy trial analysis because, as we discuss below, the presumption that pretrial delay has prejudiced the accused intensifies over time. In this case, the extraordinary 8½ year lag between Doggett's indictment and arrest clearly suffices to trigger the speedy trial enquiry; its further significance within that enquiry will be dealt with later.

As for *Barker's* second criterion, the Government claims to have sought Doggett with diligence. The findings of the courts below are to the contrary, however, and we review trial court determinations of negligence with considerable deference. . . . For six years, the Government's investigators made no serious effort to test their progressively more questionable assumption that Doggett was living abroad, and, had they done so, they could have found him within minutes. While the Government's lethargy may have reflected no more than Doggett's relative unimportance in the world of drug trafficking, it was still findable negligence, and the finding stands.

The Government goes against the record again in suggesting that Doggett knew of his indictment years before he was arrested. Were this true, *Barker*'s third factor, concerning invocation of the right to a speedy trial, would be weighed heavily against him. But here again, the Government is trying to revisit the facts. At the hearing on Doggett's speedy trial motion, it introduced no evidence challenging the testimony of Doggett's wife, who said that she did not know of the charges until his arrest, and of his mother, who claimed not to have told him or anyone else that the police had come looking for him. . . . Thus, Doggett is not to be taxed for invoking his speedy trial right only after his arrest.

III

The Government is left, then, with its principal contention: that Doggett fails to make out a successful speedy trial claim because he has not shown precisely how he was prejudiced by the delay between his indictment and trial.

A

We have observed in prior cases that unreasonable delay between formal accusation and trial threatens to produce more than one sort of harm, including "oppressive pretrial incarceration," "anxiety and concern of the accused," and "the possibility that the [accused's] defense will be impaired" by dimming memories and loss of exculpatory evidence. *Barker*, 407 U.S., at 532, 92 S. Ct., at 2193. . . . Of these forms of prejudice, "the most serious is the last, because the inability of a defendant adequately to prepare his case skews the fairness of the entire system." 407 U.S., at 532, 92 S. Ct., at 2193. Doggett claims this kind of prejudice, and there is probably no other kind that he can claim, since he was subjected neither to pretrial detention nor, he has successfully contended, to awareness of unresolved charges against him. . . .

[T]he Government claims Doggett has failed to make any affirmative showing that the delay weakened his ability to raise specific defenses, elicit specific testimony, or produce specific items of evidence. . . . *Barker* explicitly recognized that impairment of one's defense is the most difficult form of speedy trial prejudice to prove because time's erosion of exculpatory evidence and testimony "can rarely be shown." 407 U.S., at 532, 92 S. Ct., at 2193. And though time can tilt the case against either side, see *id.*, at 521, 92 S. Ct., at 2187; *Loud Hawk, supra*, 474 U.S., at 315, 106 S. Ct., at 656, one cannot generally be sure which of them it has prejudiced more severely. Thus, we generally have to recognize that excessive delay presumptively compromises the reliability of a trial in ways that neither party can prove or, for that matter, identify. While such presumptive prejudice cannot alone carry a Sixth Amendment claim without regard to the other *Barker* criteria, see *Loud Hawk, supra*, at 315, 106 S. Ct., at 656, it is part of the mix of relevant facts, and its importance increases with the length of delay.

B

This brings us to an enquiry into the role that presumptive prejudice should play in the disposition of Doggett's speedy trial claim. We begin with hypothetical and somewhat easier cases and work our way to this one.

Our speedy trial standards recognize that pretrial delay is often both inevitable and wholly justifiable. The government may need time to collect witnesses against the accused, oppose his pretrial motions, or, if he goes into hiding, track him down. We attach great weight to such considerations when balancing them against the costs of going forward with a trial whose probative accuracy the passage of time has begun by degrees to throw into question. See *Loud Hawk, supra*, at 315-317, 106 S. Ct., at 656-657. Thus, in this case, if the Government had pursued Doggett with reasonable diligence from his indictment to his arrest, his speedy trial claim would fail. Indeed, that conclusion would generally follow as a matter of course however great the delay, so long as Doggett could not show specific prejudice to his defense.

The Government concedes, on the other hand, that Doggett would prevail if he could show that the Government had intentionally held back in its prosecution of him to gain some impermissible advantage at trial. See Brief for United States 28, n.21; Tr. of Oral Arg. 28-34 (Feb. 24, 1992). That we cannot doubt. *Barker* stressed that official bad faith in causing delay will be weighed heavily against the government, 407 U.S., at 531, 92 S. Ct., at 2192, and a bad-faith delay the length of this negligent one would present an overwhelming case for dismissal.

Between diligent prosecution and bad-faith delay, official negligence in bringing an accused to trial occupies the middle ground. While not compelling relief in every case where bad-faith delay would make relief virtually automatic, neither is negligence automatically tolerable simply because the accused cannot demonstrate exactly how it has prejudiced him. It was on this point that the Court of Appeals erred, and on the facts before us, it was reversible error.

Barker made it clear that "different weights [are to be] assigned to different reasons" for delay. *Ibid.* Although negligence is obviously to be weighed more lightly than a deliberate intent to harm the accused's defense, it still falls on the wrong side of the divide between acceptable and unacceptable reasons for delaying a criminal prosecution once it has begun. And such is the nature of the prejudice presumed that the weight we assign to official negligence compounds over time as the presumption of evidentiary prejudice grows. . . . The Government, indeed, can hardly complain too loudly, for persistent neglect in concluding a criminal prosecution indicates an uncommonly feeble interest in bringing an accused to justice; the more weight the Government attaches to securing a conviction, the harder it will try to get it.

To be sure, to warrant granting relief, negligence unaccompanied by particularized trial prejudice must have lasted longer than negligence demonstrably causing such prejudice. But even so, the Government's egregious persistence in failing to prosecute Doggett is clearly sufficient. The lag between Doggett's indictment and arrest was 8½ years, and he would have faced trial 6 years earlier than he did but for the Government's inexcusable oversights. The portion of the delay attributable to the Government's negligence far exceeds the threshold needed to state a speedy trial claim; indeed, we have called shorter delays "extraordinary." See *Barker, supra*, 407 U.S., at 533, 92 S. Ct., at 2193. When the Government's negligence thus causes delay six times as long as that generally sufficient to trigger judicial review, . . . and when the presumption of prejudice, albeit unspecified, is neither extenuated, as by the defendant's acquiescence, *e.g.*, 407 U.S., at 534-536, 92 S. Ct., at 2194-2195, nor persuasively rebutted, the defendant is entitled to relief.

IV

We reverse the judgment of the Court of Appeals and remand the case for proceedings consistent with this opinion.

CASE QUESTIONS

BARKER v. WINGO

1. While discussing the procedural history of the case, the Supreme Court noted that the district court granted Barker the right to appeal "in forma pauperis." What does this mean?

2. Why did the Court say that the right to a speedy trial is unique among the constitutional protections guaranteed to an accused?

3. What two approaches did the Court consider when formulating its standard for protecting an accused's right to a speedy trial? What was the Court's response to those approaches?

4. What factors did the Court enunciate for determining whether an accused's right to a speedy trial was violated? What weight is each factor to be given in comparison to the other factors?

5. When applying the above factors to the case before it, did the Court hold that Barker's right to a speedy trial was violated? Explain.

DOGGETT v. UNITED STATES

1. If you were one of the Supreme Court Justices considering the case, would the fact that Doggett lived a "respectable" and law abiding life during six years of his delay have any bearing on your decision? Why or why not?

2. What are some examples given by the Court of common reasons for pre-trial delay that would not weigh heavily if at all against the prosecution in a speedy trial analysis?

3. What specific prejudice did Doggett show with regard to the length of his delay? What was the Court's ultimate holding as to whether Doggett was prejudiced?

HYPOTHETICAL WITH ACCOMPANYING ANALYSIS

Hypothetical

Becky was arrested for child abuse. Because she is a single-mother on a fixed income, she was unable to make bail. Raymond DeCeet, the prosecutor assigned to the case, knew that the evidence against Becky was weak and doubted he would be able to obtain a conviction. So Raymond decided to delay the trial for as long as possible by creating bogus reasons for postponements, such as the inability to locate a key witness, a delay in laboratory test results, and illness of witnesses (none of which was the truth). Raymond felt as though justice would be served even if Becky were acquitted because she would be in jail while waiting for her trial, so she would receive some punishment for a crime he was convinced she had committed.

All of Raymond's requests were granted by the trial judge, resulting in a cumulative delay of 2½ years. On only one occasion did Becky's attorney request a postponement of the trial date when Becky, who was epileptic, had a very bad seizure and was hospitalized for several weeks. The court granted her postponement but, because of an overcrowded court docket, the next available trial date was six months later.

Becky's final trial date was set for three years after her arrest. During that three-year period Becky remained in jail, and her children were placed in foster care. Additionally, Becky lost her job and was evicted from her apartment. The public defender assigned to represent Becky complained on several occasions that her rights to a speedy trial were being denied. The trial judge, however, did nothing to investigate whether Raymond's postponements were genuine and assumed that all of Raymond's requests were made in good faith. The judge ruled, therefore, that the delay was justified.

Much to Raymond's surprise, Becky was convicted of child abuse following her jury trial. Becky is now appealing her conviction and arguing that her Sixth Amendment right to a speedy trial was violated. Analyze the likelihood that Becky will succeed.

Analysis

In order to determine whether Becky's Sixth Amendment right to a speedy trial was violated, several components must be analyzed. First, it must be determined if her right to a speedy trial had attached. If so, then it must be determined whether she was denied her right to a speedy trial by examining the four factors set forth in Barker v. Wingo. Finally, if in fact her rights were violated, then she must be afforded the remedy of a dismissal of charges against her.

With regard to the first component, the right to a speedy trial attaches when an individual becomes an "accused." This occurs either by way of an arrest or formal charges such as an indictment. Because Becky had been arrested for child abuse, her arrest qualified her as an "accused," and her date of arrest set in motion the speedy trial clock.

Next, an analysis must be undertaken of the four factors set forth by the Supreme Court in Barker v. Wingo in order to determine if her right to a speedy trial was violated. In considering those factors it is helpful to list them in a chart format while applying the specific facts of this case to each particular factor:

Factor	Weighed against . . .	Explanation
Length of delay	2½ years: Prosecution 6 months: Defense	See "reason for delay" below
Reason for delay	Prosecution:	1) Request for postponement: missing witness 2) Request for postponement: laboratory results delayed 3) Request for postponement: ill witnesses

Factor	Weighed against . . .	Explanation
	Defense:	Request for postponement: accused hospitalized due to seizure
Accused's assertion of right	Prosecution	Accused, through her counsel, complained on "several occasions" about denial of right to a speedy trial
Prejudice to the accused	Prosecution	1) Accused incarcerated entire time while awaiting trial; 2) Children placed in foster care; 3) Lost job; and 4) Evicted from apartment.

An analysis of the above chart indicates the following: The overall length of delay between the period of accusation and trial was three years. This three-year period is arguably long enough to satisfy the "triggering mechanism" described in Barker to engage in further analysis. When examining the reasons for the delay, clearly the government bears the large majority of the burden for the length of delay. Of the three-year delay, 2½ years is the fault of the prosecutor, not only for requesting three postponements but for making those requests in bad faith and blatantly lying to the court to in order to delay Becky's trial. Additionally, the fact that the trial judge made no attempt to verify the prosecution's requests weighs against the government. Becky did, however, request one postponement. Even though that must be weighed against her, it would likely not be done so heavily because it was a genuine medical emergency through no fault of her own. Furthermore, the facts indicate she was only hospitalized for a "few weeks" and thus she possibly could have gone to trial sooner, but because of an overcrowded court docket, a six-month postponement was required. Therefore, it is not entirely clear how much of those six months should actually be weighed against her. Becky's counsel complained to the court on "several occasions" that her right to a speedy trial was being denied, but the trial court granted no relief. Thus, Becky clearly asserted her right and did so more than once. Finally, Becky unquestionably suffered significant prejudice from her excessive delay. Her freedom was curtailed because she was incarcerated for the three years while awaiting trial, and she suffered serious consequences in her personal life including the removal of her children from her custody, loss of her job, and eviction from her residence. Therefore, when weighing the four factors from Barker v. Wingo it is clear that Becky was denied her right to a speedy trial.

In sum, the Sixth Amendment was drafted to prevent the very type of harm and governmental manipulation that occurred in this case. Raymond, an over-zealous prosecutor, decided to manipulate the law so that he could inflict a punishment upon Becky that he felt was justified. Raymond's tactics cannot be condoned, and intentional governmental delay cannot be tolerated. Because Becky's Sixth Amendment rights were violated, the only appropriate remedy is a dismissal of all charges against her.

Mark was suspected of killing his girlfriend on Valentine's Day, 2006, after a heated argument. Investigators, however, were unable to locate the victim's body and had little more than a "hunch" to go on. After persistent efforts for over a year, police finally had probable cause and they arrested Mark for murder on May 1, 2007. Mark's trial date was set for September 1, 2007. Mark was denied bail following a hearing, and he therefore remained incarcerated. Two weeks before the September 1st trial date, Paul the prosecutor asked for a postponement because the lead detective on the case had been in a car accident and would not be available to testify for at least two or three months. The judge agreed to the postponement and set the new trial date for January 1, 2008. In late December of 2007, however, Paul left the prosecutor's office for a new job, and Richard, a "rookie" attorney in the prosecutor's office, was assigned all of Paul's outstanding cases. Richard was a bit frazzled by the added responsibilities, and he immediately requested a postponement of Mark's trial so that he could familiarize himself with the case. The judge granted the postponement and set the third trial date for March 1, 2008. A few days before the March trial date, however, two judges in that particular court became ill and, therefore, the court dockets became backlogged for a period of time. Mark's trial was continued until August 1, 2008. Meanwhile, Mark was less than thrilled that he was behind bars the entire time while awaiting his trial. On July 27, just four days before his scheduled trial date, Mark broke out of the detention facility where he was being held. He was on the run for eight months before he was eventually caught. Upon his apprehension, the trial judge set the trial date for May 1, 2009. The day before the trial date, Richard had an unexpected death in the family and requested a postponement. At that point Mark complained that he was not being given a speedy trial. The court, although granting the postponement, stated that no more postponements would be given and set trial for June 1. Mark's trial began as scheduled on June 1, 2009.

Discuss whether Mark's Sixth Amendment right to a speedy trial was violated. Be sure to address each of the four factors set forth in Barker v. Wingo. You may want to draft a chart similar to the one in the Hypothetical with Accompanying Analysis to aid in your analysis and discussion of the issue.

1. Research challenge: Research law in your jurisdiction to determine what speedy trial statutes, if any, have been enacted by the legislature. Be sure to address issues such as (1) whether a specific time limit is set within which an accused must be brought to trial; (2) at what point the speedy trial clock begins to run; (3) what happens if a trial goes beyond that statutory deadline; (4) factors that may have been set forth for determining if a speedy trial violation occurred; and (5) remedies provided to the accused for any violations of the laws.

2. What are the underlying purposes of the right to a speedy trial?

3. In your opinion, is there any such thing as a trial that is *too* speedy? In other words, can you think of circumstances under which a criminal trial could take place too quickly and actually prove to be a disadvantage to the accused? Explain.

4. Research challenge: Revisit the case dealing with the 1963 murder of Medgar Evers by Byron de la Beckwith described in Discussion Question 5 of Chapter 5, *supra*. In that case, de la Beckwith was brought to trial a third time in 1994 and convicted. On appeal, he argued that his Sixth Amendment right to a speedy trial was violated by the thirty-year delay in prosecution. What was the holding of the Supreme Court of Mississippi with regard to de la Beckwith's constitutional challenge? What was the U.S. Supreme Court's response?

5. Is the right to a speedy trial the same thing as a criminal "statute of limitations"? Why or why not?

6. Can you think of any circumstances under which the denial of a speedy trial could actually work to the accused's advantage? Explain. *See, e.g.*, Dickey v. Florida, 398 U.S. 30 (1970) and Ponzi v. Fessenden, 258 U.S. 254 (1922).

7. Bob is arrested for robbery, but the charges against him are dropped. Six months later, police obtain new evidence against him and the prosecutor reinitiates the robbery charges. Is that six-month time period between when all charges were dropped and then reinitiated to be weighed against the prosecution in a speedy trial analysis? Explain. *See* United States v. MacDonald, 456 U.S. 1 (1982).

8. Revisit the Hypothetical with Accompanying Analysis from this chapter. If Becky had been acquitted of all charges against her, would she have any legal remedies against the government and, more specifically, Raymond for the time period she spent in jail while awaiting her trial? Why or why not? Do you think she should have the right to some remedy?

True/False

1. Most state and federal jurisdictions have enacted their own laws which set specific time limits within which an accused must be brought to trial.

2. The Supreme Court in Barker v. Wingo expressly approved of the "Demand-Waiver Doctrine," whereby the speedy trial clock does not begin to run until the accused demands a trial.

3. *Any* extensive pretrial delay will be held against the prosecution when considering whether the accused was deprived of his right to a speedy trial.

4. The Sixth Amendment's Speedy Trial Clause also protects the accused from delays between when he is first suspected of a crime and when he is arrested.

5. Barker v. Wingo declared that of the four factors for analyzing a speedy trial claim, the "triggering mechanism" for the analysis is the potential prejudice to the accused.

Multiple Choice

6. Which of the following is *not* one of the factors set forth in Barker v. Wingo for determining whether the accused was denied his right to a speedy trial?

   A. Length of delay
   B. Prejudice to the accused
   C. Seriousness of the crime with which the accused is charged
   D. Reason for the delay

7. According to the Supreme Court, what is the accused's remedy for a violation of his Sixth Amendment right to a speedy trial?

   A. Dismissal of charges with the prosecution's ability to reinstate charges
   B. Dismissal of charges with no possibility of the prosecution reinitiating charges
   C. "Reimbursement" of the accused upon sentencing by deducting the number of days from his sentence that his trial was needlessly delayed
   D. The Supreme Court has established no specific remedy, but it has said a judge may take into account any violation of the right to a speedy trial when sentencing the accused for his crimes.

8. When does the right to a speedy trial attach?

   A. When the person is arrested or formal charges are brought
   B. When the person is arraigned and formally enters a plea

C. When counsel first enters his appearance on behalf of the person
D. When the person commits the crime

9. Which of the following would be an example of prejudice suffered by the accused as a result of a delay in his trial?

   A. A defense witness can no longer be located due to the delay.
   B. The accused was incarcerated the entire time while awaiting trial.
   C. The accused suffered anxiety while waiting for a resolution of the charges against him.
   D. All of the above are types of prejudice an accused could endure because of an excessive trial delay.

10. Steven is arrested for rape. His trial is continually delayed for over two years due to a backlog of court cases. In a speedy trial analysis, which side should this delay be weighed against?

    A. The prosecution, because it is the government's responsibility to bring the accused to trial in a speedy manner.
    B. The accused, because if he had not committed the rape in the first place he wouldn't be in the court system.
    C. It is within the sole discretion of the trial judge to weigh it against either side.
    D. Neither side, because a backlog of court cases is simply an imperfection of the criminal justice system for which neither side can be directly faulted.

9

Jury Trial

> "In all criminal prosecutions, the accused shall enjoy the right to a . . . trial, by an impartial jury of the State and district wherein the crime shall have been committed. . . ."
>
> **—The Sixth Amendment**

INTRODUCTION

A roll of the dice. A man's freedom, possibly his life, but certainly his future, rests in the hands of a group of strangers who are given the weighty task of deciding his fate. Our criminal justice system prides itself upon the guarantee of a jury trial, and jurors have a very important job without question. Nonetheless, some critics have argued that a jury determining a defendant's guilt or innocence essentially boils down to a roll of the dice.

But is the right to a jury trial little more than a constitutional gamble? The framers of the Constitution certainly didn't think so. Of all of the criminal protections discussed in this text, the right to a jury trial is the *only* one expressly mentioned twice: once in Article III, Section 2 of the Constitution, and again in the Sixth Amendment. (The right to a jury trial in civil cases is also explicitly preserved by the Seventh Amendment.) The Equal Protection Clause of the Fourteenth Amendment also plays a pivotal role in ensuring that a jury is comprised of members representative of the community. Furthermore, along with federal authority, each state has enacted legislation further detailing an individual's right to a jury trial.

The right to a trial by jury includes several key issues, such as determining whether an individual is entitled to a jury trial; ensuring the jury is selected in a manner consistent with the Constitution; guarding against publicity that could taint a juror's ability to remain unbiased; and determining, when applicable, whether the right to a jury trial has been properly waived by the accused. Because the right to a jury trial is very basic in nature, a proper understanding of it requires a multifaceted explanation.

STURENT *Checklist*

Jury Trial

1. Jury **applicability**:

■ Is the crime a **non-petty offense** that is **punishable** by more than **six months imprisonment**?

2. Jury **composition**:

■ Was the jury composed of at least **six** individuals who are each at least **eighteen years of age**?

3. Jury **impartiality**:

■ Was the jury able to put aside any **preconceived impressions and opinions** and render a verdict based solely on the **evidence presented** in court?

■ Did **pre-trial publicity** create a **presumption** that a juror could not be impartial after considering:
   ☐ The juror's responses during **voir dire**;
   ☐ The **nature** of the pretrial publicity; and
   ☐ The **time gap** between the height of publicity and trial?

4. Jury **selection**:

■ Was a **jury pool** selected that represents a **fair cross-section** of the community?

■ Was a jury **panel** assembled from the jury pool?

■ Did attorneys and/or the trial judge **voir dire** the panel to select members of the jury?
   ☐ Did attorneys properly exercise any **challenges for cause** in dismissing potential jurors?
   ☐ Did attorneys properly exercise any **peremptory challenges** in dismissing potential jurors?

■ Was the **Equal Protection Clause** potentially violated during the jury selection process?
   ☐ Did the challenging party make **a prima facie case** that the opposition **systematically excluded** members of a **cognizable group** from the jury panel?
   ☐ Did the opposing side offer a **non-discriminatory** reason for the exclusion?
   ☐ Did the **trial judge** consider all evidence and determine whether the challenging party adequately alleged **purposeful discrimination**?

5. Jury **waiver**:

■ Did the accused **expressly** and **intelligently waive** her right to a jury trial?

■ Did the **prosecutor consent** and did the **court approve** of the waiver?

6. Jury **verdict**:

■ Was the verdict either **unanimous** or one of the **non-unanimous** verdicts approved by the Court (i.e., 11-1; 10-2; or 9-3)?

■ Did a jury determine any fact (other than a prior conviction) that **increases the penalty beyond the statutory maximum**?

SUPREME COURT CASES

BATSON v. KENTUCKY, 476 U.S. 79 (1986)

This case requires us to reexamine that portion of *Swain v. Alabama,* 380 U.S. 202, 85 S. Ct. 824, 13 L. Ed. 2d 759 (1965), concerning the evidentiary burden placed on a criminal defendant who claims that he has been denied equal protection through the State's use of peremptory challenges to exclude members of his race from the petit jury.

I

Petitioner, a black man, was indicted in Kentucky on charges of second-degree burglary and receipt of stolen goods. On the first day of trial in Jefferson Circuit Court, the judge conducted *voir dire* examination of the venire, excused certain jurors for cause, and permitted the parties to exercise peremptory challenges. The prosecutor used his peremptory challenges to strike all four black persons on the venire, and a jury composed only of white persons was selected. Defense counsel moved to discharge the jury before it was sworn on the ground that the prosecutor's removal of the black veniremen violated petitioner's rights under the Sixth and Fourteenth Amendments to a jury drawn from a cross section of the community, and under the Fourteenth Amendment to equal protection of the laws. Counsel requested a hearing on his motion. Without expressly ruling on the request for a hearing, the trial judge observed that the parties were entitled to use their peremptory challenges to "strike anybody they want to." The judge then denied petitioner's motion, reasoning that the cross-section requirement applies only to selection of the venire and not to selection of the petit jury itself.

The jury convicted petitioner on both counts. . . .

The Supreme Court of Kentucky affirmed. . . . We granted certiorari, 471 U.S. 1052, 105 S. Ct. 2111, 85 L. Ed. 2d 476 (1985), and now reverse.

II

In *Swain v. Alabama,* this Court recognized that a "State's purposeful or deliberate denial to Negroes on account of race of participation as jurors in the administration of justice violates the Equal Protection Clause." 380 U.S., at 203-204, 85 S. Ct., at 826-27. This principle has been "consistently and repeatedly" reaffirmed, *id.,* at 204, 85 S. Ct., at 827, in numerous decisions of this Court both preceding and following *Swain.* We reaffirm the principle today.

A

More than a century ago, the Court decided that the State denies a black defendant equal protection of the laws when it puts him on trial before a jury from which members of his race have been purposefully excluded. *Strauder v. West Virginia,* 10 Otto 303, 100 U.S. 303, 25 L. Ed. 664 (1880). That decision laid the foundation for the Court's unceasing efforts to eradicate racial discrimination in the procedures used to select the venire from which individual jurors are drawn. In *Strauder,* the Court explained that the central concern of the recently ratified Fourteenth Amendment was to put an end to governmental discrimination on account of race. *Id.,* at 306-307. Exclusion of black citizens from service as jurors constitutes a primary example of the evil the Fourteenth Amendment was designed to cure.

In holding that racial discrimination in jury selection offends the Equal Protection Clause, the Court in *Strauder* recognized, however, that a defendant has no right to a "petit jury composed in whole or in part of persons of his own race." *Id.,* at 305. "The number of our races and nationalities stands in the way of evolution of such a conception" of the demand of equal protection. *Akins v. Texas,* 325 U.S. 398, 403, 65 S. Ct. 1276, 1279, 89 L. Ed. 1692 (1945). But the defendant does have the right to be tried by a jury whose members are selected pursuant to nondiscriminatory criteria. *Martin v. Texas,* 200 U.S. 316, 321, 26 S. Ct. 338, 339, 50 L. Ed. 497 (1906); *Ex parte Virginia,* 10 Otto 339, 100 U.S. 339, 345, 25 L. Ed. 676 345 (1880). The Equal Protection Clause guarantees the defendant that the State will not exclude members of his race from the jury venire on account of race, *Strauder, supra,* 100 U.S., at 305, or on the false assumption that members of his race as a group are not qualified to serve as jurors, see *Norris v. Alabama,* 294 U.S. 587, 599, 55 S. Ct. 579, 584, 79 L. Ed. 1074 (1935); *Neal v. Delaware,* 13 Otto 370, 397, 103 U.S. 370, 397, 26 L. Ed. 567 (1881).

Purposeful racial discrimination in selection of the venire violates a defendant's right to equal protection because it denies him the protection that a trial by jury is intended to secure. "The very idea of a jury is a body . . . composed of the peers or equals of the person whose rights it is selected or summoned to determine; that is, of his neighbors, fellows, associates, persons having the same legal status in society as that which he holds." *Strauder, supra,* 100 U.S., at 308; see *Carter v. Jury Comm'n of Greene County,* 396 U.S. 320, 330, 90 S. Ct. 518, 524, 24 L. Ed. 2d 549 (1970). The petit jury has occupied a central position in our system of justice by safeguarding a person accused of crime against the arbitrary exercise of power by prosecutor or judge. *Duncan v. Louisiana,* 391 U.S. 145, 156, 88 S. Ct. 1444, 1451, 20 L. Ed. 2d 491 (1968). Those on the venire must be "indifferently chosen," to secure the defendant's right under the Fourteenth Amendment to "protection of life and liberty against race or color prejudice." *Strauder, supra,* 100 U.S., at 309.

Racial discrimination in selection of jurors harms not only the accused whose life or liberty they are summoned to try. Competence to serve as a juror ultimately depends on an assessment of individual qualifications and ability impartially to consider evidence presented at a trial. See *Thiel v. Southern Pacific Co.,* 328 U.S. 217, 223-224, 66 S. Ct. 984, 987-88, 90 L. Ed. 1181 (1946). A person's race simply "is unrelated to his fitness as a juror." *Id.,* at 227, 66 S. Ct., at 989 (Frankfurter, J., dissenting). As long ago as *Strauder,* therefore, the Court recognized that by denying a person participation in jury service on account of his race, the State unconstitutionally discriminated against the excluded juror. 100 U.S., at 308; see *Carter v. Jury Comm'n of Greene County, supra,* 396 U.S., at 329-330, 90 S. Ct., at 523-524; *Neal v. Delaware, supra,* 103 U.S., at 386.

The harm from discriminatory jury selection extends beyond that inflicted on the defendant and the excluded juror to touch the entire community. Selection procedures that purposefully exclude black persons from juries undermine public confidence in the fairness of our system of justice. See *Ballard v. United States,* 329 U.S. 187, 195, 67 S. Ct. 261, 265, 91 L. Ed. 181 (1946); *McCray v. New York,* 461 U.S. 961, 968, 103 S. Ct. 2438, 2443, 77 L. Ed. 2d 1322 (1983) (Marshall, J., dissenting from denial of certiorari). Discrimination within the judicial system is most pernicious because it is "a stimulant to that race prejudice which is an impediment to securing to [black citizens] that equal justice which the law aims to secure to all others." *Strauder,* 100 U.S., at 308.

B

In *Strauder,* the Court invalidated a state statute that provided that only white men could serve as jurors. *Id.,* at 305. We can be confident that no State now has such a law. The Constitution requires, however, that we look beyond the face of the statute defining juror qualifications and also consider challenged selection practices to afford "protection against action of the State through its administrative officers in effecting the prohibited discrimination." *Norris v. Alabama, supra,* 294 U.S., at 589, 55 S. Ct. 579, 580, 79 L. Ed. 1074; see *Hernandez v. Texas,* 347 U.S. 475, 478-479, 74 S. Ct. 667, 670-71, 98 L. Ed. 866 (1954); *Ex parte Virginia, supra,* 100 U.S., at 346-347. Thus, the Court has found a denial of equal protection where the procedures implementing a neutral statute operated to exclude persons from the venire on racial grounds, and has made clear that the Constitution prohibits all forms of purposeful racial discrimination in selection of jurors. While decisions of this Court have been concerned largely with discrimination during selection of the venire, the principles announced there also forbid discrimination on account of race in selection of the petit jury. Since the Fourteenth Amendment protects an accused throughout the proceedings bringing him to justice, *Hill v. Texas,* 316 U.S. 400, 406, 62 S. Ct. 1159, 1162, 86 L. Ed. 1559 (1942), the State may not draw up its jury lists pursuant to neutral procedures but then resort to discrimination at "other stages in the selection process,". . . .

Accordingly, the component of the jury selection process at issue here, the State's privilege to strike individual jurors through peremptory challenges, is subject to the commands of the Equal Protection Clause. Although a prosecutor ordinarily is entitled to exercise permitted peremptory challenges "for any reason at all, as long as that reason is related to his view concerning the outcome" of the case to be tried, *United States v. Robinson,* 421 F. Supp. 467, 473 (Conn. 1976), mandamus granted *sub nom. United States v. Newman,* 549 F.2d 240 (CA2 1977), the Equal Protection Clause forbids the prosecutor to challenge potential jurors solely on account of their race or on the assumption that black jurors as a group will be unable impartially to consider the State's case against a black defendant.

III

The principles announced in *Strauder* never have been questioned in any subsequent decision of this Court. Rather, the Court has been called upon repeatedly to review the application of those principles to particular facts. A recurring question in these cases, as in any case alleging a violation of the Equal Protection Clause, was whether the defendant had met his burden of proving purposeful discrimination on the part of the State. *Whitus v. Georgia,* 385 U.S. 545, 550, 87 S. Ct. 643, 646-647, 17 L. Ed. 2d 599 (1967); *Hernandez v. Texas, supra,* 347 U.S., at 478-481, 74 S. Ct., at 670-672; *Akins v. Texas,* 325 U.S., at 403-404, 65 S. Ct., at 1279; *Martin v. Texas,* 200 U.S. 316, 26 S. Ct. 338, 50 L. Ed. 497 (1906). That question also was at the heart of the portion of *Swain v. Alabama* we reexamine today.

A

Swain required the Court to decide, among other issues, whether a black defendant was denied equal protection by the State's exercise of peremptory challenges to exclude members of his race from the petit jury. 380 U.S., at 209-210, 85 S. Ct., at 830. The record in *Swain* showed that the prosecutor had used the State's peremptory challenges to strike the six black persons included on the petit jury venire. *Id.*, at 210, 85 S. Ct., at 830. While rejecting the defendant's claim for failure to prove purposeful discrimination, the Court nonetheless indicated that the Equal Protection Clause placed some limits on the State's exercise of peremptory challenges. *Id.*, at 222-224, 85 S. Ct., at 837-838.

The Court sought to accommodate the prosecutor's historical privilege of peremptory challenge free of judicial control, *id.*, at 214-220, 85 S. Ct., at 832-836, and the constitutional prohibition on exclusion of persons from jury service on account of race, *id.*, at 222-224, 85 S. Ct., at 837-838. While the Constitution does not confer a right to peremptory challenges, *id.*, at 219, 85 S. Ct., at 835 (citing *Stilson v. United States,* 250 U.S. 583, 586, 40 S. Ct. 28, 29-30, 63 L. Ed. 1154 (1919)), those challenges traditionally have been viewed as one means of assuring the selection of a qualified and unbiased jury, 380 U.S., at 219, 85 S. Ct., at 835. To preserve the peremptory nature of the prosecutor's challenge, the Court in *Swain* declined to scrutinize his actions in a particular case by relying on a presumption that he properly exercised the State's challenges. *Id.*, at 221-222, 85 S. Ct., at 836-837.

The Court went on to observe, however, that a State may not exercise its challenges in contravention of the Equal Protection Clause. It was impermissible for a prosecutor to use his challenges to exclude blacks from the jury "for reasons wholly unrelated to the outcome of the particular case on trial" or to deny to blacks "the same right and opportunity to participate in the administration of justice enjoyed by the white population." *Id.*, at 224, 85 S. Ct., at 838. Accordingly, a black defendant could make out a prima facie case of purposeful discrimination on proof that the peremptory challenge system was "being perverted" in that manner. *Ibid.* For example, an inference of purposeful discrimination would be raised on evidence that a prosecutor, "in case after case, whatever the circumstances, whatever the crime and whoever the defendant or the victim may be, is responsible for the removal of Negroes who have been selected as qualified jurors by the jury commissioners and who have survived challenges for cause, with the result that no Negroes ever serve on petit juries." *Id.*, at 223, 85 S. Ct., at 837. Evidence offered by the defendant in *Swain* did not meet that standard. While the defendant showed that prosecutors in the jurisdiction had exercised their strikes to exclude blacks from the jury, he offered no proof of the circumstances under which prosecutors were responsible for striking black jurors beyond the facts of his own case. *Id.*, at 224-228, 85 S. Ct., at 838-840.

A number of lower courts following the teaching of *Swain* reasoned that proof of repeated striking of blacks over a number of cases was necessary to establish a violation of the Equal Protection Clause. Since this interpretation of *Swain* has placed on defendants a crippling burden of proof, prosecutors' peremptory challenges are now largely immune from constitutional scrutiny. For reasons that follow, we reject this evidentiary formulation as inconsistent with standards that have been developed since *Swain* for assessing a prima facie case under the Equal Protection Clause.

B

Since the decision in *Swain,* we have explained that our cases concerning selection of the venire reflect the general equal protection principle that the "invidious quality" of governmental action claimed to be racially discriminatory "must ultimately be traced to a racially discriminatory purpose." *Washington v. Davis,* 426 U.S. 229, 240, 96 S. Ct. 2040, 2048, 48 L. Ed. 2d 597 (1976). As in any equal protection case, the "burden is, of course," on the defendant who alleges discriminatory selection of the venire "to prove the existence of purposeful discrimination." *Whitus v. Georgia,* 385 U.S., at 550, 87 S. Ct., at 646-47 (citing *Tarrance v. Florida,* 188 U.S. 519, 23 S. Ct. 402, 47 L. Ed. 572 (1903)). In deciding if the defendant has carried his burden of persuasion, a court must undertake "a sensitive inquiry into such circumstantial and direct evidence of intent as may be available." *Arlington Heights v. Metropolitan Housing Development Corp.,* 429 U.S. 252, 266, 97 S. Ct. 555, 564, 50 L. Ed. 2d 450 (1977). . . .

Once the defendant makes the requisite showing, the burden shifts to the State to explain adequately the racial exclusion. *Alexander v. Louisiana,* 405 U.S., at 632, 92 S. Ct., at 1226. The State cannot meet this burden on mere general assertions that its officials did not discriminate or that they properly performed their official duties. See *Alexander v. Louisiana, supra,* 405 U.S., at 632, 92 S. Ct., at 1226; *Jones v. Georgia,* 389 U.S. 24, 25, 88 S. Ct. 4, 5, 19 L. Ed. 2d 25 (1967). Rather, the State must demonstrate that "permissible racially neutral selection criteria and procedures have produced the monochromatic result." *Alexander v. Louisiana, supra,* at 632, 92 S. Ct., at 1226; see *Washington v. Davis, supra,* 426 U.S., at 241, 96 S. Ct., at 2048.

The showing necessary to establish a prima facie case of purposeful discrimination in selection of the venire may be discerned in this Court's decisions. E.g., *Castaneda v. Partida,* 430 U.S. 482, 494-495, 97 S. Ct. 1272, 1280, 51 L. Ed. 2d 498 (1977); *Alexander v. Louisiana, supra,* 405 U.S., at 631-632, 92 S. Ct., at 1225-1226. The defendant initially must show that he is a member of a racial group capable of being singled out for differential treatment. *Castaneda v. Partida, supra,* 430 U.S., at 494, 97 S. Ct., at 1280. In combination with that evidence, a defendant may then make a prima facie case by proving that in the particular jurisdiction members of his race have not been summoned for jury service over an extended period of time. *Id.,* at 494, 97 S. Ct., at 1280. Proof of systematic exclusion from the venire raises an inference of purposeful discrimination because the "result bespeaks discrimination." *Hernandez v. Texas,* 347 U.S., at 482, 74 S. Ct., at 672-73; see *Arlington Heights v. Metropolitan Housing Development Corp., supra,* 429 U.S., at 266, 97 S. Ct., at 564.

Since the ultimate issue is whether the State has discriminated in selecting the defendant's venire, however, the defendant may establish a prima facie case "in other ways than by evidence of long-continued unexplained absence" of members of his race "from many panels." . . .

Thus, since the decision in *Swain,* this Court has recognized that a defendant may make a prima facie showing of purposeful racial discrimination in selection of the venire by relying solely on the facts concerning its selection *in his case.* These decisions are in accordance with the proposition, articulated in *Arlington Heights v. Metropolitan Housing Department Corp.,* that "a consistent pattern of official racial discrimination" is not "a necessary predicate to a violation of the Equal Protection Clause. A single invidiously discriminatory governmental act" is not "immunized by the absence of such discrimination in the making of other comparable decisions." 429 U.S., at 266, n.14, 97 S. Ct., at 564, n.14. . . .

C

The standards for assessing a prima facie case in the context of discriminatory selection of the venire have been fully articulated since *Swain.* See

Castaneda v. Partida, supra, 430 U.S., at 494-495, 97 S. Ct., at 1280; *Washington v. Davis,* 426 U.S., at 241-242, 96 S. Ct., at 2048-2049; *Alexander v. Louisiana, supra,* 405 U.S., at 629-631, 92 S. Ct., at 1224-1226. These principles support our conclusion that a defendant may establish a prima facie case of purposeful discrimination in selection of the petit jury solely on evidence concerning the prosecutor's exercise of peremptory challenges at the defendant's trial. To establish such a case, the defendant first must show that he is a member of a cognizable racial group, *Castaneda v. Partida, supra,* 430 U.S., at 494, 97 S. Ct., at 1280, and that the prosecutor has exercised peremptory challenges to remove from the venire members of the defendant's race. Second, the defendant is entitled to rely on the fact, as to which there can be no dispute, that peremptory challenges constitute a jury selection practice that permits "those to discriminate who are of a mind to discriminate." *Avery v. Georgia,* 345 U.S., at 562, 73 S. Ct., at 892. Finally, the defendant must show that these facts and any other relevant circumstances raise an inference that the prosecutor used that practice to exclude the veniremen from the petit jury on account of their race. This combination of factors in the empanelling of the petit jury, as in the selection of the venire, raises the necessary inference of purposeful discrimination.

In deciding whether the defendant has made the requisite showing, the trial court should consider all relevant circumstances. For example, a "pattern" of strikes against black jurors included in the particular venire might give rise to an inference of discrimination. Similarly, the prosecutor's questions and statements during *voir dire* examination and in exercising his challenges may support or refute an inference of discriminatory purpose. These examples are merely illustrative. We have confidence that trial judges, experienced in supervising *voir dire,* will be able to decide if the circumstances concerning the prosecutor's use of peremptory challenges creates a prima facie case of discrimination against black jurors.

Once the defendant makes a prima facie showing, the burden shifts to the State to come forward with a neutral explanation for challenging black jurors. Though this requirement imposes a limitation in some cases on the full peremptory character of the historic challenge, we emphasize that the prosecutor's explanation need not rise to the level justifying exercise of a challenge for cause. See *McCray v. Abrams,* 750 F.2d, at 1132; *Booker v. Jabe,* 775 F.2d 762, 773 (CA6 1985), cert. pending, No. 85-1028. But the prosecutor may not rebut the defendant's prima facie case of discrimination by stating merely that he challenged jurors of the defendant's race on the assumption—or his intuitive judgment—that they would be partial to the defendant because of their shared race. . . . Just as the Equal Protection Clause forbids the States to exclude black persons from the venire on the assumption that blacks as a group are unqualified to serve as jurors, *supra,* at 1716, so it forbids the States to strike black veniremen on the assumption that they will be biased in a particular case simply because the defendant is black. The core guarantee of equal protection, ensuring citizens that their State will not discriminate on account of race, would be meaningless were we to approve the exclusion of jurors on the basis of such assumptions, which arise solely from the jurors' race. Nor may the prosecutor rebut the defendant's case merely by denying that he had a discriminatory motive or "affirm[ing] [his] good faith in making individual selections." *Alexander v. Louisiana,* 405 U.S., at 632, 92 S. Ct., at 1226. If these general assertions were accepted as rebutting a defendant's prima facie case, the Equal Protection Clause "would be but a vain and illusory requirement." *Norris v. Alabama, supra,* 294 U.S. at 598, 55 S. Ct., at 583-84. The prosecutor therefore must articulate a neutral explanation related to the particular case to be tried. The trial court then will have the duty to determine if the defendant has established purposeful discrimination. . . .

V

In this case, petitioner made a timely objection to the prosecutor's removal of all black persons on the venire. Because the trial court flatly rejected the objection without requiring the prosecutor to give an explanation for his action, we remand this case for further proceedings. If the trial court decides that the facts establish, prima facie, purposeful discrimination and the prosecutor does not come forward with a neutral explanation for his action, our precedents require that petitioner's conviction be reversed. E.g., *Whitus v. Georgia,* 385 U.S., at 549-550, 87 S. Ct., at 646-47; *Hernandez v. Texas,* 347 U.S., at 482, 74 S. Ct., at 672-673; *Patton v. Mississippi,* 332 U.S., at 469, 68 S. Ct., at 187.

It is so ordered. . . .

BLAKELY v. WASHINGTON, 542 U.S. 296 (2004)

Petitioner Ralph Howard Blakely, Jr., pleaded guilty to the kidnaping of his estranged wife. The facts admitted in his plea, standing alone, supported a maximum sentence of 53 months. Pursuant to state law, the court imposed an "exceptional" sentence of 90 months after making a judicial determination that he had acted with "deliberate cruelty." App. 40, 49. We consider whether this violated petitioner's Sixth Amendment right to trial by jury.

I

Petitioner married his wife Yolanda in 1973. He was evidently a difficult man to live with, having been diagnosed at various times with psychological and personality disorders including paranoid schizophrenia. His wife ultimately filed for divorce. In 1998, he abducted her from their orchard home in Grant County, Washington, binding her with duct tape and forcing her at knifepoint into a wooden box in the bed of his pickup truck. In the process, he implored her to dismiss the divorce suit and related trust proceedings.

When the couple's 13-year-old son Ralphy returned home from school, petitioner ordered him to follow in another car, threatening to harm Yolanda with a shotgun if he did not do so. Ralphy escaped and sought help when they stopped at a gas station, but petitioner continued on with Yolanda to a friend's house in Montana. He was finally arrested after the friend called the police.

The State charged petitioner with first-degree kidnaping, Wash. Rev. Code Ann. § 9A.40.020(1) (2000). Upon reaching a plea agreement, however, it reduced the charge to second-degree kidnaping involving domestic violence and use of a firearm, see §§ 9A.40.030(1), 10.99.020(3)(p), 9.94A.125. Petitioner entered a guilty plea admitting the elements of second-degree kidnaping and the domestic-violence and firearm allegations, but no other relevant facts.

The case then proceeded to sentencing. In Washington, second-degree kidnaping is a class B felony. § 9A.40.030(3). State law provides that "[n]o person convicted of a [class B] felony shall be punished by confinement . . . exceeding . . . a term of ten years." § 9A.20.021(1)(b). Other provisions of state law, however, further limit the range of sentences a judge may impose. Washington's Sentencing Reform Act specifies, for petitioner's offense of second-degree kidnaping with a firearm, a "standard range" of 49 to 53 months. . . . A judge may impose a sentence above the standard range if he finds "substantial and compelling reasons justifying an exceptional sentence." § 9.94A.120(2). The Act lists aggravating factors that justify such a departure, which it recites to be illustrative rather than exhaustive. § 9.94A.390. Nevertheless, "[a] reason offered to justify an exceptional sentence can be considered only if it takes into account factors other than those which are used in computing the standard range sentence for the offense." *State v. Gore,* 143 Wash.2d 288, 315-316, 21 P.3d 262, 277 (2001). When a judge imposes an exceptional sentence, he must set forth findings of fact and conclusions of law supporting it. § 9.94A.120(3). A reviewing court will reverse the sentence if it finds that "under a clearly erroneous standard there is insufficient evidence in the record to support the reasons for imposing an exceptional sentence." *Id.,* at 315, 21 P.3d, at 277 (citing § 9.94A.210(4)).

Pursuant to the plea agreement, the State recommended a sentence within the standard range of 49 to 53 months. After hearing Yolanda's description of the kidnaping, however, the judge rejected the State's recommendation and imposed an exceptional sentence of 90 months—37 months beyond the standard maximum. He justified the sentence on the ground that petitioner had acted with "deliberate cruelty," a statutorily enumerated ground for departure in domestic-violence cases. § 9.94A.390(2)(h)(iii).

Faced with an unexpected increase of more than three years in his sentence, petitioner objected. The judge accordingly conducted a 3-day bench hearing featuring testimony from petitioner, Yolanda, Ralphy, a police officer, and medical experts. After the hearing, he issued 32 findings of fact, concluding:

"The defendant's motivation to commit kidnapping was complex, contributed to by his mental condition and personality disorders, the pressures of the divorce litigation, the impending trust litigation trial and anger over his troubled interpersonal relationships with his spouse and children. While he misguidedly intended to forcefully reunite his family, his attempt to do so was subservient to his desire to terminate lawsuits and modify title ownerships to his benefit.

"The defendant's methods were more homogeneous than his motive. He used stealth and surprise, and took advantage of the victim's isolation. He immediately employed physical violence, restrained the victim with tape, and threatened her with injury and death to herself and others. He immediately coerced the victim into providing information by the threatening application of a knife. He violated a subsisting restraining order." App. 48-49.

The judge adhered to his initial determination of deliberate cruelty.

Petitioner appealed, arguing that this sentencing procedure deprived him of his federal constitutional right to have a jury determine beyond a reasonable doubt all facts legally essential to his sentence. . . . We granted certiorari. 540 U.S. 965, 124 S. Ct. 429, 157 L. Ed. 2d 309 (2003).

II

This case requires us to apply the rule we expressed in *Apprendi v. New Jersey,* 530 U.S. 466, 490, 120 S. Ct. 2348, 147 L. Ed. 2d 435 (2000): "Other than the fact of a prior conviction, any fact that increases the penalty for a crime beyond the prescribed statutory maximum must be submitted to a jury, and proved beyond a reasonable doubt." This rule reflects two longstanding tenets of common-law criminal jurisprudence: that the "truth of every accusation" against a defendant "should afterwards be confirmed by the unanimous suffrage of twelve of his equals and neighbours," 4 W. Blackstone, Commentaries on the Laws of England 343 (1769), and that "an accusation which lacks any particular fact which the law makes essential to the punishment is . . . no accusation within the requirements of the common law, and it is no accusation in reason," 1 J. Bishop, Criminal Procedure § 87, p. 55 (2d ed. 1872). These principles have been acknowledged by courts and treatises since the earliest days of graduated sentencing; we compiled the relevant authorities in *Apprendi,* see 530 U.S., at 476-483, 489-490, n.15; *id.,* at 501-518, 120 S. Ct. 2348 (Thomas, J., concurring), and need not repeat them here.

Apprendi involved a New Jersey hate-crime statute that authorized a 20-year sentence, despite the usual 10-year maximum, if the judge found the crime to have been committed "'with a purpose to intimidate . . . because of race, color, gender, handicap, religion, sexual orientation or ethnicity.'" *Id.,* at 468-469, 120 S. Ct. 2348 (quoting N.J. Stat. Ann. § 2C:44-3(e) (West Supp. 1999-2000)). In *Ring v. Arizona,* 536 U.S. 584, 592-593, and n.1, 122 S. Ct. 2428, 153 L. Ed. 2d 556 (2002), we applied *Apprendi* to an Arizona law that authorized the death penalty if the judge found 1 of 10 aggravating factors. In each case, we concluded that the defendant's constitutional rights had been violated because the judge had imposed a sentence greater than the maximum he could have imposed under state law without the challenged factual finding. *Apprendi, supra,* at 491-497, 120 S. Ct. 2348; *Ring, supra,* at 603-609, 122 S. Ct. 2428.

In this case, petitioner was sentenced to more than three years above the 53-month statutory maximum of the standard range because he had acted with "deliberate cruelty." The facts supporting that finding were neither admitted by petitioner nor found by a jury. The State nevertheless contends that there was no *Apprendi* violation because the relevant "statutory maximum" is not 53 months, but the 10-year maximum for class B felonies in § 9A.20.021(1)(b). It observes that no exceptional sentence may exceed that limit. See § 9.94A.420. Our precedents make clear, however, that the "statutory maximum" for *Apprendi* purposes is the maximum sentence a judge may impose *solely on the basis of the facts reflected in the jury verdict or admitted by the defendant.* See *Ring, supra,* at 602, 122 S. Ct. 2428 ("'the maximum he would receive if punished according to the facts reflected in the jury verdict alone'"). . . . In other words, the relevant "statutory maximum" is not the maximum sentence a judge may impose after finding additional facts, but the maximum he may impose *without* any additional findings. When a judge inflicts punishment that the jury's verdict alone does not allow, the jury has not found all the facts "which the law makes essential to the punishment," Bishop, *supra,* § 87, at 55, and the judge exceeds his proper authority.

The judge in this case could not have imposed the exceptional 90-month sentence solely on the basis of the facts admitted in the guilty plea. Those facts alone were insufficient because, as the Washington Supreme Court has explained, "[a] reason offered to justify an exceptional sentence can be considered only if it takes into account factors other than those which are used in computing the standard range sentence for the offense," *Gore,* 143 Wash.2d, at 315-316, 21 P.3d, at 277, which in this case included the elements of second-degree kidnaping and the use of a firearm, see §§ 9.94A.320, 9.94A.310(3)(b). Had the judge imposed the 90-month sentence solely on the basis of the plea, he would have been reversed. See § 9.94A.210(4). The "maximum sentence" is no more 10 years here than it was 20 years in *Apprendi* (because that is what the judge could have imposed upon finding a hate crime) or death in *Ring* (because that is what the judge could have imposed upon finding an aggravator). . . .

Finally, the State tries to distinguish *Apprendi* and *Ring* by pointing out that the enumerated grounds for departure in its regime are illustrative rather than exhaustive. This distinction is immaterial. Whether the judge's authority to impose an enhanced sentence depends on finding a specified fact (as in *Apprendi*), one of several specified facts (as in *Ring*), or *any* aggravating fact (as here), it remains the case that the jury's verdict alone does not authorize the sentence. The judge acquires that authority only upon finding some additional fact.

Because the State's sentencing procedure did not comply with the Sixth Amendment, petitioner's sentence is invalid.

III

Our commitment to *Apprendi* in this context reflects not just respect for long-standing precedent, but the need to give intelligible content to the right of jury trial. That right is no mere procedural formality, but a fundamental reservation of power in our constitutional structure. Just as suffrage ensures the people's ultimate control in the legislative and executive branches, jury trial is meant to ensure their control in the judiciary. . . . *Apprendi* carries out this design by ensuring that the judge's authority to sentence derives wholly from the jury's verdict. Without that restriction, the jury would not exercise the control that the Framers intended.

Those who would reject *Apprendi* are resigned to one of two alternatives. The first is that the jury need only find whatever facts the legislature chooses to label elements of the crime, and that those it labels sentencing factors—no matter how much they may increase the punishment—may be found by the judge. This would mean, for example, that a judge could sentence a man for committing murder even if the jury convicted him only of illegally possessing the firearm used to commit it—or of making an illegal lane change while fleeing the death scene. Not even *Apprendi's* critics would advocate this absurd result. Cf. 530 U.S., at 552-553, 120 S. Ct. 2348 (O'Connor, J., dissenting). The jury could not function as circuitbreaker in the State's machinery of justice if it were relegated to making a determination that the defendant at some point did something wrong, a mere preliminary to a judicial inquisition into the facts of the crime the State *actually* seeks to punish.

The second alternative is that legislatures may establish legally essential sentencing factors *within limits*—limits crossed when, perhaps, the sentencing factor is a "tail which wags the dog of the substantive offense." *McMillan,* 477 U.S., at 88, 106 S. Ct. 2411. What this means in operation is that the law must not go *too far*—it must not exceed the judicial estimation of the proper role of the judge.

The subjectivity of this standard is obvious. Petitioner argued below that second-degree kidnaping with deliberate cruelty was essentially the same as first-degree kidnaping, the very charge he had avoided by pleading to a lesser offense. The court conceded this might be so but held it irrelevant. See 111 Wash.App., at 869, 47 P.3d, at 158. Petitioner's 90-month sentence exceeded the 53-month standard maximum by almost 70%; the Washington Supreme Court in other cases has upheld exceptional sentences 15 times the standard maximum. See *State v. Oxborrow,* 106 Wash.2d 525, 528, 533, 723 P.2d 1123, 1125, 1128 (1986) (en banc) (15-year exceptional sentence; 1-year standard maximum sentence); *State v. Branch,* 129 Wash.2d 635, 650, 919 P.2d 1228, 1235 (1996) (en banc) (4-year exceptional sentence; 3-month standard maximum sentence). Did the court go *too far* in any of these cases? There is no answer that legal analysis can provide. With *too far* as the yardstick, it is always possible to disagree with such judgments and never to refute them.

Whether the Sixth Amendment incorporates this manipulable standard rather than *Apprendi's* bright-line rule depends on the plausibility of the claim that the Framers would have left definition of the scope of jury power up to judges' intuitive sense of how far is *too far.* We think that claim not plausible at all, because the very reason the Framers put a jury-trial guarantee in the Constitution is that they were unwilling to trust government to mark out the role of the jury. . . .

    . . .

Petitioner was sentenced to prison for more than three years beyond what the law allowed for the crime to which he confessed, on the basis of a disputed finding that he had acted with "deliberate cruelty." The Framers would not have thought it too much to demand that, before depriving a man of three more years of his liberty, the State should suffer the modest inconvenience of submitting its accusation to "the unanimous suffrage of twelve of his equals and neighbours," Blackstone, *supra,* at 343, rather than a lone employee of the State.

The judgment of the Washington Court of Appeals is reversed, and the case is remanded for further proceedings not inconsistent with this opinion.

It is so ordered.

CASE QUESTIONS

BATSON v. KENTUCKY

1. How does the Court's decision in *Batson* effectively narrow the definition of a "peremptory challenge"?

2. Suppose that Hung Lee is an Asian American scheduled to go on trial for solicitation to commit murder. According to the Court's decision, is Lee entitled to have at least *some* Asian Americans on his jury? Explain.

3. Which side bears the burden of raising the issue that potential jurors have been excluded from the panel on account of race? If that burden is met, what happens next?

4. Is a defendant permitted to consider past practices of the prosecuting attorney in order to support a claim of discrimination in the jury selection process for *his* case? *Must* a defendant rely on such information in order to succeed on a *Batson* claim?

5. Given the Court's holding, what procedurally would be the next step in Batson's case? Did the Court find that the prosecutor impermissibly excluded jurors on account of race? Explain.

6. How did the Court's holding in *Batson* affect the prior decision of Swain v. Alabama, 380 U.S. 202 (1965)?

BLAKELY v. WASHINGTON

1. How did the trial judge overstep his authority when imposing Blakely's sentence?

2. What rule of law was established in Apprendi v. New Jersey, 530 U.S. 466 (2000), and how did it impact the Court's holding in this case?

3. What narrow exception did *Apprendi* recognize? Why do you think this was an exception?

4. How did the Court's holding in this case protect the defendant's right to a jury trial? Explain.

HYPOTHETICAL WITH ACCOMPANYING ANALYSIS

Hypothetical

Brad is currently on trial for first-degree, premeditated murder. The case has been very controversial from the outset. The prosecution claims that Brad murdered his wife after a heated argument, while the defense argues that Mary took her own life after Brad had told her he was unhappy with their marriage and wanted a divorce. The trial lasted almost three weeks, and the jury was sequestered the entire time. At the conclusion of the case, the bailiff escorted the jurors into the jury room to begin deliberations. The bailiff held the door as the jurors filed one at a time into the small room. As Sarah and Heather, the last two jurors, walked past the bailiff he said to them, "Brad is *so* guilty of killing his wife. I think it's pretty obvious, don't you?" Neither juror replied to the bailiff's question.

A few hours later the judge received a note from the jury, which read: "Two jurors wish to speak with the judge. They overheard something related to the case and need advice." The judge summoned Sarah and Heather into the courtroom with both attorneys and Brad present. When the judge asked them to elaborate on what had happened, Sarah explained what the bailiff had said. She also informed the judge that she had told the other jurors about the bailiff's remarks. The following then occurred:

> **Judge:** Let me ask each of you, has what you heard affected your ability to decide this case in an impartial and unbiased manner?
>
> **Sarah:** I don't think so.
>
> **Heather:** I guess not.
>
> **Judge:** Well neither one of you seems very sure of your answers.
>
> **Heather:** Well, it's just that, I mean, the bailiff is around cases like this all the time, isn't he? And, well, I would just think that he knows what he's talking about, that's all.
>
> **Sarah:** But I know it's not his decision, it's our decision.
>
> **Judge:** That is absolutely correct. And as for your comment ma'am, you're right, he does see a lot of criminal cases but you need to remember that he is neither a lawyer nor an expert in the law. And it's your job to decide the case based on the evidence presented and *only* the evidence presented. So, do you think you can still deliberate in an unbiased manner?
>
> **Sarah:** Yes.
>
> **Heather:** Umm, okay.

Both women returned to the jury room to deliberate. Less than two hours later the jury found Brad guilty of first-degree murder.

Brad is now challenging his conviction and arguing that his Sixth Amendment right to a jury trial was compromised. Discuss whether Brad's arguments have merit.

Analysis

The Sixth Amendment provides that "in all criminal prosecutions, the accused shall enjoy the right to a . . . trial, by an impartial jury[.]" The issue in this case

is whether Brad was denied his constitutional right to an *impartial* jury in light
of the bailiff's comments and the impact they may have had on the jurors.

In Irvin v. Dowd, 366 U.S. 717 (1961), a case dealing with the impact of
pre-trial publicity on individual jurors, the Supreme Court explained that a jury
must base its decision "on the evidence presented in court." Numerous facts
support Brad's argument that his Sixth Amendment rights were violated. The
remark made by the bailiff to the two jurors was extremely prejudicial, since
it concluded that Brad was guilty and asked the jurors to confirm that conclusion. When the judge summoned the two jurors into the courtroom, Heather
appeared to have been influenced by the bailiff's remarks since, in her words,
"he knows what he's talking about." Additionally, when he first asked the
two jurors if they could deliberate the case in an impartial manner, their
answers were tentative at best. Further supporting Brad's argument is the fact
that Sarah told the judge she had shared the bailiff's remarks with the rest of
the jury, yet the judge did nothing to inquire as to whether any of the other
jurors might have been prejudiced. Finally, the fact that the murder trial was
very controversial yet it took the jury less than two hours to render a verdict
supports the position that at least some of the jurors could have been influenced
by the bailiff's remarks.

The prosecutor could attempt to argue that after fully exploring the issue
before the judge, both jurors ultimately said that they could continue to deliberate in an unbiased manner. However, the reliance that at least one of the jurors
admittedly put in the bailiff's remarks, the fact that the judge failed to question
any of the other jurors, and the speed of the verdict following the bailiff's
remarks in combination suggest that at least *some* members of the jury could
not remain impartial during deliberations. Therefore, Brad's Sixth Amendment
rights to an impartial jury were violated.

Bryan is the city's most notorious businessman turned drug dealer who is scheduled to go on trial for a laundry list of drug and weapons offenses. At first the jury selection process was running very smoothly, with each side using its challenges to narrow down the respective jurors who would decide Bryan's fate. But all of a sudden things changed dramatically. Dirk, Bryan's defense attorney, objected to the prosecutor using two peremptory challenges to strike potential jurors #16 and #22 from the jury. When the judge asked Dirk to elaborate on his objection, he explained: "Your Honor, I believe the prosecutor is attempting to exclude all homosexuals from the jury, and my client argues that this violates his Sixth Amendment right to a jury that is representative of the community." "Wait a minute," the judge inquired, "what even makes you believe these two individuals are homosexuals in the first place?" Dirk explained that during *voir dire*, in response to a question of whether the juror or anyone close to the juror had been charged with a crime, #16 answered that his "ex-boyfriend" had once been charged with a misdemeanor; and, when asked about each potential juror's employment, #22 had stated that she and her "life partner" were the founders and CEOs of a lesbian adoption agency.

Before the judge could respond to Dirk's allegations, Patty, the prosecutor, interjected: "Your Honor, Dirk's argument that I am excluding potential jurors based on their sexual orientation is preposterous!" "Then why *did* you exclude them?" Dirk demanded. "Well, as for #16, he just looked to me like he wouldn't be able to pay attention and focus during the trial. We have all said that this trial could last two or three weeks, and did you see the way he's been fidgeting in his seat the whole morning? I just don't think he could sit still and give this case his undivided attention. As for #22, given her job and the fact that she has worked in the Peace Corps, she just appears way too liberal for me, and I am trying to seat more conservative jurors." "Say what you want," Dirk replied curtly, "but I know what you're *really* up to, and I object to it."

Assume you are the trial judge in this case. How would you respond to Dirk's challenge and why? Draft a detailed opinion based on relevant Sixth Amendment law that you will deliver to the parties in this case expressing your ruling.

1. What is jury nullification? Find an example of a case where jury nullification occurred. Do you agree with this principal of law? Why or why not? *See, e.g.,* Woodson v. North Carolina, 428 U.S. 280, n.29 (1976) and Roberts v. Louisiana, 428 U.S. 325 (1976).

2. Research challenge: Familiarize yourself with the case of Scott Peterson, a California man who was convicted of murdering his wife and unborn child in 2002. How many potential jurors were summoned for that case and why? What do you anticipate were some of the questions asked to potential jurors during *voir dire*?

3. In which of the following scenarios could a successful constitutional challenge occur based on *Batson* and subsequent cases? (a) A female defendant challenging the prosecution's exclusion of women from the jury; (b) A Caucasian male defendant challenging the prosecution's exclusion of African Americans from the jury; (c) A prosecutor challenging defense counsel's exclusion of Caucasian men from the jury, where the defendant is an African American male. *See* Powers v. Ohio, 499 U.S. 400 (1991), Georgia v. McCollum, 505 U.S. 42 (1992), and JEB v. Alabama ex rel. TB, 511 U.S. 127 (1994).

4. Are there any types of cases where you feel as though *you* could not be completely unbiased as a juror? What kinds of cases, if any, and why?

5. In today's society where the media plays such a prevalent role, do you think we run the risk of compromising a defendant's right to an impartial jury given the amount of pretrial publicity some cases receive? What potential solutions could serve to balance the competing interests of the First Amendment right to freedom of the press versus the Sixth Amendment right to an impartial jury? How did Sam Sheppard, a prominent doctor famously accused of murdering his wife and the man about which the popular movie and television series "The Fugitive" was loosely based, grapple with these issues? *See* Sheppard v. Maxwell, 384 U.S. 333 (1966).

6. Revisit the Supreme Court's decision in Batson v. Kentucky. Do you see any potential problems with the Court's opinion in terms of a "snowball effect"? What if attorneys purposefully excluded individuals from a jury because of their economic status, age, political affiliation, religion, or ethnicity; would that be challengeable under *Batson* and its progeny?

7. What impact does plea bargaining have on a defendant's right to a trial by jury? What are the advantages of disadvantages of plea bargaining? What if plea bargaining were abolished; how do you think it would affect the nation's criminal justice system? Explain.

8. Can a criminal defendant be *forced* to have a jury trial? What if she does not want one? Explain. *See* Singer v. United States, 380 U.S. 24 (1965).

9. What are some methods by which jurisdictions obtain a list of potential jurors representing a cross-section of the community? Could a blind person serve on a jury? A deaf person? A person suffering from the beginning stages of Alzheimer's disease? Why or why not?

10. Why might an individual choose to waive her right to a jury trial and be tried by a judge? Can you think of any types of cases where a defendant might be more likely to seek a court trial rather than a jury trial?

11. What are the purposes of sequestering a jury? What are the advantages and disadvantages of doing so? In the double homicide trial of O.J. Simpson, his jury was sequestered for over nine months. Do you think this is fair? Explain.

12. Tom is on trial for burglary. Two alternate jurors were empanelled and both were used to replace regular jurors during the second week of trial when one juror fell ill and the other had a death in the family. During the third

week of trial another juror is excused after the judge learns that she did outside research on Tom's case. There are no alternates left to replace her. What happens next in Tom's trial?

13. Jury consultants are individuals who pick juries as their occupation. They learn to monitor a person's behavior, body language, etc. The costs of employing such experts can be phenomenal. Do you agree with the use of these individuals? Is this fair to the indigent defendant who cannot afford such "high tech" methods of jury selection? Explain.

True/False

Read the below hypothetical and answer the questions that follow:

Stephanie, the mother of three young children, has been charged with numerous counts of child abuse. During the jury selection process, the prosecutor uses peremptory challenges to exclude eight men from the jury.

1. Stephanie must first make a *prima facie* case of purposeful discrimination, and then the burden will shift to the prosecutor to offer a gender-neutral explanation for excluding the men.

2. Stephanie cannot succeed in her complaint about the prosecutor's exclusion of men because Stephanie is not a member of the group being excluded.

3. Stephanie cannot succeed in her complaint about the prosecutor's exclusion of men because men are not a class traditionally discriminated against and thus entitled to constitutional protection.

4. Stephanie is permitted to use statistical information from past cases in which the same prosecuting attorney systematically excluded men from the jury where women were defendants in similar types of cases.

5. Stephanie is constitutionally entitled to a jury with at least *some* men on it because men make up a majority of the population.

Multiple Choice

6. For which of the following crimes would an individual most likely *not* be constitutionally entitled to a jury trial?

   A. A felony with a maximum potential penalty of one year in jail
   B. A misdemeanor with a maximum potential penalty of two years in jail
   C. A felony with a maximum potential penalty of nine months in jail
   D. A misdemeanor with a potential fine of $5,000

7. Tanya has been charged with robbery. During *voir dire* all jurors admit that they have previous knowledge of the case due to media attention, but they all confirm individually that they could render an unbiased verdict and that their opinions were not swayed by the media attention. Tanya is then tried before a jury of three men and three women. After deliberations, the jury unanimously finds her guilty of robbery, which carries a maximum penalty of twenty years imprisonment. In imposing a sentence, the judge declares that she is guilty of "aggravated robbery" because she used a handgun during the commission of the crime, and he therefore sentences her to twenty-five

years imprisonment. Which will be Tanya's best argument that her constitutional right to a jury trial was violated?

    A. The jurors who served on her case had been exposed to facts of her case prior to trial through the media.

    B. Her jury was comprised of only six individuals.

    C. The judge impermissibly increased Tanya's sentence by finding another element of the crime without the jury having determined it first.

    D. Tanya has no plausible arguments to make.

8. Which of the following would be unconstitutional under the Sixth Amendment?

    A. A jury comprised of six individuals where all vote for conviction

    B. A jury comprised of twelve individuals where nine vote for conviction

    C. A jury comprised of six individuals where five vote for conviction

    D. All of the above would unconstitutionally infringe on an individual's right to a jury trial.

9. Walter Buchanan, the mayor of a very small town, has been charged with embezzling millions of dollars from the town. The citizens of the community are outraged by the accusations against Walter, and the case has received extensive media coverage for almost a year. Walter's trial is set to begin in just a few months, and he is concerned that the amount of publicity will negatively affect his right to an impartial jury. What could Walter do in order to ensure that his constitutional right is protected?

    A. Walter could request a change of venue to a location where the case has received less media attention.

    B. Walter could have his attorney extensively question potential jurors during *voir dire* to ensure they would be impartial.

    C. Walter could do either A or B.

    D. Walter could do both A and B.

10. Which of the following statements with regard to jury selection is accurate?

    A. Attorneys are entitled to an unlimited number of "for cause" and "peremptory" challenges.

    B. Attorneys are entitled to a limited number of "for cause" and "peremptory" challenges.

    C. Attorneys are entitled to an unlimited number of "for cause" challenges and a limited number of "peremptory" challenges.

    D. Attorneys are entitled to a limited number of "for cause" challenges and an unlimited number of "peremptory" challenges.

10

Confrontation

"In all criminal prosecutions, the accused shall enjoy
the right . . . to be confronted with the witnesses against
him[.]"

—The Sixth Amendment

INTRODUCTION

"It is always more difficult to tell a lie about a person 'to his face' than 'behind
his back.'" So said Justice Scalia in the 1988 Supreme Court case of Coy v. Iowa.
His remark strikes at the very heart of the Confrontation Clause: the guarantee
that the criminal defendant will be able to confront her accusers face to face.
Forcing someone to look you in the eye and blame you for a crime is a very
powerful thing indeed, and, according to the framers of the Constitution, it is an
essential ingredient to the fair operation of our nation's criminal justice system.

Issues that deal with the Confrontation Clause commonly fall into one of
two categories: First we consider when a trial can be conducted either without
the defendant's presence or participation. Within this category are the common
scenarios of when the defendant either fails to attend trial and it is conducted in
her absence; or, when she is so disruptive during the trial process that measures
must be taken to eliminate the disruption, thereby affecting her right of
confrontation.

Second, questions also arise as to when a witness' testimony will be permitted in court in a manner other than live testimony in front of the defendant.
Once again, two common scenarios occur—first, when hearsay evidence is admitted at trial against the defendant; and second, where children witnesses or
victims of sexual abuse are permitted to testify in a manner other than a face-to-
face confrontation in order to protect the child from the trauma of having to
testify in the presence of the alleged perpetrator.

The Confrontation Clause is perhaps the most literal of all of the protections
afforded to the criminal defendant in the Bill of Rights. Because our society
places such great importance on the right to (1) compel the live testimony of
witnesses, (2) observe their demeanor on the stand, and (3) cross-examine them

195

in order to judge their credibility, the issues in this chapter raise serious concerns. Courts have constantly been attempting to strike a balance between protecting the accused's right to confrontation while ensuing that our justice system operates in a fair and realistic manner.

STUDENT Checklist

Confrontation

1. **Defendant's** presence at trial:

■ Did the defendant **voluntarily** fail to attend her trial so that it could be conducted in her absence (i.e., **in abstentia**)?
or

■ Although physically present, did the defendant act in such a **disruptive** manner that the trial judge was compelled to:
Bind and gag the defendant;
Cite the defendant for **contempt of court**; or
Remove the defendant until she promised to conduct herself properly?

2. **Witness'** presence at trial:

■ Did the prosecution seek to admit **hearsay** evidence against the defendant
or

■ Did the prosecution seek to have a **child** witness of **sexual abuse** testify in a manner other than direct face-to-face confrontation?

SUPREME COURT CASES

MARYLAND v. CRAIG, 497 U.S. 836 (1990)

This case requires us to decide whether the Confrontation Clause of the Sixth Amendment categorically prohibits a child witness in a child abuse case from testifying against a defendant at trial, outside the defendant's physical presence, by one-way closed circuit television.

I

In October 1986, a Howard County grand jury charged respondent, Sandra Ann Craig, with child abuse, first and second degree sexual offenses, perverted sexual practice, assault, and battery. The named victim in each count was a 6-year-old girl who, from August 1984 to June 1986, had attended a kindergarten and prekindergarten center owned and operated by Craig.

In March 1987, before the case went to trial, the State sought to invoke a Maryland statutory procedure that permits a judge to receive, by one-way closed circuit television, the testimony of a child witness who is alleged to be a victim of child abuse. To invoke the procedure, the trial judge must first "determin[e] that testimony by the child victim in the courtroom will result in the child suffering serious emotional distress such that the child cannot reasonably communicate." Md. Cts. & Jud. Proc. Code Ann. § 9-102(a)(1)(ii) (1989). Once the procedure is invoked, the child witness, prosecutor, and defense counsel withdraw to a separate room; the judge, jury, and defendant remain in the courtroom. The child witness is then examined and cross-examined in the separate room, while a video monitor records and displays the witness' testimony to those in the courtroom. During this time the witness cannot see the defendant. The defendant remains in electronic communication with defense counsel, and objections may be made and ruled on as if the witness were testifying in the courtroom.

In support of its motion invoking the one-way closed circuit television procedure, the State presented expert testimony that the named victim as well as a number of other children who were alleged to have been sexually abused by Craig, would suffer "serious emotional distress such that [they could not] reasonably communicate," § 9-102(a)(1)(ii), if required to testify in the courtroom. App. 7-59. . . .

Craig objected to the use of the procedure on Confrontation Clause grounds, but the trial court rejected that contention, concluding that although the statute "take[s] away the right of the defendant to be face to face with his or her accuser," the defendant retains the "essence of the right of confrontation," including the right to observe, cross-examine, and have the jury view the demeanor of the witness. App. 65-66. The trial court further found that, "based upon the evidence presented . . . the testimony of each of these children in a courtroom will result in each child suffering serious emotional distress . . . such that each of these children cannot reasonably communicate." *Id.*, at 66. The trial court then found the named victim and three other children competent to testify and accordingly permitted them to testify against Craig via the one-way closed circuit television procedure. The jury convicted Craig on all counts. . . .

We granted certiorari to resolve the important Confrontation Clause issues raised by this case. 493 U.S. 1041, 110 S. Ct. 834, 107 L. Ed. 2d 830 (1990).

II

The Confrontation Clause of the Sixth Amendment, made applicable to the States through the Fourteenth Amendment, provides: "In all criminal prosecutions, the accused shall enjoy the right . . . to be confronted with the witnesses against him."

We observed in *Coy v. Iowa* that "the Confrontation Clause guarantees the defendant a face-to-face meeting with witnesses appearing before the trier of fact." 487 U.S., at 1016, 108 S. Ct., at 2801. . . . This interpretation derives not only from the literal text of the Clause, but also from our understanding of its historical roots. . . .

We have never held, however, that the Confrontation Clause guarantees criminal defendants the *absolute* right to a face-to-face meeting with witnesses against them at trial. Indeed, in *Coy v. Iowa,* we expressly "le[ft] for another day . . . the question whether any exceptions exist" to the "irreducible literal meaning of the Clause: 'a right to *meet face to face* all those who appear and give evidence *at trial.*' " 487 U.S., at 1021, 108 S. Ct., at 2803 (quoting *Green, supra,* 399 U.S., at 175, 90 S. Ct., at 1943 (Harlan, J., concurring)). The procedure challenged in *Coy* involved the placement of a screen that prevented two child witnesses in a child abuse case from seeing the defendant as they testified against him at trial. See 487 U.S., at 1014-1015, 108 S. Ct., at 2799-2800. In holding that the use of this procedure violated the defendant's right to confront witnesses against him, we suggested that any exception to the right "would surely be allowed only when necessary to further an important public policy"—*i.e.*, only upon a showing of something more than the generalized, "legislatively imposed presumption of trauma" underlying the statute at issue in that case. *Id.*, at 1021, 108 S. Ct., at 2803; see also *id.*, at 1025, 108 S. Ct., at 2805 (O'Connor, J., concurring). We concluded that "[s]ince there ha[d] been no individualized findings that these particular witnesses needed special protection, the judgment [in the case before us] could not be sustained by any conceivable exception." *Id.*, at 1021, 108 S. Ct., at 2803. Because the trial court in this case made individualized findings that each of the child witnesses needed special protection, this case requires us to decide the question reserved in *Coy*. . . .

. . . [T]he right guaranteed by the Confrontation Clause includes not only a "personal examination," 156 U.S., at 242, 15 S. Ct., at 339, but also "(1) insures that the witness will give his statements under oath—thus impressing him with the seriousness of the matter and guarding against the lie by the possibility of a penalty for perjury; (2) forces the witness to submit to cross-examination, the 'greatest legal engine ever invented for the discovery of truth'; [and] (3) permits the jury that is to decide the defendant's fate to observe the demeanor of the witness in making his statement, thus aiding the jury in assessing his credibility." *Green, supra,* 399 U.S., at 158, 90 S. Ct., at 1935 (footnote omitted).

The combined effect of these elements of confrontation—physical presence, oath, cross-examination, and observation of demeanor by the trier of fact—serves the purposes of the Confrontation Clause by ensuring that evidence admitted against an accused is reliable and subject to the rigorous adversarial testing that is the norm of Anglo-American criminal proceedings. . . .

Although face-to-face confrontation forms "the core of the values furthered by the Confrontation Clause," *Green,* 399 U.S., at 157, 90 S. Ct., at 1934, we have nevertheless recognized that it is not the *sine qua non* of the confrontation right. . . .

For this reason, we have never insisted on an actual face-to-face encounter at trial in *every* instance in which testimony is admitted against a defendant. Instead, we have repeatedly held that the Clause permits, where necessary, the admission of certain hearsay statements against a defendant despite the defendant's inability to confront the declarant at trial. . . .

In sum, our precedents establish that "the Confrontation Clause reflects a *preference* for face-to-face confrontation at trial," *Roberts, supra,* 448 U.S., at 63, 100 S. Ct., at 2537 (emphasis added; footnote omitted), a preference that "must occasionally give way to considerations of public policy and the necessities of the case," *Mattox, supra,* 156 U.S., at 243, 15 S. Ct., at 339-340. . . . Thus, though we reaffirm the importance of face-to-face confrontation with witnesses appearing at trial, we cannot say that such confrontation is an indispensable element of the Sixth Amendment's guarantee of the right to confront one's accusers. . . .

That the face-to-face confrontation requirement is not absolute does not, of course, mean that it may easily be dispensed with. As we suggested in *Coy,* our precedents confirm that a defendant's right to confront accusatory witnesses may be satisfied absent a physical, face-to-face confrontation at trial only where denial of such confrontation is necessary to further an important public policy and only where the reliability of the testimony is otherwise assured. See 487 U.S., at 1021, 108 S. Ct., at 2803 (citing *Roberts, supra,* 448 U.S. at 64, 100 S. Ct., at 2538; *Chambers, supra,* 410 U.S. at 295, 93 S. Ct., at 1045); *Coy, supra,* 487 U.S., at 1025, 108 S. Ct., at 2805 (O'Connor, J., concurring).

III

Maryland's statutory procedure, when invoked, prevents a child witness from seeing the defendant as he or she testifies against the defendant at trial. We find it significant, however, that Maryland's procedure preserves all of the other elements of the confrontation right: The child witness must be competent to testify and must testify under oath; the defendant retains full opportunity for contemporaneous cross-examination; and the judge, jury, and defendant are able to view (albeit by video monitor) the demeanor (and body) of the witness as he or she testifies. Although we are mindful of the many subtle effects face-to-face confrontation may have on an adversary criminal proceeding, the presence of these other elements of confrontation—oath, cross-examination, and observation of the witness' demeanor—adequately ensures that the testimony is both reliable and subject to rigorous adversarial testing in a manner functionally equivalent to that accorded live, in-person testimony. These safeguards of reliability and adversariness render the use of such a procedure a far cry from the undisputed prohibition of the Confrontation Clause: trial by *ex parte* affidavit or inquisition, see *Mattox,* 156 U.S., at 242, 15 S. Ct., at 389; see also *Green,* 399 U.S., at 179, 90 S. Ct., at 1946 (Harlan, J., concurring) ("[T]he Confrontation Clause was meant to constitutionalize a barrier against flagrant abuses, trials by anonymous accusers, and absentee witnesses"). Rather, we think these elements of effective confrontation not only permit a defendant to "confound and undo the false accuser, or reveal the child coached by a malevolent adult," *Coy, supra,* 487 U.S., at 1020, 108 S. Ct., at 2802, but may well aid a defendant in eliciting favorable testimony from the child witness. Indeed, to the extent the child witness' testimony may be said to be technically given out of court (though we do not so hold), these assurances of reliability and adversariness are far greater than those required for admission of hearsay testimony under the Confrontation Clause. See *Roberts,* 448 U.S., at 66, 100 S. Ct., at 2539. We are therefore confident that use of the one-way closed circuit television procedure, where necessary to further an important state interest, does not impinge upon the truth-seeking or symbolic purposes of the Confrontation Clause.

The critical inquiry in this case, therefore, is whether use of the procedure is necessary to further an important state interest. The State contends that it has a substantial interest in protecting children who are allegedly victims of child abuse from the trauma of testifying against the alleged perpetrator and that its statutory procedure for receiving testimony from such witnesses is necessary to further that interest.

We have of course recognized that a State's interest in "the protection of minor victims of sex crimes from further trauma and embarrassment" is a "compelling" one. . . . "[W]e have sustained legislation aimed at protecting the physical and emotional well-being of youth even when the laws have operated in the sensitive area of constitutionally protected rights." *Ferber, supra,* 458 U.S., at 757, 102 S. Ct., at 3354. . . .

We likewise conclude today that a State's interest in the physical and psychological well-being of child abuse victims may be sufficiently important to outweigh, at least in some cases, a defendant's right to face his or her accusers in court. That a significant majority of States have enacted statutes to protect child witnesses from the trauma of giving testimony in child abuse cases attests to the widespread belief in the importance of such a public policy. . . . Thirty-seven States, for example, permit the use of videotaped testimony of sexually abused children; 24 States have authorized the use of one-way closed circuit television testimony in child abuse cases; and 8 States authorize the use of a two-way system in which the child witness is permitted to see the courtroom and the defendant on a video monitor and in which the jury and judge are permitted to view the child during the testimony.

The statute at issue in this case, for example, was specifically intended "to safeguard the physical and psychological well-being of child victims by avoiding, or at least minimizing, the emotional trauma produced by testifying." *Wildermuth v. State,* 310 Md. 496, 518, 530 A.2d 275, 286 (1987). . . .

Given the State's traditional and "'transcendent interest in protecting the welfare of children,'" *Ginsberg,* 390 U.S., at 640, 88 S. Ct., at 1281 (citation omitted), and buttressed by the growing body of academic literature documenting the psychological trauma suffered by child abuse victims who must testify in court . . . we will not second-guess the considered judgment of the Maryland Legislature regarding the importance of its interest in protecting child abuse victims from the emotional trauma of testifying. Accordingly, we hold that, if the State makes an adequate showing of necessity, the state interest in protecting child witnesses from the trauma of testifying in a child abuse case is sufficiently important to justify the use of a special procedure that permits a child witness in such cases to testify at trial against a defendant in the absence of face-to-face confrontation with the defendant.

The requisite finding of necessity must of course be a case-specific one: The trial court must hear evidence and determine whether use of the one-way closed circuit television procedure is necessary to protect the welfare of the particular child witness who seeks to testify. . . . The trial court must also find that the child witness would be traumatized, not by the courtroom generally, but by the presence of the defendant. . . . Denial of face-to-face confrontation is not needed to further the state interest in protecting the child witness from trauma unless it is the presence of the defendant that causes the trauma. In other words, if the state interest were merely the interest in protecting child witnesses from courtroom trauma generally, denial of face-to-face confrontation would be unnecessary because the child could be permitted to testify in less intimidating surroundings, albeit with the defendant present. Finally, the trial court must find that the emotional distress suffered by the child witness in the presence of the defendant is more than *de minimis,* i.e., more than "mere nervousness or excitement or some reluctance to testify,". . . .

To be sure, face-to-face confrontation may be said to cause trauma for the very purpose of eliciting truth, cf. *Coy, supra,* 487 U.S., at 1019-1020, 108 S. Ct., at 2802-03, but we think that the use of Maryland's special procedure, where necessary to further the important state interest in preventing trauma to child witnesses in child abuse cases, adequately ensures the accuracy of the testimony and preserves the adversary nature of the trial. See *supra,* at 3166-3167. Indeed, where face-to-face confrontation causes significant emotional distress in a child witness, there is evidence that such confrontation would in fact *disserve* the Confrontation Clause's truth-seeking goal. . . .

In sum, we conclude that where necessary to protect a child witness from trauma that would be caused by testifying in the physical presence of the defendant, at least where such trauma would impair the child's ability to communicate, the Confrontation Clause does not prohibit use of a procedure that, despite the absence of face-to-face confrontation, ensures the reliability of the evidence by subjecting it to rigorous adversarial testing and thereby preserves the essence of effective confrontation. Because there is no dispute that the child witnesses in this case testified under oath, were subject to full cross-examination, and were able to be observed by the judge, jury, and defendant as they testified, we conclude that, to the extent that a proper finding of necessity has been made, the admission of such testimony would be consonant with the Confrontation Clause.

IV

The Maryland Court of Appeals held, as we do today, that although face-to-face confrontation is not an absolute constitutional requirement, it may be abridged only where there is a " 'case-specific finding of necessity.' " 316 Md., at 564, 560 A.2d, at 1126 (quoting *Coy, supra,* 487 U.S., at 1025, 108 S. Ct., at 2805 (O'Connor, J., concurring)). Given this latter requirement, the Court of Appeals reasoned that "[t]he question of whether a child is unavailable to testify . . . should not be asked in terms of inability to testify in the ordinary courtroom setting, but in the much narrower terms of the witness's inability to testify in the presence of the accused." 316 Md., at 564, 560 A.2d, at 1126 (footnote omitted). "[T]he determinative inquiry required to preclude face-to-face confrontation is the effect of the presence of the defendant on the witness or the witness's testimony." *Id.,* at 565, 560 A.2d, at 1127. The Court of Appeals accordingly concluded that, as a prerequisite to use of the § 9-102 procedure, the Confrontation Clause requires the trial court to make a specific finding that testimony by the child in the courtroom *in the presence of the defendant* would result in the child suffering serious emotional distress such that the child could not reasonably communicate. *Id.,* at 566, 560 A.2d, at 1127. This conclusion, of course, is consistent with our holding today.

In addition, however, the Court of Appeals interpreted our decision in *Coy* to impose two subsidiary requirements. First, the court held that "§ 9-102 ordinarily cannot be invoked unless the child witness initially is questioned (either in or outside the courtroom) in the defendant's presence." *Id.,* at 566, 560 A.2d, at 1127; see also *Wildermuth,* 310 Md., at 523-524, 530 A.2d, at 289 (personal observation by the judge should be the rule rather than the exception). Second, the court asserted that, before using the one-way television procedure, a trial judge must determine whether a child would suffer "severe emotional distress" if he or she were to testify by *two*-way closed circuit television. 316 Md., at 567, 560 A.2d, at 1128.

Reviewing the evidence presented to the trial court in support of the finding required under § 9-102(a)(1)(ii), the Court of Appeals determined that "the finding of necessity required to limit the defendant's right of confrontation through invocation of § 9-102 . . . was not made here." *Id.,* at 570-571, 560 A.2d, at 1129. The Court of Appeals noted that the trial judge "had the benefit only of expert testimony on the ability of the children to communicate; he did not question any of the children himself, nor did he observe any child's behavior on the witness stand before making his ruling. He did not explore any alternatives to the use of one-way closed-circuit television." *Id.,* at 568, 560 A.2d, at 1128 (footnote omitted). The Court of Appeals also observed that "the testimony in this case was not sharply focused on the effect of the defendant's presence on the child witnesses." *Id.,* at 569, 560 A.2d, at 1129. . . .

. . . So long as a trial court makes such a case-specific finding of necessity, the Confrontation Clause does not prohibit a State from using a one-way closed circuit television procedure for the receipt of testimony by a child witness in a child abuse case. Because the Court of Appeals held that the trial court had not made the requisite finding of necessity under its interpretation of "the high threshold required by [*Coy*] before § 9-102 may be invoked," 316 Md., at 554-555, 560 A.2d, at 1121 (footnote omitted), we cannot be certain whether the Court of Appeals would reach the same conclusion in light of the legal standard we establish today. We therefore vacate the judgment of the Court of Appeals of Maryland and remand the case for further proceedings not inconsistent with this opinion.

It is so ordered.

DAVIS v. WASHINGTON and HAMMON v. INDIANA, 547 U.S. 813 (2006)

These cases require us to determine when statements made to law enforcement personnel during a 911 call or at a crime scene are "testimonial" and thus subject to the requirements of the Sixth Amendment's Confrontation Clause.

I

A

The relevant statements in *Davis v. Washington,* No. 05-5224, were made to a 911 emergency operator on February 1, 2001. When the operator answered the initial call, the connection terminated before anyone spoke. She reversed the call, and Michelle McCottry answered. In the ensuing conversation, the operator ascertained that McCottry was involved in a domestic disturbance with her former boyfriend Adrian Davis, the petitioner in this case:

> **911 Operator:** Hello.
> **Complainant:** Hello.
> **911 Operator:** What's going on?
> **Complainant:** He's here jumpin' on me again.
> **911 Operator:** Okay. Listen to me carefully. Are you in a house or an apartment?
> **Complainant:** I'm in a house.
> **911 Operator:** Are there any weapons?
> **Complainant:** No. He's usin' his fists.
> **911 Operator:** Okay. Has he been drinking?
> **Complainant:** No.
> **911 Operator:** Okay, sweetie. I've got help started. Stay on the line with me, okay?
> **Complainant:** I'm on the line.
> **911 Operator:** Listen to me carefully. Do you know his last name?
> **Complainant:** It's Davis.
> **911 Operator:** Davis? Okay, what's his first name?
> **Complainant:** Adrian.
> **911 Operator:** What is it?
> **Complainant:** Adrian.
> **911 Operator:** Adrian?
> **Complainant:** Yeah.
> **911 Operator:** Okay. What's his middle initial?
> **Complainant:** Martell. He's runnin' now.

App. in No. 05-5224, pp. 8-9.

As the conversation continued, the operator learned that Davis had "just r[un] out the door" after hitting McCottry, and that he was leaving in a car with someone else. *Id.*, at 9-10. McCottry started talking, but the operator cut her off, saying, "Stop talking and answer my questions." *Id.*, at 10. She then gathered more information about Davis (including his birthday), and learned that Davis had told McCottry that his purpose in coming to the house was "to get his stuff," since McCottry was moving. *Id.*, at 11-12. McCottry described the context of the assault, *id.*, at 12, after which the operator told her that the police were on their way. "They're gonna check the area for him first," the operator said, "and then they're gonna come talk to you." *Id.*, at 12-13.

The police arrived within four minutes of the 911 call and observed McCottry's shaken state, the "fresh injuries on her forearm and her face," and her "frantic efforts to gather her belongings and her children so that they could leave the residence." 154 Wash.2d 291, 296, 111 P.3d 844, 847 (2005) (en banc).

The State charged Davis with felony violation of a domestic no-contact order. "The State's only witnesses were the two police officers who responded to the 911 call. Both officers testified that McCottry exhibited injuries that appeared to be recent, but neither officer could testify as to the cause of the injuries." *Ibid*. McCottry presumably could have testified as to whether Davis was her assailant, but she did not appear. Over Davis's objection, based on the Confrontation Clause of the Sixth Amendment, the trial court admitted the recording of her exchange with the 911 operator, and the jury convicted him. . . . We granted certiorari. 546 U.S. ___, 126 S. Ct. 552, 163 L. Ed. 2d 459 (2005).

B

In *Hammon v. Indiana,* No. 05-5705, police responded late on the night of February 26, 2003, to a "reported domestic disturbance" at the home of Hershel and Amy Hammon. 829 N.E.2d 444, 446 (Ind. 2005). They found Amy alone on the front porch, appearing "'somewhat frightened,'" but she told them that "'nothing was the matter,'" *id.*, at 446, 447. She gave them permission to enter the house, where an officer saw "a gas heating unit in the corner of the living room" that had "flames coming out of the . . . partial glass front. There were pieces of glass on the ground in front of it and there was flame emitting from the front of the heating unit." App. in No. 05-5705, p. 16.

Hershel, meanwhile, was in the kitchen. He told the police "that he and his wife had 'been in an argument' but 'everything was fine now' and the argument 'never became physical.'" 829 N.E.2d, at 447. By this point Amy had come back inside. One of the officers remained with Hershel; the other went to the living room to talk with Amy, and "again asked [her] what had occurred." *Ibid.;* App. in No. 05-5705, at 17, 32. Hershel made several attempts to participate in Amy's conversation with the police, see *id.*, at 32, but was rebuffed. The officer later testified that Hershel "became angry when I insisted that [he] stay separated from Mrs. Hammon so that we can investigate what had happened." *Id.*, at 34. After hearing Amy's account, the officer "had her fill out and sign a battery affidavit." *Id.*, at 18. Amy handwrote the following: "Broke our Furnace & shoved me down on the floor into the broken glass. Hit me in the chest and threw me down. Broke our lamps & phone. Tore up my van where I couldn't leave the house. Attacked my daughter." *Id.*, at 2.

The State charged Hershel with domestic battery and with violating his probation. Amy was subpoenaed, but she did not appear at his subsequent bench trial. The State called the officer who had questioned Amy, and asked him to recount what Amy told him and to authenticate the affidavit. Hershel's counsel repeatedly objected to the admission of this evidence. See *id.*, at 11, 12, 13, 17, 19, 20, 21. At one point, after hearing the prosecutor defend the affidavit because it was made "under oath," defense counsel said, "That doesn't give us the opportunity to cross examine [the] person who allegedly drafted it. Makes me mad." *Id.*, at 19. Nonetheless, the trial court admitted the affidavit as a "present sense impression," *id.*, at 20, and Amy's statements as "excited utterances" that "are expressly permitted in these kinds of cases even if the declarant is not available to testify." *Id.*, at 40. The officer thus testified that Amy

informed me that she and Hershel had been in an argument. That he became irrate [sic] over the fact of their daughter going to a boyfriend's house. The argument became . . . physical after being verbal and she informed me that Mr. Hammon, during the verbal part of the argument was breaking things in the living room and I believe she stated he broke the phone, broke the lamp, broke the front of the heater. When it became physical he threw her down into the glass of the heater.

. . .

She informed me Mr. Hammon had pushed her onto the ground, had shoved her head into the broken glass of the heater and that he had punched her in the chest twice I believe. *Id.,* at 17-18.

The trial judge found Hershel guilty on both charges, *id.,* at 40. . . . We granted certiorari. 546 U.S. ____, 126 S. Ct. 552, 163 L. Ed. 2d 459 (2005).

II

The Confrontation Clause of the Sixth Amendment provides: "In all criminal prosecutions, the accused shall enjoy the right . . . to be confronted with the witnesses against him." In *Crawford v. Washington,* 541 U.S. 36, 53-54, 124 S. Ct. 1354, 158 L. Ed. 2d 177 (2004), we held that this provision bars "admission of testimonial statements of a witness who did not appear at trial unless he was unavailable to testify, and the defendant had had a prior opportunity for cross-examination." A critical portion of this holding, and the portion central to resolution of the two cases now before us, is the phrase "testimonial statements." Only statements of this sort cause the declarant to be a "witness" within the meaning of the Confrontation Clause. See *id.,* at 51, 124 S. Ct. 1354. It is the testimonial character of the statement that separates it from other hearsay that, while subject to traditional limitations upon hearsay evidence, is not subject to the Confrontation Clause.

Our opinion in *Crawford* set forth "[v]arious formulations" of the core class of " 'testimonial' " statements, *ibid.,* but found it unnecessary to endorse any of them, because "some statements qualify under any definition," *id.,* at 52, 124 S. Ct. 1354. Among those, we said, were "[s]tatements taken by police officers in the course of interrogations," *ibid.;* see also *id.,* at 53, 124 S. Ct. 1354. The questioning that generated the deponent's statement in *Crawford*—which was made and recorded while she was in police custody, after having been given *Miranda* warnings as a possible suspect herself—"qualifies under any conceivable definition" of an " 'interrogation,' " 541 U.S., at 53, n.4, 124 S. Ct. 1354. . . .

Without attempting to produce an exhaustive classification of all conceivable statements—or even all conceivable statements in response to police interrogation—as either testimonial or nontestimonial, it suffices to decide the present cases to hold as follows: Statements are nontestimonial when made in the course of police interrogation under circumstances objectively indicating that the primary purpose of the interrogation is to enable police assistance to meet an ongoing emergency. They are testimonial when the circumstances objectively indicate that there is no such ongoing emergency, and that the primary purpose of the interrogation is to establish or prove past events potentially relevant to later criminal prosecution.

III

A

In *Crawford,* it sufficed for resolution of the case before us to determine that "even if the Sixth Amendment is not solely concerned with testimonial hearsay, that is its primary object, and interrogations by law enforcement officers fall squarely within that class." *Id.,* at 53, 124 S. Ct. 1354. Moreover, as we have just described, the facts of that case spared us the need to define what we meant by "interrogations." The *Davis* case today does not permit us this luxury of indecision. The inquiries of a police operator in the course of a 911 call are an interrogation in one sense, but not in a sense that "qualifies under any conceivable definition." We must decide, therefore, whether the Confrontation Clause applies only to testimonial hearsay; and, if so, whether the recording of a 911 call qualifies.

The answer to the first question was suggested in *Crawford,* even if not explicitly held:

> The text of the Confrontation Clause reflects this focus [on testimonial hearsay]. It applies to "witnesses" against the accused—in other words, those who "bear testimony." 1 N. Webster, An American Dictionary of the English Language (1828). "Testimony," in turn, is typically "a solemn declaration or affirmation made for the purpose of establishing or proving some fact." *Ibid.* An accuser who makes a formal statement to government officers bears testimony in a sense that a person who makes a casual remark to an acquaintance does not. 541 U.S., at 51, 124 S. Ct. 1354. . . .

The question before us in *Davis,* then, is whether, objectively considered, the interrogation that took place in the course of the 911 call produced testimonial statements. When we said in *Crawford, supra,* at 53, 124 S. Ct. 1354, that "interrogations by law enforcement officers fall squarely within [the] class" of testimonial hearsay, we had immediately in mind (for that was the case before us) interrogations solely directed at establishing the facts of a past crime, in order to identify (or provide evidence to convict) the perpetrator. The product of such interrogation, whether reduced to a writing signed by the declarant or embedded in the memory (and perhaps notes) of the interrogating officer, is testimonial. . . . A 911 call, on the other hand, and at least the initial interrogation conducted in connection with a 911 call, is ordinarily not designed primarily to "establis[h] or prov [e]" some past fact, but to describe current circumstances requiring police assistance.

The difference between the interrogation in *Davis* and the one in *Crawford* is apparent on the face of things. In *Davis,* McCottry was speaking about events *as they were actually happening,* rather than "describ [ing] past events," *Lilly v. Virginia,* 527 U.S. 116, 137, 119 S. Ct. 1887, 144 L. Ed. 2d 117 (1999) (plurality opinion). Sylvia Crawford's interrogation, on the other hand, took place hours after the events she described had occurred. Moreover, any reasonable listener would recognize that McCottry (unlike Sylvia Crawford) was facing an ongoing emergency. Although one *might* call 911 to provide a narrative report of a crime absent any imminent danger, McCottry's call was plainly a call for help against bona fide physical threat. Third, the nature of what was asked and answered in *Davis,* again viewed objectively, was such that the elicited statements were necessary to be able to *resolve* the present emergency, rather than simply to learn (as in *Crawford*) what had happened in the past. That is true even of the operator's effort to establish the identity of the assailant, so that the dispatched officers might know whether they would be encountering a violent felon. See, e.g., *Hiibel v. Sixth Judicial Dist. Court of Nev., Humboldt Cty.,* 542 U.S. 177, 186, 124 S. Ct. 2451, 159 L. Ed. 2d 292 (2004). And finally, the difference in the level of formality between the two interviews is striking. Crawford was responding calmly, at the station house, to a series of questions, with the officer-interrogator taping and making notes of her answers; McCottry's frantic answers were provided over the phone, in an environment that was not tranquil, or even (as far as any reasonable 911 operator could make out) safe.

We conclude from all this that the circumstances of McCottry's interrogation objectively indicate its primary purpose was to enable police assistance to meet an ongoing emergency. She simply was not acting as a *witness;* she was not *testifying.* . . .

B

Determining the testimonial or nontestimonial character of the statements that were the product of the interrogation in *Hammon* is a much easier task, since they were not much different from the statements we found to be testimonial in *Crawford.* It is entirely clear from the circumstances that the interrogation was part of an investigation into possibly criminal past conduct—as, indeed, the testifying officer expressly acknowledged, App. in No. 05-5705, at 25, 32, 34. There was no emergency in progress; the interrogating officer testified that he had heard no arguments or crashing and saw no one throw or break anything, *id.,* at 25. When the officers first arrived, Amy told them that things were fine, *id.,* at 14, and there was no immediate threat to her person. When the officer questioned Amy for the second time, and elicited the challenged statements, he was not seeking to determine (as in *Davis*) "what is happening," but rather "what happened." Objectively viewed, the primary, if not indeed the sole, purpose of the interrogation was to investigate a possible crime—which is, of course, precisely what the officer *should* have done.

It is true that the *Crawford* interrogation was more formal. It followed a *Miranda* warning, was tape-recorded, and took place at the station house, see 541 U.S., at 53, n.4, 124 S. Ct. 1354. While these features certainly strengthened the statements' testimonial aspect—made it more objectively apparent, that is, that the purpose of the exercise was to nail down the truth about past criminal events—none was essential to the point. It was formal enough that Amy's interrogation was conducted in a separate room, away from her husband (who tried to intervene), with the officer receiving her replies for use in his "investigat[ion]." App. in No. 05-5705, at 34. What we called the "striking resemblance" of the *Crawford* statement to civil-law *ex parte* examinations, 541 U.S., at 52, 124 S. Ct. 1354, is shared by Amy's statement here. Both declarants were actively separated from the defendant-officers forcibly prevented Hershel from participating in the interrogation. Both statements deliberately recounted, in response to police questioning, how potentially criminal past events began and progressed. And both took place some time after the events described were over. Such statements under official interrogation are an obvious substitute for live testimony, because they do precisely *what a witness does* on direct examination; they are inherently testimonial. . . .

IV

Respondents in both cases, joined by a number of their *amici,* contend that the nature of the offenses charged in these two cases—domestic violence—requires greater flexibility in the use of testimonial evidence. This particular type of crime is notoriously susceptible to intimidation or coercion of the victim to ensure that she does not testify at trial. When this occurs, the Confrontation Clause gives the criminal a windfall. We may not, however, vitiate constitutional guarantees when they have the effect of allowing the guilty to go free. Cf. *Kyllo v. United States,* 533 U.S. 27, 121 S. Ct. 2038, 150 L. Ed. 2d 94 (2001) (suppressing evidence from an illegal search). But when defendants seek to undermine the judicial process by procuring or coercing silence from witnesses and victims, the Sixth Amendment does not require courts to acquiesce. While defendants have no duty to assist the State in proving their guilt, they *do* have the duty to refrain from acting in ways that destroy the integrity of the criminal-trial system. We reiterate what we said in *Crawford:* that "the rule of forfeiture by wrongdoing . . . extinguishes confrontation claims on essentially equitable grounds." 541 U.S., at 62, 124 S. Ct. 1354 (citing *Reynolds,* 98 U.S., at 158-159). That is, one who obtains the absence of a witness by wrongdoing forfeits the constitutional right to confrontation. . . .

We have determined that, absent a finding of forfeiture by wrongdoing, the Sixth Amendment operates to exclude Amy Hammon's affidavit. The Indiana courts may (if they are asked) determine on remand whether such a claim of forfeiture is properly raised and, if so, whether it is meritorious.

. . .

We affirm the judgment of the Supreme Court of Washington in No. 05-5224. We reverse the judgment of the Supreme Court of Indiana in No. 05-5705, and remand the case to that Court for proceedings not inconsistent with this opinion.

It is so ordered.

CASE QUESTIONS

MARYLAND v. CRAIG

1. What are the underlying purposes of the Confrontation Clause as explained by the Court?

2. How does the rule regarding the admissibility of hearsay impact the Confrontation Clause?

3. What must a trial court specifically determine prior to permitting a child witness to testify in a manner other than a face-to-face confrontation with a defendant?

4. What competing interests are being balanced in this case? On which side does the Court come down? Do you agree with the Court's decision? Explain.

5. Based on the Court's holding, will *all* children victims/witnesses be entitled to testify via a mechanism similar to the one-way closed circuit television? Explain.

DAVIS v. WASHINGTON

1. Why do you think the victims in *Davis* and *Hammon* failed to testify in their respective trials? What reason(s) could have contributed to their failure to appear?

2. How is it determined whether a statement is considered "testimonial evidence"? Provide some examples of what is/is not considered testimonial evidence. Why does it matter whether a statement is testimonial or not?

3. How did the Court use its prior precedent in Crawford v. Washington, 541 U.S. 36 (2004) to reach its holdings in *Davis* and *Hammon*? Why did the Court

reach opposite results in the two cases when applying the law in *Crawford* to the facts in each case?

4. What two related issues did the Court have to decide?

5. Why do you think the Court might have chosen to consider the facts in *Davis* and *Hammon* together as companion cases?

HYPOTHETICAL WITH ACCOMPANYING ANALYSIS

Hypothetical

Jim, a well-known physician, has been charged with illegally prescribing pain-killers to patients in order to make a profit. In fact, one of his patients overdosed and almost died as a result. Jim was able to post bond prior to trial. At the end of the first day of trial, Jim was informed by both his attorney and the judge that he needed to return to court the following morning at 8:00 a.m. sharp for the continuation of his trial. The next morning, however, Jim was nowhere to be found. Despite extensive efforts to locate him by the prosecution and defense, it appeared as though Jim had skipped bail and headed out of town. The trial judge decided to continue the trial even without Jim. During the remainder of the trial four of his former patients testified against him, and Jim's defense attorney cross-examined each witness. After four days of trial the case went to the jury. The judge instructed the jury not to assume guilt from the fact that Jim was not present at trial. Jim was convicted *in abstentia* on all counts.

Jim was eventually apprehended and incarcerated. On appeal, Jim is now arguing that his right to confrontation was violated because, although he was informed he had to report back to court the next morning, he was never specifically informed by the judge that the trial would continue without him. Therefore, Jim maintains he was precluded from confronting any witnesses against him. Will Jim succeed in his argument? Explain your answer in detail.

Analysis

The Confrontation Clause of the Sixth Amendment provides that "[i]n all criminal prosecutions, the accused shall enjoy the right . . . to be confronted with witnesses against him[.]" This right has typically encompassed situations in which the defendant is not present for trial; a witness is either not physically present and the witness' hearsay statement is admitted; or, the witness is permitted to testify in a manner other than a direct face-to-face confrontation with the accused.

In the instant case we are dealing with a situation in which the defendant was not present for his entire trial. Although a trial should be conducted *only* in the defendant's presence, a trial of a defendant *in abstentia* will be permitted under certain circumstances. Those circumstances include a defendant who has voluntarily failed to attend trial, or a defendant who is so disruptive during the trial process that removal from court or other measures become necessary. Jim's case falls within the former scenario because he voluntarily absented himself from trial. Both the judge and defense attorney explicitly told Jim that he was required to attend the next day of trial. Jim, however, decided to flee rather than stand trial. There is no evidence to indicate that he missed trial for reasons beyond his control. Diaz v. United States, 223 U.S. 442 (1912) has explained that if a trial has begun with the defendant present and he then voluntarily absents himself, the trial can continue in his absence because the defendant has, in effect, waived his right to be present at trial. Additionally, Jim will not succeed in his argument that the trial judge had an obligation to specifically tell him the trial would continue in his absence. A trial court is under no such obligation and a defendant should know that once a trial has begun, if the defendant takes flight, that the trial will likely continue in his absence. Taylor v. United States, 414 U.S. 17 (1973).

In conclusion, Jim's Sixth Amendment right to confrontation was not violated by the completion of his trial *in abstentia*.

Steve, a county police officer, was on traffic patrol one day and running radar in the hopes of catching someone in way too much of a hurry. His unmarked patrol car was cleverly hidden behind some overgrown bushes in a residential neighborhood when a car flew right past him. His radar indicated that the vehicle was traveling 52 miles per hour in a posted 25 mile-per-hour zone. Steve immediately pursued the vehicle, activating his lights and sirens, and he pulled it over to the shoulder of the road. Steve then began to exit his patrol car. Before he could get both feet on the ground, Melanie, the young woman who was driving the vehicle, ran up to him in a complete panic. "Oh thank goodness!" she exclaimed. "I just saw a man kidnap a child! You have to do something!" "What? Okay ma'am, calm down," Steve replied. "Now tell me again what happened, but slow down and please try to give me as much detail as you can." The woman took a deep breath and began: "Well, I was just on Pine Street and there was this car ahead of me driving really slowly. All of a sudden the car stopped. The driver grabbed this little girl who was jumping rope on the sidewalk and shoved her into the car. She kept screaming 'Help! Let me go!' Then he just took off. I didn't have my cell phone with me and I panicked, so I drove as fast as I could so I could get to the police station and tell someone what happened. Please officer, you *have* to help!"

Steve immediately radioed the patrol center and relayed what the woman had told him, along with a detailed description she had given him of the vehicle. Within an hour the vehicle was located and Carl, the driver, was apprehended. The young girl was found safe, although she had a few bruises from when Carl had forced her into the vehicle.

Carl is currently on trial for kidnapping and related offenses. During his trial the prosecutor called Steve to the stand and asked him to repeat the conversation he had with Melanie, because Melanie had moved out of state and could not be located for trial. Carl objected and argued that allowing Steve to testify as to what Melanie had said would violate his Sixth Amendment rights to confrontation. Discuss whether Carl will succeed in his argument.

1. Matt and Will are codefendants being tried jointly for an armed bank robbery. Neither defendant testifies at trial. The prosecution introduces into evidence a confession that Matt gave to police the day after the robbery in which he said, "Yeah, I robbed the bank with Will, but it was all his idea and he's the one who brought the gun." Will objects and argues that allowing Matt's confession to be admitted at trial when Matt is not going to testify will violate his right to confrontation. Can Will prevail in his argument? *See* Bruton v. United States, 391 U.S. 123 (1968).

2. Revisit the previous Discussion Question. If you were the trial judge, in what way(s) could you resolve the issue so that Matt's confession would

be admissible at trial against him without potentially violating Will's Sixth Amendment right to confrontation?

3. Research challenge: Familiarize yourself with the bizarre case of Ira Einhorn, a man accused of murdering his ex-girlfriend Holly Maddux in Philadelphia in 1977. What did Einhorn to do essentially waive his Sixth Amendment right to confrontation? What was the ultimate outcome of his case?

4. (a) Garrett is on trial for incest. The prosecution calls Dr. Anderson to testify and repeat on the stand what Jennifer, the 3-year-old victim, had told him regarding the alleged abuse at a previous doctor's appointment. Jennifer does not take the stand, and Garrett objects to the admission of the testimony. (b) Becky is on trial for sexually exploiting Cindy, her 14-year-old daughter. Cindy testifies at trial, but Becky claims she is denied her right effectively cross-examine Cindy because Becky did not have access to social service records including previous statements made by Cindy regarding potential abuse. In which situation, if either, will the respective defendants have a valid argument that their right to confrontation was violated? *See* Pennsylvania v. Ritchie, 480 U.S. 39 (1987) and Idaho v. Wright, 497 U.S. 805 (1990).

5. How disruptive does a defendant's behavior have to be before she will be removed from trial and it will continue in her absence? *See, e.g.,* Illinois v. Allen, 397 U.S. 337 (1970).

6. Research challenge: In the mid-1980s, family members Violet Amirault, Gerald Amirault, and Cheryl Amirault LaFave were convicted in a Massachusetts court of various sexual offenses against several young children at a daycare center their family owned and operated. How did the children witnesses testify against the Amiraults at trial? How did their unique method of testimony potentially conflict with the defendants' right to confrontation? *See* Commonwealth v. Amirault, 677 N.E.2d 652 (Mass. 1997) and Commonwealth v. Amirault, 535 N.E.2d 193 (Mass. 1989).

7. Brandon is on trial for drug trafficking, conspiracy to distribute drugs, and weapons offenses. The large majority of the prosecution's evidence came from "Bob" (not his real name), one of the key players in Brandon's drug enterprise. Bob turned Brandon in and gave the authorities a wealth of information implicating Brandon. At trial the prosecution declines to call Bob as a witness, arguing that his identity needs to remain anonymous in order to protect Bob's safety and to ensure that other suspects in the drug enterprise could be brought to justice. Brandon argues he has a right to confront Bob and examine the prosecution's most crucial witness against him. Which side will prevail? *See, e.g.,* Rovario v. United States, 353 U.S. 53 (1957).

8. Research challenge: What does your jurisdiction do with regard to handling the testimony of a child witness? Locate the relevant statute(s).

9. Courts are generally permitted, given compelling circumstances, to conduct trials in the defendant's absence *unless* it is a capital offense. *See, e.g.,* Diaz v. United States, 223 U.S. 442 (1912). Why do you think death penalty

cases are treated differently from all other criminal cases in this regard? *See* Chapter 11, *infra*.

10. Revisit the Hypothetical for Student Analysis from this chapter. Would it have made any difference in your analysis if Melanie had been available to testify at trial? Explain.

11. What is a "rape shield statute" and what is its purpose? How might such a statute conflict with an accused's right to confrontation? *See* Olden v. Kentucky, 488 U.S. 227 (1988).

12. Research challenge: Familiarize yourself with the case of Mark Jensen, a Wisconsin man convicted in 2008 of poisoning his wife a decade before. How did his case, dubbed "The Letter from the Grave" case by media, center around a Confrontation Clause issue? What was the outcome regarding that issue? Do you agree? *See* State v. Jensen, 727 N.W.2d 518 (Wis. 2007).

True/False

Read the below hypothetical and answer the questions that follow:

Asheville is a small town that has been the subject of a string of recent hate crimes. The police have had little luck finding who is responsible for the crimes, so they decided to set up a telephone hotline where citizens could call in tips. One afternoon an individual called the hotline. The operator identified herself as an employee of the local police department, and the caller stated he wished to remain anonymous. "No problem," replied the operator, "so what is it you'd like to tell me?" "Well, I know who burned down that church last week. It was Colin Jenkins. He came over to my house after it was done and was bragging about it." "And how did he do it?" asked the operator. The caller then provided details about how Colin planned and executed his crimes, and the caller hung up without ever giving his name. Several weeks later, Colin Jenkins was arrested for arson.

1. If the operator is called to the stand and asked to repeat what the caller said, the admission of this testimony would constitute hearsay.

2. The caller's statement would not be considered "testimonial" evidence for purposes of the Confrontation Clause because he was calling to report a past crime rather than to seek assistance in an immediate emergency.

3. The Confrontation Clause would not apply to the above hypothetical because the operator never learned the identity of the caller.

4. The caller's statement would most likely be inadmissible in court against Colin because it is not inherently reliable, and Colin had no opportunity to cross-examine the caller about his statement.

5. Colin's right to cross-examination was satisfied because the operator asked the caller to provide details, so the operator in effect cross-examined the caller for Colin.

Multiple Choice

6. What unique facts in Maryland v. Craig led the Court to hold that a defendant's right to confrontation could be limited under certain conditions?

   A. The fact that the witness in that case was a child
   B. The fact that the witness in that case had been a victim of sexual abuse
   C. Both the fact that the witness was a child and had been a victim of sexual abuse
   D. The fact that the witness did not want to testify in front of the defendant

7. Which of the following is *not* one of the underlying purposes of the Confrontation Clause?

   A. To ensure that a victim has the constitutional right to confront the defendant and testify as to the impact the crime had on the victim's life
   B. To ensure that a witness will give statements under oath, thus impressing the seriousness of the matter on the witness
   C. To require the witness to submit to cross-examination
   D. To provide the jury with the opportunity to observe the witness' demeanor and judge the witness' overall credibility

8. According to Maryland v. Craig, what must a trial court find *before* permitting a child to testify in a manner other than direct face-to-face confrontation with the accused?

   A. That the child witness would be traumatized by having to testify specifically in the presence of the defendant
   B. That the emotional distress suffered by the child witness in the presence of the defendant is more than mere nervousness or reluctance to testify
   C. Neither A nor B
   D. Both A and B

9. Which of the following factors would likely be the *most* important when determining whether a statement is "testimonial" for the purposes of the Confrontation Clause?

   A. Whether the statement was made by a victim of a crime
   B. The location of the witness when making the statement
   C. Whether the witness was *Mirandized* prior to making the statement
   D. Whether the primary purpose of the statement was to explain an ongoing emergency or to produce facts revealing a past crime

10. Which of the following circumstances could potentially result in a violation of the defendant's Sixth Amendment right to confrontation?

    A. Conducting a trial in the defendant's absence
    B. Conducting a trial with the defendant present but bound and gagged because of her disruptive behavior
    C. Admitting hearsay evidence against the defendant that cannot be established as reliable
    D. All of the above could result in a violation of the defendant's right to confrontation.

III

The Post-Trial Process

11

Cruel and Unusual Punishment

"Excessive bail shall not be required, nor excessive fines imposed, nor cruel and unusual punishments inflicted."
—**The Eighth Amendment**

INTRODUCTION

Death is different. One simple sentence, three little words that speak volumes about the ultimate price to pay for committing a crime: The price of life.

Cruel and unusual punishment isn't *all* about the death penalty of course. In fact, when our nation was first formed the use of the death penalty wasn't even controversial. Rather, the Cruel and Unusual Punishment Clause of the Eighth Amendment was seen more as a prohibition on torture. In the 1800s, however, organized opposition to the death penalty began, and the Eighth Amendment provided the vehicle to accomplish that opposition. Fast forwarding another hundred or so years, it seems as though today whenever we hear the phrase "cruel and unusual punishment," we automatically think of the death penalty and little else. But as we'll see in this chapter, the Eighth Amendment covers circumstances that have nothing to do with taking an individual's life.

When it comes to cruel and unusual punishment, the most significant case to date is undoubtedly Furman v. Georgia, 408 U.S. 238 (1972). Why? Because it declared that the death penalty was being imposed in an unconstitutional manner, and it single-handedly put a national freeze on the death penalty for over a decade. It sent legislatures in 37 jurisdictions back to the drawing board, either to rewrite their death penalty laws or to abolish the death penalty altogether. And practically speaking, it took 629 inmates who were on death row at that time and gave them automatic reprieves—their sentences were commuted to life in prison. Basically, a mad scramble occurred. So if one case could wreak havoc on a nation, why omit it from this book? The numbers speak for themselves: The opinion is a massive 232 pages, and all nine Justices wrote separately to express their views. It is truly a monster of a case that cannot be whittled down to ten or so pages. But *Furman*'s message and significance is easily understood when reading Gregg v. Georgia, a case four years after *Furman* in which the Court approved of new standards for the imposition of the death penalty that are followed in many states to this day.

Of all the constitutional provisions related to criminal procedure, this one has likely seen the most evolution, controversy, and raw emotion. Never has a nation been so divided or so passionate about the interpretation of four words: CRUEL AND UNUSUAL PUNISHMENT.

STUDENT *Checklist*

Cruel and Unusual Punishment

PUNISHMENT GENERALLY

1. Did the government seek to punish the appropriate **conduct**?

■ Did government improperly punish **status** rather than properly punishing **antisocial behavior**?

2. Was the **punishment imposed** cruel and unusual?

■ Was the imposed punishment **significantly disproportionate** to the crime when considering:
   The **gravity of the offense** and the **harshness of the penalty**;
   Sentences imposed on **other criminals** in the **same jurisdiction**; and
   Sentences imposed for the **same crime** in **other jurisdictions**?

3. With regard to **prisoners:**

■ Did prison officials exhibit a **deliberate indifference** to **serious medical needs** of the prisoner?

■ Was the prisoner denied the **minimum necessities for civilized existence**?

■ Was the prisoner exposed to the **wanton and unnecessary infliction of pain**?

THE DEATH PENALTY

1. Was the individual **eligible** for the death penalty?

■ **Eighteen** years of age at the time of the crime

■ **Not mentally retarded**

■ **Not legally insane**

2. Did the defendant commit a **crime** that was punishable by death?*

■ **Premeditated murder**

■ **Felony murder** if
   The defendant directly **caused the death** of the victim
   or

The defendant did not actually cause the death but he either (a) had the **intent to kill** or (b) was a **major participant** in a felony where death resulted and the defendant exhibited a **reckless indifference to human life**

3. Were **procedural safeguards** imposed to ensure that the death penalty wasn't imposed in an **arbitrary and capricious** manner, such as:

■ A **bifurcated trial** (including a **guilt phase** and a **sentencing phase**)

■ The jury's ability to **weigh aggravating** and **mitigating factors**

■ The ability to **avoid** the death penalty if desired (i.e., no **mandatory death penalty** as punishment)

■ Jury given **clear and detailed standards** as to when the death penalty would be appropriate

■ An **automatic appeal** of a death sentence

*Note: Both the federal government and various state governments permit the death penalty for crimes other than murder, including aggravated kidnapping, aircraft hijacking, espionage, treason, and drug trafficking. The Supreme Court, however, has never directly ruled on the constitutionality of executing someone for the commission of those crimes.

SUPREME COURT CASES

GREGG v. GEORGIA, 428 U.S. 153 (1976)

The issue in this case is whether the imposition of the sentence of death for the crime of murder under the law of Georgia violates the Eighth and Fourteenth Amendments.

I

The petitioner, Troy Gregg, was charged with committing armed robbery and murder. In accordance with Georgia procedure in capital cases, the trial was in two stages, a guilt stage and a sentencing stage. The evidence at the guilt trial established that on November 21, 1973, the petitioner and a traveling companion, Floyd Allen, while hitchhiking north in Florida were picked up by Fred Simmons and Bob Moore. Their car broke down, but they continued north after Simmons purchased another vehicle with some of the cash he was carrying. While still in Florida, they picked up another hitchhiker, Dennis Weaver, who rode with them to Atlanta, where he was let out about 11 p.m. A short time later the four men interrupted their journey for a rest stop along the highway. The next morning the bodies of Simmons and Moore were discovered in a ditch nearby.

On November 23, after reading about the shootings in an Atlanta newspaper, Weaver communicated with the Gwinnett County police and related information concerning the journey with the victims, including a description of the car. The next afternoon, the petitioner and Allen, while in Simmons' car, were arrested in Asheville, N.C. In the search incident to the arrest a .25-caliber pistol, later shown to be that used to kill Simmons and Moore, was found in the petitioner's pocket. After receiving the warnings required by Miranda v. Arizona, 384 U.S. 436, 86 S. Ct. 1602, 16 L. Ed. 2d 694 (1966), and signing a written waiver of his rights, the petitioner signed a statement in which he admitted shooting, then robbing Simmons and Moore. He justified the slayings on grounds of self-defense. The next day, while being transferred to Lawrence-ville, Ga., the petitioner and Allen were taken to the scene of the shootings. Upon arriving there, Allen recounted the events leading to the slayings. His version of these events was as follows: After Simmons and Moore left the car, the petitioner stated that he intended to rob them. The petitioner then took his pistol in hand and positioned himself on the car to improve his aim. As Simmons and Moore came up an embankment toward the car, the petitioner fired three shots and the two men fell near a ditch. The petitioner, at close range, then fired a shot into the head of each. He robbed them of valuables and drove away with Allen. . . .

. . . The jury found the petitioner guilty of two counts of armed robbery and two counts of murder.

At the penalty stage, which took place before the same jury, neither the prosecutor nor the petitioner's lawyer offered any additional evidence. Both counsel, however, made lengthy arguments dealing generally with the propriety of capital punishment under the circumstances and with the weight of the evidence of guilt. The trial judge instructed the jury that it could recommend either a death sentence or a life prison sentence on each count. The judge further charged the jury that in determining what sentence was appropriate the jury was free to consider the facts and circumstances, if any, presented by the parties in mitigation or aggravation. . . .

[T]he jury returned verdicts of death on each count.

The Supreme Court of Georgia affirmed the convictions and the imposition of the death sentences for murder. 233 Ga. 117, 210 S.E.2d 659 (1974). After reviewing the trial transcript and the record, including the evidence, and comparing the evidence and sentence in similar cases in accordance with the requirements of Georgia law, the court concluded that, considering the nature of the crime and the defendant, the sentences of death had not resulted from prejudice or any other arbitrary factor and were not excessive or disproportionate to the penalty applied in similar cases. . . .

We granted the petitioner's application for a writ of certiorari limited to his challenge to the imposition of the death sentences in this case as "cruel and unusual" punishment in violation of the Eighth and the Fourteenth Amendments. 423 U.S. 1082, 96 S. Ct. 1090, 47 L. Ed. 2d 93 (1976).

II

Before considering the issues presented it is necessary to understand the Georgia statutory scheme for the imposition of the death penalty. The Georgia statute, as amended after our decision in Furman v. Georgia, 408 U.S. 238, 92 S. Ct. 2726, 33 L. Ed. 2d 346 (1972), retains the death penalty for six categories of crime: murder, kidnaping for ransom or where the victim is harmed, armed robbery rape, treason, and aircraft hijacking. 6 Ga. Code Ann. §§ 26-1101, 26-1311, 26-1902, 26-2001, 26-2201, 26-3301 (1972). The capital defendant's guilt or innocence is determined in the traditional manner, either by a trial judge or a jury, in the first stage of a bifurcated trial.

If trial is by jury, the trial judge is required to charge lesser included offenses when they are supported by any view of the evidence. Sims v. State, 203 Ga. 668, 47 S.E.2d 862 (1948). See Linder v. State, 132 Ga. App. 624, 625, 208 S.E.2d 630, 631 (1974). After a verdict, finding, or plea of guilty to a capital crime, a presentence hearing is conducted before whoever made the determination of guilt. The sentencing procedures are essentially the same in both bench and jury trials. At the hearing:

> (T)he judge (or jury) shall hear additional evidence in extenuation, mitigation, and aggravation of punishment, including the record of any prior criminal convictions and pleas of guilty or pleas of nolo contendere of the defendant, or the absence of any prior conviction and pleas: Provided, however, that only such evidence in aggravation as the State has made known to the defendant prior to his trial shall be admissible. The judge (or jury) shall also hear argument by the defendant or his counsel and the prosecuting attorney . . . regarding the punishment to be imposed. § 27-2503. (Supp. 1975).

The defendant is accorded substantial latitude as to the types of evidence that he may introduce. See Brown v. State, 235 Ga. 644, 647-650, 220 S.Ed.2d 922, 925-926 (1975). Evidence considered during the guilt stage may be considered during the sentencing stage without being resubmitted. Eberheart v. State, 232 Ga. 247, 253, 206 S.E.2d 12, 17 (1974).

In the assessment of the appropriate sentence to be imposed the judge is also required to consider or to include in his instructions to the jury "any mitigating circumstances or aggravating circumstances otherwise authorized by law and any of (10) statutory aggravating circumstances which may be supported by the evidence. . . ." § 27-2534.1(b) (Supp. 1975). The scope of the nonstatutory aggravating or mitigating circumstances is not delineated in the statute. Before a convicted defendant may be sentenced to death, however, except in cases of treason or aircraft hijacking, the jury, or the trial judge in cases tried without a jury, must find beyond a reasonable doubt one of the 10 aggravating circumstances specified in the statute. The sentence of death may be imposed only if the jury (or judge) finds one of the statutory aggravating circumstances and then elects to impose that sentence. § 26-3102 (Supp. 1975). If the verdict is death, the jury or judge must specify the aggravating circumstance(s) found. § 27-2534.1(c) (Supp. 1975). In jury cases, the trial judge is bound by the jury's recommended sentence. §§ 26-3102, 27-2514 (Supp. 1975).

In addition to the conventional appellate process available in all criminal cases, provision is made for special expedited direct review by the Supreme Court of Georgia of the appropriateness of imposing the sentence of death in the particular case. . . .

IV

We now consider whether Georgia may impose the death penalty on the petitioner in this case.

A

While Furman did not hold that the infliction of the death penalty per se violates the Constitution's ban on cruel and unusual punishments, it did recognize that the penalty of death is different in kind from any other punishment imposed under our system of criminal justice. Because of the uniqueness of the death penalty, Furman held that it could not be imposed under sentencing procedures that created a substantial risk that it would be inflicted in an arbitrary and capricious manner. Mr. Justice White concluded that "the death penalty is exacted with great infrequency even for the most atrocious crimes and . . . there is no meaningful basis for distinguishing the few cases in which it is imposed from the many cases in which it is not." 408 U.S., at 313, 92 S. Ct., at

2764 (concurring). Indeed, the death sentences examined by the Court in Furman were "cruel and unusual in the same way that being struck by lightening is cruel and unusual. For, of all the people convicted of (capital crimes), many just as reprehensible as these, the petitioners (in Furman were) among a capriciously selected random handful upon whom the sentence of death has in fact been imposed. . . . (T)he Eighth and Fourteenth Amendments cannot tolerate the infliction of a sentence of death under legal systems that permit this unique penalty to be so wantonly and so freakishly imposed." Id., at 309-310, 92 S. Ct., at 2762 (Stewart, J., concurring).

Furman mandates that where discretion is afforded a sentencing body on a matter so grave as the determination of whether a human life should be taken or spared, that discretion must be suitably directed and limited so as to minimize the risk of wholly arbitrary and capricious action. . . .

Jury sentencing has been considered desirable in capital cases in order "to maintain a link between contemporary community values and the penal system a link without which the determination of punishment could hardly reflect 'the evolving standards of decency that mark the progress of a maturing society.'" But it creates special problems. Much of the information that is relevant to the sentencing decision may have no relevance to the question of guilt, or may even be extremely prejudicial to a fair determination of that question. This problem, however, is scarcely insurmountable. Those who have studied the question suggest that a bifurcated procedure—one in which the question of sentence is not considered until the determination of guilt has been made—is the best answer. . . .

But the provision of relevant information under fair procedural rules is not alone sufficient to guarantee that the information will be properly used in the imposition of punishment, especially if sentencing is performed by a jury. Since the members of a jury will have had little, if any, previous experience in sentencing, they are unlikely to be skilled in dealing with the information they are given. . . . To the extent that this problem is inherent in jury sentencing, it may not be totally correctible. It seems clear, however, that the problem will be alleviated if the jury is given guidance regarding the factors about the crime and the defendant that the State, representing organized society, deems particularly relevant to the sentencing decision. . . .

While some have suggested that standards to guide a capital jury's sentencing deliberations are impossible to formulate, the fact is that such standards have been developed. When the drafters of the Model Penal Code faced this problem, they concluded "that it is within the realm of possibility to point to the main circumstances of aggravation and of mitigation that should be weighed *and weighed against each other* when they are presented in a concrete case." ALI, Model Penal Code § 201.6, Comment 3, p. 71 (Tent. Draft No. 9, 1959) (emphasis in original). While such standards are by necessity somewhat general, they do provide guidance to the sentencing authority and thereby reduce the likelihood that it will impose a sentence that fairly can be called capricious or arbitrary. Where the sentencing authority is required to specify the factors it relied upon in reaching its decision, the further safeguard of meaningful appellate review is available to ensure that death sentences are not imposed capriciously or in a freakish manner.

In summary, the concerns expressed in Furman that the penalty of death not be imposed in an arbitrary or capricious manner can be met by a carefully drafted statute that ensures that the sentencing authority is given adequate information and guidance. As a general proposition these concerns are best met by a system that provides for a bifurcated proceeding at which the sentencing authority is apprised of the information relevant to the imposition of sentence and provided with standards to guide its use of the information.

We do not intend to suggest that only the above-described procedures would be permissible under Furman or that any sentencing system constructed along these general lines would inevitably satisfy the concerns of Furman, for each distinct system must be examined on an individual basis. Rather, we have embarked upon this general exposition to make clear that it is possible to construct capital-sentencing systems capable of meeting Furman's constitutional concerns.

B

We now turn to consideration of the constitutionality of Georgia's capital-sentencing procedures. In the wake of Furman, Georgia amended its capital punishment statute, but chose not to narrow the scope of its murder provisions. See Part II, Supra. Thus, now as before Furman, in Georgia "(a) person commits murder when he unlawfully and with malice aforethought, either express or implied, causes the death of another human being." Ga. Code Ann., § 26-1101(a) (1972). All persons convicted of murder "shall be punished by death or by imprisonment for life." § 26-1101(c) (1972).

Georgia did act, however, to narrow the class of murderers subject to capital punishment by specifying 10 statutory aggravating circumstances, one of which must be found by the jury to exist beyond a reasonable doubt before a death sentence can ever be imposed. In addition, the jury is authorized to consider any other appropriate aggravating or mitigating circumstances. § 27-2534.1(b) (Supp. 1975). The jury is not required to find any mitigating circumstance in order to make a recommendation of mercy that is binding on the trial court, see § 27-2302 (Supp. 1975), but it must find a Statutory aggravating circumstance before recommending a sentence of death.

These procedures require the jury to consider the circumstances of the crime and the criminal before it recommends sentence. No longer can a Georgia jury do as Furman's jury did: reach a finding of the defendant's guilt and then, without guidance or direction, decide whether he should live or die. Instead, the jury's attention is directed to the specific circumstances of the crime: Was it committed in the course of another capital felony? Was it committed for money? Was it committed upon a peace officer or judicial officer? Was it committed in a particularly heinous way or in a manner that endangered the lives of many persons? In addition, the jury's attention is focused on the characteristics of the person who committed the crime: Does he have a record of prior convictions for capital offenses? Are there any special facts about this defendant that mitigate against imposing capital punishment (E.g., his youth, the extent of his cooperation with the police, his emotional state at the time of the crime). As a result, while some jury discretion still exists, "the discretion to be exercised is controlled by clear and objective standards so as to produce non-discriminatory application." Coley v. State, 231 Ga. 829, 834, 204 S.E.2d 612, 615 (1974).

As an important additional safeguard against arbitrariness and caprice, the Georgia statutory scheme provides for automatic appeal of all death sentences to the State's Supreme Court. That court is required by statute to review each sentence of death and determine whether it was imposed under the influence of passion or prejudice, whether the evidence supports the jury's finding of a statutory aggravating circumstance, and whether the sentence is disproportionate compared to those sentences imposed in similar cases. § 27-2537(c) (Supp. 1975).

In short, Georgia's new sentencing procedures require as a prerequisite to the imposition of the death penalty, specific jury findings as to the circumstances of the crime or the character of the defendant. Moreover, to guard further against a situation comparable to that presented in Furman, the Supreme Court of Georgia compares each death sentence with the sentences imposed on similarly situated defendants to ensure that the sentence of death in a particular case is not disproportionate. On their face these procedures seem to satisfy the concerns of Furman. No longer should there be "no meaningful basis for distinguishing the few cases in which (the death penalty) is imposed from the many cases in which it is not." 408 U.S., at 313, 92 S. Ct., at 2764 (White, J., concurring). . . .

V

The basic concern of Furman centered on those defendants who were being condemned to death capriciously and arbitrarily. Under the procedures before the Court in that case, sentencing authorities were not directed to give attention to the nature or circumstances of the crime committed or to the character or record of the defendant. Left unguided, juries imposed the death sentence in a way that could only be called freakish. The new Georgia sentencing procedures, by contrast, focus the jury's attention on the particularized nature of the crime and the particularized characteristics of the individual defendant. While the jury is permitted to consider any aggravating or mitigating circumstances, it must find and identify at least one statutory aggravating factor before it may impose a penalty of death. In this way the jury's discretion is channeled. No longer can a jury wantonly and freakishly impose the death sentence; it is always circumscribed by the legislative guidelines. In addition, the review function of the Supreme Court of Georgia affords additional assurance that the concerns that prompted our decision in *Furman* are not present to any significant degree in the Georgia procedure applied here.

For the reasons expressed in this opinion, we hold that the statutory system under which Gregg was sentenced to death does not violate the Constitution. Accordingly, the judgment of the Georgia Supreme Court is affirmed.

It is so ordered.

BAZE v. REES, 553 U.S. ____ (2008)

Like 35 other States and the Federal Government, Kentucky has chosen to impose capital punishment for certain crimes. As is true with respect to each of these States and the Federal Government, Kentucky has altered its method of execution over time to more humane means of carrying out the sentence. That progress has led to the use of lethal injection by every jurisdiction that imposes the death penalty.

Petitioners in this case—each convicted of double homicide—acknowledge that the lethal injection procedure, if applied as intended, will result in a humane death. They nevertheless contend that the lethal injection protocol is unconstitutional under the Eighth Amendment's ban on "cruel and unusual punishments," because of the risk that the protocol's terms might not be properly followed, resulting in significant pain. They propose an alternative protocol, one that they concede has not been adopted by any State and has never been tried.

The trial court held extensive hearings and entered detailed Findings of Fact and Conclusions of Law. It recognized that "[t]here are no methods of legal execution that are satisfactory to those who oppose the death penalty on moral, religious, or societal grounds," but concluded that Kentucky's procedure "complies with the constitutional requirements against cruel and unusual punishment." App. 769. The State Supreme Court affirmed. We too agree that petitioners have not carried their burden of showing that the risk of pain from maladministration of a concededly humane lethal injection protocol, and the failure to adopt untried and untested alternatives, constitute cruel and unusual punishment. The judgment below is affirmed.

I

A

By the middle of the 19th century, "hanging was the 'nearly universal form of execution' in the United States." *Campbell v. Wood,* 511 U.S. 1119, 114 S. Ct. 2125, 128 L. Ed. 2d 682 (1994). . . . In 1888, following the recommendation of a commission empaneled by the Governor to find " 'the most humane and practical method known to modern science of carrying into effect the sentence of death,' " New York became the first State to authorize electrocution as a form of capital punishment. *Glass v. Louisiana,* 471 U.S. 1080, 1082, and n.4, 105 S. Ct. 2159, 85 L. Ed. 2d 514 (1985) (Brennan, J., dissenting from denial of certiorari); Denno, *supra,* at 373. By 1915, 11 other States had followed suit, motivated by the "well-grounded belief that electrocution is less painful and more humane than hanging." *Malloy v. South Carolina,* 237 U.S. 180, 185, 35 S. Ct. 507, 59 L. Ed. 905 (1915).

Electrocution remained the predominant mode of execution for nearly a century, although several methods, including hanging, firing squad, and lethal gas were in use at one time. Brief for Fordham University School of Law et al. as *Amici Curiae* 5-9 (hereinafter Fordham Brief). Following the 9-year hiatus in executions that ended with our decision in *Gregg v. Georgia,* 428 U.S. 153, 96 S. Ct. 2909, 49 L. Ed. 2d 859 (1976), however, state legislatures began responding to public calls to reexamine electrocution as a means of assuring a humane death. See S. Banner, The Death Penalty: An American History 192-193, 296-297 (2002). In 1977, legislators in Oklahoma, after consulting with the head of the anesthesiology department at the University of Oklahoma College of Medicine, introduced the first bill proposing lethal injection as the State's method of execution. See Brief for Petitioners 4; Fordham Brief 21-22. A total of 36 States have now adopted lethal injection as the exclusive or primary means of implementing the death penalty, making it by far the most prevalent method of execution in the United States. It is also the method used by the Federal Government. . . .

Of these 36 States, at least 30 (including Kentucky) use the same combination of three drugs in their lethal injection protocols. See *Workman v. Bredesen,* 486 F.3d 896, 902 (C.A. 6 2007). The first drug, sodium thiopental (also known as Pentathol), is a fast-acting barbiturate sedative that induces a deep, comalike unconsciousness when given in the amounts used for lethal injection. App. 762-763, 631-632. The second drug, pancuronium bromide (also known as Pavulon), is a paralytic agent that inhibits all muscular-skeletal movements and, by paralyzing the diaphragm, stops respiration. *Id.,* at 763. Potassium chloride, the third drug, interferes with the electrical signals that stimulate the contractions of the heart, inducing cardiac arrest. *Ibid.* The proper administration of the first drug ensures that the prisoner does not experience any pain associated with the paralysis and cardiac arrest caused by the second and third drugs. *Id.,* at 493-494, 541, 558-559. . . .

II

The Eighth Amendment to the Constitution, applicable to the States through the Due Process Clause of the Fourteenth Amendment, see *Robinson v. California,*

370 U.S. 660, 666, 82 S. Ct. 1417, 8 L. Ed. 2d 758 (1962), provides that "[e]xcessive bail shall not be required, nor excessive fines imposed, nor cruel and unusual punishments inflicted." We begin with the principle, settled by *Gregg,* that capital punishment is constitutional. See 428 U.S., at 177, 96 S. Ct. 2909 (joint opinion of Stewart, Powell, and Stevens, JJ.). It necessarily follows that there must be a means of carrying it out. Some risk of pain is inherent in any method of execution—no matter how humane—if only from the prospect of error in following the required procedure. It is clear, then, that the Constitution does not demand the avoidance of all risk of pain in carrying out executions.

Petitioners do not claim that it does. Rather, they contend that the Eighth Amendment prohibits procedures that create an "unnecessary risk" of pain. Brief for Petitioners 38. Specifically, they argue that courts must evaluate "(a) the severity of pain risked, (b) the likelihood of that pain occurring, and (c) the extent to which alternative means are feasible, either by modifying existing execution procedures or adopting alternative procedures." *Ibid.* Petitioners envision that the quantum of risk necessary to make out an Eighth Amendment claim will vary according to the severity of the pain and the availability of alternatives, Reply Brief for Petitioners 23-24, n.9, but that the risk must be "significant" to trigger Eighth Amendment scrutiny, see Brief for Petitioners 39-40; Reply Brief for Petitioners 25-26.

Kentucky responds that this "unnecessary risk" standard is tantamount to a requirement that States adopt the " 'least risk' " alternative in carrying out an execution, a standard the Commonwealth contends will cast recurring constitutional doubt on any procedure adopted by the States. Brief for Respondents 29, 35. Instead, Kentucky urges the Court to approve the " 'substantial risk' " test used by the courts below. *Id.,* at 34-35.

A

This Court has never invalidated a State's chosen procedure for carrying out a sentence of death as the infliction of cruel and unusual punishment. In *Wilkerson v. Utah,* 99 U.S. 130, 25 L. Ed. 345 (1879), we upheld a sentence to death by firing squad imposed by a territorial court, rejecting the argument that such a sentence constituted cruel and unusual punishment. *Id.,* at 134-135. We noted there the difficulty of "defin[ing] with exactness the extent of the constitutional provision which provides that cruel and unusual punishments shall not be inflicted." *Id.,* at 135-136. Rather than undertake such an effort, the *Wilkerson* Court simply noted that "it is safe to affirm that punishments of torture, . . . and all others in the same line of unnecessary cruelty, are forbidden" by the Eighth Amendment. *Id.,* at 136. By way of example, the Court cited cases from England in which "terror, pain, or disgrace were sometimes superadded" to the sentence, such as where the condemned was "embowelled alive, beheaded, and quartered," or instances of "public dissection in murder, and burning alive." *Id.,* at 135. In contrast, we observed that the firing squad was routinely used as a method of execution for military officers. *Id.,* at 137. What each of the forbidden punishments had in common was the deliberate infliction of pain for the sake of pain—"superadd[ing]" pain to the death sentence through torture and the like.

We carried these principles further in *In re Kemmler,* 136 U.S. 436, 10 S. Ct. 930, 34 L. Ed. 519 (1890). There we rejected an opportunity to incorporate the Eighth Amendment against the States in a challenge to the first execution by electrocution, to be carried out by the State of New York. *Id.,* at 449, 10 S. Ct. 930. In passing over that question, however, we observed that "[p]unishments are cruel when they involve torture or a lingering death; but the punishment of death is not cruel within the meaning of that word as used in the Constitution.

It implies there something inhuman and barbarous, something more than the mere extinguishment of life." *Id.*, at 447, 10 S. Ct. 930. We noted that the New York statute adopting electrocution as a method of execution "was passed in the effort to devise a more humane method of reaching the result." *Ibid.*

B

Petitioners do not claim that lethal injection or the proper administration of the particular protocol adopted by Kentucky by themselves constitute the cruel or wanton infliction of pain. Quite the contrary, they concede that "if performed properly," an execution carried out under Kentucky's procedures would be "humane and constitutional." Brief for Petitioners 31. That is because, as counsel for petitioners admitted at oral argument, proper administration of the first drug, sodium thiopental, eliminates any meaningful risk that a prisoner would experience pain from the subsequent injections of pancuronium and potassium chloride. See Tr. of Oral Arg. 5; App. 493-494 (testimony of petitioners' expert that, if sodium thiopental is "properly administered" under the protocol, "[i]n virtually every case, then that would be a humane death").

Instead, petitioners claim that there is a significant risk that the procedures will *not* be properly followed—in particular, that the sodium thiopental will not be properly administered to achieve its intended effect—resulting in severe pain when the other chemicals are administered. Our cases recognize that subjecting individuals to a risk of future harm—not simply actually inflicting pain—can qualify as cruel and unusual punishment. To establish that such exposure violates the Eighth Amendment, however, the conditions presenting the risk must be "*sure or very likely* to cause serious illness and needless suffering," and give rise to "sufficiently *imminent* dangers." *Helling v. McKinney,* 509 U.S. 25, 33, 34-35, 113 S. Ct. 2475, 125 L. Ed. 2d 22 (1993) (emphasis added). We have explained that to prevail on such a claim there must be a "substantial risk of serious harm," an "objectively intolerable risk of harm" that prevents prison officials from pleading that they were "subjectively blameless for purposes of the Eighth Amendment." *Farmer v. Brennan,* 511 U.S. 825, 842, 846, and n.9, 114 S. Ct. 1970, 128 L. Ed. 2d 811 (1994). . . .

C

Much of petitioners' case rests on the contention that they have identified a significant risk of harm that can be eliminated by adopting alternative procedures, such as a one-drug protocol that dispenses with the use of pancuronium and potassium chloride, and additional monitoring by trained personnel to ensure that the first dose of sodium thiopental has been adequately delivered. Given what our cases have said about the nature of the risk of harm that is actionable under the Eighth Amendment, a condemned prisoner cannot successfully challenge a State's method of execution merely by showing a slightly or marginally safer alternative.

Permitting an Eighth Amendment violation to be established on such a showing would threaten to transform courts into boards of inquiry charged with determining "best practices" for executions, with each ruling supplanted by another round of litigation touting a new and improved methodology. Such an approach finds no support in our cases, would embroil the courts in ongoing scientific controversies beyond their expertise, and would substantially intrude on the role of state legislatures in implementing their execution procedures—a role that by all accounts the States have fulfilled with an earnest desire to provide for a progressively more humane manner of death. See *Bell v. Wolfish,* 441 U.S. 520, 562, 99 S. Ct. 1861, 60 L. Ed. 2d 447 (1979) ("The wide range of 'judgment calls' that meet constitutional and statutory requirements are confided to officials outside of the Judicial Branch of Government"). Accordingly, we reject petitioners' proposed "unnecessary risk" standard. . . .

Instead, the proffered alternatives must effectively address a "substantial risk of serious harm." *Farmer, supra,* at 842, 114 S. Ct. 1970. To qualify, the alternative procedure must be feasible, readily implemented, and in fact significantly reduce a substantial risk of severe pain. If a State refuses to adopt such an alternative in the face of these documented advantages, without a legitimate penological justification for adhering to its current method of execution, then a State's refusal to change its method can be viewed as "cruel and unusual" under the Eighth Amendment.

III . . .

A

Petitioners contend that there is a risk of improper administration of thiopental because the doses are difficult to mix into solution form and load into syringes; because the protocol fails to establish a rate of injection, which could lead to a failure of the IV; because it is possible that the IV catheters will infiltrate into surrounding tissue, causing an inadequate dose to be delivered to the vein; because of inadequate facilities and training; and because Kentucky has no reliable means of monitoring the anesthetic depth of the prisoner after the sodium thiopental has been administered. Brief for Petitioners 12-20.

As for the risk that the sodium thiopental would be improperly prepared, petitioners contend that Kentucky employs untrained personnel who are unqualified to calculate and mix an adequate dose, especially in light of the omission of volume and concentration amounts from the written protocol. *Id.,* at 45-46. The state trial court, however, specifically found that "[i]f the manufacturers' instructions for reconstitution of Sodium Thiopental are followed, . . . there would be minimal risk of improper mixing, despite converse testimony that a layperson would have difficulty performing this task." App. 761. We cannot say that this finding is clearly erroneous, see *Hernandez v. New York,* 500 U.S. 352, 366, 111 S. Ct. 1859, 114 L. Ed. 2d 395 (1991) (plurality opinion), particularly when that finding is substantiated by expert testimony describing the task of reconstituting powder sodium thiopental into solution form as "[n]ot difficult at all. . . . You take a liquid, you inject it into a vial with the powder, then you shake it up until the powder dissolves and, you're done. The instructions are on the package insert." 5 Tr. 695 (Apr. 19, 2005).

Likewise, the asserted problems related to the IV lines do not establish a sufficiently substantial risk of harm to meet the requirements of the Eighth Amendment. Kentucky has put in place several important safeguards to ensure that an adequate dose of sodium thiopental is delivered to the condemned prisoner. The most significant of these is the written protocol's requirement that members of the IV team must have at least one year of professional experience as a certified medical assistant, phlebotomist, EMT, paramedic, or military corpsman. App. 984. Kentucky currently uses a phlebotomist and an EMT, personnel who have daily experience establishing IV catheters for inmates in Kentucky's prison population. *Id.,* at 273-274; Tr. of Oral Arg. 27-28. Moreover, these IV team members, along with the rest of the execution team, participate in at least 10 practice sessions per year. App. 984. These sessions, required by the written protocol, encompass a complete walk-through of the execution procedures, including the siting of IV catheters into volunteers. *Ibid.* In addition, the protocol calls for the IV team to establish both primary and backup lines and to prepare two sets of the lethal injection drugs before the execution commences. *Id.*, at 975. These redundant measures ensure that if an insufficient dose of sodium thiopental is initially administered through the primary line, an additional dose can be given through the backup line before the last two drugs are injected. *Id.*, at 279-280, 337-338, 978-979.

The IV team has one hour to establish both the primary and backup IVs, a length of time the trial court found to be "not excessive but rather necessary," *id.*, at 762, contrary to petitioners' claim that using an IV inserted after any "more than ten or fifteen minutes of unsuccessful attempts is dangerous because the IV is almost certain to be unreliable," Brief for Petitioners 47. And, in any event, merely because the protocol gives the IV team one hour to establish intravenous access does not mean that team members are required to spend the entire hour in a futile attempt to do so. The qualifications of the IV team also substantially reduce the risk of IV infiltration.

In addition, the presence of the warden and deputy warden in the execution chamber with the prisoner allows them to watch for signs of IV problems, including infiltration. Three of the Commonwealth's medical experts testified that identifying signs of infiltration would be "very obvious," even to the average person, because of the swelling that would result. App. 385-386. See *id.*, at 353, 600-601. Kentucky's protocol specifically requires the warden to redirect the flow of chemicals to the backup IV site if the prisoner does not lose consciousness within 60 seconds. *Id.*, at 978-979. In light of these safeguards, we cannot say that the risks identified by petitioners are so substantial or imminent as to amount to an Eighth Amendment violation.

B

Nor does Kentucky's failure to adopt petitioners' proposed alternatives demonstrate that the Commonwealth's execution procedure is cruel and unusual.

First, petitioners contend that Kentucky could switch from a three-drug protocol to a one-drug protocol by using a single dose of sodium thiopental or other barbiturate. Brief for Petitioners 51-57. That alternative was not proposed to the state courts below. As a result, we are left without any findings on the effectiveness of petitioners' barbiturate-only protocol, despite scattered references in the trial testimony to the sole use of sodium thiopental or pentobarbital as a preferred method of execution. See Reply Brief for Petitioners 18, n.6.

In any event, the Commonwealth's continued use of the three-drug protocol cannot be viewed as posing an "objectively intolerable risk" when no other State has adopted the one-drug method and petitioners proffered no study showing that it is an equally effective manner of imposing a death sentence. See App. 760-761, n.8 ("Plaintiffs have not presented any scientific study indicating a better method of execution by lethal injection"). Indeed, the State of Tennessee, after reviewing its execution procedures, rejected a proposal to adopt a one-drug protocol using sodium thiopental. The State concluded that the one-drug alternative would take longer than the three-drug method and that the "required dosage of sodium thiopental would be less predictable and more variable when it is used as the sole mechanism for producing death. . . ." *Workman*, 486 F.3d, at 919 (Appendix A). We need not endorse the accuracy of those conclusions to note simply that the comparative efficacy of a one-drug method of execution is not so well established that Kentucky's failure to adopt it constitutes a violation of the Eighth Amendment. . . .

Petitioners' barbiturate-only protocol, they contend, is not untested; it is used routinely by veterinarians in putting animals to sleep. Moreover, 23 States, including Kentucky, bar veterinarians from using a neuromuscular paralytic agent like pancuronium bromide, either expressly or, like Kentucky, by specifically directing the use of a drug like sodium pentobarbital. See Brief for Dr. Kevin Concannon et al. as *Amici Curiae* 18, n.5. If pancuronium is too cruel for animals, the argument goes, then it must be too cruel for the condemned inmate. Whatever rhetorical force the argument carries, see *Workman, supra,* at 909 (describing the comparison to animal euthanasia as "more of a debater's point"), it overlooks the States' legitimate interest in providing for a quick, certain death. . . . [I]n any event other methods approved by veterinarians—such as stunning the animal or severing its spinal cord, see 6 Tr. 758-759 (Apr. 20, 2005)—make clear that veterinary practice for animals is not an appropriate guide to humane practices for humans.

Petitioners also fault the Kentucky protocol for lacking a systematic mechanism for monitoring the "anesthetic depth" of the prisoner. Under petitioners' scheme, qualified personnel would employ monitoring equipment, such as a Bispectral Index (BIS) monitor, blood pressure cuff, or EKG to verify that a prisoner has achieved sufficient unconsciousness before injecting the final two drugs. The visual inspection performed by the warden and deputy warden, they maintain, is an inadequate substitute for the more sophisticated procedures they envision. Brief for Petitioners 19, 58.

At the outset, it is important to reemphasize that a proper dose of thiopental obviates the concern that a prisoner will not be sufficiently sedated. All the experts who testified at trial agreed on this point. The risks of failing to adopt additional monitoring procedures are thus even more "remote" and attenuated than the risks posed by the alleged inadequacies of Kentucky's procedures designed to ensure the delivery of thiopental. See *Hamilton v. Jones,* 472 F.3d 814, 817 (C.A.10 2007) *(per curiam); Taylor v. Crawford,* 487 F.3d 1072, 1084 (C.A.8 2007).

But more than this, Kentucky's expert testified that a blood pressure cuff would have no utility in assessing the level of the prisoner's unconsciousness following the introduction of sodium thiopental, which depresses circulation. App. 578. Furthermore, the medical community has yet to endorse the use of a BIS monitor, which measures brain function, as an indication of anesthetic awareness. . . . The asserted need for a professional anesthesiologist to interpret the BIS monitor readings is nothing more than an argument against the entire procedure, given that both Kentucky law, see Ky. Rev. Stat. Ann. § 431.220(3), and the American Society of Anesthesiologists' own ethical guidelines, see Brief for American Society of Anesthesiologists as *Amicus Curiae* 2-3, prohibit anesthesiologists from participating in capital punishment. Nor is it pertinent that the use of a blood pressure cuff and EKG is "the standard of care in surgery requiring anesthesia," as the dissent points out. *Post,* at _____. Petitioners have not shown that these supplementary procedures, drawn from a different context, are necessary to avoid a substantial risk of suffering. . . .

Kentucky has adopted a method of execution believed to be the most humane available, one it shares with 35 other States. Petitioners agree that, if administered as intended, that procedure will result in a painless death. The risks of maladministration they have suggested—such as improper mixing of chemicals and improper setting of IVs by trained and experienced personnel—cannot remotely be characterized as "objectively intolerable." Kentucky's decision to adhere to its protocol despite these asserted risks, while adopting safeguards to protect against them, cannot be viewed as probative of the wanton infliction of pain under the Eighth Amendment. Finally, the alternative that petitioners belatedly propose has problems of its own, and has never been tried by a single State.

Throughout our history, whenever a method of execution has been challenged in this Court as cruel and unusual, the Court has rejected the challenge.

Our society has nonetheless steadily moved to more humane methods of carrying out capital punishment. The firing squad, hanging, the electric chair, and the gas chamber have each in turn given way to more humane methods, culminating in today's consensus on lethal injection. *Gomez v. United States Dist. Court for Northern Dist. of Cal.*, 503 U.S. 653, 657, 112 S. Ct. 1652, 118 L. Ed. 2d 293 (1992) (Stevens, J., dissenting); App. 755. The broad framework of the Eighth Amendment has accommodated this progress toward more humane methods of execution, and our approval of a particular method in the past has not precluded legislatures from taking the steps they deem appropriate, in light of new developments, to ensure humane capital punishment. There is no reason to suppose that today's decision will be any different.

The judgment below concluding that Kentucky's procedure is consistent with the Eighth Amendment is, accordingly, affirmed.

It is so ordered.

Justice GINSBURG, with whom Justice SOUTER joins, dissenting.

It is undisputed that the second and third drugs used in Kentucky's three-drug lethal injection protocol, pancuronium bromide and potassium chloride, would cause a conscious inmate to suffer excruciating pain. Pancuronium bromide paralyzes the lung muscles and results in slow asphyxiation. App. 435, 437, 625. Potassium chloride causes burning and intense pain as it circulates throughout the body. *Id.*, at 348, 427, 444, 600, 626. Use of pancuronium bromide and potassium chloride on a conscious inmate, the plurality recognizes, would be "constitutionally unacceptable." *Ante*, at _____.

The constitutionality of Kentucky's protocol therefore turns on whether inmates are adequately anesthetized by the first drug in the protocol, sodium thiopental. Kentucky's system is constitutional, the plurality states, because "petitioners have not shown that the risk of an inadequate dose of the first drug is substantial." *Ante*, at _____. I would not dispose of the case so swiftly given the character of the risk at stake. Kentucky's protocol lacks basic safeguards used by other States to confirm that an inmate is unconscious before injection of the second and third drugs. I would vacate and remand with instructions to consider whether Kentucky's omission of those safeguards poses an untoward, readily avoidable risk of inflicting severe and unnecessary pain. . . .

I agree with petitioners and the plurality that the degree of risk, magnitude of pain, and availability of alternatives must be considered. I part ways with the plurality, however, to the extent its "substantial risk" test sets a fixed threshold for the first factor. The three factors are interrelated; a strong showing on one reduces the importance of the others.

Lethal injection as a mode of execution can be expected, in most instances, to result in painless death. Rare though errors may be, the consequences of a mistake about the condemned inmate's consciousness are horrendous and effectively undetectable after injection of the second drug. Given the opposing tugs of the degree of risk and magnitude of pain, the critical question here, as I see it, is whether a feasible alternative exists. Proof of "a slightly or marginally safer alternative" is, as the plurality notes, insufficient. *Ante*, at _____. But if readily available measures can materially increase the likelihood that the protocol will cause no pain, a State fails to adhere to contemporary standards of decency if it declines to employ those measures. . . .

II

. . . Other than using qualified and trained personnel to establish IV access, however, Kentucky does little to ensure that the inmate receives an effective dose of sodium thiopental. After siting the catheters, the IV team leaves the execution chamber. *Id.*, at 977. From that point forward, only the warden and deputy warden remain with the inmate. *Id.*, at 276. Neither the warden nor the deputy warden has any medical training.

The warden relies on visual observation to determine whether the inmate "appears" unconscious. *Id.*, at 978. In Kentucky's only previous execution by lethal injection, the warden's position allowed him to see the inmate best from the waist down, with only a peripheral view of the inmate's face. See *id.*, at 213-214. No other check for consciousness occurs before injection of pancuronium bromide. Kentucky's protocol does not include an automatic pause in the "rapid flow" of the drugs, *id.*, at 978, or any of the most basic tests to determine whether the sodium thiopental has worked. No one calls the inmate's name, shakes him, brushes his eyelashes to test for a reflex, or applies a noxious stimulus to gauge his response.

Nor does Kentucky monitor the effectiveness of the sodium thiopental using readily available equipment, even though the inmate is already connected to an electrocardiogram (EKG), *id.*, at 976. A drop in blood pressure or heart rate after injection of sodium thiopental would not prove that the inmate is unconscious, see *id.*, at 579-580; *ante,* at _____ - _____ (plurality opinion), but would signal that the drug has entered the inmate's bloodstream, see App. 424, 498, 578, 580; 8 Tr. 1099 (May 2, 2005). Kentucky's own expert testified that the sodium thiopental should "cause the inmate's blood pressure to become very, very low," App. 578, and that a precipitous drop in blood pressure would "confir[m]" that the drug was having its expected effect, *id.*, at 580. Use of a blood pressure cuff and EKG, the record shows, is the standard of care in surgery requiring anesthesia. *Id.*, at 539.

A consciousness check supplementing the warden's visual observation before injection of the second drug is easily implemented and can reduce a risk of dreadful pain. Pancuronium bromide is a powerful paralytic that prevents all voluntary muscle movement. Once it is injected, further monitoring of the inmate's consciousness becomes impractical without sophisticated equipment and training. Even if the inmate were conscious and in excruciating pain, there would be no visible indication.

Recognizing the importance of a window between the first and second drugs, other States have adopted safeguards not contained in Kentucky's protocol. . . .

These checks provide a degree of assurance—missing from Kentucky's protocol—that the first drug has been properly administered. They are simple and essentially costless to employ, yet work to lower the risk that the inmate will be subjected to the agony of conscious suffocation caused by pancuronium bromide and the searing pain caused by potassium chloride. The record contains no explanation why Kentucky does not take any of these elementary measures.

The risk that an error administering sodium thiopental would go undetected is minimal, Kentucky urges, because if the drug was mistakenly injected into the inmate's tissue, not a vein, he "would be awake and screaming." Tr. of Oral Arg. 30-31. See also Brief for Respondents 42; Brief for State of Texas et al. as *Amici Curiae* 26-27. That argument ignores aspects of Kentucky's protocol that render passive reliance on obvious signs of consciousness, such as screaming, inadequate to determine whether the inmate is experiencing pain.

First, Kentucky's use of pancuronium bromide to paralyze the inmate means he will not be able to scream after the second drug is injected, no matter how much pain he is experiencing. Kentucky's argument, therefore, appears to rest on the assertion that sodium thiopental is itself painful when injected into tissue rather than a vein. See App. 601. The trial court made no finding on that point, and Kentucky cites no supporting evidence from executions in which it is known that sodium thiopental was injected into the inmate's soft tissue. *See, e.g., Lightbourne,* 969 So. 2d, at 344 (describing execution of Angel Diaz).

Second, the inmate may receive enough sodium thiopental to mask the most obvious signs of consciousness without receiving a dose sufficient to achieve a surgical plane of anesthesia. See 7 Tr. 976 (Apr. 21, 2005). If the drug is injected too quickly, the increase in blood pressure can cause the inmate's veins to burst after a small amount of sodium thiopental has been administered. Cf. App. 217 (describing risk of "blowout"). Kentucky's protocol does not specify the rate at which sodium thiopental should be injected. The executioner, who does not have any medical training, pushes the drug "by feel" through five feet of tubing. *Id.,* at 284, 286-287. In practice sessions, unlike in an actual execution, there is no resistance on the catheter, see *id.,* at 285; thus the executioner's training may lead him to push the drugs too fast.

"The easiest and most obvious way to ensure that an inmate is unconscious during an execution," petitioners argued to the Kentucky Supreme Court, "is to check for consciousness prior to injecting pancuronium [bromide]." Brief for Appellants in No.2005-SC-00543, p. 41. See also App. 30 (Complaint) (alleging Kentucky's protocol does not "require the execution team to determine that the condemned inmate is unconscious prior to administering the second and third chemicals"). The court did not address petitioners' argument. I would therefore remand with instructions to consider whether the failure to include readily available safeguards to confirm that the inmate is unconscious after injection of sodium thiopental, in combination with the other elements of Kentucky's protocol, creates an untoward, readily avoidable risk of inflicting severe and unnecessary pain.

CASE QUESTIONS

GREGG v. GEORGIA

1. In Part IV.A of its opinion, the Court quoted Justice Stewart's concurring opinion in Furman v. Georgia that the death sentences were "cruel and unusual in the same way that being struck by lightning is cruel and unusual." What do you think Justice Stewart meant by his remark?

2. What are the advantages and disadvantages discussed by the Court of having a jury determine whether the death penalty is an appropriate sentence?

3. How did Georgia specifically redraft its death penalty statute to rectify the concerns brought about in Furman v. Georgia? What safeguards were put in place after *Furman* was decided?

BAZE v. REES

1. According to the Petitioners, what three factors should be considered when determining whether the Eighth Amendment prohibits a certain punishment? Should each factor be weighed equally? What was the Court's response to the Petitioners' argument?

2. What reasons does the Court give for declining to become involved in determining whether a "slightly" or "marginally safer" alternative procedure than the one used in Kentucky is feasible?

3. Are the Petitioners arguing that lethal injection is *per se* cruel and unusual punishment? Explain.

4. What safeguards have been put in place by Kentucky to ensure that the first drug is administered properly? What does Justice Ginsburg say about those safeguards in her dissent?

HYPOTHETICAL WITH ACCOMPANYING ANALYSIS

Hypothetical

Mark, Ron, and Jay are buddies who like to get into mischief. One day the three decide to rob a bank. While sitting around sipping coffee, they work out the logistics of the robbery: Mark and Ron, both armed with shotguns, will enter the bank. Mark will hold the gun on any customers while Ron aims his gun at the bank tellers and demands money. Jay, meanwhile, will be waiting outside of the bank in the getaway car. None of the men specifically discuss their desire to kill anyone during the robbery, but Jay tells his friends he wants it to be a "clean, quick" robbery.

On the day of the robbery everything seems to be going according to plan. The men pull up in their vehicle, and Jay waits in the car with the engine running. Mark enters the bank first and yells, "This is a robbery, everybody down!" Ron enters immediately behind him, walks up to the tellers brandishing his gun, and says, "Put the money in the bag, and no funny business." He collects a large bag of cash from the tellers, and the two men bolt for the door. On their way out, however, an off-duty police officer happens to be entering the bank to deposit his paycheck. The officer quickly realizes that a robbery is in progress, and he draws his service revolver. The felons panic, and gunfire erupts. When the smoke clears, the police officer is dead. Mark and Ron run out of the bank, jump into the getaway car and flee the scene, filling Jay in on what transpired. They are captured a short time later. Subsequent ballistics tests conclusively determine that the bullets fired from Ron's gun struck and killed the officer. Mark also fired his weapon, but all of his shots missed.

All three men were charged with felony murder. Following their trials, they were each convicted and sentenced to death. They are now appealing, arguing that the imposition of the death penalty for their crimes constitutes cruel and unusual punishment and, therefore, violates the Eighth Amendment. Argue the likelihood that each one will succeed.

Analysis

The Eighth Amendment protects an individual from "cruel and unusual punishment." Part of what the amendment seeks to protect is punishment that is "greatly disproportionate" to the crime committed. Weems v. United States, 217 U.S. 349 (1910). When determining whether the imposition of the death penalty is disproportionate to the crime, each case must be considered on an individual basis. Lockett v. Ohio, 438 U.S. 586 (1978). Therefore, we must look at the culpability of Mark, Ron, and Jay separately as opposed to assuming that all men are equally deserving of the death penalty. Enmund v. Florida, 458 U.S. 782 (1982).

In cases of felony murder, a defendant may receive the death penalty if: (a) he committed the murder; or (b) even though he did not actually commit the murder, he either had the intent to kill or he was a major participant in the felony and exhibited a reckless indifference to human life. Tison v. Arizona, 481 U.S. 137 (1987). We will now apply that standard to the conduct of Mark, Ron, and Jay.

First, we consider Ron's participation in the felony murder. Under the standards set forth in *Tison*, Ron is clearly eligible for the death penalty because he actually killed the off-duty police officer.

Next we examine Mark's conduct. Mark did not actually kill the police officer. However, when considering the standard that felons who did not kill may be sentenced to death if they either had the intent to kill or were major participants who exhibited a reckless indifference to human life, the evidence supports the fact that Mark's death sentence was appropriate. Mark was a "major participant" in the felony: He willingly took part in the planning and execution of an armed bank robbery where he entered the bank and brandished his weapon. That alone could give rise to a reasonable inference that Mark had the intent to kill if necessary, or at the very least that he "exhibited a reckless indifference to human life." Additionally, during the exchange of gunfire Mark attempted to kill the officer even though his shots missed, which shows his "intent to kill." In sum, Mark's argument that his death sentence violates cruel and unusual punishment merely because he was not the trigger-man is extremely weak and will not succeed.

Finally, Jay's participation as the getaway driver must be examined. Jay could attempt to argue that he was not a major participant in the robbery since he never entered the bank and was never armed. However, a stronger argument to the contrary exists, since he helped plan the robbery, he knew his cofelons would be armed, and he was on the scene as the getaway driver. When determining whether Jay had the intent to kill, the evidence is weaker. At no time did he express his desire for anyone to be killed, and his comments to his cofelons that he wanted the robbery to be "clean" and "quick" suggest the opposite. However, Jay will still be eligible for the death penalty if he "exhibited a reckless indifference to human life." In Enmund v. Florida, the Supreme Court struck down a death sentence for the getaway driver during a burglary and murder where there was no evidence the defendant knew that a murder would occur. The facts in our case are similar to those in *Enmund*. The prosecutor could attempt to argue that knowingly taking part in an armed bank robbery is sufficient to satisfy this requirement, but Jay also has a strong argument to the contrary in light of the Court's holding in *Edmund*. Although Jay helped plan the robbery and acted as the getaway driver, he has a strong argument that his actions were not so outrageous that they exhibited a reckless indifference to human life. In sum, a court would likely determine that Jay's death sentence was disproportionate to his participation in the crime. Although his conviction for felony murder will stand, the imposition of the death penalty will be struck down as violating his Eighth Amendment rights.

In conclusion, Ron and Mark will not succeed in arguing that the death penalty violates their Eighth Amendment rights. Jay, on the other hand, will have a much more persuasive argument, and a court would likely hold that the imposition of the death penalty in his case amounts to cruel and unusual punishment.

HYPOTHETICAL FOR STUDENT ANALYSIS

Jodi and Laurie are female inmates at the Women's Correctional Facility ("WCF"). Jodi was sentenced to five years incarceration for various drug offenses, and Laurie was sentenced to twelve years incarceration for aggravated assault. Shortly after both women arrived at WCF to begin their sentences, they learned that they were pregnant.

Jodi wishes to keep her child, and she has requested that prison officials at WCF provide her with appropriate prenatal care. Laurie, on the other hand, wishes to terminate her pregnancy. She has accordingly asked WCF officials to provide her with the transportation to a facility where she could obtain an elective abortion. Laurie concedes that her reasons for wanting the abortion are purely personal and her health is not at risk because of the pregnancy. Both prisoners have stated that they will pay for all expenses related to their requests.

The WCF has a written policy that female inmates are entitled to "basic necessary medical care." The WCF has interpreted this language to exclude any pregnancy related services unless the inmate can make a direct showing that her health will be jeopardized if she does not receive the services. The WCF has taken the position that neither Jodi nor Laurie has made the required showing. It has, therefore, refused both of their requests.

Jodi and Laurie are challenging the WCF's actions. They specifically argue that the denial of their requests amounts to cruel and unusual punishment under the Eighth Amendment. Discuss their likelihood of success.

DISCUSSION QUESTIONS

1. Jeremy and Butch are cellmates who are each serving prison sentences of more than twenty years. Jeremy is a habitual smoker. On a typical day he smokes more than three packs of cigarettes. The prison where both men are housed has proposed a complete smoking ban in the facility. Butch is in favor of the ban, because he claims that allowing Jeremy to chain smoke and exposing Butch to the second-hand smoke violates his Eighth Amendment rights. Jeremy, on the other hand, argues that prohibiting him from smoking amounts to cruel and unusual punishment. Which side do you agree with? *See* Helling v. McKinney, 509 U.S. 25 (1993).

2. In the late 1990s, China enforced "strike-hard" anticrime legislation which made numerous crimes punishable by death. In 2001, Lu Feng and Chen Jing were convicted of embezzling $60 million from investors, and both were sentenced to death for their crimes. Do you agree with their punishments? Explain.

3. During the 1800s, public executions were common. In today's society, do you think public executions could potentially have a deterrent effect on murder? What about televised executions? Pay per view?

4. Do you think it is cruel and unusual punishment to execute an individual: (a) who commits a crime other than murder? *See* Coker v. Georgia, 433 U.S. 584 (1977) and Kennedy v. Louisiana, 128 S. Ct. 2641 (2008); (b) who is insane? *See* Ford v. Wainwright, 477 U.S. 399 (1986); (c) who is mentally retarded? *See* Atkins v. Virginia, 536 U.S. 304 (2002); (d) who was under eighteen years old at the time the crime was committed? *See* Roper v. Simmons, 543 U.S. 551 (2005).

5. Revisit the above discussion question. After locating the Supreme Court cases cited therein, what trends do you see in the Supreme Court's position on the death penalty? Based on those trends, what predictions can you make, if any, as to the potential future of the death penalty in our nation?

6. Do you think the death penalty is currently being imposed in a racially biased manner? Explain. *See, e.g.*, McClesky v. Kemp, 481 U.S. 279 (1987).

7. Cassidy is a public high school freshman with a history of behavioral problems. Recently, she stole a final exam and distributed it to her classmates. In accordance with school procedures, Cassidy was paddled more than twenty times for her actions. Cassidy argues that her punishment violates her Eighth Amendment rights against cruel and unsual punishment. Do you agree? *See* Ingraham v. Wright, 430 U.S. 651 (1978).

8. In your opinion, should all death row inmates be entitled to mandatory DNA testing prior to their executions if they so desire? What are the advantages and disadvantages of such testing?

9. Blake is a suspected serial killer who is currently on death row for murdering a prostitute. He is now on trial for another murder, and the state has again sought the death penalty. Following his conviction and during the sentencing phase of his case, the prosecutor attempted to introduce evidence that Blake had already been sentenced to death for the previous murder. Blake's defense attorney objected, arguing that if the jury were to find out Blake was already on death row, it would be more likely to impose a second death sentence rather than life imprisonment. Do you agree with Blake's attorney? *See* Romano v. Oklahoma, 512 U.S. 1 (1994).

10. Assume your jurisdiction has recently enacted a law that makes the death penalty mandatory for *any* conviction of murder (in any degree). The legislature's theory behind the law is that if all cases of murder result in a death sentence, then the death penalty cannot be applied arbitrarily. Do you think the law violates the Eighth Amendment? Explain. *See* Woodson v. North Carolina, 428 U.S. 280 (1976).

11. Research challenge: Many critics of the death penalty argue that executions are cruel and barbaric in the way they are carried out. How does the case of Pedro Medina, a man executed in Florida in 1997, lend support to this position? Can you find any other similar examples?

12. Excluding cases of felony murder, do you think that individuals who did not directly murder someone but nonetheless caused or contributed to a victim's death should be eligible for the death penalty? For example, a drug dealer who sells drugs to a young teenager and the teenager overdoses and dies? Or a husband who hires a hit man to kill his wife? Explain.

13. Vince has just been convicted of the double homicide of a young mother and her three-year-old daughter. The brutal murders took place when Vince broke into the victims' house late one night during a burglary. At the sentencing phase of his case, the prosecutor called William to the stand, the husband and father of the victims, to testify as to the impact that the deaths had on his life. Vince's attorney objects, arguing that William's testimony has no relevance either to Vince or the circumstances of the crime. Will Vince's attorney prevail? *Compare* Booth v. Maryland, 482 U.S. 496 (1987) *with* Payne v. Tennessee, 501 U.S. 808 (1991).

14. Revisit the Hypothetical for Student Analysis from this chapter. In addition to any potential Eighth Amendment claims the prisoners may have, what other constitutional arguments could the prisoners make that their rights were violated?

15. Willie Francis was convicted of murder in 1945 and sentenced to death. On May 3, 1946, he was placed in Louisiana's electric chair. The executioner threw the switch, but because the chair malfunctioned, Willie did not die. (It was later determined that the malfunction had been caused by an intoxicated guard who had wired the chair wrong.) He was returned to his cell and another death warrant was issued. Willie appealed his case to the Supreme Court, arguing that it would constitute cruel and unusual punishment to subject him to a second execution procedure. If you were one of the Supreme Court Justices, how would you rule? Why? *See* Louisiana ex rel. Francis v. Resweber, 329 U.S. 459 (1947).

16. Research challenge: What did Illinois Governor George Ryan do in 2003 that created so much controversy regarding the death penalty? Do you agree with his actions? Explain.

17. Jeremy is a recovering alcoholic. Recently, the state he lives in enacted a law making it a misdemeanor punishable by up to six months' imprisonment to be a known alcoholic. Jeremy has been arrested under the law even though he hasn't had a drink for over a year and he regularly attends AA meetings. He is challenging the law, arguing that it violates the Eighth Amendment's protection against cruel and unusual punishment. Will Jeremy's argument succeed? *See* Robinson v. California, 370 U.S. 660 (1962).

True/False

1. Any individual who knowingly participates in a felony where death results is eligible for the death penalty.

2. A "bifurcated trial" in death penalty cases is one in which the charges submitted to the jury are divided between murder and manslaughter.

3. When determining whether the death penalty is an appropriate punishment, aggravating factors weigh in favor of imposing death, while mitigating factors weigh against imposing death.

4. The Supreme Court has recognized that the definition of what constitutes cruel and unusual punishment may change as society evolves and changes.

5. The death penalty is an appropriate punishment for any form of homicide.

Multiple Choice

6. In order to be eligible for the death penalty, the Supreme Court has said that an individual *must* be eighteen years of age:

    A. At the time the crime is committed
    B. At the time of arrest
    C. At the time of the guilty verdict
    D. At the time of the execution

7. The Eighth Amendment prohibits the government from:

    A. Punishing the status of an individual rather than overt criminal behavior
    B. Imposing punishment that is significantly disproportionate to the offense committed
    C. Denying prisoners basic necessities or ignoring their serious medical needs
    D. All of the above

8. Brandon is thirteen years old and is known for being a "prankster." One day after school Brandon put smoke bombs in all of the neighborhood mailboxes. When caught, Brandon admitted to his parents that he did it for "kicks" and didn't care if he caused any property damage or if anyone got hurt because of his prank. As punishment, his parents whipped him with a leather belt and confined him to his room for one month. Were Brandon's Eighth Amendment rights violated?

    A. Yes, because his punishment was disproportionate to the conduct being punished.

    B. Yes, because his status as a prankster is being punished rather than the actual conduct of putting smoke bombs in mailboxes.

    C. Yes, because whipping him constituted the wanton and unnecessary infliction of pain.

    D. No

9. The Supreme Court has said that it violates the Eighth Amendment to execute someone who is:

    A. Legally insane

    B. Mentally retarded

    C. Neither A nor B violates the Eighth Amendment

    D. Both A and B violate the Eighth Amendment

10. Which is one of the procedural safeguards implemented by the Georgia legislature following Furman v. Georgia and discussed in Gregg v. Georgia?

    A. The sentencing jury was required to weigh aggravating and mitigating factors before determining whether death is an appropriate penalty.

    B. The case was conducted using a bifurcated process.

    C. A sentence of death would result in an automatic appeal to the Georgia Supreme Court.

    D. All of the above were put in place by the legislature and discussed by the Court in Gregg v. Georgia.

12

Sentencing and Appeals

INTRODUCTION

Lock 'em up and throw away the keys. Is that what we should do once someone has been convicted of a crime? It's often difficult enough to figure out if a person is guilty beyond a reasonable doubt. But once that much has been determined, the question then becomes, "What do we do with that person"? Issues dealing with sentencing and appeals, therefore, inevitably arise.

Sentencing generally refers to the consequences imposed upon an offender for his crimes. A convicted criminal can receive a number of potential sentences, such as incarceration, fines, restitution, probation, or community service, just to name a few. The list is virtually endless. Those sentences theoretically serve a variety of purposes, including retribution, deterrence, rehabilitation, and incapacitation. Determining the *appropriate* sentence, however, is rarely easy. Exactly where is that imaginary line drawn in the sand to separate what *is* a constitutionally permissible sentence and what *is not*?

Appeals, in turn, are legal challenges of a conviction in a higher court, a process with which the average person has a hazy picture at best. Television shows from *Matlock* to *Law & Order* have given us an "education" over the decades as to what a trial is all about: the defendant anxiously awaiting his fate; witnesses fidgeting on the stand as they testify; attorneys passionately arguing to the jury; and the godlike judge maintaining order and dignity amidst potential chaos. When it comes to appeals, however, most of us are in uncharted territory. Often appeals don't have the high drama that trials do, so we find ourselves uninterested in what they are all about. Intimidating terms such as "habeas corpus" and "post-conviction petitions" make us shy away even further from any desire to understand the appellate process. But appeals can be just as significant as the trial itself, if not more so. For the trial affects one individual and one individual alone: the defendant. The law established on appeal, on the other hand, has the potential of impacting a large segment of the population, or even at times the entire nation.

Sentencing and appeals each include a vast body of case law and generate many controversial issues, yet aside from the establishment of the Supreme Court in Article III, neither is directly mentioned in the Constitution or the Bill of Rights. Nonetheless, a number of constitutional protections are relevant: the Fifth and Fourteenth Amendment rights to due process; the Sixth Amendment right to counsel and the right to have elements of an offense determined by a jury; the Fourteenth Amendment right to equal protection; and the Eighth Amendment prohibition against cruel and unusual punishment. Even at times the First Amendment rights to freedom of speech and association, which are traditionally associated with civil rather than criminal law, are implicated when sentencing is enhanced for hate crimes.

In light of the huge significance that sentencing and appeals have on our criminal justice system, don't end your constitutional analysis at the moment the jury says "Guilty." Instead, keep your Constitution handy, and don't throw away the keys quite yet either.

STUDENT *Checklist*

Sentencing and Appeals

SENTENCING

1. Fifth/Fourteenth Amendment Due Process Clauses

■ Was the defendant given **procedural protections** before **revoking probation** or **parole**?

■ Did the defendant receive a **higher sentence** following an **appeal and reversal** of the conviction due to **vindictiveness** for taking the appeal?

2. Sixth Amendment right to counsel

■ Was the defendant provided counsel at the **critical stage** of **sentencing**?

■ Did a court consider providing the defendant with counsel during **parole revocation proceedings** depending upon the **complexity of the issues** involved?

3. Sixth Amendment right to a jury trial

■ Did the **jury** determine **beyond a reasonable doubt** any fact that **increases the maximum punishment** beyond the statutory maximum (other than **prior convictions**)?

4. Eighth Amendment protection against cruel & unusual punishment

■ Was the imposed sentence **significantly disproportionate** to the crime when considering:

    The **gravity of the offense** and the **harshness of the penalty**;

    Sentences imposed on **other criminals** in the **same jurisdiction**; and

    Sentences imposed for the **same crime** in **other jurisdictions**?

5. Fourteenth Amendment Equal Protection Clause

■ Was the defendant **incarcerated** because of his **inability to pay** a fine?

APPEALS

1. Fifth/Fourteenth Amendment Due Process rights

■ Was the defendant provided with **counsel** on his first **appeal as of right**?

2. Fourteenth Amendment Equal Protection Clause

■ Was the defendant **discriminated against** in the appeals process due to his **poverty**? (e.g., right to **counsel** on appeal as of right or right to be provided with a **trial transcript** if that transcript was central to pursuing a meaningful appeal)

SUPREME COURT CASES

EWING v. CALIFORNIA, 538 U.S. 11 (2003)

In this case, we decide whether the Eighth Amendment prohibits the State of California from sentencing a repeat felon to a prison term of 25 years to life under the State's "Three Strikes and You're Out" law.

I

A

California's three strikes law reflects a shift in the State's sentencing policies toward incapacitating and deterring repeat offenders who threaten the public safety. The law was designed "to ensure longer prison sentences and greater punishment for those who commit a felony and have been previously convicted of serious and/or violent felony offenses." Cal. Penal Code Ann. § 667(b) (West 1999). On March 3, 1993, California Assemblymen Bill Jones and Jim Costa introduced Assembly Bill 971, the legislative version of what would later become the three strikes law. The Assembly Committee on Public Safety defeated the bill only weeks later. Public outrage over the defeat sparked a voter initiative to add Proposition 184, based loosely on the bill, to the ballot in the November 1994 general election.

On October 1, 1993, while Proposition 184 was circulating, 12-year-old Polly Klaas was kidnaped from her home in Petaluma, California. Her admitted killer, Richard Allen Davis, had a long criminal history that included two prior kidnaping convictions. Davis had served only half of his most recent sentence (16 years for kidnaping, assault, and burglary). Had Davis served his entire sentence, he would still have been in prison on the day that Polly Klaas was kidnaped.

Polly Klaas' murder galvanized support for the three strikes initiative. Within days, Proposition 184 was on its way to becoming the fastest qualifying initiative in California history. . . .

California thus became the second State to enact a three strikes law. . . . Between 1993 and 1995, 24 States and the Federal Government enacted three strikes laws. *Ibid.* Though the three strikes laws vary from State to State, they share a common goal of protecting the public safety by providing lengthy prison terms for habitual felons.

B

California's current three strikes law consists of two virtually identical statutory schemes "designed to increase the prison terms of repeat felons." *People v. Superior Court of San Diego Cty. ex rel. Romero,* 13 Cal. 4th 497, 504, 53 Cal. Rptr. 2d 789, 917 P.2d 628, 630 (1996) *(Romero).* When a defendant is convicted of a felony, and he has previously been convicted of one or more prior felonies defined as "serious" or "violent" in Cal. Penal Code Ann. §§ 667.5 and 1192.7 (West Supp. 2002), sentencing is conducted pursuant to the three strikes law. Prior convictions must be alleged in the charging document, and the defendant has a right to a jury determination that the prosecution has proved the prior convictions beyond a reasonable doubt. § 1025; § 1158 (West 1985).

If the defendant has one prior "serious" or "violent" felony conviction, he must be sentenced to "twice the term otherwise provided as punishment for the current felony conviction." § 667(e)(1) (West 1999); § 1170.12(c)(1) (West Supp. 2002). If the defendant has two or more prior "serious" or "violent" felony convictions, he must receive "an indeterminate term of life imprisonment." § 667(e)(2)(A) (West 1999); § 1170.12(c)(2)(A) (West Supp. 2002). . . .

Under California law, certain offenses may be classified as either felonies or misdemeanors. These crimes are known as "wobblers." Some crimes that would otherwise be misdemeanors become "wobblers" because of the defendant's prior record. For example, petty theft, a misdemeanor, becomes a "wobbler" when the defendant has previously served a prison term for committing specified theft-related crimes. § 490 (West 1999); § 666 (West Supp. 2002). Other crimes, such as grand theft, are "wobblers" regardless of the defendant's prior record. See § 489(b) (West 1999). Both types of "wobblers" are triggering offenses under the three strikes law only when they are treated as felonies. Under California law, a "wobbler" is presumptively a felony and "remains a felony except when the discretion is actually exercised" to make the crime a misdemeanor. *People v. Williams,* 27 Cal.2d 220, 229, 163 P.2d 692, 696 (1945) (emphasis deleted and internal quotation marks omitted).

In California, prosecutors may exercise their discretion to charge a "wobbler" as either a felony or a misdemeanor. Likewise, California trial courts have discretion to reduce a "wobbler" charged as a felony to a misdemeanor either before preliminary examination or at sentencing to avoid imposing a three strikes sentence. . . . In exercising this discretion, the court may consider "those factors that direct similar sentencing decisions," such as "the nature and circumstances of the offense, the defendant's appreciation of and attitude toward the offense, . . . [and] the general objectives of sentencing." *Ibid.* (internal quotation marks and citations omitted).

California trial courts can also vacate allegations of prior "serious" or "violent" felony convictions, either on motion by the prosecution or *sua sponte. Romero, supra,* at 529-530, 53 Cal. Rptr. 2d 789, 917 P.2d, at 647-648. In ruling whether to vacate allegations of prior felony convictions, courts consider whether, "in light of the nature and circumstances of [the defendant's] present felonies and prior serious and/or violent felony convictions, and the particulars of his background, character, and prospects, the defendant may be deemed outside the [three strikes'] scheme's spirit, in whole or in part." *People v. Williams,* 17 Cal. 4th 148, 161, 69 Cal. Rptr. 2d 917, 948 P.2d 429, 437 (1998). Thus, trial courts may avoid imposing a three strikes sentence in two ways: first, by reducing "wobblers" to misdemeanors (which do not qualify as triggering offenses), and second, by vacating allegations of prior "serious" or "violent" felony convictions.

C

On parole from a 9-year prison term, petitioner Gary Ewing walked into the pro shop of the El Segundo Golf Course in Los Angeles County on March 12, 2000. He walked out with three golf clubs, priced at $399 apiece, concealed in his pants leg. A shop employee, whose suspicions were aroused when he observed Ewing limp out of the pro shop, telephoned the police. The police apprehended Ewing in the parking lot.

Ewing is no stranger to the criminal justice system. In 1984, at the age of 22, he pleaded guilty to theft. The court sentenced him to six months in jail (suspended), three years' probation, and a $300 fine. In 1988, he was convicted of felony grand theft auto and sentenced to one year in jail and three years' probation. After Ewing completed probation, however, the sentencing court reduced the crime to a misdemeanor, permitted Ewing to withdraw his guilty plea, and dismissed the case. In 1990, he was convicted of petty theft with a prior and sentenced to 60 days in the county jail and three years' probation. In 1992, Ewing was convicted of battery and sentenced to 30 days in the county jail and two years' summary probation. One month later, he was convicted of theft and sentenced to 10 days in the county jail and 12 months' probation. In January 1993, Ewing was convicted of burglary and sentenced to 60 days in the county jail and one year's summary probation. In February 1993, he was convicted of possessing drug paraphernalia and sentenced to six months in the county jail and three years' probation. In July 1993, he was convicted of appropriating lost property and sentenced to 10 days in the county jail and two years' summary probation. In September 1993, he was convicted of unlawfully possessing a firearm and trespassing and sentenced to 30 days in the county jail and one year's probation.

In October and November 1993, Ewing committed three burglaries and one robbery at a Long Beach, California, apartment complex over a 5-week period. He awakened one of his victims, asleep on her living room sofa, as he tried to disconnect her video cassette recorder from the television in that room. When she screamed, Ewing ran out the front door. On another occasion, Ewing accosted a victim in the mailroom of the apartment complex. Ewing claimed to have a gun and ordered the victim to hand over his wallet. When the victim resisted, Ewing produced a knife and forced the victim back to the apartment itself. While Ewing rifled through the bedroom, the victim fled the apartment screaming for help. Ewing absconded with the victim's money and credit cards.

On December 9, 1993, Ewing was arrested on the premises of the apartment complex for trespassing and lying to a police officer. The knife used in the robbery and a glass cocaine pipe were later found in the back seat of the patrol car used to transport Ewing to the police station. A jury convicted Ewing of first-degree robbery and three counts of residential burglary. Sentenced to nine years and eight months in prison, Ewing was paroled in 1999.

Only 10 months later, Ewing stole the golf clubs at issue in this case. He was charged with, and ultimately convicted of, one count of felony grand theft of personal property in excess of $400. See Cal. Penal Code Ann. § 484 (West Supp. 2002); § 489 (West 1999). As required by the three strikes law, the prosecutor formally alleged, and the trial court later found, that Ewing had been convicted previously of four serious or violent felonies for the three burglaries and the robbery in the Long Beach apartment complex. See § 667(g) (West 1999); § 1170.12(e) (West Supp. 2002).

At the sentencing hearing, Ewing asked the court to reduce the conviction for grand theft, a "wobbler" under California law, to a misdemeanor so as to avoid a three strikes sentence. See §§ 17(b), 667(d)(1) (West 1999); § 1170.12(b)(1) (West Supp. 2002). Ewing also asked the trial court to exercise its discretion to dismiss the allegations of some or all of his prior serious or violent felony convictions, again for purposes of avoiding a three strikes sentence. See *Romero,* 13 Cal. 4th, at 529-531, 53 Cal. Rptr. 2d 789, 917 P.2d, at 647-648. Before sentencing Ewing, the trial court took note of his entire criminal history, including the fact that he was on parole when he committed his latest offense. The court also heard arguments from defense counsel and a plea from Ewing himself.

In the end, the trial judge determined that the grand theft should remain a felony. The court also ruled that the four prior strikes for the three burglaries and the robbery in Long Beach should stand. As a newly convicted felon with two or more "serious" or "violent" felony convictions in his past, Ewing was sentenced under the three strikes law to 25 years to life. . . .

II

A

The Eighth Amendment, which forbids cruel and unusual punishments, contains a "narrow proportionality principle" that "applies to noncapital sentences." . . . We have most recently addressed the proportionality principle as applied to terms of years in a series of cases beginning with *Rummel v. Estelle, supra.*

In *Rummel,* we held that it did not violate the Eighth Amendment for a State to sentence a three-time offender to life in prison with the possibility of parole. *Id.,* at 284-285, 100 S. Ct. 1133. Like Ewing, Rummel was sentenced to a lengthy prison term under a recidivism statute. Rummel's two prior offenses were a 1964 felony for "fraudulent use of a credit card to obtain $80 worth of goods or services," and a 1969 felony conviction for "passing a forged check in the amount of $28.36." *Id.,* at 265, 100 S. Ct. 1133. His triggering offense was a conviction for felony theft—"obtaining $120.75 by false pretenses." *Id.,* at 266, 100 S. Ct. 1133.

This Court ruled that "[h]aving twice imprisoned him for felonies, Texas was entitled to place upon Rummel the onus of one who is simply unable to bring his conduct within the social norms prescribed by the criminal law of the State." *Id.,* at 284, 100 S. Ct. 1133. The recidivism statute "is nothing more than a societal decision that when such a person commits yet another felony, he should be subjected to the admittedly serious penalty of incarceration for life, subject only to the State's judgment as to whether to grant him parole." *Id.,* at 278, 100 S. Ct. 1133. We noted that this Court "has on occasion stated that the Eighth Amendment prohibits imposition of a sentence that is grossly disproportionate to the severity of the crime." *Id.,* at 271, 100 S. Ct. 1133. But "[o]utside the context of capital punishment, successful challenges to the proportionality of particular sentences have been exceedingly rare." *Id.,* at 272, 100 S. Ct. 1133. Although we stated that the proportionality principle "would . . . come into play in the extreme example . . . if a legislature made overtime parking a felony punishable by life imprisonment," *id.,* at 274, n.11, 100 S. Ct. 1133, we held that "the mandatory life sentence imposed upon this petitioner does not constitute cruel and unusual punishment under the Eighth and Fourteenth Amendments," *id.*, at 285, 100 S. Ct. 1133. . . .

Three years after *Rummel,* in *Solem v. Helm,* 463 U.S. 277, 279, 103 S. Ct. 3001, 77 L. Ed. 2d 637 (1983), we held that the Eighth Amendment prohibited "a life sentence without possibility of parole for a seventh nonviolent felony." The triggering offense in *Solem* was "uttering a 'no account' check for $100." *Id.*, at 281, 103 S. Ct. 3001. We specifically stated that the Eighth Amendment's ban on cruel and unusual punishments "prohibits . . . sentences that are disproportionate to the crime committed," and that the "constitutional principle of proportionality has been recognized explicitly in this Court for almost a century." *Id.*, at 284, 286, 103 S. Ct. 3001. The *Solem* Court then explained that three factors may be relevant to a determination of whether a sentence is so disproportionate that it violates the Eighth Amendment: "(i) the gravity of the offense and the harshness of the penalty; (ii) the sentences imposed on other criminals in the same jurisdiction; and (iii) the sentences imposed for commission of the same crime in other jurisdictions." *Id.*, at 292, 103 S. Ct. 3001.

Applying these factors in *Solem,* we struck down the defendant's sentence of life without parole. We specifically noted the contrast between that sentence and the sentence in *Rummel,* pursuant to which the defendant was eligible for parole. 463 U.S., at 297, 103 S. Ct. 3001; see also *id.*, at 300, 103 S. Ct. 3001 ("[T]he South Dakota commutation system is fundamentally different from the parole system that was before us in *Rummel*"). Indeed, we explicitly declined to overrule *Rummel:* "[O]ur conclusion today is not inconsistent with *Rummel v. Estelle.*" 463 U.S., at 303, n.32, 103 S. Ct. 3001; see also *id.*, at 288, n.13, 103 S. Ct. 3001 ("[O]ur decision is entirely consistent with this Court's prior cases— including *Rummel v. Estelle*"). . . .

B

For many years, most States have had laws providing for enhanced sentencing of repeat offenders. *See, e.g.,* U.S. Dept. of Justice, Bureau of Justice Assistance, National Assessment of Structured Sentencing (1996). Yet between 1993 and 1995, three strikes laws effected a sea change in criminal sentencing throughout the Nation. These laws responded to widespread public concerns about crime by targeting the class of offenders who pose the greatest threat to public safety: career criminals. As one of the chief architects of California's three strikes law has explained: "Three Strikes was intended to go beyond simply making sentences tougher. It was intended to be a focused effort to create a sentencing policy that would use the judicial system to reduce serious and violent crime." Ardaiz, California's Three Strikes Law: History, Expectations, Consequences, 32 McGeorge L. Rev. 1, 12 (2000) (hereinafter Ardaiz).

Throughout the States, legislatures enacting three strikes laws made a deliberate policy choice that individuals who have repeatedly engaged in serious or violent criminal behavior, and whose conduct has not been deterred by more conventional approaches to punishment, must be isolated from society in order to protect the public safety. Though three strikes laws may be relatively new, our tradition of deferring to state legislatures in making and implementing such important policy decisions is longstanding. . . .

When the California Legislature enacted the three strikes law, it made a judgment that protecting the public safety requires incapacitating criminals who have already been convicted of at least one serious or violent crime. Nothing in the Eighth Amendment prohibits California from making that choice. To the contrary, our cases establish that "States have a valid interest in deterring and segregating habitual criminals." *Parke v. Raley,* 506 U.S. 20, 27,

113 S. Ct. 517, 121 L. Ed. 2d 391 (1992); *Oyler v. Boles,* 368 U.S. 448, 451, 82 S. Ct. 501, 7 L. Ed. 2d 446 (1962) ("[T]he constitutionality of the practice of inflicting severer criminal penalties upon habitual offenders is no longer open to serious challenge"). Recidivism has long been recognized as a legitimate basis for increased punishment. . . .

California's justification is no pretext. Recidivism is a serious public safety concern in California and throughout the Nation. According to a recent report, approximately 67 percent of former inmates released from state prisons were charged with at least one "serious" new crime within three years of their release. See U.S. Dept. of Justice, Bureau of Justice Statistics, P. Langan & D. Levin, Special Report: Recidivism of Prisoners Released in 1994, p. 1 (June 2002). In particular, released property offenders like Ewing had higher recidivism rates than those released after committing violent, drug, or public-order offenses. *Id.,* at 8. Approximately 73 percent of the property offenders released in 1994 were arrested again within three years, compared to approximately 61 percent of the violent offenders, 62 percent of the public-order offenders, and 66 percent of the drug offenders. *Ibid.* . . .

The State's interest in deterring crime also lends some support to the three strikes law. We have long viewed both incapacitation and deterrence as rationales for recidivism statutes: "[A] recidivist statute['s] . . . primary goals are to deter repeat offenders and, at some point in the life of one who repeatedly commits criminal offenses serious enough to be punished as felonies, to segregate that person from the rest of society for an extended period of time." *Rummel, supra,* at 284, 100 S. Ct. 1133. Four years after the passage of California's three strikes law, the recidivism rate of parolees returned to prison for the commission of a new crime dropped by nearly 25 percent. . . .

To be sure, California's three strikes law has sparked controversy. Critics have doubted the law's wisdom, cost-efficiency, and effectiveness in reaching its goals. . . . This criticism is appropriately directed at the legislature, which has primary responsibility for making the difficult policy choices that underlie any criminal sentencing scheme. We do not sit as a "superlegislature" to second-guess these policy choices. It is enough that the State of California has a reasonable basis for believing that dramatically enhanced sentences for habitual felons "advance[s] the goals of [its] criminal justice system in any substantial way." See *Solem,* 463 U.S., at 297, n.22, 103 S. Ct. 3001.

III

Against this backdrop, we consider Ewing's claim that his three strikes sentence of 25 years to life is unconstitutionally disproportionate to his offense of "shoplifting three golf clubs." Brief for Petitioner 6. We first address the gravity of the offense compared to the harshness of the penalty. At the threshold, we note that Ewing incorrectly frames the issue. The gravity of his offense was not merely "shoplifting three golf clubs." Rather, Ewing was convicted of felony grand theft for stealing nearly $1,200 worth of merchandise after previously having been convicted of at least two "violent" or "serious" felonies. Even standing alone, Ewing's theft should not be taken lightly. His crime was certainly not "one of the most passive felonies a person could commit." *Solem, supra,* at 296, 103 S. Ct. 3001 (internal quotation marks omitted). To the contrary, the Supreme Court of California has noted the "seriousness" of grand theft in the context of proportionality review. See *In re Lynch,* 8 Cal.3d 410, 432, n.20, 105 Cal. Rptr. 217, 503 P.2d 921, 936, n.20 (1972). Theft of $1,200 in property is a felony under federal law, 18 U.S.C. § 641, and in the vast majority of States. See App. B to Brief for Petitioner 21a.

That grand theft is a "wobbler" under California law is of no moment. Though California courts have discretion to reduce a felony grand theft charge to a misdemeanor, it remains a felony for all purposes "unless and until the trial court imposes a misdemeanor sentence." *In re Anderson,* 69 Cal. 2d 613, 626, 73 Cal. Rptr. 21, 447 P.2d 117, 126 (1968) (Tobriner, J., concurring). . . . Under California law, the reduction is not based on the notion that a "wobbler" is "conceptually a misdemeanor." *Necochea v. Superior Court,* 23 Cal. App. 3d 1012, 1016, 100 Cal. Rptr. 693, 695 (1972). Rather, it is "intended to extend misdemeanant treatment to a potential felon." *Ibid.* In Ewing's case, however, the trial judge justifiably exercised her discretion not to extend such lenient treatment given Ewing's long criminal history.

In weighing the gravity of Ewing's offense, we must place on the scales not only his current felony, but also his long history of felony recidivism. Any other approach would fail to accord proper deference to the policy judgments that find expression in the legislature's choice of sanctions. In imposing a three strikes sentence, the State's interest is not merely punishing the offense of conviction, or the "triggering" offense: "[I]t is in addition the interest . . . in dealing in a harsher manner with those who by repeated criminal acts have shown that they are simply incapable of conforming to the norms of society as established by its criminal law." *Rummel,* 445 U.S., at 276, 100 S. Ct. 1133; *Solem, supra,* at 296, 103 S. Ct. 3001. To give full effect to the State's choice of this legitimate penological goal, our proportionality review of Ewing's sentence must take that goal into account.

Ewing's sentence is justified by the State's public-safety interest in incapacitating and deterring recidivist felons, and amply supported by his own long, serious criminal record. Ewing has been convicted of numerous misdemeanor and felony offenses, served nine separate terms of incarceration, and committed most of his crimes while on probation or parole. His prior "strikes" were serious felonies including robbery and three residential burglaries. To be sure, Ewing's sentence is a long one. But it reflects a rational legislative judgment, entitled to deference, that offenders who have committed serious or violent felonies and who continue to commit felonies must be incapacitated. The State of California "was entitled to place upon [Ewing] the onus of one who is simply unable to bring his conduct within the social norms prescribed by the criminal law of the State." *Rummel, supra,* at 284, 100 S. Ct. 1133. Ewing's is not "the rare case in which a threshold comparison of the crime committed and the sentence imposed leads to an inference of gross disproportionality." *Harmelin,* 501 U.S., at 1005, 111 S. Ct. 2680 (Kennedy, J., concurring in part and concurring in judgment).

We hold that Ewing's sentence of 25 years to life in prison, imposed for the offense of felony grand theft under the three strikes law, is not grossly disproportionate and therefore does not violate the Eighth Amendment's prohibition on cruel and unusual punishments. The judgment of the California Court of Appeal is affirmed.

It is so ordered.

DOUGLAS v. CALIFORNIA, 372 U.S. 353 (1963)

Petitioners, Bennie Will Meyes and William Douglas, were jointly tried and convicted in a California court on an information charging them with 13 felonies. A single public defender was appointed to represent them. At the commencement of the trial, the defender moved for a continuance, stating that the case was very complicated, that he was not as prepared as he felt he should be because he was handling a different defense every day, and that there was a conflict of interest between the petitioners requiring the appointment of separate counsel for each of them. This motion was denied. Thereafter, petitioners dismissed the defender, claiming he was unprepared, and again renewed motions for separate counsel and for a continuance. These motions also were denied, and petitioners were ultimately convicted by a jury of all 13 felonies, which included robbery, assault with a deadly weapon, and assault with intent to commit murder. Both were given prison terms. Both appealed as of right to the California District Court of Appeal. That court affirmed their convictions. 187 Cal. App. 2d 802, 10 Cal. Rptr. 188. Both Meyes and Douglas then petitioned for further discretionary review in the California Supreme Court, but their petitions were denied without a hearing. 187 Cal. App. 2d, at 813, 10 Cal. Rptr., at 195. We granted certiorari. 368 U.S. 815, 82 S. Ct. 71, 7 L. Ed. 2d 23.

Although several questions are presented in the petition for certiorari, we address ourselves to only one of them. The record shows that petitioners requested, and were denied, the assistance of counsel on appeal, even though it plainly appeared they were indigents. In denying petitioners' requests, the California District Court of Appeal stated that it had "gone through" the record and had come to the conclusion that "no good whatever could be served by appointment of counsel." 187 Cal. App. 2d 802, 812, 10 Cal. Rptr. 188, 195. The District Court of Appeal was acting in accordance with a California rule of criminal procedure which provides that state appellate courts, upon the request of an indigent for counsel, may make "an independent investigation of the record and determine whether it would be of advantage to the defendant or helpful to the appellate court to have counsel appointed. . . . After such investigation, appellate courts should appoint counsel if in their opinion it would be helpful to the defendant or the court, and should deny the appointment of counsel only if in their judgment such appointment would be of no value to either the defendant or the court." People v. Hyde, 51 Cal.2d 152, 154, 331 P.2d 42, 43.

We agree, however, with Justice Traynor of the California Supreme Court, who said that the "(d)enial of counsel on appeal (to an indigent) would seem to be a discrimination at least as invidious as that condemned in Griffin v. People of State of Illinois. . . ." People v. Brown, 55 Cal.2d 64, 71, 9 Cal. Rptr. 816, 357 P.2d 1072, 1076 (concurring opinion). In Griffin v. Illinois, 351 U.S. 12, 76 S. Ct. 585, 100 L. Ed. 891, we held that a State may not grant appellate review in such a way as to discriminate against some convicted defendants on account of their poverty. There, as in Draper v. Washington, 372 U.S. 487, 83 S. Ct. 774, the right to a free transcript on appeal was in issue. Here the issue is whether or not an indigent shall be denied the assistance of counsel on appeal. In either case the evil is the same: discrimination against the indigent. For there can be no equal justice where the kind of an appeal a man enjoys "depends on the amount of money he has." Griffin v. Illinois, supra, at p. 19, 76 S. Ct., at p. 591.

In spite of California's forward treatment of indigents, under its present practice the type of an appeal a person is afforded in the District Court of Appeal hinges upon whether or not he can pay for the assistance of counsel. If he can the appellate court passes on the merits of his case only after having the full benefit of written briefs and oral argument by counsel. If he cannot the appellate court is forced to prejudge the merits before it can even determine whether counsel should be provided. At this stage in the proceedings only the barren record speaks for the indigent, and, unless the printed pages show that an injustice has been committed, he is forced to go without a champion on appeal. Any real chance he may have had of showing that his appeal has hidden merit is deprived him when the court decides on an ex parte examination of the record that the assistance of counsel is not required.

We are not here concerned with problems that might arise from the denial of counsel for the preparation of a petition for discretionary or mandatory review beyond the stage in the appellate process at which the claims have once been presented by a lawyer and passed upon by an appellate court. We are dealing only with the first appeal, granted as a matter of right to rich and poor alike (Cal. Penal Code §§ 1235, 1237), from a criminal conviction. We need not now decide whether California would have to provide counsel for an indigent seeking a discretionary hearing from the California Supreme Court after the District Court of Appeal had sustained his conviction (see Cal. Const., Art. VI, § 4c; Cal. Rules on Appeal, Rules 28, 29), or whether counsel must be appointed for an indigent seeking review of an appellate affirmance of his conviction in this Court by appeal as of right or by petition for a writ of certiorari which lies within the Court's discretion. But it is appropriate to observe that a State can, consistently with the Fourteenth Amendment, provide for differences so long as the result does not amount to a denial of due process or an "invidious discrimination." Williamson v. Lee Optical of Oklahoma, 348 U.S. 483, 489, 75 S. Ct. 461, 465, 99 L. Ed. 563; Griffin v. Illinois, supra, p. 18, 76 S. Ct., p. 590. Absolute equality is not required; lines can be and are drawn and we often sustain them. See Tigner v. Texas, 310 U.S. 141, 60 S. Ct. 879, 84 L. Ed. 1124; Goesaert v. Cleary, 335 U.S. 464, 69 S. Ct. 198, 93 L. Ed. 163. But where the merits of the one and only appeal an indigent has as of right are decided without benefit of counsel, we think an unconstitutional line has been drawn between rich and poor.

When an indigent is forced to run this gantlet of a preliminary showing of merit, the right to appeal does not comport with fair procedure. In the federal courts, on the other hand, an indigent must be afforded counsel on appeal whenever he challenges a certification that the appeal is not taken in good faith. Johnson v. United States, 352 U.S. 565, 77 S. Ct. 550, 1 L. Ed. 2d 593. The federal courts must honor his request for counsel regardless of what they think the merits of the case may be; and "representation in the role of an advocate is required." Ellis v. United States, 356 U.S. 674, 675, 78 S. Ct. 974, 975, 2 L. Ed. 2d 1060. In California, however, once the court has "gone through" the record and denied counsel, the indigent has no recourse but to prosecute his appeal on his own, as best he can, no matter how meritorious his case may turn out to be. The present case, where counsel was denied petitioners on appeal, shows that the discrimination is not between "possibly good and obviously bad cases," but between cases where the rich man can require the court to listen to argument of counsel before deciding on the merits, but a poor man cannot. There is lacking that equality demanded by the Fourteenth Amendment where the rich man, who appeals as of right, enjoys the benefit of counsel's examination into the record, research of the law, and marshalling of arguments on his behalf, while the indigent, already burdened by a preliminary determination that his case is without merit, is forced to shift for himself. The indigent, where the record is unclear or the errors are hidden, has only the right to a meaningless ritual, while the rich man has a meaningful appeal.

We vacate the judgment of the District Court of Appeal and remand the case to that court for further proceedings not inconsistent with this opinion. It is so ordered.

Judgment of the District Court of Appeal vacated and case remanded.

Mr. Justice CLARK, dissenting.

I adhere to my vote in Griffin v. Illinois, 351 U.S. 12, 76 S. Ct. 585, 100 L. Ed. 891 (1956), but, as I have always understood that case, it does not control here. It had to do with the State's obligation to furnish a record to an indigent on appeal. There we took pains to point out that the State was free to "find other means of affording adequate and effective appellate review to indigent defendants." Id., at 20, 76 S. Ct., at 591. Here California has done just that in its procedure for furnishing attorneys for indigents on appeal. We all know that the overwhelming percentage of in forma pauperis appeals are frivolous. Statistics of this Court show that over 96% of the petitions filed here are of this variety. California, in the light of a like experience, has provided that upon the filing of an application for the appointment of counsel the District Court of Appeal shall make "an independent investigation of the record and determine whether it would be of advantage to the defendant or helpful to the appellate court to have counsel appointed." People v. Hyde, 51 Cal.2d 152, 154, 331 P.2d 42, 43 (1958). California's courts did that here and after examining the record certified that such an appointment would be neither advantageous to the petitioners nor helpful to the court. It, therefore, refused to go through the useless gesture of appointing an attorney. In my view neither the Equal Protection Clause nor the Due Process Clause requires more. I cannot understand why the Court says that this procedure afforded petitioners "a meaningless ritual." To appoint an attorney would not only have been utter extravagance and a waste of the State's funds but as surely "meaningless" to petitioners.

With this new fetish for indigency the Court piles an intolerable burden on the State's judicial machinery. Indeed, if the Court is correct it may be that we should first clean up our own house. We have afforded indigent litigants much less protection than has California. Last term we received over 1,200 in forma pauperis applications in none of which had we appointed attorneys or required a record. Some were appeals of right. Still we denied the petitions or dismissed the appeals on the moving papers alone. At the same time we had hundreds of paid cases in which we permitted petitions or appeals to be filed with not only records but briefs by counsel, after which they were disposed of in due course. On the other hand, California furnishes the indigent a complete record and if counsel is requested requires its appellate courts either to (1) appoint counsel or (2) make an independent investigation of that record and determine whether it would be of advantage to the defendant or helpful to the court to have counsel appointed. Unlike Lane v. Brown, 372 U.S. 477, 83 S. Ct. 768, decision in these matters is not placed in the unreviewable discretion of the Public Defender or appointed counsel but is made by the appellate court itself. . . .

There is an old adage which my good Mother used to quote to me, i.e., "People who live in glass houses had best not throw stones." I dissent. . . .

CASE QUESTIONS

EWING v. CALIFORNIA

1. What is a "wobbler"? What impact does it have on the three strikes law?

2. What factors should a court consider when determining whether a sentence violates the Eighth Amendment prohibition against cruel and unusual punishment? What did the Court hold with regard to each of those factors in *Ewing*?

3. What were the basic facts and holdings of the Court's earlier opinions in Rummel v. Estelle, 445 U.S. 263 (1980) and Solem v. Helm, 463 U.S. 277 (1983)? How did the facts of *Ewing* fit into the previously established precedent of *Rummel* and *Solem*?

4. In *Ewing* the Supreme Court failed to reach a majority opinion. The opinion contained within this text is Justice O'Connor's plurality opinion. How does that impact any potential precedent established by this case?

5. Do you agree with the Court's holding in this case? Why or why not?

DOUGLAS v. CALIFORNIA

1. Why did the Court rely on the Equal Protection Clause of the Fourteenth Amendment when deciding this case rather than the Sixth Amendment right to counsel?

2. Can you foresee any potential "snowball effect" from the Court's decision? If so, what?

3. How did the Court explicitly limit its holding in the case?

4. What were the specific grounds of Justice Clark's dissent? What did he mean by his comments that "we should first clean up our own house" and "people who live in glass houses had best not throw stones"?

HYPOTHETICAL WITH ACCOMPANYING ANALYSIS

Hypothetical

Amy, an unemployed and uneducated 27-year-old woman, was found guilty by a jury of welfare fraud. According to a statute, her maximum potential sentence was ten years incarceration and/or a $10,000 fine. At her sentencing Amy requested counsel, but her request was denied. The judge told Amy that "having an attorney present wouldn't make any difference." The judge then sentenced Amy to all ten years incarceration and a $10,000 fine. He additionally placed her on probation for five years following the completion of her sentence, during which time he required Amy to obtain her high school GED and to make every effort to obtain suitable employment. The following exchange then took place:

> **Amy:** Excuse me sir, I ain't got no money. How am I supposed to pay that $10,000?
> **Judge:** Well, if you can't pay the fine then you shall be sentenced to an additional month of incarceration for each thousand dollars that you are unable to pay.
> **Amy:** Uh, one more thing sir. School just ain't for me. I ain't even made it past the ninth grade.
> **Judge:** Education, young lady, is the key to the future. If you ever expect to turn your life around, then you *must* get an education.

Amy's sentencing was then concluded. Amy wishes to appeal her sentence, but she cannot afford an attorney and the judge told her she was not entitled to an attorney on appeal unless she could pay the fees herself.

Discuss any potential violations that occurred in Amy's case, specifying which amendment applies to each particular violation.

Analysis

Several constitutional amendments offer protections during the sentencing and appeals phases of a criminal case. In Amy's case specifically, numerous such violations occurred. Each violation will be discussed separately along with the applicable constitutional provision.

The first violation occurred when Amy was denied the right to counsel at her sentencing. The Sixth Amendment right to counsel extends to the critical stage of sentencing proceedings in a criminal case. Mempa v. Rhay, 389 U.S. 128 (1967). The judge's refusal to provide her with counsel, therefore, violated her constitutional rights. The second violation was the increase of Amy's sentence by one month "for each thousand dollars" of the fine that she was unable to pay. Amy's Fourteenth Amendment equal protection rights prohibit the judge from incarcerating Amy solely for inability to pay a fine, which is essentially what the judge did by increasing her sentence solely on account of her indigency. Williams v. Illinois, 399 U.S. 235 (1970). The third and final violation occurred when Amy was denied the right to counsel on appeal. Amy's Fourteenth Amendment due process and equal protection rights were both violated because Amy is constitutionally entitled to counsel on her first appeal as of right. She cannot be discriminated against because of her inability to afford counsel on the appeal. Douglas v. California, 372 U.S. 353 (1963).

During her sentencing the judge imposed the conditions on Amy's probation that she obtain her GED and she find employment. Amy protested the first condition, stating that school wasn't for her. Under the Fourteenth Amendment Due Process Clause, a judge may impose conditions on probation that are reasonably related to the offense and the goals of the sentence. Because Amy was convicted of welfare fraud and her lack of an education and employment could have very likely contributed to her reasons for committing the offense, the judge's conditions were reasonably related to the offense. The two conditions imposed upon Amy during her period of probation, therefore, did not violate her constitutional rights.

In sum, Amy's constitutional rights were violated during her sentencing and her efforts to appeal her sentence. In all likelihood, any single error would entitle her to a new sentencing. However, the cumulative effect of *all* of the errors would virtually guarantee Amy a new sentencing free of the constitutional errors committed throughout the initial proceedings.

Jack is a 23-year-old father of three children who is no stranger to the law. In the past five years he fathered his children with three different women, and he refuses to stop his partying lifestyle in favor of being a responsible parent. In fact, he had been charged with the misdemeanor of child neglect on at least four prior occasions. The straw that broke the camel's back came when Jack left his daughters (who were 5, 3, and 18 months old at the time) in his car so that he could attend a bonfire keg party. Temperatures reached near freezing in the car. The girls would have likely died had a passerby not heard crying coming from the car and immediately called the authorities. Based on that incident Jack was charged with child abuse, to which he plead guilty. At Jack's sentencing the judge took special note of the pattern of neglect and abuse and the fact that Jack appeared entirely unwilling to change his behavior. Therefore, the judge sentenced Jack to three years incarceration and then an additional five years of supervised probation. As a condition of that probation the judge stated that Jack was "not permitted to father any additional children without the express prior consent of the Court."

Jill is a 42-year-old mother of two teenagers. While admittedly having an affair she became pregnant. The last thing Jill needed was to start all over again with a baby when her children were practically grown. Shortly after giving birth to a boy, Jill went to a large department store and left him in the toy aisle of the store along with a note requesting someone to "take good care of him." The boy was found unharmed a short time later, and it was soon discovered that the baby was Jill's. Following a trial she was found guilty of child abandonment and a variety of lesser offenses. Since Jill had never been in trouble with the law before, the judge showed some leniency on her during the sentencing. Jill was sentenced to probation for five years and she was ordered "not to become pregnant during her period of probation."

Jack and Jill have challenged their respective sentences. Specifically, they each allege that the conditions of their probation are unconstitutional. Discuss the likelihood of success in each case. Additionally, if you reach different conclusions in each case, be sure to discuss why you did so.

DISCUSSION QUESTIONS

1. Several states currently have laws permitting the chemical castration of convicted sex offenders. Do you agree with such laws? Why or why not? What constitutional provisions discussed within this text might the laws violate?

2. In Europe, "day fines" exist, where the amount an offender is fined depends in part upon the offender's income. What are the advantages and disadvantages of a day fine? Which method do you think is better—the European method, or the method primarily used in the United States whereby the fine is for a fixed amount based solely on the offense?

3. What is a "mandatory minimum sentence"? What crime(s) in your jurisdiction have such sentences? Why do you think the legislature required mandatory minimum sentences for those offenses?

4. In more recent times "boot camps" have become a method of punishment for youthful offenders as opposed to incarceration. What do these boot camps do in order to rehabilitate offenders? How does the case of Martin Lee Anderson, a fourteen-year-old boy sent to a Florida boot camp for probation violation in 2006, illustrate the potential dangers of boot camps? What ultimately happened to the guards in the Anderson case?

5. Research challenge: Marie Noe, a Pennsylvania resident in her seventies, was convicted in 1999 of horrific crimes that occurred decades before. What were the circumstances of her crimes, and what was her controversial sentence? Do you agree with the sentence? Explain.

6. Can *any* criminal case be appealed to the U.S. Supreme Court? What is the process by which parties attempt to have their case heard before the high Court, and what is the likelihood that the Court will take a case?

7. Research challenge: Who is Megan Kanka, and what is "Megan's Law" all about? Do you agree with the law?

8. What is the difference between "plain error" and "harmless error" when it comes to grounds for appealing a criminal conviction? Compare and contrast the two concepts.

9. Research challenge: Familiarize yourself with the cases of James Byrd, Jr., and Matthew Sheppard, two victims of horrific hate crimes in 1998. Since that time numerous jurisdictions have passed laws allowing enhanced sentences for hate crimes. Do you agree with those laws? Are they constitutional? *See, e.g.,* Wisconsin v. Mitchell, 508 U.S. 476 (1993).

10. Research challenge: Our nation has long struggled with determining the appropriate punishment for juvenile offenders and consistently enforcing that punishment. Take, for example, two school shootings: one committed by Luke Woodham in 1997, and the other jointly committed by Andrew Golden and Mitchell Johnson less than one year later. What sentences did theses offenders receive? Do you foresee any problems when comparing their respective sentences? Which, if either, do you think is appropriate and why?

TEST BANK

True/False

1. Evidence of a defendant's character may *not* be considered at sentencing.

2. There is no federal constitutional right to appeal a criminal conviction.

3. A pre-sentence report is a tool to aid the judge in determining the appropriate sentence for a convicted offender prior to imposing a sentence.

4. Concurrent sentences for convictions run at the same time, whereas consecutive sentences run one after the other.

5. Allocution refers to the right of the defendant to be sentenced by a jury rather than a judge.

Multiple Choice

6. Matt was convicted of assault. The judge imposed probation as punishment. The judge:

    A. May not revoke Matt's probation unless Matt commits another crime
    B. May not impose other sanctions on Matt along with the probation, such as a fine or restitution
    C. May revoke Matt's probation without giving Matt the opportunity for a hearing
    D. May impose conditions on Mat in addition to probation, such as maintaining employment or staying in school

7. A sanction whereby the offender is ordered to compensate the victim for any injuries the victim suffered is called:

    A. A fine
    B. Restitution
    C. Retribution
    D. Damages

8. Cheyenne was convicted of embezzlement and sentenced to five years' incarceration. Her convicted was reversed on appeal. Following her second trial she was sentenced to fifteen years' incarceration for the same crime. Under which of the following circumstances would her increased sentence potentially violate her due process rights?

    A. At trial #1 she was sentenced by the judge; at trial #2 she was sentenced by the same judge.
    B. A trial #1 she was sentenced by a jury; at trial #2 she was sentenced by another jury.

    C. At trial #1 she was sentence by a jury; at trial #2 she was sentenced by a judge.

    D. All of the above scenarios would violate her due process rights.

9. If a defendant appeals her criminal conviction, which of the following rights is the defendant *not* constitutionally entitled to on appeal?

    A. The right to counsel on the defendant's first appeal "as of right"

    B. The right to counsel on the defendant's subsequent discretionary appeals

    C. The right to a trial transcript for use on appeal if the defendant is indigent

    D. The defendant is constitutionally entitled to all of the rights described above.

10. A procedure by which an individual in official custody challenges the legality of his incarceration is called:

    A. A petition for post-conviction relief

    B. Ineffective assistance of counsel

    C. A writ of habeas corpus

    D. A de novo appeal

TABLE OF CASES

Principal cases indicated by italics.